CW01212814

WILLIAM SCHAW LINDSAY

WILLIAM SCHAW LINDSAY
VICTORIAN ENTREPRENEUR

BILL LINDSAY

AMBERLEY

To my wife Sue for all her forbearance and support.

Half-title page: Painting of Lindsay's vessels, Swedish National Maritime Museum, Stockholm. Inv. Number SM 20028. Artist unknown. From left: *Coromandel, Barrackpore, Cossipore, Tynemouth, Robert Lowe* (broadside on), *W S Lindsay, Dinapore, Gladiator, Jenny Lind, Mirzapore, Alipore, c.*1855.

First published 2023

Amberley Publishing
The Hill, Stroud
Gloucestershire, GL5 4EP

www.amberley-books.com

Copyright © Bill Lindsay, 2023

The right of Bill Lindsay to be identified as the Author of this work has been asserted in accordance with the Copyright, Designs and Patents Act 1988.

All rights reserved. No part of this book may be reprinted or reproduced or utilised in any form or by any electronic, mechanical or other means, now known or hereafter invented, including photocopying and recording, or in any information storage or retrieval system, without the permission in writing from the Publishers.

British Library Cataloguing in Publication Data.
A catalogue record for this book is available from the British Library.

ISBN 978 1 3981 1525 5 (hardback)
ISBN 978 1 3981 1526 2 (ebook)

1 2 3 4 5 6 7 8 9 10

Typesetting by SJmagic DESIGN SERVICES, India.
Printed in the UK.

Contents

Foreword by J. D. Davies   8
Acknowledgements   9
Introduction: A True Story   10

Part One: At Sea (1815–1841)   11
  1 The Old Man   11
  2 A Mother Besieged   12
  3 Liverpool Docks   18
  4 Ship's Apprentice   21
  5 Icy Surrounds   25
  6 Desertion   29
  7 The Bullying Mate Leaves   32
  8 Ship's Steward   33
  9 Pestilence on board   35
10 Promotion   36
11 The Sick Sheikh   38
12 The Commodore and the Monkey   41
13 The Ambush   43
14 After-effects of a Hurricane   45

Part Two: Journey to Success (1841–1852)   50
15 Reminiscing   50
16 The Fairer Sex   52
17 Limerick Docks   57
18 A New Start   58
19 The Lighthouse   61
20 Partners in Iron   63
21 The Road to a Fortune   66
22 Building the Empire   68
23 Shipowner and Father   71
24 Free Trade   80

25	The Gold Box	82
26	Queen Victoria's Rebuke	84
27	Caroline Chisholm	85
28	Auxiliary Steamers	91

Part Three: Politics and Shipping (1852–1854)   **96**
29	Monmouth Contest: Buying Votes	96
30	Dartmouth Contest: Up against the Admiral	103
31	Tynemouth Contest: Close-Run Victory	108
32	The Marchioness and her Dog	110
33	The University of Life	115
34	An Overworked Mind	116

Part Four: The Crimean War (1854–1856)   **123**
35	Transport Ships	123
36	Underwater Explosives	130
37	Tables without Legs	133
38	Transport Ships for the French	135
39	The Naval Scapegoat	137
40	Administrative Reform Association	144

Part Five: Shipping Business Continues (1856–1861)   **149**
41	Mail Service to Calcutta via the Cape	149
42	Manor by the Thames	155
43	Brunel's Giant Ship	159
44	The Portuguese Loan	162
45	Parliamentary Royal Commissions	164
46	Explorers and Republicans	168
47	Bride Ships	173
48	Paxton's Wallpaper	176
49	Soporific Parliamentarians	179
50	Insights on Four Prime Ministers	180
51	No Confidence Vote	187

Part Six: American Civil War (1861–1865)   **190**
52	Atlantic Crossing	190
53	Hudson River to Niagara Falls	195
54	What the Dickens!	199
55	Lincoln's Ham	202
56	French Naval Threat	204
57	Onset of the American Civil War	211
58	Threat of War with the United States	219
59	Support for the Confederate Independence	225
60	Blockade Running	227

Contents

61	Building a Confederate Navy Funding, Supplying	230
62	The Emperor's Messenger	235
63	Suppliers' Greed	246
64	Emancipation of Slaves	246
65	Overwork and Stroke	249

Part Seven: Maritime Historian and Author (1865–1877)   252

66	Recovery	252
67	Changing Tack Galbraiths, Building, Farming	253
68	Tales by the Riverbank	258
69	Winter House by the Sea	262
70	Admiralty Reform	264
71	The Navy, Past and Present	267
72	My Son, his University Life, and Marriage	270
73	Maritime 'Magnum Opus'	273
74	Coffin Ships	275

Epilogue   281

Appendix I	Timeline	291
Appendix II	List of ships owned, or part-owned, by Lindsay	294
Appendix III	Ships owned, or possibly owned, by Lindsay's partners	296
Appendix IV	Voyages of the *Tynemouth* during the Crimean War with details of cargo and troops	297
Appendix V	Business affairs	298
Appendix VI	Estate of William Schaw Lindsay at his death in 1877	298
Appendix VII	William Schaw Lindsay's family tree	300

Notes	302
Sources and Bibliography	336
List of Illustrations	342
Index	345

Foreword by J. D. Davies

The Victorian age produced many larger-than-life figures whose lives and achievements still resound today. Others, though, who were celebrated in their own time, are now forgotten. William Schaw Lindsay was one such man, and in this fascinating study his descendant Bill Lindsay has done an impressive job of restoring an eminent Victorian to public attention.

Lindsay's is a genuine rags-to-riches story: orphaned as a child and then seeking a living as the proverbial cabin boy, he made a hugely successful career for himself in shipping and commerce by dint of sheer hard work and determination. At one time he owned one of the largest merchant shipping companies in the world, and his own vessels assisted in the transportation of the British and French armies during the Crimean War. He knew many of the greatest men of the age, from Gladstone and Disraeli to Brunel, Abraham Lincoln, and the Emperor Napoleon III.

Never afraid to court controversy or take an unpopular stance, he strongly advocated the recognition of the Confederacy during the American Civil War; using Lindsay's own papers and opinions, the author presents a provocative alternative explanation for the origins of that conflict.

Sadly, his public career was effectively ended by illness before his fiftieth birthday, but in retirement he still managed to write a four-volume history of merchant shipping.

Basing his account on Lindsay's substantial archive, the author has adopted a fresh and lively approach to his subject, to present Lindsay as a real person with genuine emotions and ambitions. In doing so he has splendidly revived the life and reputation of a forgotten Victorian giant.

David Davies
Historian, Author, and Chairman of
the Society for Nautical Research[1]

Acknowledgements

This book has been quite a task, exciting much of the time, discovering fascinating information in Lindsay's papers. I first came across my forefather in print while reading Michael Clark's article on him entitled 'W S Lindsay: Righting the Wrongs of a Radical Shipowner'.

Along the way I was grateful for the help of others, particularly the librarians at the Caird Library at the National Maritime Museum in Greenwich, London, where the papers are stored.

I was also greatly assisted by Robert Cutts in Bristol, who helped with the transcription, research, and valuable advice, and by Dr Martin Bellamy from Glasgow Museums and Glasgow University who set me on the right road.

Encouragement to write this book came from Frank Gallagher, Gill Hoffs, Peter King, the late Ronald McKie, Crosbie Smith, Stephanie Zarach and my Lindsay cousins. In addition, I was aided by friends and relatives who kindly read my drafts: my wife Sue, my sister and twin brother, my cousin Patrick Lindsay and my colleagues Sarah Carrick, Laurence Cowley, and Michael Rhodes.

I am very grateful to David Davies for writing the foreword. Dr Sam Willis, Charles Priestley, Peter King, and Professor Andrew Lambert kindly reviewed the manuscript.

My relative Peter Phillips gave me the portrait of Lindsay (on the cover). Many thanks. Thanks also to Alan Bradford for restoring the portrait. I appreciated Martin Turner's (of design27.studio) help with ideas for the cover of the book.

My thanks too to Ingrid Ulfstedt at the Swedish Maritime Museum in Stockholm for the use of the painting they hold of the Lindsay fleet.

I wish to thank Amberley Publishing and especially Shaun Barrington in having faith in me and pressing ahead with publication.

This book could not have been written without Hilda Kirkwood's efforts.

Bill Lindsay

Introduction: A True Story

Lindsay's journals provide fascinating first-hand insights into merchant shipping in Victorian days, mismanagement of the Crimean War, and European involvement in the American Civil War. Much of the information is previously unpublished.

But it is more than that. It is a story of how a man, who came from nothing, created one of the largest maritime businesses in Victorian times. This was achieved in the new era of ocean-going steamships.

Clever Boys of our Time who Became Famous Men[1] provides a stirring precis:

William Shaw [sic] Lindsay,

A poor friendless orphan, cabin boy, great shipowner, and member of parliament.

Can we now, in this hasty glance at the career of William Lindsay, realise the two extremes in the life of that extraordinary man?

First, the poor orphan boy shovelling coals in the hold of a steamer ... and then seven weeks' weary wandering from ship to ship in the fruitless hope of being taken on board as a cabin-boy – without food, without rest – save such as could be obtained on doorsteps...

That is one extreme; now look at the other. Author, Magistrate, Member of Parliament, Millionaire!

Why, it seems a fable – it seems too improbable to be true; but it is true, nevertheless.

Part One
At Sea
(1815–1841)

1 The Old Man

In 1877, a man sits beneath an elm tree beside the river Thames. He is sixty-one and in a wheelchair. The stroke that changed his life happened twelve years before, when he was in his prime. As a shipowner and an active Member of Parliament, he was known and respected throughout the land and beyond. But an embattled early life on the high seas and years of continuous hard work have taken their toll.

Most days, when the weather is fine, he can be seen at a portable writing table. His journals have multiplied over the years, and he has written several novels. He has recently completed his greatest work, a reference book on merchant shipping, which was painstakingly researched. Reviews of the book have pleased him. For a man with a limited education, and from a poor background, they are praise indeed. Although not called on so much nowadays, his expertise on shipping has been sought by governments over the years.

The vista before him pleases him. This is his favourite place. He is a man who relaxes with water nearby. After all, his whole life has been spent either on water, or near it. Cows wander in the fields in front of him. Behind him is his manor house in Shepperton. Although he is privileged to own such a magnificent home, he worked hard to earn the money to purchase it.

The lawns stretch down to the river, and the pasture opposite is full of wildflowers in the spring and summer. The hill in the distance behind the fields is covered in trees which stand out on the horizon. The bells of the church nearby are often the only sound that can be heard.

Before his stroke he used to travel into London city centre to work. It's only eighteen miles away. However, the roads are rough, and journeys can be delayed, especially in bad weather. Journeys are easier now. He lobbied his friends to fund a railway link to the village so that travel to the City is easier.

He has helped to improve the village. He has built a school and houses. The cemetery is full, so he has set aside some of his land for future burials. He has sold all but one of his ships, and his company to his partners. This has enabled him to invest in the houses and in farms. It has also meant that he has been able to build a winter retreat by the sea.

As an invalid, he realises what a burden he is to his wife, but the firm he founded has made him a rich man and he can afford servants to help with the household duties. They have been married for thirty-four years and their only son is now twenty-eight.

Their son, however, is a big disappointment to him. He has done what he can to encourage him to make his own way in life. But the boy is lazy, and his mother protects him.

The old man overcame many challenges to become famous in his day. Few people from his background become Members of Parliament. His near-death experiences at sea have taught him to count his blessings, but he has still striven to achieve greater things. He knows that he is fortunate to have lived as long as he has. He has had a long time to reflect on his life...

2 A Mother Besieged

Sixty-one years earlier. It is December 1815. The storm shows no sign of abating. The wind howls straight in from the sea nearby. The west coast of Scotland is a harsh place during a winter storm.[1] A woman is about to give birth to her fifth child. She is homeless and is staying at her brother-in-law's house in Ayr. He is a prominent figure in the town, a clergyman, and lives in a manse in the old town. Her husband[2] is a merchant who has struggled to make a living and is prone to speculate in business. He has difficulty supporting his family and by all accounts he has abandoned them. In despair, he has turned to drink and is destined to die a few years later.

During the night of the 19th of December, while the storm was raging at its height, the woman gave birth to a child she named after her well-loved brother-in-law. That was how I, William Schaw Lindsay, came into this world.

A few months after I was born, my mother Mary[3] moved to Glasgow with four of us. One of my sisters stayed behind with our aunt and uncle. Mary managed to rent out a house in the Gorbals to lodgers, and she was then able to feed and house us. Mother strove to bring us up in respectability. Few people, however, were aware of her struggles. My two elder brothers managed to get employment and, although their wages were very small, it helped.

Glasgow's population was only 147,000 in those days. Life for the poor, in overcrowded housing, was miserable, and was influenced by sickness and early death. Indeed, the average age of death in Glasgow was in the low 40s for both men and women. My own brothers died young; Alexander at 18, and Peter at 37.

The Napoleonic Wars had just ended,[4] and the French Revolution was still in people's memories. Indeed, there was a growing concern amongst the ruling classes in Britain that a revolution could occur here.

A week of strikes and unrest commenced in protest at the Government's handling of the economy in Scotland and a national strike was proposed by the protesters. 60,000 workers stopped work in the mid-west of Scotland. Rumours spread of an uprising that would be joined by the French. In Greenock, not far from Glasgow further down the River Clyde, the army was called in to put an end to the insurgency and order was restored, but only after eight people were killed and a dozen others injured.

I was of course too young to understand all this. One day, when I was a small child, I saw a toy in the shop window and was enchanted by it.

"Mother, can I have a sixpence to buy that wooden top?" I asked.

She gently dissuaded me. But I would not be put off. I demanded to have it.

"You can't," she insisted.

I flew into a rage, crying with anger and disappointment. Throwing her arms around me, her eyes full of tears, she said, "My dear boy, I would give you all you want, but I have not a sixpence in the wide world, and at this moment know not where to get one."

Taken aback, I was brought to my senses and felt very ashamed. I sobbed for forgiveness, and said "Mother, I will never ask again."

Although I was then only five, I never forgot the incident. From that moment I felt I was a child of poverty, and it was up to me to make my own way in life. This lesson was to stand me in good stead in the years to come.

In 1825 my mother died and at the age of ten I became an orphan. But I was lucky. My Uncle William and Aunt Janet gave me a home. Janet was my mother's sister. My uncle sent me to Ayr Academy where I was able to make good the sparse schooling as I had received in Gorbals. My time at the academy was brief but beneficial. It shaped the rest of my life. My gratitude to my dear uncle and aunt for giving me a loving home and education is unbounded.

Numbers at the Academy rose from 420 before I joined to nearly 600 when I left. The numbers however declined soon after, to fewer than 400, mainly due to an outbreak of cholera in 1832, which I was fortunate to miss.[5]

The school abounded with interesting characters. There was James Gray, who taught arithmetic, who was nicknamed 'Fisty' because he only had one hand. That didn't stop him using it to discipline us, however. Old Robert Taylor, the writing master known as 'Ranting Rob', was everlastingly sucking sugar candy, and kissing the little girls for good behaviour. James Ridley taught English. He stressed the importance of morality and sobriety but did not follow his own advice and got drunk most nights on whisky toddies.

No doubt, their teaching left a mark on me. The greatest influence on me, however, was Reverend Dr John Smyth Memes, the school's Rector. Dr Memes threw himself into his work with enthusiasm. He took over classes in Mathematics, Natural Philosophy, and Geography. He added History,

Botany, and English. He had his own peculiarities. So engrossed in his teaching, he often forgot to wash his face and hands, and usually neglected his dressing too, his trousers were hardly ever tucked into his boots. The Rector sought to improve all his pupils. He was a dedicated teacher and often held his classes at extra hours, as early as six a.m., teaching for 12 hours with few breaks. He assisted us with our debates and solved our difficulties. Dr Memes also ensured that the Academy was provided with globes and maps of the World. These encouraged me to travel.

Although my uncle, Reverend Schaw, hoped that I would follow in his footsteps into the church, my aunt quickly saw that my character was ill equipped to do so, and she persuaded her husband to stop trying to encourage me on that path. Nevertheless, I greatly venerated him.[6] Reverend Schaw was Minister of the United Secession Church in Ayr. Born in 1770 in Falkirk, he had come to Ayr in 1801 from Lochwinnoch eighteen miles from Glasgow, where he had been ordained in 1795. He accepted a call to the recently formed congregation in Ayr. He had started preaching in the open air. Under his ministry, and amid a growing population, the congregation increased by degrees, until in 1836 it had a membership of 400.[7]

His calling to the church started when he was young. During his boyhood he had experienced near-death experiences on two occasions. Once, attempting to draw a bucket up from a pond in the main street in Falkirk,

Rev William Schaw *c.*1830: Lindsay's uncle.

the bucket was too heavy for him, he lost his balance and fell into the pond. Fortunately, a passer-by witnessed it and rescued him. On another occasion, he was playing on ice, and it gave way beneath him. The water was very deep but after a considerable struggle he got hold of the bank and extricated himself. Both these deliverances prompted him to turn to God.[8]

In 1830, aged fifteen, I decided not to be a burden to my uncle and aunt any longer, and I moved back to Glasgow hoping to live with my brothers or sisters.[9] I had hoped to gain employment in my brother Peter's office, or in that of one of his friends. I experienced anything but a warm reception. Peter was a clever man, but too fond of company, and his many good qualities were counteracted by a jealous and bad-hearted wife.[10] They did everything in their power to hinder me.

I was occasionally allowed to dine with them, but more often I ate in the kitchen, or in a small bedroom which had been grudgingly allocated to me. Peter never appeared to seek out employment for me, as he had often promised he would. In fact, I soon saw that Peter's wife had resolved that my brother should have nothing whatever to do with me, as she anxiously watched for an opportunity to throw me out of the house. Being at a loss for an excuse, she contrived to make one up, and charged me with stealing. My young blood boiled at the accusation. I could not restrain myself. I told her plainly what I thought of her. It resulted in a most serious quarrel and I was turned out, and ran away from the house. The hatred was mutual. I never saw them again. They both died some four or five years later. Their end was most miserable. Peter had become a half-witted fool through drink and the harassing effects of a worthless and faithless wife. She closed her days raving mad, also brought on by excessive drinking.

My sister Helen,[11] aged 19, also lived in Glasgow. She had at that time been married for some years to Mr. Thomas Christie[12] who was a scholar and a gentleman, but exceedingly hard-hearted, and lazy. She gave me shelter and food, but her husband demanded that I should work for them, which I readily did in his office.

My employment was not confined to desk duties. Mr Christie was a person of great eccentricity, and amongst his numerous hobbies he had at that time a taste for keeping chickens. He had no convenient place to keep them except the coal cellar, and a small green plot in front of the house, where it was necessary to watch them carefully, or otherwise they were certain to be stolen. This duty fell to me, so I was obliged to rise at four o'clock in the morning "to air the chickens" on the green until eight o'clock when it was time to leave for the office. The whole brood was afterwards daily locked up in the cellar. As might be expected, the chickens did not thrive, and proved a waste of money like most hobbies. Orders were given to dispose of them, and the business of taking them to Candleriggs Market was placed upon me.

Rising early, I went about my task, and although I certainly didn't relish the job of standing in a public place shouting, "Cocks and hens for sale", I completed it. Old Christie, for he was a full twenty years older than my sister, must have noticed that I appeared sulky, because after the affair he was more than usually harsh and severe with me. No doubt he felt that his brother-in-law Peter had a greater obligation than he had to keep and maintain me.

I had had enough of relying on my siblings to assist me. In truth, I felt that I was nobody's child. Nobody was under any obligation to keep me, nor care for me. As no one took an interest in me, my only option was to take care of myself. I was about sixteen, slender but strong, and tall for my age.

With a small bundle of clothes, and with a small amount of money, about five shillings, I set off for the dock to start a life at sea. Had I known what difficulties lay ahead, I would not have gone. It may have been a strange choice, for few in our family had been sailors, but the sea had been close-by all my life.

I recalled one incident which may have influenced my decision. I was a little boy and could not have been more than seven years of age. My cousin Peter Belch[13] was then a tall handsome, powerful man, fully six feet high. He was dressed in full naval uniform, going, as I afterwards understood, to take command of a Gun Boat that was lying at the Tail of the Bank[14] off Greenock. He had called upon my dear Mother, his aunt, on his way. I recollect that he lifted me upon his shoulders, raising me up easily as I could lift a child's doll. It was one of those incidents that one never forgets.

I remembered too, how I felt heading towards the dockside. I was alone in the world. No one cared for me, still less loved me. I had no father. No mother. Nor did I have any friends. I was a child of poverty.

I chose to board a steamer, a relatively new innovation, sailing for Liverpool. My dear sisters, Helen and Mary stocked me with an excellent outfit and gave me five pounds, some odd shillings besides, more than enough to pay not merely my passage to Liverpool but keep me there for a while until I could obtain a ship. However, the five pounds disappeared and only the odd shillings remained. What became of the five pounds I never could ascertain, but I expect it was stolen by a young sailor who accompanied me.[15]

Once on deck, I was asked for my fare. I had heard that the fare was four shillings which I submitted. Alas, I was mistaken. The amount due was six shillings. This I didn't have, and when I explained this to the ship's mate, I was told to remain where I was.

Waiting fearfully for an hour, I was again joined by the mate, this time accompanied by the Master. I explained my predicament. The Master listened closely while the mate searched me. The Master asked me to give him all the money I had, which I did, and I was ordered to go below, and report to the engineer.

This order I obeyed with alacrity. The engineer handed me over to the stokers and they in turn handed me into the coal bunkers where I found plenty of work.[16] I soon saw what I had to do. The coals were collected in a heap and required trimming towards a hole from which they were shovelled by the firemen into the furnaces. I plied away lustily for a couple of hours,

Part One: At Sea

"*The poor boy, shut up amid the dust and heat of the boiler-room, experiencing the sensations of a first voyage.*"—p. 149.

Lindsay working his passage to Liverpool in the engine room of the steamer. Johnson, J., *Clever Boys of our Time who Became Famous Men*.

and soon won the good graces of the stokers who gave me a portion of their dinner. Never had I before, nor have I since, eaten a meal with greater relish. I felt that I had worked for it. In this manner was I employed till the steamer arrived at Liverpool. I had been very seasick during the night, for the sea was somewhat rough. I however did not complain and always managed to keep sufficient supply of coals at a particular hole, ready for the stokers, and thus I won their favour.

When about to quit the vessel, the master called me to him, and kindly handed me back all the money I had given to him, saying "You have worked for your passage, and worked for it well."

That was one of the proudest moments I had ever up to that period experienced. I had not only worked for my dinner but worked for my passage too! I left the ship with a feeling of far less despondency than might have been expected under the circumstances of a poor boy cast adrift in a strange place, without the most distant idea of what I was to do.

3 Liverpool Docks

St. George's Dock was a forest of ships' masts. As one of the most important ports in Britain, Liverpool was a bustling trading centre. A major harbour for handling slaves in earlier days, now outlawed, it had expanded even more, as it became an important port for cotton, located close to the textile mills of Lancashire, linking itself to Manchester by railway. For a teenager alone, it was a daunting place.

I sallied forth off the steamer with my bundle under my arm.[17] Where I was to go, I didn't know, but I followed the crowd, and soon found myself at the upper side of the St. George's Dock not far from the centre of the town. There I sat myself down on the top of one of those mooring posts which lined the Quay and began to ponder upon my position. I had never been allowed to think for myself before. Now necessity compelled me. Well, I thought, there is not much chance of getting employment in any office, as I know no one and no one knows me. I arrived at the conclusion that there was no alternative for me but to seek a position on board a ship, even though I was utterly ignorant of a ship's duties. I knew no one connected with shipping, nor any other business in the town or docks.

However, I had to do something. Necessity is indeed the mother of invention, and the great stimulant to exertion. With the little money I had, I realised if I did not soon obtain work, I might starve. To think of going back to Glasgow or writing to any of my relatives for money or assistance was out of the question, so I immediately started by boarding the first ship I saw in St. George's Dock. I enquired whether they wanted a boy. No boy was wanted. "Far too many boys now" was one of the first replies I received.

From ship to ship I persevered in my enquiries during the whole of that weary day until dusk, but no boy was wanted in any of the vessels. For the most part I was gruffly ordered on shore. I already began to despair, but I stuck at it. A penny biscuit, and a ladle full of water at the neighbouring pump, sufficed both for dinner and supper, and as I feared that my limited means would soon disappear, I took refuge for the night in one of the sheds

Part One: At Sea

of the Princes' Parade. Placing my little bundle under my head for a pillow, I found a good resting place during the first night in that great maritime seat of commerce. I slept soundly, very soundly, and rose at five the following morning, as well refreshed as if I had lain upon a soft bed.

I renewed my visits again from ship to ship, and during the course of that day, boarded every vessel of reasonable size in the St George's and Queen's Dock. Unfortunately, my efforts were no more successful than the previous day.

Some warned me to beware of the police "who had their eyes upon me". I felt that I had done no wrong, but that the shelter of a police office would actually be better than the open sheds of the Prince's pier, were it not that it might leave a stain upon my character. Many told me to "go to the devil", and when one Master of a great North American-built craft politely threatened to kick my arse for bothering him, adding civilly that I go to Hell. I thought he might reach there before me, but I said nothing.

From many, however, I received kind replies, but the shipping business was very depressed, and able seamen were so abundant that there seemed little prospect of any employment falling to my lot. That was indeed a miserable day. I was lonely and wearied, dirty, and sad, when towards dusk I slipped away to the shed to rest myself for the night. I again slept soundly, and at sunrise got up with renewed energy, and once more I commenced my task of hunting for employment.

For eight days, day after day, my labours in search of employment were incessant, but unavailing. My spirits, and my energy, though often depressed, never left me. I had by that time visited every ship in the docks. Some of them I had applied to several times.

On the Sunday morning I washed my shirt in a canal at the outskirts of the town. I dried it at a brick kiln near the canal. After this, I had my breakfast in a miserable house in one of the narrow streets with which Liverpool abounds. It consisted of a basin of soup, i.e., hot water with some greens swimming on the surface, and a small spoonful of fat, or rather the refuse salt "slush" collected on board ships and sold by the cook at the end of the voyage. This delicacy with a hard biscuit and a penny roll was a sumptuous meal.

After breakfast, I attended Church in a floating chapel[18] moored in the Salthouse Dock. I well remember the sermon. It was upon the vanity of all things human. "Lay not up for yourself treasures upon earth" was the text of the apparently sincere but humble preacher. I remember too, that there was a collection after the sermon on that day. Two rough looking men went round collecting from the congregation with a box. What object it was for, I do not now remember, but out of my limited capital I contributed a penny with a ready hand and no grudging heart. It was the orphan's mite.

My visit to the canal revealed a somewhat better resting place for the night than that in the Prince's Parade shed. At the brickyard where I dried my shirt, I found a quantity of old straw which served as a bed, and the heat from the smoking kilns made for a comparatively excellent bedroom,

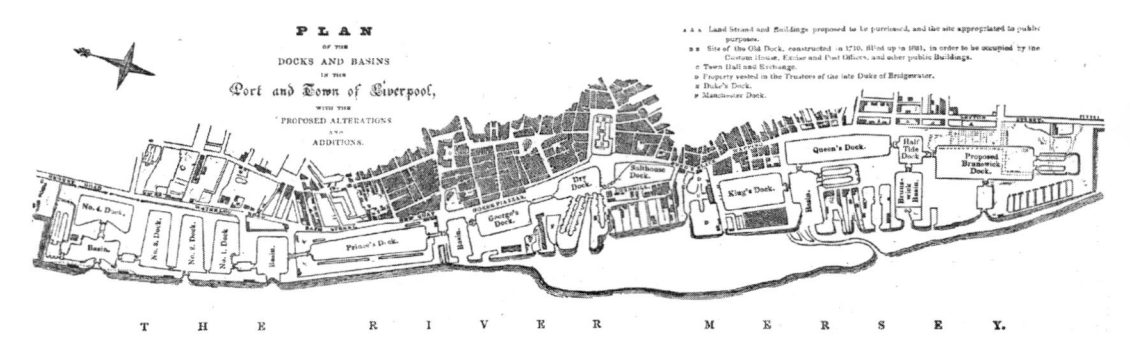

Plan of the docks and basins in the port and town of Liverpool with the proposed alterations and additions. *The Penny Magazine*, p. 173, 1832.

although open to the sky. Here I slept for four or five nights, with, at times, many homeless mortals like myself. I soon discovered that my companions were a parcel of the greatest thieves and blackguards that any great city could furnish. In addition to the roasting of potatoes at the kilns, they often roasted chickens, which it was impossible for them to procure by honest means. One night they had a special feast, including a ham and a bottle of wine. It is doing them no injustice to suspect that these were stolen. I felt that the sooner I quitted their company the better, otherwise I could follow in their ways.

Once more I was therefore obliged to take refuge in the Prince's Parade sheds until good fortune gave me part of a bed in a humble but honest lodging house. It was during one of my walks around the Dock that I saw an old man before me in the dress of a rigger, with a bag on his shoulder from which some of his tools had slipped unperceived. I ran, picked them up, and handed them to him. He thanked me, and asked what I did? I told him my simple story.

He seemed to feel sorry for me and told me to follow him to the ship where he was employed. I did so. He then said if I would help him in his work, he would share his "grub" and his bed with me. To this I most readily agreed. Never did I enter upon my work with a greater relish. It was a pleasure. Tarring ropes, twisting spun yarn, cleaning coils of ropes, and similar employment. But I no longer ate the bread of idleness. I was working for my dinner. The old man's lodgings were very humble, but his bed, though of straw, had a clean covering and, if there were no carpets on the floor, there was no dirt to complain of. For nearly three weeks I was thus employed and was very happy. I never knew my patron by any other name than Thomas or old Tom. At the end of that time, he sailed as boatswain of a ship, and to my very deep regret he could not take me with him. He tried to get a job on board for me, but his efforts were unsuccessful. The vessel had all her apprentices engaged, and the Master could not make room for me. From that day I never heard of poor old Tom again.

I was once more left to my own resources, but my capital had slightly diminished during those three weeks. Tom had offered me half a crown on parting, but I was too proud to take it from him, and I knew that he could little afford to part with it.

For more than two weeks my exertions to find work were again unceasing, but without avail. To such distress was I at last driven, that after being long without any food, I was compelled to beg – beg for what I could get, either in halfpence or bread. But I was a useless beggar for I only managed to get sufficient to keep me alive. The struggles between pride and poverty with starvation were then very severe. I refused to write to my brother and his wife, nor even to my sister or her husband. I would sooner have expired through utter want, than stoop to such a humiliation.

I was conscious that if I ever hinted to my good old Uncle and his excellent wife that I needed help my wishes would have been at once complied with. "But why," I used to say to myself "why should I trouble them. They have been too kind to me already, and I cannot, and will not distress them by describing my position, or even telling them where I am. No. No. I must not and will not. I must struggle on."

Nothing is so lonely, none so truly solitary, as the unemployed who seek work amidst the busy haunts of men. There is no greater wilderness to the unknown and unhappy wanderer than the crowd and crush of human beings in some mighty assembly of men. No country lane as dull as Lord Street in Liverpool, when all the people who pass you, don't know you, and care for you no more than the stones upon which they tread.

It was upon one of those days when I was reduced to the last extremity, while making a third or fourth attempt to obtain employment in a ship, named the *Isabella*,[19] that an old gentleman, who I afterwards ascertained to be a Scotsman, seemed to take compassion upon me. He asked various questions, all of which I answered in a simple straightforward manner but avoided mentioning the name of any of my relations. He promised to do all he could for me, and on the following day, I had the satisfaction to learn that he had succeeded in obtaining for me a berth as an apprentice for four years on board that ship.

So began my life at sea. It was 1833, I was seventeen and the world lay before me.

4 Ship's Apprentice

I stood on the deck. I had only been on board a day, and I was getting used to my surroundings. The ship was commanded by a Captain Thomas Tait[20] who seemed to be a friendly little man. The chief mate on the other hand, was a foolhardy Scottish fellow named McCastle,[21] a proud silly youth. He was only twenty years of age, and, as I was soon to find out, a tyrant and a bully.

The ship, the *Isabella*, was a "flush-decked" ship of about 450 tons built in Nova Scotia, only some three or four years old[22] but as proved afterwards, far gone with dry rot in her stern's timbers. I learnt very soon that I had joined a very rotten ship. One of my jobs was to carry away decayed timbers as the carpenter cut them out, or rather dug them out, from the stern frames. I often heard men say, "This craft will be a coffin for some poor fellows." I was determined, however, to stick with her, as I knew that there was little chance of getting other employment.

The crew numbered twenty-one. Living quarters were very cramped, and either very hot in a warm climate, or very cold in cooler ones. It was often mouldy, full of maggots, and rats abounded. In the tropics, mosquitoes were everywhere. We cabin boys on board were known by our nicknames which derived from the names of our hometowns. Willie Hall was known as "Derby". A fine handsome gentle boy, he was a gentleman's son. Jamie heralded from Leith and was nicknamed "Colehill" which was a well-known part of that port, and, like the place, he was filthy and dishonest. He was a little, dark dirty fellow, but very active, well meaning, and with a keen spirit. "Liverpool" was the nickname of one of the other boys for obvious reasons. He was a great lounging cheeky lad who his father, an honest industrious tailor, could not improve. He soon reverted to drinking and stealing. The crew laughed at his drinking. But no amount of punishment could stop his stealing. I was known as "Glasgow".

The vessel was a fast-sailing ship, and on that first journey travelled from Liverpool to Demerara, in British Guyana, in the West Indies in 30 days. On arrival the crew set to work offloading the cargo. From five o'clock in the morning until eight at night, we set about receiving sugars, or breaking out huge casks of coals in the suffocating hold. We also rolled casks down the wharf ready for shipment, and piled barrels of sugar in stores. Any slacking caused the mate to soundly beat us.

It wasn't long before a new cargo was loaded, and the ship set sail for London. It was my first visit to the mighty capital. It left a big impression on me. I wrote to my aunt and uncle in Ayr, explaining how happy I was. Even though life on board was hard, it compared favourably to living rough in Liverpool Docks, and to when I lived with my brother and his despicable wife.

For two and a half years the ship sailed between London and Demerara, principally to the capital, Georgetown. Our stay in either port was never more than ten days. Time was spent off-loading and loading cargo. It was a tough life.

McCastle's bullying knew no bounds. All the sailors suffered. There was a very fine young man on board named Thomas Richards. He was a tall, muscular, handsome youth, but very quiet, one who knew his duty as an able seaman, and always performed it well. He was much respected by all of us, but because he was quiet, and never answered back, McCastle picked on him, and forced him to do work which the other seamen would baulk at. Tom never complained when McCastle hurled insults to him.

One day in the West Indies, McCastle overstepped the mark. He had been victimising Tom more than usual, and when he, with a dreadful oath, called him the son of a whore, he seemed to have touched a most tender nerve.

Part One: At Sea

"My mother was no whore" exclaimed Tom, "Sir, don't call her so again."

"Huh," said McCastle with a contemptuous sneer. But, enraged with Tom for daring to reply, he repeated the offensive words, adding "She could be little better to produce such a son of a whore as you."

"I warn you Mr. McCastle," Tom calmly replied, "my mother was a virtuous woman, and much too good for her wicked son. But if, Mr. McCastle, I am bad, and have become an outcast, I have some love for my mother left. Although I am your slave, you shall not say anything against my mother's memory. So, if you repeat those words, I will make you suffer for it."

Anyone in their right mind would understand fully that he meant what he said. But the First Officer had no such comprehension. He was boiling with rage.

"Son of a whore," roared McCastle, "how dare..."

The word "dare" had scarcely been uttered, when the muscular arm of Richards was uplifted, and with one single blow of his clenched fist he laid McCastle senseless on the deck. The boatswain, who was nearly as great a ruffian as the mate himself, together with the second mate, hearing the scuffle, rushed to the assistance of McCastle.

"Stand back," exclaimed Tom, "by God, if you lay one finger on me, I will stretch you by his side."

"That despicable villain," he added with a terrible calmness, "that miserable tyrant called my mother, my good and virtuous mother a whore, and I swear by the God that lives in that blue sky, that unless he now, once and for ever, confesses he lied, as he has done a thousand times, he shall never rise from the deck a living man."

McCastle, returning to his senses, made a struggle to rise. Richards clapped his naked foot upon the neck of the prostrate Mate, which it held with the grip of a vice.

"Own to your lies, your infamous lies," roared Tom in a burst of rage. The second mate and boatswain sprung to the aid of their superior. But the enraged sailor never moved an inch from his position, and with one swing of his arm sent the boatswain right through an open gangway, head over heels into the river; the second blow pitched the second mate down the main hatchway into the hold, where luckily, he fell on some soft bales, or he would certainly have been killed.

Then Richards, drawing the long knife which usually hung from his side in a leather case, lifted it over his head, and bending down, was prepared to thrust it right into the heart of McCastle. The glittering steel and the wild look of the enraged seaman put the fear of God into the mate. He implored Tom, in the most grovelling manner, not to kill him.

"Spare me Tom! Oh! Spare my life. I did not mean it. I beg your pardon."

"Not my pardon," replied Tom, "you are my master, but admit that you lied when you called my mother, my poor dear gentle mother a whore."

"I do Tom, I do," exclaimed the mate looking very worried, "you will forgive me, I know you will."

"So, you have agreed you lied – you have admitted" replied Tom, in a somewhat mollified tone, "that my mother was good and virtuous. For once in your life, you have spoken the truth, and I forgive you."

And then the man relaxed his hold of McCastle, sheathed his knife, and turning aside sat down on a spar, and wept like a child.

The cowardly mate shrank away to his cabin, washed his hands and face, slipped into a boat alongside and pulled ashore in order to obtain a warrant to seize poor Tom for the assault. The boatswain was none the worse for his sudden and somewhat awkward somersault overboard. The old scoundrel received a good ducking which he richly deserved. He would have met his end if a shark had caught him. Of all the wicked reprobates and persecutors that ever trod a deck, he assuredly was the worst. The old blackguard used to flog us cabin boys daily. I, especially, never escaped a single day. He seemed to delight in it.

On that same evening, Richards was apprehended, dragged on shore, and thrown into prison. The following day he was taken before a magistrate, who after hearing the simple statement of the facts, dismissed the complaint. He recommended that Richards should receive his discharge from our ship if he desired it. This arrangement was equally satisfactory to both Tom and Mr. McCastle. The coward was afraid for his life, and justly so after what had happened.

I had no idea just how dangerous life at sea was then. Little did I know that death was an ever-present fact of life for sailors.

That year, when I set off on my first journey, there were nearly one and a half thousand shipwrecks. As a result of so many losses a Select Committee on Shipwrecks[23] was created a few years later to address the issue. Their report showed that between the years of 1833 and 1835 the entire crews of 81 vessels were lost, and the estimated number of seamen that lost their lives in those vessels was over two and a half thousand; significantly more must have died in the other shipwrecks. Drunkenness contributed towards the loss of many ships.

Our Captain had to rely on charts that were unreliable since many coastlines had not been accurately surveyed and charted. The depth of the water was often inaccurate, so we had to rely on measurements using lead weights, difficult in rough seas.

Navigation was notoriously difficult too. Sextants could be troublesome to use, particularly in bad weather. Good navigators were essential. Many ships had incompetent Captains and Officers, and we were in their hands. Mapping journeys by marking the position of the ship on charts, had to take account of the ship's speed, wind speed and direction, latitude, and longitude, as well as sand banks, rocks, and other hazards. Any errors could be disastrous. Collisions, particularly in rivers and harbours, were not uncommon.

Of course, our ship, like all such vessels, was wooden and had no bulkheads. It was over a quarter of a century years before significant numbers of iron-clad sailing ships began to be built. Other aspects of ship design, including the incorporation of lifejackets, safety lines and other safety features, also had to wait. They were sadly lacking during my time at sea. Seafarers were constantly at risk of being swept overboard in rough weather and, although we had a long boat on board, we did not have a proper lifeboat.

Other accidents were a regular occurrence, falling from rigging for instance. We often had fights amongst the crew, and these could result in injury. Most of our crew did not know how to swim and so the risk of drowning was always present.

We all were prone to various diseases, such as yellow fever and cholera, and these could be fatal. Epidemics were common. Scurvy, due to lack of vitamin C, was rife. It was easily preventable by providing fresh food, especially citrus juice, but sometimes we did not have access to these.

Rats and lice on board ship caused ill health too. Typhus was spread by a louse that lived in dirty conditions, especially filthy clothing, and bedding. Although we kept the ship tidy, we paid little attention to keeping our vessel clean. Most men slept on the deck or the forecastle and bedding soon became filthy and infested. We tried our best to minimise this by sleeping in hammocks. In the cramped conditions on board ship, if any of us was infected with typhus it could easily spread to the entire crew.

Physical fitness was essential. If we showed any sign of weakness it was exploited. Bullying and punishment was commonplace. We were often lonely, depressed and even suicidal but we dared not show any signs of this. We were trapped, however, because our poor pay meant that most of us had to stay with our trade. It was difficult to save up enough money to be able to retire, but this was the trade I had chosen, and I had to persevere with it.

5 Icy Surrounds

In the autumn of 1835, we were sailing off the East coast of Canada, having collected wood which was needed to make barrels for sugar when we returned to the West Indies. Lumber was in short supply in Demerara, and the best price for lumber was in Nova Scotia, Canada.

The wood came to our rescue in a storm. The ship grounded on a reef of rocks, and although there was no loss of life, the *Isabella* was considerably damaged. Indeed, had she not been laden with wood, she would have sunk. We made for St Andrews, the port nearby, and the ship was hauled upon a gridiron[24] in the dockyard, where repairs could take place.[25] The cargo was then unloaded and sold. The damage took two and a half months to repair.

We set off once again to load timber in a nearby timber yard. By now, it was the depths of winter. The extreme cold, and the harsh treatment from the mate, McCastle, caused several of the crew to desert the ship. Among those deserters was "Liverpool".

I slept in the forecastle and, as the bow had to be kept open to allow for loading the cargo, it was open to the elements. Sleeping quarters were bitterly cold. We tried to warm the place by lighting a fire in an old iron pot, but we derived little warmth from it. As there was no chimney for the smoke to escape, we had to choose between being suffocated or frozen. Our clothes were frozen stiff. Indeed, our trousers were so stiff, they could be stood upright. The only way to unfreeze them was to take them to the ship's galley. On deck, blankets in the hammocks froze to each other and, when breathed on during the night, ice formed a fringe on the necks of the crew.

Willie Hall or rather "Derby" and I were great buddies. He appeared to be two or three years younger than me. Late one afternoon he had been sent by McCastle to clean out the long boat which was being towed astern. It was absolutely freezing. The boat rocked vigorously from side to side in the strong wind. The cleaning had to be done so Willie persisted. He knew that if he didn't do a good job, he would pay for it. The mate severely punished the crew if he saw any blemishes.

He hadn't been cleaning for long when he noticed he was adrift. Somehow the line tying the boat to the ship had come apart. He knew he was in trouble. No amount of shouting and waving could catch the ship's crew's attention. He saw the ship disappear as the wind and tide took him. Soon the ship was no longer in view. The sun disappeared behind the horizon. There were no lights and darkness enveloped him. He was frightened out of his wits. It wasn't long before the cold took a grip of him. He shivered continuously. He could find no warmth anywhere. Gradually he fell into a faint and collapsed.

When Willie didn't appear in the forecastle at tea-time 6 o'clock, enquiries were made about him, and it was then discovered that the long boat had gone adrift with him in it. It was quite dark and blowing a gale right down the bay. No one could have heard his cries when the boat broke adrift, and as there were no oars in her, his situation must indeed have been helpless. Moreover, no one knew at what time the boat had drifted. All we could assume was it must have been around 4 o'clock when Willie was in the boat. The wind was blowing so strong that by the time he was missed, the boat might have drifted six or seven miles out to sea.

Orders were immediately given to lower away the quarter boat[26] in search of him. This was rapidly done. The second mate, with two seamen and me, proceeded in the boat to search for poor Willie. Our task was highly dangerous and almost hopeless. We rowed as fast as we could. Each spray of the waves, as it dashed over our bows, froze as it fell into our boat. As we rowed, we shouted at full stretch of our voices. The night was so dark, and we couldn't see further than ten yards. Our shouts were the only means whereby we could let Willie know a helping hand was near. For three hours we rowed, and rowed continuously, but the bleak wind, which whistled over our heads, brought no response to our calls.

Numb, exhausted, and wearied we rested on our oars in order to decide what was best to be done. There appeared, however, no other course but to proceed still further down the bay. Once more we rowed with renewed vigour, for another hour. By that time, we had drawn close to a small island, not far from the mainland, which we reckoned might be a likely place that Willie's boat had drifted.

We decided to pull for this spot, beach our boat, and rest there for a while until the moon rose, which was then in her last quarter. As there was no appearance of any habitation close at hand, we ran up and down the beach to keep ourselves warm. In calm way we passed the time until nearly midnight, when we launched our boat and renewed our search. By this time the moon rose and aided our search. We closely inspected every corner of the bay, and after two hours of continuous searching we were delighted to discover a boat high and dry on a sand bank, about two miles from the land. As we approached the vessel, we were alarmed and dismayed to receive no response to our repeated calls.

The sand bank was long and flat, and as the tide had been ebbing, we couldn't approach nearer than fifty yards of the boat. I was so anxious to discover whether it was the missing long boat, and if Willie was really in her or not, that I leaped into the water to find out. I soon saw by the painted white line round her, that she was indeed the lost boat. But when I drew closer, I discovered poor Willie stretched along her bottom covered in a sheet of ice. I was horrified. Poor boy, he had fallen asleep – a sleep of which is often fatal.

The second mate, and another seaman, was by his side in a moment. He opened Willie's jacket and placed his hand upon his chest. There was still warmth, and Willie looked so calm and so placid, we felt sure that he was still alive.

I will never forget the scene of that night. The dark barren hills in the distance; the rough sea of the bay covered with floating masses of ice; the clear blue sky overhead with the waning moon flitting rapidly behind long flakes of greyish clouds. Calm and still in the boat, with his auburn ringlets frozen to his handsome brow – the peaceful appearance of the dead or dying boy, with his delicate features more interesting than in the happiest moments of his life, were altogether so striking that they could not fail to make a lasting impression.

We tenderly, but hastily, carried him to our boat, and then pulled for the nearest shore. Fortunately, we landed at a spot not more than half a mile from the only house which was to be found for miles around. It was a small, substantial, though somewhat straggling farmhouse built of logs. It was several minutes before we could make anyone hear us. We heard voices inside the cottage, debating what was to be done. Visitors of any kind were rare in those parts, and at that untimely hour of the morning, our visit naturally caused alarm.

At length, a middle-aged woman opened the door. A ray of the moon at that instant, shone on the death-like appearance of Willie, who lay supported on our knees. She required no further explanation. She was a woman, with all the maternal feelings of a mother. She saw in a moment we needed her aid and welcomed us in. It was such a welcome that only a mother could give. Not one more word was spoken. The woman seized upon the unconscious boy and assisted by two young women, who appeared to be her daughters, carried him away. The husband and his two grown-up sons welcomed us into the kitchen, or great hall.

A glorious fire, comprised of large and well-seasoned billets of wood, was soon kindled. The house, which had seemed so desolate from the outside, with its log walls cemented with mud, and its heavily thatched roof, was now full of comfort within. The walls inside were whitewashed. Red curtains decorated the small openings which served the purpose of windows. Over the great mantelpiece were suspended a couple of muskets and, beneath those, various tin culinary utensils lay, so bright that they looked like silver. On each side of the large fireplace stood two great easy chairs made of wood from the neighbouring forest, with pieces of carpet stuffed with wool – rather cumbersome in appearance, but most comfortable.

In one corner were an antiquated cheese press, a great stone, and a screw. In another was a cupboard dresser for the dishes, plates, cups, saucers, etc, all neatly arranged. Overhead and dangling from the beams were great long bunches of dried onions, hams, sides of bacon and an infinite number of similar edible goods.

The master of that humble home welcomed us sailors to his fireside and proceeded to feed us and offered us rum. One of his daughters came in to fetch some hot water from the kettle which stood before the fire. The second mate insisted upon snatching a kiss "out of regard for her father". This, however, was honestly given and bonnily received, and away tripped the simple-hearted girl, to aid her mother in their mission of love by tending to the frozen boy. The great care and unwearied attentions of that good mother and her daughters had been the means of preserving poor Willie's life. Their gentle treatment had succeeded.

We greatly needed rest when the farmer and his household resumed the labours of the day. They kindly supplied us with beds, and we slept soundly until noon. By that time Willie had been completely restored.

Thanking the generous and kind-hearted benefactors with all our hearts, we launched our boat, and proceeded on our way back to the long boat. The wind still blew in the same direction. It was impossible to tow the long boat, in which Willie was cast adrift, so we hauled her as high up the beach as we could and rowed back to the ship. It was a very hard pull as the wind was against us, but we arrived at 8 o'clock that same evening.

McCastle was happy that Willie had been saved but he was furious that his rescuers had taken so long, and that we hadn't brought back the long boat. Indeed, he seemed more concerned about its safety, and arranged for it to be collected. He swore at us and took his anger out on me, flogging me with a rope's end when I got on deck. He didn't touch the older rescuers. Forgetting my position as a junior, I retaliated. I snatched a billet of wood and felled the mate to the deck. Relatively unscathed and rather taken aback, the mate's flogging and kicking thereafter was far less severe than before.

However, Willie was not destined to live a long life. On a subsequent voyage from Demerara to Liverpool, I had the misfortune to lose my only true friend and companion.

It had been blowing a strong gale for two or three days, but on the day that he was lost the weather had suddenly changed from gale to calm, with a clear blue sky overhead. After my duty on watch, I was aroused from my sleep by a rush along the deck, and a startling cry of "man overboard!" I leapt from my hammock, and without waiting an instant to dress, sprung upon the deck. No sooner had I got there I knew that all was over. Willie was not far away, but he was sinking, and evidently quite unconscious. He made no effort to save himself and did not seem even to notice the rope which had been thrown out to him. Before the long boat could be lowered, he was many fathoms under water.

I never forgot his last look. I thought the drowning boy recognised me. But he must have lost consciousness before he made his last gasp and sank. As he sank, he clasped his hands. The water was as clear as crystal, and I saw the body sinking many, many fathoms below the surface. His death affected me deeply.

Willie had been sent to loosen the jib and had either been violently thrown from the jib-boom through the uneasy motion of the ship, or had missed his hold, and for a time sank under the bow of the vessel, and thus was rendered unconscious. Everyone on board felt his loss.

6 Desertion

On our return voyage to London, that same year, 1835, the sudden death of our excellent commander Captain Tait shocked the crew. It was felt the more acutely, as the person taking over was McCastle.

Tait was never a very fit man, and the change from the severe cold in Canada to the excess heat in the West Indies had been the main cause of his death. The burial of the captain took place the day after his death.[27] This ceremony was the first that I had witnessed at sea. It was calm and still. The sky was of that clear blue which is only be seen in tropical climates. Not a cloud was visible. A strong red glare from the sun's rays spread along the whole western horizon and danced in alternate gold and silver streaks on the smooth undulating waters of the deep blue Atlantic.

The carpenter had made a rough coffin, in which the body of the late Commander was laid, with sufficient cannon shot at the lower end, to sink it. The whole ship's crew was assembled around the coffin. We all showed our respect for the late Captain, except McCastle, who, it was obvious, only pretended to be affected. He moaned and blubbered his way reading the service. When it came to saying, "earth to earth", he blundered by saying "earth to water", which raised almost a smile from little Colehill. At this flagrant outrage upon his authority McCastle showed his true colours. He stopped short the service, looked daggers at the poor boy, and struck him a violent cuff on the side of his head, saying "there, take that, you infernal young imp, for laughing at your Captain."

In almost the same breath he ordered the slip rope to be withdrawn, and the coffin was launched into the deep feet first. It sank some ten or twelve feet then bobbed up again, and a moment after filling with water, gradually sank lower and lower, until it was lost in sight. The ship lay so still, and the water was so clear, that we watched the coffin for many fathoms, slowly sinking, never to rise again.

When we arrived in London all the seamen quitted the ship, and none of them could be persuaded to return to her, except the Boatswain. My life was very miserable. I had no option but to serve out the term of my apprenticeship. If I ran away there was nothing for me to do, and I might once more be reduced to sleep in sheds as I had done in Liverpool, and perhaps beg for bread in the streets.

McCastle was a canny fellow. He reserved his tyranny for when the owners of the ship were not around. They had no idea of his cruelty. He hoodwinked them, and they confirmed his appointment to Captain. The second mate was promoted to fill the vacancy caused by McCastle's elevation, and a new Second Officer was appointed. The Boatswain continued to serve in his former post. The sudden and unexpected promotion of McCastle in no way improved him. He had little knowledge, and he was vain, overbearing, and arrogant. These, added to his meanness, meant that he was the worst of Masters.

Life on board was so miserable that I considered suicide. Despite toiling diligently on my daily tasks, I saw no reward. In fact, it appeared that the harder I worked the harder the beatings.

Whilst in Georgetown I took my chance and escaped at night. It is 1836 and I was now twenty. Yet again, as before in Liverpool Docks, I had little but the clothes I stood up in. By daylight I was far away from the ship. I managed to secure a job in a plantation. Living amongst the slaves, I was made welcome. This, however, was not the type of employment which I wanted and, when offered a situation of £4 per month on board of a schooner then lying at Georgetown, I readily accepted it, not doubting that the *Isabella* had by that time sailed for England. This offer was made to me by an individual who was then on a short visit to the Planter, and who described himself as the manager and part-owner of the schooner. He was, I found afterwards, by birth a Spaniard, but he spoke a little English.

I agreed to accompany him on the following day to the schooner, which then lay at anchor a little below the fort at Georgetown. *Isabella* was still anchored some two miles distant, and I was disappointed and greatly alarmed when I saw that she had not sailed.

Part One: At Sea

When I arrived on the schooner, I was excited to see that it was one of the most beautiful vessels I had ever seen. She was a long vessel, quite wide and very shallow. She was brigantine rigged.[28] She was evidently of American build but hoisted Portuguese colours.

Her bulwarks were full of port holes, which might be used in action or just for show, but I thought I could trace marks of gun carriage wheels on her deck; on the forward deck, in her bows, was a circular plate of iron, partly hidden, inserted in the deck, as if it could be used for a heavy swivel gun.

The crew were a sad contrast to the beautiful craft in which they sailed. They were a set of the dirtiest, laziest, and most reckless looking follows I had ever seen. Their only employment appeared to that of keeping the schooner clean. They lounged on deck one half of the day, either sleeping, or drinking, playing cards or dice, or smoking their pipes. In fact, they seemed to do pretty much as they pleased. They were evidently all foreigners, though some of them spoke a little broken English. The Commander and the Chief Officer were evidently British, as they spoke with a Scottish accent, although they usually spoke in Spanish. They spoke kindly to me, but I had some strange misgivings about them and the ship.

I had hoped that by now the *Isabella* had sailed and that I had escaped detection. Unfortunately, this wasn't to be. On the second day I was recognised by a visiting clerk who had seen me before. That afternoon I was taken off the ship as a deserter. At the port I was interrogated. I described the reason why I had absconded from the *Isabella*. McCastle was sent for. He admitted that I knew my duty and performed it well, and overall reported favourably on my character. It was explained to me that my desertion would be overlooked if I returned with McCastle to the ship. This I refused to do. As it happened the second mate had been discharged due to his failings, and therefore a vacancy occurred to fill the role. It was offered to me, and as I felt a promotion might lessen McCastle's cruelty to me, I reluctantly accepted.

A few years later, I learned I had had a lucky escape. The schooner I nearly joined was a pirate slaver![29] Her skipper was one of the most depraved and desperate characters that ever trod a deck. He had, it was said, in his career massacred more human beings than any other buccaneer. This infamous miscreant perished as he deserved, upon the scaffold.

The business of a slaver was bad enough, but the more dreadful occupation of this arch-pirate was to attack the regular slavers and rob them of their slaves on board. Whenever they resisted, of course they were captured by force of arms. The carnage in those bloody encounters was truly dreadful. Rather than yield to such an enemy, the slavers would sometimes blow up their craft with the whole of their living cargo, with men, women and children chained down in the hold. Slaves, when captured, were of course sold in the markets, precisely as they would have been, and the pirate slavers would reap the rewards.

Had I not been discovered as a deserter, my life would have changed considerably and I may well have ended up on the gallows.

7 The Bullying Mate Leaves

The journey back to England under McCastle's command wasn't without incident. It was evident that he was not a good Navigator. We headed for Liverpool.

As we approached St. George's Channel, between Ireland and Wales, the ship encountered very severe weather. We lost all our sails and were very nearly wrecked on Skerry Rocks. McCastle seemed quite bewildered as we approached land. It took three days[30] seeking shelter around the coast before we at last docked at Beaumaris. I was astonished that we had been able to escape the many dangerous rocks at all.

After repairing our sails, and putting the *Isabella* in order, we sailed again, but we had not been more than ten hours at sea when we encountered another severe gale. This continued without ceasing for three days, and our ship had to run for the Clyde as she became very leaky. When we reached Greenock, the cargo was landed and the old ship was ordered into dock for extensive repairs. It was soon discovered that the dry rot had set in throughout the ship. How she held together for so long was astonishing.

It was here that McCastle left the *Isabella*. The owners gave him another command.[31] I, of course, was not disappointed to see him go. I didn't hear of him until ten years later when I learnt that he had died of brain fever off the coast of Africa.[32]

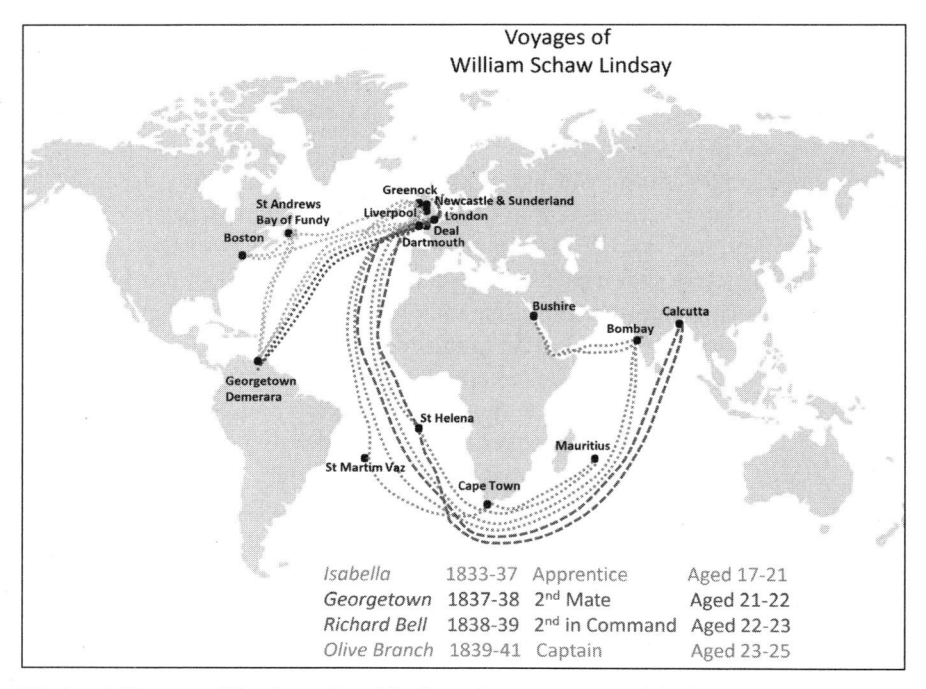

Isabella	1833-37	Apprentice	Aged 17-21
Georgetown	1837-38	2nd Mate	Aged 21-22
Richard Bell	1838-39	2nd in Command	Aged 22-23
Olive Branch	1839-41	Captain	Aged 23-25

Lindsay's Voyages. The Suez Canal had not been constructed in Lindsay's days at sea, so journeys to the Far East were via the Cape of Good Hope, South Africa.

Whilst the ship was undergoing repairs, I visited my uncle and aunt in Ayr, though I never revealed the many hardships I had suffered. It would have caused them much unhappiness. The four-week stay was a pleasant break, and I had a cheerful time with them.

Following my leave, I returned to the *Isabella,* where significant progress had been made with her repairs. A further two months later that year, 1836, she had been completely refitted and we sailed again for Demerara. Our new commander was Captain Dinning,[33] who was familiarly known under the name of Honest Jock Dinning. He was indeed an honest fellow, and a thorough sailor. I found a very different prospect before me, compared to McCastle's captaincy.

8 Ship's Steward

It was during the dreadful gales that occurred at the start of 1837 that I met with an accident which nearly cost me my life. It shortened one of my legs a full inch and a quarter. I was twenty-one.

The *Isabella,* on her way once again to the West Indies, had cleared land and was off the West Coast of Ireland when she encountered a tremendous storm. The captain, exhausted after a long stint, had thrown himself down on a couch in his cabin. As it was the chief mate's watch below, I, as Second Officer, oversaw the ship. It was between midnight and two in the morning. The ship was close hauled and under close-reefed top sails – reefed foresail, and mizzen. She was a 'flush ship', and along the quarter deck on either side, there was a row of water casks lashed to the rail stanchions.[34]

I stood with my elbow resting on the capstan, watching the motion of the ship. The gale came in fearful gusts, lulling for a few minutes, and then bursting forth with increased violence. The fury of the hurricane directed against our frail barque[35] and threatened to capsize her. My orders were not to shorten sail without calling the captain. For my own part I rather gloried in a stiff gale and felt a secret delight in seeing the ship driving through it, lashing the green seas right over her bows, driving through every wave, and then rising and shaking herself like some frolicsome water dog, ready for another plunge.

A gust of extraordinary violence was fast approaching. Nevertheless, I stood my ground as I did not want to disturb the captain. The fierce wind hit us, and the ship heeled over. The heavy sea which struck the ship carried away with it the entire range of water casks that had been lashed to windward. One of them was dashed right through the skylight into the cabin and, in its course, crushed the mahogany table inside to pieces and destroyed the whole of the one side of the cabin bulkheads.

The other casks went smack through the bulwarks, carrying overboard two of the seamen, who, poor fellows, were not seen again. In fact, they must have been killed instantaneously by the blow, and their mangled bodies launched into the raging sea. The edge of another of the casks, as it dashed across the deck, caught me on the left leg, tore open the fleshy part of my thigh, and dislocated the kneecap from the knee. The cask also hit my right thigh with full force, and it broke in two, a few inches above the knee. I lay flat out on the deck. My life had been spared, as if by a miracle. When I was picked up, I was found entangled in some ropes. These had prevented me from being washed overboard. Captain Dinning and the Chief Officer were on deck in an instant.

"Where is Lindsay?" shouted the commander. No one could tell. For a while it was thought that I had been swept overboard with the other two seamen. It was fully five minutes before they discovered me among the ropes. They thought I was dead and carried me below to one of the cabins. I had suffered dreadfully. Two of my ribs had been broken; my right leg was so doubled up that the foot rested on my chest, and the thigh bone protruded through the flesh. My body was a complete wreck. When I recovered my senses, I was unable to utter a word, and believed I was going to die. I was placed under the care of our steward, Robert, a native West Indian.

Although immediate danger to the ship appeared to be over, her position was still much too perilous for the Captain and the First Officer to leave the deck. The gale continued for two further days and all hands were on deck to ensure that the ship didn't flounder. Only Robert was able to attend to me.

Most merchant vessels did not carry a surgeon except when there were a few passengers on board. There wasn't one on board. There was however a medicine chest in the cabin with an abundance of ointments and dressings, together with a book of directions on how they should be applied. Robert, who could read, studied the manual attentively and succeeded in bandaging my left thigh in such a manner that in time it healed. The kneecap as well as the ribs, somehow or other got into their proper places, and I was cured as effectually as if I had been under the treatment of the most skilful medical practitioner.

My right leg was the most difficult part to manage. To adjust this properly the steward was sorely puzzled for more than two hours after the accident despite all his skill and ingenuity. He however succeeded in getting the bone back through the flesh, through which it protruded, but the agony I suffered during that operation was beyond description. It was subsequently found that Robert had reset it without lacerating any of the sinews or opening any of the arteries. This ingenious and surprising feat would no doubt have astonished some medics. Perhaps the steward, if he had to perform a similar operation a second time, would not be quite so successful.

There were however no splints, nor bandages, in the medical stores. Splints were formed from mouldings on the cabin doors, and from panelling. One of my shirts was torn into rollers which served as bandages. The steward struggled against the lurching and rolling of the ship to carry out his work and at length the operation was completed by blocking my leg between the side of the bed and the ceiling of the ship, so that it could not move. After two hours the work was done.

For the rest of the voyage, which lasted two months, I lay constantly on my back, and by the time our ship anchored off Georgetown, I had just managed to creep on deck with the assistance of the steward and another man. In Georgetown I obtained medical advice, and much to his surprise, the Doctor said that, under the circumstances, an excellent job had been made of the splice for my leg.

I was, however, not contented with the "splice", and thinking that I might be lame for life, later consulted the opinion of Sir Astley Cooper,[36] the eminent surgeon at the London Hospital. I asked him if it would be advisable to have my leg re-set. Sir Astley looking me hard in the face, and, with a smile, said "Ah! That is just like you sailors; keep your leg as it is, it will never spoil your dancing." I followed his advice.

As it was, there was great excitement in Britain when we had arrived back from the West Indies. The whole country was celebrating Queen Victoria's accession to the throne in June that year. At the end of the voyage, I rewarded Robert, with all I could give, which was my entire earnings from that voyage.

My cure was indeed miraculous. It took some months to accomplish, but in the process of time, it was so perfect that I never experienced any ill-effects from those serious injuries, apart from a slight limp.

9 Pestilence on board

At Georgetown, in Demerara, yellow fever raged. In that same year, 1837, I had been transferred to another of the *Isabella's* owner's ships. She was the *Georgetown*. A vessel of 500 tons, newly built. Her commander was Captain Michael Keane[37] and I was again Second Officer.[38] One of the cabin passengers, an intelligent and gentlemanly man, had, during the outbound passage, expressed great alarm about the disease. His visit to the colony was intended to be a very hurried one. He wished to visit an estate which he was interested in.

On the second day of the ship's arrival, I met him on the wharf. He said how disappointed he was with the place and the climate, but remarked he never felt in better health and spirits, and that he was then on his way to dine with a friend a few miles from the town. The following day I heard that the man was dead and buried!

That very evening the man had been seized with the first symptoms of the disease – a violent pain across the temple. By midnight the black vomit followed. At 2 o'clock in the morning, he was a corpse. By noon he was in his grave. In those climates it was dangerous to keep the dead body above ground for more than twelve hours, when it could possibly be avoided. The speed with which death followed the first attack shocked me.

During the many voyages we made to the West Indies, we had lost none of our crew to that terrible disease. Indeed, it had assumed a very mild form for many years, and, in some seasons, there were no deaths from yellow fever at all, even amongst the native population. The ravages, however, made during that season, were far worse than the previous healthy ten years. For a time, work of all kinds was suspended, and most of the well-to-do people left town and took refuge in the country. Our crew had, however, no such means of escape.

One by one our crew was seized with the fever and fell victims. The mortality was as great, or nearly so, on board many of the other ships which lay at anchor. The air was clear, the sky transparent, and the weather supremely beautiful. But in the thin haze which hovered over the town, and the river, extending to the flat and marshy plains which for miles skirted either bank, there lurked an air of impending doom. The bloom of spring and the gloom of death were in such great contrast. Death could strike at any moment and two cases out of three were fatal. I, however, was the only one on board the *Georgetown* to wholly escape the disease or some symptom of it. One morning, when I awoke, I found two of my shipmates had died in their hammocks, and yet I had escaped the malady, although they lay close to where I slept. Out of a crew of thirty-one, no fewer than sixteen had died in the short space of three or four weeks.

Our Captain, Keane, was also attacked, and so violent were the symptoms that no one had the slightest hopes of his recovery. He himself, however, seemed not to worry about death, and his only thought was that if he died, he might be buried with naval honours! He recovered, but it was a long time before he was fully fit.

When it came to the burials, they were pitiful affairs. It was difficult to get local help to bury the dead. I attended the so-called funeral of the ship's carpenter. His body, placed in a rough shell, was carried in a cart dragged by a mule to the churchyard, situated in a low swampy ground, and was deposited there. The shallow grave was about two feet deep. It was full of water and land crabs lay ready for their prey.

10 Promotion

In 1838, with great difficulty, a sufficient crew was mustered to carry the *Georgetown* back to London. There, the chief mate, Thomas Millman, was appointed to the command of the *Richard Bell*, which was in the process of loading cargo to Calcutta, India. He offered me the situation of Chief Officer, in that vessel, which offer I accepted.[39]

Mr. Anderson, the owner of the vessel, in recognition of my services, gave me my release from apprenticeship, and presented me with five pounds. However, when I applied to Captain Keane to give me the usual written reference, he refused. When I pressed him to do so, he seized a pen, cocked his hat on one side, as was his habit when he was put out, and wrote as follows:

> This is to certify that Mr. W.S. Lindsay has served under me as Second Officer, one voyage to and from Demerara, in the ship *Georgetown*.

Part One: At Sea

He is a thorough sailor, knows his duty, and does it. But more I cannot say in his favour, for though he is sober and attentive, he is without exception the sauciest scamp that ever trod a deck and is certain to finish his career either on the gallows, or at the Admiralty as First Lord. Signed, Keane.

"There" he said, "as you must, and will have it, take that," handing me the document "and much good may it do you."

It was the first and last character reference that I received. Happily, I wasn't in need of it in the future.

During my time in Calcutta, serving on the *Richard Bell*, and whilst on the banks of the river Hooghly, I picked up a Hindu skull. I carefully preserved it and took it home to show an anthropologist. As is well known, it has been the custom from time immemorial for Hindus to cast their dead into the Ganges and into its branch, the Hooghly, which in their eyes are sacred. It is nevertheless a muddy, filthy river, far worse than the Thames, and almost as bad as the Clyde. These corpses were daily seen in great numbers, of all ages and sexes, and in every stage of putrification, floating up and down, with every ebb and flow of the tide, being excellent food for the alligators, and for vultures and carrion crows.

Our ship anchored a good way down the river. She had a cargo on board and was on the way to England. A passenger and I went ashore to try our hands in shooting some of the vultures and crows which thrived in the place.

The old pilot warned us about tigers which were in the vicinity, but we accepted the risk. Although footprints proved that the animals were around, we were not troubled by them. We would have taken him more seriously had we seen anyone carried off by one of the tigers. As indeed we saw happen later. We fired our guns at the birds on numerous occasions, but our powder and shot were wasted.

The banks of the creeks, which had been dry for some time, were littered with bones, and skulls of various kinds. Seeing a skull cleaner than the rest, and having an excellent row of teeth, which a dentist would have coveted, I picked it up, and rolled it carefully in my handkerchief. I presented it with a solemn face to the old pilot, so he could have it for his dinner. The joke succeeded, and everyone joined in the laughter. One of the seamen washed it carefully, and as the steward thought it quite an ornament, he placed it on a shelf at the foot of my bed.

After the day's excursion, I was quite tired, so I went to bed for a rest. The skull provoked a dream. I dreamt that the Hindu came into the room and demanded my head, as I had his. I replied saying that the Hindu would look odd with a Scotsman's head. This didn't worry him and, he drew a cutlass from his belt, and with one blow, whipped off my head.

I was awoken abruptly by the steward, with a cry that "dinner awaits". I gave the man a right roasting for putting the skull at the bottom of my bed. I ordered the ghostly ornament to be stowed away in an empty locker where it lay undisturbed for more than five months; and there it might have remained totally forgotten had I not, after receiving the command of the *Olive Branch*, formed the acquaintance of the anthropologist in Sunderland to whom it was later presented.

The *Richard Bell* lay at Newcastle docks, so I made my way there by stagecoach from Sunderland. It was a beautiful Sunday afternoon towards the end of July 1839. I travelled there to get some charts, and other odds and ends which I had left on board the ship. I remembered my promise to the anthropologist, and taking the skull from the locker, I wrapped it in my silk pocket handkerchief. The coach returned to Sunderland about seven or eight in the evening. It was full inside, but I secured the only vacant seat on the top. The "all right" was given, and away rumbled the stagecoach, four-in-hand, across Newcastle bridge and up the main street of Gateshead, which was somewhat steep and roughly paved.

The coach had just reached the top of the hill, when away slipped the skull from my handkerchief, tumbling down the street which we had just climbed, to the amazement and horror of the crowd of passers-by, who were returning from Church. I was however determined not to lose my precious possession, so I shouted to the coachman to pull up, whilst I got down to chase after the skull.[40] After a lengthy run, I finally caught it, with many onlookers watching suspiciously, and returned in triumph, to my seat on the coach. I had to relate the whole history of the skull to the other passengers, so that they didn't think I was a body snatcher.

Having collected my possessions from the *Richard Bell*, I took command of the *Olive Branch*, a barque of 400 tons, which was about to be fitted out on a voyage to Cape Town and Mauritius. So it was that I was placed in command of a ship trading to India. I was very proud of my achievement. My new title, 'Captain Lindsay' resonated well. I was only 23.

11 The Sick Sheikh

My first command of the *Olive Branch* during 1839 was uneventful.[41] We sailed from Newcastle to Cape Town via Dartmouth.[42] From South Africa we journeyed to Mauritius and returned to Newcastle via St Helena.

It was towards the latter end of 1840 that I sailed once more with the *Olive Branch*. My destination on this voyage was Bombay with a cargo of coals, bottles, and various descriptions of glassware. We were a long time in clearing the English Coast. The weather was very stormy, and we were unfortunate to encounter a succession of adverse gales. For fifteen days and nights I beat with the old ship in the Straits of Dover against a westerly gale, and under double reefed topsails. It was indeed miserably cold, bleak work, and my prudence in adopting such a course was somewhat questionable. I was however young and full of life and spirit, and whilst other ships lay snugly at anchor in the Downs, I was resolved to go ahead. On the sixteenth

Part One: At Sea

The *Olive Branch* on a stamp from Ciskei, South Africa, in a series on sail troopships.

day I sighted the Isle of Wight. We were then favoured with a slant of wind from the north which enabled us to weather away Ushant and clear the land.

The *Olive Branch* sailed on to Bombay without incident. Having arrived, it was difficult to secure a cargo however the East India Company wished to have coals delivered to their army stationed on the Island of Karrack[43] in the Arabian Gulf. Although the navigation in those parts was dangerous, I took on the cargo.

On Christmas Day 1840, I wrote to my brother-in-law congratulating him on news of his marriage to my sister Mary. I said that I was to sail to the Middle East the following day on 'Government service'.[44] The voyage took much longer than expected due to adverse winds and the intricate navigation.

On route, early one morning when the *Olive Branch* was getting underway on the eastern shores of the Gulf, a native boat pulled alongside, and a person who seemed to be important came on board. Using sign language, he implored me to accompany him on shore. At first, I positively declined, but the man pointed to a large building in the centre of the town which lay opposite my ship. Holding my hand to his head, and placing both hands on his stomach, the man imitated a person vomiting. He indicated that someone important was very ill and needed treatment. Grabbing the medicine chest, I followed the stranger ashore. I ordered four sailors to follow me in another boat so I could return to my ship.

Hurrying through filthy narrow streets, lined with miserable clay houses, we came to a large house. It was owned by the local Sheikh. At the walled entrance two shabby guards stood shouldering old rifles. As the stranger and I passed them, we were saluted. We proceeded through a long and narrow, dark passage until we came to an apartment where we were ushered in.

The Sheikh lay surrounded by his courtiers. The cries of many female voices in trepidation were heard from an adjoining room. The noise was very disconcerting, so the first thing I did was to remove the women. They were very reluctant to go. Eventually all was quiet, so assuming as serious and knowledgeable a face as possible I took the Sheikh's hand and felt his pulse. Then, looking firstly at the patient, then his courtiers, I indicated the seriousness of the case. I however signalled I would be able to help.

I made my patient stick out his tongue. I looked up his nose; turned up his eyelids, felt the beating of his heart, and placed my hand on his stomach. The Sheikh was a large man, evidently more than six feet tall, very muscular, and between forty and fifty years of age. His stomach appeared to be unusually swollen and very hard. It was obvious that the man had been gorging himself, and the food would not digest.

Amongst the medications in the Medical Chest were calomel[45] and jalap,[46] which were the universal remedies of all internal complaints on board ship. It was to these that I turned. I paced up and down, taking my time to decide what to give my patient. I then asked one of the attendants for a cup of water into which I put the medicines. In view of the man's size, I made sure that there was a sufficiently large amount.

The Sheikh did not seem to relish the smell or the taste but, when I made signs that he would die unless he swallowed it, he gulped it down. Such a large dose had never been given. It very speedily flattened his stomach and never had he undergone so complete a clearing out!

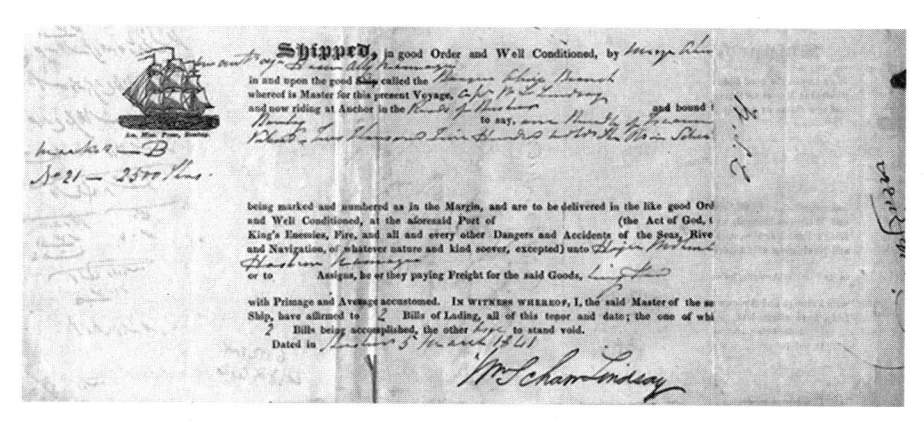

Olive Branch Bill of Lading at Bushire 1841. The Lindsay family.

Part One: At Sea

By the afternoon the Sheikh was feeling much better. He forced me to accept a couple of Arab horses and a Persian shawl as a reward for his treatment. I later sold the horses in Karrack, and the latter I took home, and presented it some two or three years later to my aunt Janet Schaw.

Word of the cure spread throughout the town. A great crowd had assembled at the gate of the Palace, anxious to see me when I came out. Very little trade was carried out in the area and so Europeans were relatively unknown. I was a great curiosity. They followed me to the beach, shrieking and cheering me at the top of their voices. They surrounded me, taking time to examine my clothes, and were especially struck by my pocket watch. At last, I was able to drag myself away, make for my boat and set off for the *Olive Branch*.

12 The Commodore and the Monkey

So it was, after six weeks, in the spring of 1841, that my ship arrived in the vicinity of its destination, Karrack Island, in the Arabian Gulf.[47]

A contingent of the East India Company army was encamped there. It consisted of the 16th Infantry Regiment and a detachment of the 2nd Bombay Artillery. Most of the men were Indian sepoys[48] except the Officers who were English. With its cargo of coals on board, the *Olive Branch* served as a refuelling ship for the small fleet which was occupied surveying the coast or suppressing local pirates. We were anchored off Karrack for four months.

In charge of the Honourable East India Company's Indian Navy in the Persian Gulf was Commodore Brucks,[49] a meticulous sailor who knew no fear. He was quite a character, an eccentric to the extreme. He was about 60 or 65 and one of the dirtiest looking Officers I had ever seen. A short man, not more than five foot two, he wore exceedingly high heeled boots – rather unusual for a sailor – in order to make him appear taller than he really was. He seemed to hold soap and fresh water in utter abhorrence. Apparently, he never washed his hands or face for a week and his shirt lasted him a fortnight.

For some reason I got on very well with him. He confided in me and told me a great many stories about the stupidity of his own Officers and the impertinence of the Military Officers on shore, accompanied with details which I would much rather not have heard. He had a special detestation of them, and there certainly was no love lost between them.

During my stay, an amusing incident occurred. I had been there about six weeks, when Colonel Davies, who was Commander-in-Chief, ordered a grand review of the forces under him. The day was to be concluded with various athletic games and other amusements. Prior to the event, I stayed at the camp with one of the Officers who had become my friend. He had a terrible grudge against the Commodore who had once insulted him.

A horse was kept on shore for the use of the Commodore. He was a wretched horseman, and although rather rotund, was very fond of a gallop. Somehow, he managed to remain on the horse at whatever speed he went. The horse itself was a long-legged skeleton of a brute and would have made very little if sold as horsemeat.

I had a monkey on board my ship and, without my knowledge or permission the Officer took the monkey on shore and handed it over to one of the native tailors. He proceeded to dress it in clothes similar to the Commodore's: a blue coat with three stripes on the right cuff and a cocked hat decorated with the tip of a feather from the tail of a goose.

Another Officer had a dark greyhound much like the Commodore's gangly horse. A saddle with stirrups was made to fit the dog and a cloth, resembling the one which was thrown across the Commodore's horse when in full dress, completed the caparison. When everything was prepared, both these animals were secured under lock and key, to be called upon when needed.

The weather on the morning of the review was excellent. The Officers' wives wore their best clothes and were seated under a covered platform which had been erected for them. These ladies had no love for the Commodore either. He prided himself in plain speaking and he had never attempted to conceal his hatred and contempt for the female sex.

The review passed off splendidly. The soldiers performed their drills magnificently, which drew approval from the Commander-in-Chief. They even seemed to satisfy the critical Commodore who, although he had no special duty on shore, was galloping about in full dress and in high spirits on his long-legged horse.

Everybody happily settled down to enjoy the athletics that were to follow the review. Their enjoyment rose to an unspeakable height, when to the astonishment and delight of everybody, with one single exception, the monkey lashed to the back of the greyhound rushed into the ring: the exact copy of the Commodore on his skeleton horse. There could be no mistake about the identity.

The ladies could not restrain themselves. They laughed, waved their handkerchiefs, and literally screamed with delight. Even the Officers for a moment forgot the strict rules of discipline and joined in the fun. The men, seeing the excited state of their superiors, joined in the clamour with shouts of laughter which rang on all sides.

The dog, with the monkey on his back, ran around and around the ring in a state of feverish excitement, greatly increased by the noise. The soldiers took special care to keep the ring clear so that everyone should have an opportunity to see the spectacle of the model Commodore.

One peel of laughter followed another. This rose into a perfect frenzy when a most irate Commodore rushed on horseback into the ring. When he appeared, Colonel Davies felt it necessary to respect the Commodore's rank and to quieten the crowd, even though he himself had difficulty in containing his laughter. He gave orders to the troops to dismiss and to return to quarters which they promptly obeyed, evidently well pleased with amusements of the day.

Commodore Brucks was extremely angry. He threatened to report the matter at once to headquarters at Bombay. He vowed that he would have a court martial. In his opinion half the Officers ought to be shot, and the other half dismissed from the Service forthwith. Colonel Davies promised an immediate inquiry but, although great efforts were made to discover the culprits, they were never found. He ascertained that the monkey belonged to me, but he was not able to find out who took the animal from my ship. As I was a favourite with the Commodore, the Colonel was satisfied that I was not involved.

The Commodore was not often on shore after this incident, and he never again rode on his long-legged horse.

13 The Ambush

On my return, I found all was well on board the *Olive Branch*. I learnt that there were good prospects of obtaining a large amount of bullion to be transported as freight, so I delayed the departure of the ship for ten days. I wasn't disappointed. The surrounding area was in a heightened state. There were rumours of war. Indeed, the First Anglo-Afghan War had recently broken out.[50] Many of the native chiefs and merchants were fearful that hostilities might extend to the area, and they were anxious to transport their riches to a safer place. My ship was the only British merchantman in the Gulf, and it was conveniently placed to undertake the task.[51]

It was on an excursion to a town some three miles from Bushire to fetch a considerable quantity of currency, which awaited collection, that I nearly lost my life once again.

Although I need not have attended to the transportation myself, I decided to go. A native Officer accompanied me with twelve native soldiers. Nothing worthy of note occurred until we were on our return journey, within a mile of the fortifications of Bushire. The sun had set, but it was not quite dark. There was a clear sky, and the moon was in her first quarter. It was a lovely evening. For protection I had taken with me a small pistol which I carried in my side pocket, and which I had loaded before starting on our return to Bushire. I did this as a precaution even though I did not anticipate any danger.

The money, consisting of gold and silver coins, was enclosed in strong canvas bags sealed and marked by their owners together with the amount of money. Each of the soldiers carried one of the bags slung across his shoulders and marched in order, two in a line. I walked by their side conversing with the native Officer who spoke a little English.

The countryside was devoid of houses or huts. The local population lived in greater security within the confines of their fortified towns. The soil was sandy without any vegetation except for large quantities of tall brushwood which grew in clumps on the summits of the numerous little hillocks, lining the path. Due to the possible impending war, the neighbourhood was more than usually infested by a nomadic tribe of marauders.

As I walked along, smoking a cigar, and chatting with the native Officer, I suddenly heard a loud yell that immediately warned the soldiers, for they instantly threw down the bags of currency in a heap and formed a solid square around it, shouldering their rifles ready for defence.

The yell seemed to come from behind the hillocks, and from there almost immediately sprung a tribesman brandishing a sword which glittered brightly in the twilight. The man made a dash at my left shoulder, with the intent to kill me instantly. This he assuredly would have done had I not instantly taken a step backwards. The sword, instead of catching me on the shoulder, ripped through my coat inflicting a severe wound across my chest from which the blood flowed freely.

Feeling that the blow was not mortal, and, never losing my presence of mind, I drew my pistol fully cocked, and aimed it at the marauder. The man threw his arms up in the air and cast a wild imploring glance to the heavens.

I fired. The robber fell, with a yell. No sooner had he fallen, than the soldiers heard a commotion. The tribesmen were in full retreat. Our troop did not remain to see if the man I had shot was killed, or only wounded. We were conscious that we were still in danger as it was evident that the man who had fallen had many followers. They were panic-stricken at the sudden fall of their leader but could return at any moment.

The soldiers shouldered the bullion and marched off at full speed towards the safety of Bushire not far away. The following day a strong detachment of soldiers was sent in search of the body of the tribe's leader, but none was found. Indeed, I never heard whether the chief I had shot was killed or not.

My wound was very painful, but it was not dangerous. As it was a clean cut, it soon healed, having been washed and dressed by a native surgeon. The scar, however, remained on my chest for the rest of my life.

Having shipped all the money, the *Olive Branch* set sail for Bombay. The currency on board amounted to no less than £300,000 in coins. I, however, discovered, on the passage down the Gulf, that the bags really contained a much greater amount than was stated. The reason for this was obvious. The rascally Persians, in order to defraud me of my small freight commission of about one quarter per cent, entered a sum that was less than what the bags really contained. Therefore, instead of the £300,000, there was no doubt more than £400,000 on board.

A secure place had been built in the after-hold of the ship to store the bags, and a large portion was also stowed in the state rooms of my cabin. Whether through the friction of the ship at sea, or the insufficient strength of the bag, one of them broke, and the coins tumbled out upon the floor of the cabin. The contents marked upon the bag 2,000 local coins, and the receipt, or Bill of Lading, corresponded with that amount. I ordered a fresh bag to be made, and in counting the coins to ascertain that the amount as correct, I found to my surprise that instead of 2,000, the bag contained no fewer than 2,890!

I was at a loss for what to do. I argued with myself whether I should just replace the bag with only the 2,000 and keep the surplus of 890.

I even went further though, and thought, "These fellows will only pay me a freight commission on £300,000. They have knowingly and wilfully defrauded me of my commission on any balance over and above that sum, I have given receipts for a specified amount, and the owners could only claim delivery of that sum, and no more. I should surely be justified, if, upon my arrival at Bombay, I opened the bags and counted out the amount due. I might thus, all at once, realise a princely fortune, and return home with a handsome independence for life."

I decided however, although I had been cheated, the money was their property. I could not cheat them of what was theirs.

I subsequently related the circumstances to the firm, to which my ship was consigned at Bombay, and was told that I was "a young fool" for my pains. However, my conscience told me that I was right, and I never regretted the course which I took.

14 After-effects of a Hurricane

When in Bombay I found that available freights to England had considerably improved, and accordingly I loaded a cargo of cotton and seeds for Liverpool.

I realised I had become a petty tyrant on my ship. I had a temper which I had difficulty controlling. I was a hardened young man. Although I was never tempted by alcohol, I was in the habit of routinely swearing. I felt it was my duty to my employers to drive the crew hard. I wanted them to know the difference between right and wrong.[52] Perhaps the life I had led, the companions whom I had mingled with in the forecastle of the *Isabella*, and the sufferings and hardships I had endured, together with the tyrannical treatment I had experienced when a boy, all contributed to my strict behaviour.

The passage on the *Olive Branch* from Bombay to England passed with nothing worthy of note, until we drew near the Cape of Good Hope. We were sailing a hundred miles or so south of Algoa Bay.[53] The weather up until then had been fair and favourable, but the barometer gave indications of an approaching gale. The wind was blowing from the south, veering from S.S.E. to S.S.W, and consequently the Cape was leeward. We could be in danger of being driven on to the shore. Towards nightfall, I summoned all hands to shorten sail. No sooner had I done this than the gale increased dramatically, and I was obliged to call upon the men again to double reef the topsails and furl the mainsail. The ship heeled over dreadfully at times in the sudden gusts, as they howled and whistled through the rigging.

By midnight the gale had increased to almost a hurricane. The sky was densely overcast with dark clouds, and the only light we had was from the phosphorescent wave as it dashed its thick spray over the deck or poured in vast volumes through the gangway upon every lurch of the ship.

I felt that there was more canvas on the vessel than she could safely carry, but as the land was to the leeward and as it was impossible to go on the opposite tack, we had no course left other than to carry sufficient sail to go ahead and escape the rocky shoreline. To heave to, as I would have done in any other position, would have been certain destruction. The ship then would have driven bodily upon the coast.

At about one in the morning, I was forced again to call all hands to take another reef in the topsails. I next had the topsails lashed to the yards, double sheeted and double tacked to foresail. Having taken these extraordinary precautions, and having bent a storm trysail, which was also firmly lashed to the mizzen boom, I sent the watch below until we had weathered the Cape. I now felt that it was a case of life or death. No sail should be furled. They must stay as they were, until either the canvas blew away, or the masts went over the sides, or the Cape was cleared. I disclosed my concern to no one but took a fixed position on the quarter deck where I could watch the progress of the ship and direct the helmsman.

The gale showed no sign of lessening. At times it blew harder than ever and threw the ship so far over that she made far less progress ahead than we could have wished. At other times the speed was truly terrific, and I often felt as if the *Olive Branch* was about to capsize. The waves rolled as if each would swallow up the little barque and every third one, as it curled along with its great feathery cap, seemed like some huge monster of the deep sent for our destruction. But again and again, the good ship rode over them, dashing through some, skirting over others and was like a wild thing sporting with the raging sea which played so furiously with her. The spars bent and cracked, the rigging rustled and the ship herself groaned under the fearful load she was under, but all kept firm and onwards she went on the course I had indicated.

The whole of that night and the following day the gale raged with unabated fury. I never left my post. A cup of coffee and a biscuit sufficed for all my wants. The crew wondered why I was acting strangely. They did not know the danger they were in. I kept my own counsel. I scarcely opened my lips except occasionally to give an order to the helmsman or to secure some odds and ends. The second night looked as if it might be more dreadful than the first, even though the clouds overhead were not quite as dense. On that night I would not allow any of the hands to turn in but kept them all at fixed posts upon deck. Though land had not been sighted I knew that somewhere between midnight and two in the morning we should be close to the Cape promontory.

It was a night of dreadful suspense. I was wet, worn out and exhausted but dared not shut my eyes. I was riveted to one spot and stood fixed as if I

Part One: At Sea

was made of stone. My spirits, however, never flagged, and my nerve never failed me.

Midnight passed then one o'clock and two o'clock. Each hour seemed to last for ever. Three o'clock approached and nothing was seen. I was beginning to hope and feel that we must have travelled to the west of the Cape though I was determined to keep my watch until daylight. Suddenly, the clouds cleared, and the moon burst forth and shone on the waters, but it was to reveal an appalling sight.

"Land! Half a beam on the lee bow," roared the seaman on lookout.

My nerves shook, and my spirit left me, but it was only for a moment.

"Steady!" I exclaimed to the helmsman. "Keep her as she goes."

One glance at the land over which the white waves were breaking, proved that it was "touch and go". The slightest movement off course and our destruction was inevitable, as it was a rugged coast.

Nearer and nearer, we drew, and still the ship, though dragged to leeward, went ahead but agonisingly slowly. Another half hour later and the ship was abreast of the Cape, not a hundred yards from the outer point at which the sea broke furiously, dashing its white foam far over the cliffs behind it.

At that moment a terrible rip was heard. The foresail had split into shreds sounding like the cracking of many coach whips. I sprang to the helm, seized the wheel and threw it hard over. The good ship responded. The action paid off. At that moment I saw to my delight the rocks had passed us by. We had weathered the Cape and were safe!

No sooner was this accomplished than my wearied spirit gave way. I shook like a leaf and felt tears trickling in large drops down my cheeks. My lips were covered with blood. During the hours of intense anxiety, whilst I had stood on the quarter dock watching the progress of the ship, I had subconsciously bit them until they drew blood. The *Olive Branch* was now running before the wind with the whole of the Atlantic Ocean ahead of us. We were beyond all danger from the land and had simply to steer a straight course before the gale.

There was nothing which required my attention longer on deck. Leaving directions therefore with the crew to disentangle the foresail and set another in its place, I went down below to my small cabin, where I had not been during the two preceding nights. There, a lamp was dimly burning. The rolling of the vessel which had completely deranged the few articles of furniture, and the heavy spray from the sea, which had found its way through the skylight and companionway into the cabin, was slopping backwards and forwards on the floor. It was altogether a miserable appearance.

There was a small mirror which hung from a nail driven in the bulkhead. I took one glance at it and turned away with a shudder from my own image. The blood from my lips had saturated my collar and partially stained the front of my shirt. My unshaven beard was rough, and dirty. My hair was uncombed, and the curls were matted in lumps on my head and forehead. The spray of the sea had whitened my rough overcoat and the salty scales were congealed on my face. I looked wrinkled and shrivelled like an old man. My eyes were blood-shot and stood out from their sockets. My appearance was so hideous I could not bear to look at myself.

Mentally I felt exhausted and humbled. If there is a God, I thought, He had spared us. My ship had avoided being dashed upon those rocks which we all had so miraculously escaped.

Weakened beyond belief, I dropped onto my knees, and my head fell upon my sea-chest which stood in one corner of the small cabin. I did not pray, but I remained a long time in this position, and I rose cold and stiff. I mechanically threw off my outer clothes and flung myself into bed, overwhelmed with fatigue and anxiety. I fell asleep and did not wake until the following noon.

I awoke a changed man, my eyes opened to a new world. I felt like someone waking from a long and harassing dream. The ordeal resulted in something of an epiphany. For the first time I read the Bible that my Reverend Uncle had given me and compared it to Thomas Paine's *'The Rights of Man'*. I concluded that Paine's book was such drivel that, in disgust I threw it into the sea, resolving to be less of a tyrant.

About ten days after rounding the Cape of Good Hope, the *Olive Branch* arrived at the island of Saint Helena where we cast anchor for twenty-four hours so that we could replenish our stock of fresh water and procure some fresh provisions for the crew. On the island, I visited the farmhouse where the great Napoleon[54] had been detained as an exile and his body buried nearby, twenty years earlier. The grave was in a spot which was everything any man could wish for as his last resting-place. In a little valley, rich in greenery, close to a spring and over-shadowed by the branches of two graceful willows, lay the ashes of the immortal Napoleon. A plain flagstone surrounded by light iron railings was inscribed with the simple words "Napoleon Bonaparte", with the age at which he died. This was all that marked the spot where lay the body of the person who, in his lifetime had changed dynasties, overthrown monarchies, establishing Kingdoms of his own and, during his ambitious career, had shed the blood of millions.[55]

Soon after my ship sailed for home on an uneventful voyage. and we arrived safely in Liverpool. I had saved a little money, some two or three hundred pounds. As I was anxious for a short rest on shore after the arduous life I had led, I decided to give up the command of the vessel, and wrote to Messrs. Greenwell & Sacker, the owners, announcing my resolution. They did not object to my resignation but were so pleased with what I had done that they told me whenever I was tired of the shore, they would give me the command of another ship.

Part One: At Sea

Some three or four years later, I was settled in London, as a ship broker, with a rapidly increasing business. Amongst the various ships placed under my charge was my old *Olive Branch*. She had been sold to a shipowner in Stockton, who for many years afterwards, sent her to me for charter. I gained many a commission out of her until she was lost in 1851, at the mouth of the St Lawrence River. Little did her owners know at that time that the *Olive Branch* was my first and last command at sea.

My life at sea was over. It was 1841. I was twenty-five.

Part Two

Journey to Success
(1841–1852)

15 Reminiscing

Having arrived in Liverpool, the port I had started out from nine or so years ago, I determined to track down those men who had helped me in my time of need.

I traced the kindly elderly Scottish gentleman who had helped me secure a place on the *Isabella* and who provided provisions for ships from his small shop. He had not the slightest recollection of assisting me. Nevertheless, I rewarded him with a Persian shawl to present to his wife.[1]

Next, I went to the canal to revisit the places I remembered from the dark days living rough. There, in the canal, I had washed my only shirt. I went to the brick kilns where I had slept and where boys had feasted on stolen roasted chickens and roasted potatoes. I assumed that half the boys had ended up in Botany Bay, and that the rest of them had either been hanged or had died.

I next paid a visit to the baker's shop where I used to buy my daily meals, in the form of a penny biscuit, and the pump where I had so often quenched my thirst. I once again visited the floating chapel where I had attended Church and out of my scanty resources had nevertheless contributed one penny in aid of that humble sanctuary for the destitute. I then retraced my steps to the Princes Parade and to the open sheds in which I had slept night after night. There I found my initials which I had cut on the brick wall.

Having visited all these well-remembered places, I sought out Tom the Rigger. His humble dwelling was occupied by strangers who had never heard of him. I wanted so much to reward him for all his past kindness to me, but even after a full day of searching, I could not find him.

Nine years had made little or no change to these places which I had become so familiar with. They brought back recollections as vivid as if they had only happened the day before.

Part Two: Journey to Success

I reflected on my treatment. How my family had turned their backs on me. How I had to fend for myself at a young age. How those people outlawed by society are likely to become reckless and turn to crime, and how the erring child should be gently led on the right path. These profound thoughts filled my mind.

I then decided to make my way to Glasgow. The same line of steamers, belonging to Messrs. Burns[2] of Glasgow, continued to ply between that port and Liverpool. Curiously enough, I returned on the identical boat in which I had worked my passage to Liverpool all those years earlier. I did not recognise any of the crew, but I observed the captain was the same, although I did not approach him.

Remarkably, no sooner had I arrived on board than I saw an old shipmate of mine, Dugald McDonald, who had been a steward on the *Isabella*. Dugald did not recognise me but recalled events when I recounted them to him. We discussed various members of the crew from the old days. Jock Dinning, our skipper at that time, was dead. So was his brother, Long Dave, the carpenter. They had both died in the ship on the coast of Africa. That petty tyrant McCastle had also died a miserable death by brain fever. Jenkins, the mate, had been promoted to the command of a barque called the *Thistle* trading to Berbice near Demerara.

"And as to your old fellow apprentice Liverpool," said Dugald, "I saw him on the quay there a minute ago."

He had scarcely uttered the words, when he further exclaimed: "There he is!" pointing to a great swinging fellow dressed in trousers and a red shirt, but without a jacket or waistcoat, swaggering on the quay, quite drunk, with a couple of women who appeared to be prostitutes of the lowest order, walking on either side of him.

The passage went smoothly and on arrival in Glasgow I paid a visit to my sister Helen. She gave me a warm welcome this time. Her elderly husband, Thomas Christie, had died four years earlier and she had been well provided for. The episode selling chickens in the market was not discussed. I stayed for a few days.

I then visited the house in Portland Street, where my brother Peter and his despicable wife had lived. I did not dream of entering it, as it was occupied by strangers, but I stood full ten minutes on the opposite side of the street, remembering the misery that I had endured in those earlier times. Both had died.

I was also keen to visit the house in which my mother had died when I was nine. My sister Mary, my brother Peter and I had been by her side when she passed away. I had been mortified by her loss and felt quite alone. The house had been pulled down, and a great row of stately tenements had been erected on the site in a continuous line for more than half a mile up the long street.

Not far from the old Cathedral, and at the head of a street named after Saint Mungo, stood a somewhat handsome and fashionable detached house called Parson's Green. It was by far the best in that quarter. Here a young lady called Helen Stewart lived with her brother Robert. I had met her briefly a few years earlier at a party whilst I was on leave from my ship and had been quite taken with her. I felt I was not on good enough terms to visit her then, but one or two months later I mustered enough courage to call on her and received a most kindly welcome from Miss Craig who acted the part of a parent. Robert, a man of liberal and extended views and of extraordinary determination of character, also gave me a friendly reception.

16 The Fairer Sex

I had written to my aunt and uncle in Ayr indicating that I would be visiting Scotland after my return voyage from India and received an invitation from them to stay. So, after my stay in Glasgow I took the stagecoach to Ayr where the good old Clergyman, Reverend Schaw, was awaiting my arrival. I was returning a confident twenty-five-year-old. My old aunt gave me a warm reception. So much had taken place in my life since I was last there ten years ago, yet nothing had changed in the Manse.[3] The ornaments and furniture were the same. The dining room was the same sombre place, reserved for people of importance. Both aunt and uncle were now in their 70s and very much stuck in their ways.

In my aunt's estimation however, I had become a great man. I was a "Captain of an Indiaman" as she delighted in calling me. My Reverend Uncle was very happy too. He was truly delighted and very proud to see me.

I spent two months of pleasure and enjoyment at the quiet Manse. I had many invitations to tea parties, but these were insipid affairs, and they were something new to me. My hand shook with trepidation when I had to pass the cups and teacakes to the young ladies. My nerve, unlike when attacked by marauders or facing a gale off the Cape, lost its firmness. I was self-conscious particularly because of my slight limp and my rather uncouth manners. However, marriageable men were scarce commodities in Ayr, and many of the mothers who had no dowries to bestow upon their daughters considered me perfection. There were usually eight or ten single ladies of various ages for every single man, and to keep all of them supplied round the room with cups and cakes with an unsteady hand, and no fine words, was no easy matter.

I could not dance or sing. The ladies at one tea party pressed me to sing which I did. Never again! I gave up in embarrassment. I tried instead to help out by turning the leaves of the music book, but I couldn't read music, lost my way and that ended up in further embarrassment.

Before long I tired of the quiet life in Ayr. An idle life and an active mind were not the most harmonious companions. I became anxious and fidgety to return to my old work again, laborious as it was. I therefore wrote to Greenwell & Sacker to find out if the new ship was ready which they had promised me the command of. The answer was not satisfactory. She was ready, but they had sold her. The fact was that Greenwell & Sacker had extended their business

Part Two: Journey to Success

beyond their means and the depressed times were pinching them. They could not conveniently hold more ships than they already had. Of course, I did not urge them to keep their promise but patiently waited another month amusing myself as best I could in Ayr.

I pondered over many things and amongst others, that which proved perhaps one of the wisest of my life. I thought of Helen Stewart. As I was due to visit Glasgow that month, I decided to call at her brother Robert's home in Parsons Green. Very much on the back foot, as I didn't know if she had feelings for me, I decided to ask for her guardian Miss Craig. I rang the doorbell and handed in card entitled 'Captain Lindsay' to the servant girl. I was ushered into the front room to wait.

The old lady was not more than five minutes, but it seemed an hour. However much of my apprehension vanished when she entered the room. She was so kind, so agreeable, and so affable in her manners that I was at once reassured by her honest, warm-hearted reception. She remembered me.

At length I asked how Miss Stewart and her sister Miss Margaret[4] were. It was a bold question, but the old lady answered it by pulling the bell and sending for them to come upstairs. They came but I could say little or nothing to them. I was tongue-tied. Helen was somewhat coy and retired and seemed almost as nervous as I was. Margaret was very talkative and asked a great many questions as to where I had been and what had happened to me. I answered as best I could. At last, we parted and, as I told Miss Craig that I was returning to Ayr the following day, she asked me to tea that evening. This invitation I gladly accepted.

I was less nervous on my return to the house. I found Robert there from whom I received a most hearty welcome. I also met Mrs Craig,[5] the elder sister, who was a widow. I saw her there for the first time and admired her as one of the most beautiful women I had ever beheld. She could not at that time have been more than twenty-seven or twenty-eight years of age. I was struck by her intellectual and classical appearance with her dark and brilliant eyes. I might have fallen in love with her in preference if I had had the chance.

I met others in the family and enjoyed myself amazingly. The family was quite invigorated, but Helen seemed rather demure. However, she seemed overall to be pleased with my company and with the few foolish things I said to her.

Robert talked to me about ships and coal, also on civic matters, for he was at that time contemplating entering the Town Council. Before long we would enter into business together.

I was due to leave the following day but somehow or other I was persuaded to stay. An afternoon excursion was arranged, a trip into the country, during which I talked a great many things to Helen, but to all of which, I got no answer except a laugh or a monosyllabic "yes" or "no". As to popping the question, that was indeed out of the question. I had no more nerve to do that than I had ability to fly. Hints were dropped by family members about finding a suitable house for Helen and me, but I felt that it was my duty to maintain a wife in the circumstances that she was accustomed to. I did not at that time feel that I was able to guarantee that. Nevertheless, I kept thinking of Helen and wrote anonymous poems to her. I stayed in Glasgow a further six days, every day growing less nervous.

When I returned to Ayr, my aunt wondered why I had been absent so long. I hinted at the reason and my practical aunt expressed surprise, suggesting that I ought to marry the daughter of Shipowner Mr Greenwell. I would not countenance the idea though.

I had not been in Ayr a week when I resolved to write to Helen Stewart a letter to pop the question. I did so. It was a bold step, but I made it a condition that she should wait until I was able to maintain a wife. I was not sure how long the wait would be. I rather suspected it would be two years; I did not inform Helen of this. The letter was very short and business like. It commenced "My dear Miss Helen" and ended with "be so good as to favour me with an answer in due course of post." I had no idea whether she would do so, still less that her answer would be a "yes". But it was. She accepted my offer on the condition I had stipulated, and the contract was sealed. Her letter commenced with "My dear Mr. William".

Another idle month in Ayr passed pleasantly enough. Every third day or so I had a letter to write to Helen[6] and received one from her, in which correspondence we eventually dropped the "Miss" and "Mr".

I also had a very pleasant trip to Millport, a sea-bathing resort on the Clyde where Mrs. Craig had taken a house for the season. Helen had gone on a month's visit to see her. It was there I was bold enough to steal my first kiss from my fiancée. There we talked about future happiness and of wedded bliss. In later years, however, Helen[7] told me that compared with what she heard from others, I was the coldest lover it was possible to conceive. I thought perhaps she had acquired her experience to some extent from novel reading.

The month soon passed. I wrote again to Greenwell & Sacker. They had no vessel for me, but they said that in another month two small vessels belonging to them would be in Limerick and that they would like me to proceed there and superintend the unloading of the cargoes and see to the repairs that would be necessary before they were again sent to sea. This I felt would be an opportunity for me. I would be paid all the time and have something to do in the way of business, so I readily consented to go.

Many years later I was to recall an incident with Mrs Richard Greenwell, the wife of my old friend and employer. She was a showy and fine-looking woman, somewhat sharp at times, but not a person of any ability above the ordinary view of persons of her position in society. However, the brains of very ordinary persons frequently produce sparkling arguments. I remember this in her case.

One evening an old bachelor, who had been enjoying her husband's hospitality, raised an argument with her husband, after we had adjourned to the drawing room, as to the relative importance of the duties of man and

Part Two: Journey to Success

William Schaw Lindsay c.1850.

Lindsay's wife, Helen Lindsay née Stewart, shown with their son William Stewart Lindsay.

Lindsay's sister-in-law Christina Craig née Stewart.

woman. I thought when he spoke of man as the higher order, because he found the means of supporting the wife and children, that his arguments were neither gracious nor well timed.

Mrs Greenwell, as well as the remaining guests, seemed to be also of that opinion, but for a time she bore his remarks with a great deal of equanimity. Some remarks however seemed to have touched her feelings to the quick – she was the mother of a large family – for suddenly she interrupted him, saying with a sneer: "Ah Mr So&So, you think that making money is the chief aim of a man and that, because it is a man's duty to make it, he must be superior to a woman. But when he doesn't make it," she sarcastically asked – the old bachelor had never made a sixpence in his life – "what status will you give to him then?"

This was a poser of a rather personal nature but he avoided it, saying that men were at the head of all important undertakings in the army, navy, colleges, and so forth.

Warming as she spoke, Mrs Greenwell replied: "Quite true, man is the great educator; he also teaches the monkey, and the bear, how to dance, taming even the wild beasts of the forest and bringing them under his control. For all this you give him credit, and I daresay he deserves it, but you might

Part Two: Journey to Success

give at least give equal credit to the woman who spends day after day, night after night – long weary nights – week after week, month after month, and year after year, taming the wildest of all animals – man!!"

I did not know if the idea was original – I never heard it used before or since, but it had the effect of completely silencing the old bachelor. For the remainder of that night at least he held his tongue about man's superiority.[8]

17 Limerick Docks

I saw in this Limerick business a glimpse of something in the future, though I could not say what it was. It would however give me an insight into how to conduct business on shore and, if I settled matters about the two ships to the satisfaction of Greenwell & Sacker, they might find me some other more permanent employment.[9] Accordingly, when the time arrived, I went to Ireland in good spirits. I made sure I was able to handle accounts and business correspondence. I studied book-keeping by double-entry with enthusiasm. I bought a book which gave me a smattering of Maritime Law.

Then, at the little dockyard at Ayr, where I had become acquainted with one of the partners, I soon made myself a tolerably good master of the prices of oak timber, pitch pine planks, tar, and oakum. I familiarised myself with the cost of employment, the wages of carpenters, caulkers, and blacksmiths, so that the Irish tradesmen could not cheat me in the repairs of the two vessels which were to be placed under my charge. My old school-fellow Jamie Davidson, who was a clerk in Cowan's Bank [10] gave me an inkling on how to handle banking.

When, therefore, I left for Limerick Docks in 1842 I had picked up a considerable amount of knowledge in connection with the business ahead of me, and I felt that it would require a pretty sharp Irishman to get the better of me.

I was, however, in need of all my knowledge, as the agents into whose hands the vessels had placed were notorious scamps. One of the skippers of the brigs was a thorough drunkard and the other a merry-hearted fool who never washed his face from the first week I saw him. Although he was not an absolute drunkard like his colleague, he was always in so muddled a state that I could never get two words of common-sense out of him. Between the agents and these two worthies I soon saw that my employers were likely to be fleeced to a considerable extent if I did not carefully watch them.

I advised my employers of a way forward. I took charge of unloading the cargoes myself. I also suggested that the two skippers be dismissed and that I would be allowed to appoint other Masters in their places, also to send the ships away again on whatever voyage I thought would pay the best. I received thanks from the Company and these actions were agreed to.

When the agents continued to try to cheat me, pocketing discounts from the ships' accounts which they had no right to pocket and making private bargains with the tradesmen about the stores, I discharged them too. One of them called me "the damndest Scotsman that ever came to Ireland". By this time, I had gained a fair knowledge of how shipping business was conducted in Limerick. So, as I thought it was of no use putting my employers to the expense of any further Agency Commissions, I took the matter entirely in my own hands, and became sole agent for the ships myself.

This step seemed to please them even more than any other I had taken. I had all the work done by contract. I arranged supplies and provisions in all the stores at the lowest prices, appointed new Masters, fitted the ships out complete for sea and determined the fares for passengers to North America. After much hard work, I had despatched them, all in order, in about three months from my arrival in Limerick. At that time, Limerick was an important embarkation port for people emigrating particularly to the United States of America to seek a better life.[11]

After settling all their accounts, I forwarded full particulars to my employers in Sunderland, and advised them that I was about to return to Ayr, at which place I should be happy to hear from them. Shortly after my arrival there I received a most flattering and pleasing letter from them in which they informed me that Mr. Greenwell had taken an interest in a large colliery in the neighbourhood of Hartlepool that was about to be opened. He offered me the agency at a salary of £150 a year and I readily accepted.

My services, they said, would be required in Hartlepool, where I was to take up my residence, in about six weeks' time. I had now some prospects of being able to maintain a wife. That had been my aim. With a light heart I visited Glasgow to communicate to Helen Stewart the good tidings. I daresay she was not dazzled with the amount of the income, but I felt that, with economy, we should be able to live respectably on it.

18 A New Start

As the newly appointed Agent for the colliery, I now had a new business to learn: the value of coals, the way they were shipped, the best markets for them, and similar details. I soon got to grips with these difficulties, and when I settled down in Hartlepool in 1842 aged 26, I had a very fair idea of what I had to do.[12]

The town had for centuries fallen into decay. It stood upon a promontory of land on the Northeast coast, about twenty miles south of Newcastle. The only buildings of note consisted of a church which stood upon the cliffs and one or two gothic houses which had not been washed or painted for years. In these resided the well-to-do, namely the clergyman and Old Vollum[13] the Banker, who had been Mayor for years. The rest of the locals were mainly fishermen. Old Vollum was also Director of the Docks which had been opened several years previously. He was "Master of all he surveyed" and ruled with a rod of iron. He was the most bad-tempered old dog I ever met.

I had not been there long before I saw the need for reform. I attended Parish meetings and challenged the Church Rates[14] which were being overcharged. Old Vollum and the council took umbrage at my interference but, with growing support from the public, I won through, and the Rates were reduced.

The Castle Eden Coal Company was an extensive concern and more than £100,000 had been sunk into the undertaking. They had opened offices for me in a new house on the Town Wall. About a quarter of a mile from the office, on the cliff, facing the sea a pretty row of houses had just been built. Still a bachelor, I took one of these and furnished it as neatly as I could from the money I had saved while at sea.

I employed a housekeeper, Mary, to act as cook and housemaid. She thought that I would never marry, so she was set for life, living in a house which she regarded as pretty much her own property. She had a habit of being rather free with my whisky decanter when visitors called but after a while, I stopped that by locking up the spirits.

There were quite a few characters in Hartlepool calling at my house. Most were rather too fond of drink. Old Vollum's son Will, unlike his father, appeared to be a gentleman and well educated but a terrible drunkard. Many of them met an untimely death. Several years later Old Vollum one night after a dinner party walked into the Dock mistaking it for the entrance to the Bank and was drowned. George Rowell, one morning, was found standing on his head at the foot of the cliff over which he had tumbled the night before, his neck broken and as stiff as the cliff itself. His brother Tom became an imbecile bankrupt through drink. Only Turnbull,[15] the Lawyer, became more of a true friend and helped me carry reforms in the town. He later became the mayor.

Making a success of selling Castle Eden Coal was not an easy task. As it was a new colliery, the coal had not been tried and tested so I had to find a market for it. The most sought-after trade came from King's Lynn, Portsmouth, and Shoreham. There were a great number of collieries competing for the business. Unlike other Agents, or "fitters", who used to bribe the Masters of these colliers with ever increasing amounts of money, I decided to adopt a different approach. I aimed to be first on board the ships as they entered the Docks. I made every effort to induce the Masters to agree to load, I then put a "stiffening keel" of coal[16] into them without delay so that they could not be coaxed or bought off by other parties. By the end of six months, I had fairly established the Castle Eden Coals, and obtained for them an extensive circle of shippers.

Now that I was earning a steady wage, I wanted to get married. I had of course carried on a regular correspondence with Helen[17] at Parsons Green and the day of our wedding was fixed for 12 November 1843. That time approached. Not a soul in Hartlepool had any idea of my intentions. Even Mary, my housekeeper, did not know that I was engaged. I had no time for a honeymoon, and no money to spare for it. I arranged to go to Glasgow on one day, get married on the succeeding day and return to Hartlepool with my wife on the day after.

On the morning of 11 November, I told Mary that I was going North by the 10 o'clock train. "And" I added, "Mary you must have the house in good order for I shall be back with your mistress in a couple of days or so."

"My Mistress, Sir!" exclaimed Mary, her mouth gaping open with the utmost astonishment.

"Yes," I said, "see to have my luggage at the train," and off I went to the office to get my letters before leaving. Mary remained stock still, as I passed her, lost in wonder.

I caught the train to Newcastle, and then on to Carlisle. The railway was not connected to Glasgow so from there I would travel on by mail coach. The coach left at one in the morning and, as I arrived at Carlisle at 8 o'clock at night, I thought I might as well have a few hours in bed at the coach house. I made sure to leave instructions that I was to be called at a quarter to twelve. Imagine my feelings however when I was awakened by the bugle of the coach, then just on the point of starting. I jumped out of bed clutching my clothes in my hand and rushed downstairs with nothing on but my drawers. The driver was on his seat. I begged him to stay just one minute until my luggage was down and without any ceremony, jumped into my seat inside the coach much to the horror of a couple of ladies, happily elderly ones, who were the only other passengers inside. I of course begged a thousand pardons from turning the inside of the mail into a dressing room but, when I told them that it was my wedding day and they became informed of the cause of my undressed state, they were mollified and graciously forgave me.

It was a cold, weary drive, I thought the coach would never get to Glasgow, but it kept to time, and was there at 9 a.m. Our wedding was to be at one o'clock. I drove straight to my sister Mrs. Christie's, where I found Dr Schaw and his wife. Uncle had come to perform the ceremony.

Our wedding day was somewhat the same as weddings usually are. Friends on both sides assembled. There was much laughter, a good deal of crying and a due portion of seriousness.

When the wedding was over, we set off by train for Edinburgh amidst a shower of old shoes and other symbols of good luck. We got to Edinburgh happily where we remained all night and started for Newcastle the next day. We stayed at Gateshead on the second night at the old-fashioned Inn where I used to put up when the *Olive Branch* was fitting out in the Tyne. Helen did not seem to relish that old Inn. The roofs were too low, and the passages too intricate. But it had been a favourite lodging house of mine for it was scrupulously clean, and the old landlord and his maiden sisters were all attention and kindness.

On the following afternoon we left for Hartlepool. As I did not want all and sundry to see us, I took a circuitous route home which was muddy. My wife wondered where I was leading her. Even though it was muddy outside, it was comfortable and homely inside. My neighbours had prepared a nice little supper and a roaring fire for us.

Next morning, I was as hard at work at my office, and as early down at the Docks, as if no event of importance had happened to me. People could not believe that I had been all the way to Glasgow in so short a time and brought home a wife.

19 The Lighthouse

Though my work in connection with the Castle Eden Colliery was considerable, it did not occupy all my time, and I was determined in my spare time to carry out reforms that I deemed necessary in the Town.[18] The first was to have the borough brought under the Municipal Corporations Act.[19] That I achieved, greatly assisted by Turnbull, after much hard work.

Next, I succeeded in designating Hartlepool as a Port Town.[20] That was a great triumph, and as it was then only ranked as a creek of the port of Stockton. My next step was to have it created an independent port. I carried that also, but strange as it may appear, I had a tremendous opposition to overcome from Old Vollum and all the old residents. They hated all change, which they dreaded, and they hated me with a degree of vehemence it was scarcely possible to imagine.

My third task was to erect a Lighthouse on the Heugh, or promontory. At that time there was only one small harbour light on the pier-end, which was only lit at half flood. It was not visible further than half a mile at sea, and was entirely obscured by the headland, so that vessels entering from the north could not see it. Navigation into the entrance to the harbour was also dangerous. During the winter season that part of the coast was often strewn with wrecks, and many most melancholy scenes had been witnessed by me during my short residence there.

One of these disasters occurred shortly after I was married, in the following January. I was aroused from my bed about four o'clock one morning by the cry that a ship had struck on the reef of the rocks under the Heugh, and not further than two hundred yards from the spot where I lived.

When I got out, it was blowing a fearful gale. The sea was breaking right over the cliffs, and the foam was washed right up to the door of my house. The moon was in her last quarter and through the mist I could see a barque of about 400 tons with her foremast washed away, rolling to and fro on the outside of the reef.

Several townspeople had gathered, but they could do nothing to save the people on board. We did what we could with life rockets[21] as no boat could survive in such a sea and, even if she could, it would have been impossible to reach the barque. But to no avail. Every successive wave dashed her farther and farther onto the reef. She must have been a strong vessel for she held together more than a couple of hours. At last, her main and mizzen masts went over the sides with a fearful crash, thereby lightening the ship which drove nearer and nearer to the perpendicular cliffs as the tide rose.

By seven o'clock her bows and her hull were torn to pieces as she settled on the rocks, with every wave dashing right over her. Piece by piece her hull then began to give way and, as daylight opened out, we could see the crew clinging to the wreck. One by one they were washed away, drowned, or killed by being dashed against the rocks. One person, with a rope tied round his waist and clasping a woman in his arms, attracted our attention. We supposed that they were the Master and his wife. Shortly after they shared the fate of the others and by nine o'clock the strong barque was broken in a thousand pieces.[22] The spectacle was a most heartrending one. If there had been a lighthouse on the Heugh it would not have happened. From that morning my resolution was fixed.

To enable this reform, I had to obtain a significant number of signatures on a petition to be submitted. One day, whilst obtaining these signatures, I met Old Vollum face to face. He could not pass me. He seemed too much excited to speak. But at length he could contain himself no longer.

"Sir," he said, "you are a nuisance to the place. Such upstarts as you will ruin it. Taxing us, Sir, is ruining us Sir. You are a low-minded cur Sir. You do this to annoy me Sir. I will pay you off yet Sir for this. You will go to the dogs, Sir. To the low kennels, whence you came. Allow me to tell you, Sir, that you are a low-minded upstart cur."

I stared at him and, with a sneer, and a sardonic laugh, I exclaimed. "You, ruin me? You! Why I shall be in high esteem amongst my fellows when you are rotting in your unknown grave."

And saying these words, I turned upon my heel and walked away. Many years later when I returned to Hartlepool, I rambled through the old church yard, and saw the old man's tombstone, and that of his son who had been drowned when drunk in the Docks. It was the only reference to him.

After significant opposition from Old Vollum and the Council, a Lighthouse was erected. It is visible from far out to sea. For years the Heugh Lighthouse was known to the fishermen and pilots by no other name than "Lindsay's Light". I received little recognition for my efforts though; the council grabbed the credit.

Indeed, an article in *The Newcastle Guardian and Tyne Mercury*, dated Saturday, October 16th, 1847, described the lavish supper which was organised to celebrate the building of the Lighthouse:

The supper party ... committed the injustice of suppressing all reference to the gentleman whose health ought to have formed the chief topic of the evening; and yet, how are we to believe that Messrs Denton, Rowell, Belk, and Vollum, forgot the debt of gratitude under which the town is laid to Mr. Lindsay for this great boon.

Why, the men who now take all the credit to themselves in this matter were the very parties who were at the outset its strongest opponents.

Part Two: Journey to Success

The Lighthouse at Hartlepool by J. S. Holmes.

Mr. Belk and Mr. Rowell petitioned against it, Mr. Denton refused to sign the memorial in its favour; the Hartlepool Dock and Railway Company would not move in the business, and it was principally owing to the services rendered by Mr. Lindsay – to his strenuous and public-spirited efforts both in Hartlepool and with the Trinity Board in London – that the result has been accomplished.

20 Partners in Iron

The business of the Castle Eden Colliery rapidly increased under my agency, and the profits proved satisfactory to my employers. After I had been there a year and a half, I thought I might safely ask for an increase of £50 to my annual salary. I well remember making the application by letter. My request was refused. I was most put off with this, as I thought that I had more than earned it. I kept my thoughts to myself though as I did not want to risk being replaced.[23]

At this time, I saw however an opportunity to partner with my brother-in-law Robert Stewart. He had trained in accountancy before acquiring his father's iron and coal business at Cleland, a few miles East of Glasgow. He was at a loss to find buyers for his pig iron[24] and I had seen that a great deal was sold in Newcastle. I had some success with this, earning a commission of between £300 and £400 a year.

Robert Stewart, Lord Provost of Glasgow (1851–1854) (after Daniel Macnee), by David Gauld (1867–1936).

Part Two: Journey to Success

This encouraged me to make another request to the owners of the Castle Eden Colliery, for an increase in my salary to £200, but it was granted with a grudge. I had managed to secure sales even though the quality of their coal was of an inferior kind. But they did not appreciate all the hard work that went into selling between 500 and 1,000 tons every day.

After I had left the Company, the trade fell off and before long their losses were ruinous. They were in debt to such an extent that the same colliery which had cost £115,000 was sold for only £20,000.

The additional sale of Scottish pig iron was much more profitable for me. With a little tact, the sale of 2,000 tons was an easy affair, and on that I received one per cent commission paid punctually by Robert's Company. It was less troublesome too, compared to selling coal where I had to board colliers early in the morning and then chase the skippers for payment.

I began to think seriously about giving up the Castle Eden Agency altogether, and about setting up in Newcastle as an Iron Agent. There were various reasons for this. Helen's health was not good, and the place did not agree with her, though she seldom complained. My work was not very pleasant. My employers, if they were satisfied, never showed it.

At this time however there was one event that affected me greatly: the strike amongst the pitmen in the north of England.[25] The Castle Eden Colliery issued orders that if the men did not resume work on a certain day they were to be turned out of their cottages.

As the men refused to leave the cottages on the morning however, I was ordered to go with a gang of men to the Colliery. I did not agree with this task. I have always had a strong love of people, and to see families turned out in the lane, and their prized possessions flung into the mud, was soul destroying. It was the first and only time I was stoned. That day was altogether the most unsatisfactory of my life. When I got home, I told Helen all the details of the day and, reiterating all my reasons, I told her that I had serious thoughts of resigning my situation. She, poor girl, cried. "What are we to do?" she said. "You cannot depend on always being able to sell iron in Newcastle, and should that fail, what are we to do?"

Quite true I said to myself. What are we to do? I could not go to sea again and leave her on her own; her health was far too delicate to allow her to go with me. That was a long and dreary night, but the more I turned it over in my mind, the more resolved I became to resign.

With a somewhat faltering spirit I wrote a courteous letter to my employers stating my intentions to settle in Newcastle as agent there for the sale of Mr. Stewart's iron and offering my services if I could be useful to them in that place.

In due course I received a much more polite letter than I had been accustomed from them. My resignation was of course accepted, but much to my amazement, they informed me that they wanted an agent in London, and they offered me the situation at £400 per annum.

I was indeed agreeably surprised and so was my wife when I took the letter home and read it to her. This appointment was a certainty; an income upon which I could depend, and a wide field was opened for me. Moreover, I knew that a great deal of Scottish pig iron was sold in London and, as long as I obtained the full market price for it, Robert would not care whether it was sold there, or in Newcastle. I, of course, gladly accepted the offer.

21 The Road to a Fortune

Within a month of this offer, my wife and I moved to London.[26] We travelled by express train. It was March 1845. I was twenty-eight. Although full of concerns whether I would be able to make a success of the job, since I had no connections in London, I was still optimistic. Through a school friend Willie McKay who worked in London at the Stationery Office, we were able to obtain lodgings in Brompton, opposite the Royal Brompton Hospital then being built.

On the following morning I proceeded to the city where I met Mr. Cook and Mr. Gladstone, the London owners of the Castle Eden Colliery, at the warehouse in St. Paul's Church Yard. Mr Gladstone had found a suitable office at No. 35 Abchurch Lane, and I accompanied him there to take possession and commence my duties forthwith. It comprised of a single back room on the ground floor, of a reasonable size but exceedingly dark. In it there were three desks, one for a boy who was to be my sole clerk, another for myself and one more for Mr. Gladstone. He knew so many people in London and was so well acquainted with the mode of transacting business that his presence and advice was invaluable to me.

One condition I made in my agreement with the Castle Eden Company was that, though I was not to sell coal for anyone else, I had full liberty to act on my own account as a Commission Agent or Broker for the sale of Iron. I therefore added to the agency the business of a Ship and Insurance Broker.[27]

On that very day – that very morning – I commenced business and my first job was to procure a Directory and take from it names of all the Coal Merchants. That afternoon I began my rounds amongst them. I did not get on very well that day for all I saw made me understand that they always bought their coal on the market, and they had no desire to change. They said that our coal was unknown and that it did not suit them to buy entire cargoes; they would rather pick and choose from existing suppliers. I got home about 8 o'clock at night tired, and considerably bad-tempered. At the end of the month, after visiting all the merchants in East and West London, I was beginning to fear that I would be obliged to give it up and go and settle in Newcastle.

When my wife hinted that we ought to take a house of our own, as it was very expensive living in lodgings, I could not agree with her. However, on one Sunday afternoon she persuaded me to go and see one which had caught

Part Two: Journey to Success

her fancy. It was a house, St. Peter's Villa, situated at Percy Cross, Fulham. It suited our purpose exactly and, having met and bargained with the owner, we agreed to lease the property.

The next morning when I got to my office at Abchurch Lane, I sat quietly down, and turned various matters over seriously in my mind. After some thought, I saw an opportunity to make a success of my business. I realised that at the Castle Eden Colliery there was another seam of coal; hard coal which would suit steamships. I suggested that the Company adopt this approach and send me a cargo here in London to be tested at the dockyards.

In due course a cargo arrived. After an infinite deal of labour and trouble, I got the government authorities to give an order to test its qualities and report to them accordingly. I took care to attend at Woolwich Dock Yard to see the coal tested. The report was favourable. It was transmitted to Somerset House, and after some fifty applications I obtained a copy of the report.

My field of operations now changed. From the Coal Merchants of London, I turned my attention to the great consumers of steam coals, such as the Peninsular and Oriental Steam Company, the West India Royal Mail Steam Packet Company and to those mercantile houses which shipped steam coals to foreign ports. Day after day I toiled amongst the shippers and consumers of coals in steam navigation. No one knew me and after many calls which resulted in failure, I finally made a breakthrough.

One day I had the good fortune to see Mr. James Allan, the Secretary to the Peninsular and Oriental Company.[28] Our conversation led to Glasgow coal, then Glasgow people, and I found that he knew Robert. I had a long chat with him. From that hour the tide turned.

Before me, I saw the path which led to a fortune. It was a market that was new and wide open. I knew that competition would follow, but I felt up to it and few grasped the significance. I learnt from Mr. Allan that his Company never bought coals at a price delivered on board at a port of shipment. The only way his Company bought the coals was at the port where they were consumed. He very kindly gave me a list of these coaling stations and told me the price they were ready to pay for steam coals delivered at Southampton, Gibraltar, Malta, Alexandria, Aden, Bombay, Singapore, Calcutta, and Hong Kong. He said he would take, as a start to test their quality, one or two cargoes at any of the above-named places, at the price he had indicated.

Shipbrokers began to come to my office in Abchurch Lane to offer me ships for charter. In time shipowners themselves began to find their way to me and, as I could talk to them about ships, how they were managed, how they were sailed and could tell them from personal knowledge about many ports in the world, we became somewhat familiar. The shipbrokers of London could not do so as they had all been brought up in Counting Houses. By coming to me direct they saved the broker's commission, and thereby got a higher freight for their vessels. I felt however that this was not fair to the shipbrokers and, in justice to them I was compelled to become a broker on my own account.

I also found another opportunity: that of fixing a return freight. Little by little I became known to merchants as the broker most likely to find them vessels at the lowest rates for return goods, as the outward freight was in my own hands. This led me naturally enough into the regular business of coal-shipper and shipbroker.

I set up agency partnership in Sunderland, with Lumsden & Byers[29] and in Liverpool with Lamport & Holt.[30] I kept up a daily correspondence with both Companies. They also corresponded daily with each other. Thus, we all knew what was going on in our own line of business in London, Liverpool, and Sunderland. Lamport soon found more strangers walking up his stairs in the shape of shipowners wanting freights, or of merchants requiring ships. Byers also found more Sunderland shipowners entering his office, for they knew he received a daily report from London and Liverpool of the principal freights in these markets. I worked hard to carry out any charter with good merchants Byers sent to me. Lamport did the same.

Of course, I had some extremely hard work at first, but at the end of the first year I found that I had cleared profits of nearly £1,000 on shipments of coals and brokerages on the vessels.

The second year my business increased to double that amount. By then my single-roomed office became too small and I was obliged to move to two rooms at No.11 Abchurch Lane, and to take a regular clerk to assist my two boys. At the end of the third year, I had established a splendid and lucrative position, as my business by that time yielded me £10,000 per annum.

All was gained bit by bit by hard work and close attention to it. My maxim was "Work! Work! Work!" and to "do to others as I would be done unto."

22 Building the Empire

My wife and I had resided in our house at St Peter's Villa in Fulham for three years when we decided, in 1851, to move to a larger house. It was called Mornington Lodge, in the Northern part of Fulham. The rent for the former was £50 per year and for the latter £160 per year. There was some reluctance to agree to the rent as I was a young man of 35, and the owner was not sure that I could guarantee the funds. We settled in and made suitable improvements to the house.

Many merchants in those days invested in ships. Much of their goods came from abroad, so ships were needed to import their wares. Some of the merchants overstretched themselves however and went into debt. One such man was a cobbler, an industrious man who, by hard work mending shoes in Sunderland, had saved some two or three hundred pounds. He invested it in a small ship and borrowed the remainder of the purchase money. This small ship was chartered by me for delivery of coals to Marseilles, and for grain for the return journey.[31]

Part Two: Journey to Success

The Master of the vessel, however, was unable to secure grain at a profit in Marseilles and was obliged to take on the loss-making cargo. The cobbler wrote to me explaining his ill fortune. He told me that the lender, who was a hard man, had given him notice that he would need to sell off the ship to repay him.

As I had chartered the ship from him, I felt obliged to help him. I asked him what losses he had incurred, and he replied £170. I was at that time not very rich, for I was then struggling, but the cobbler was very poor, so I sent him a private letter enclosing him a cheque for £170 and told him not to say anything to anybody about the matter.

The poor man however was so surprised with the receipt of the money that he could not contain himself. To keep it a secret was impossible for him. He went around Sunderland for a whole week telling the story to everybody. I soon became favourably known at that port.

That act proved one of the main reasons for my rapid rise as a shipbroker in London. Various Sunderland ship owners wrote to me to find employment for their vessels and my business with that port increased so rapidly that I was obliged to open a regular agency there. Before long I opened another agency, this time in Liverpool.

The Companies in Newcastle and Liverpool that I had association with worked on the same principle that I did, not one of speculation but of treating our customers' business as if it was our own. We were careful not to overstretch ourselves. Our customers appreciated the way our business was conducted and as a result it flourished.

I was favoured in another way by the famine[32] of 1846 and 1847. This created an enormous demand for vessels to carry grain to this country from the Black Sea and the Mediterranean ports and from the ports of the United States and Canada. I also held the great bulk of the grain charters from the Levant,[33] from the Danube, and especially from Alexandria.

So rapidly did my business increase and so enormous was its extent, all by adhering to sound principles and by unwearied industry, that during the 15 months of that extraordinary importation of grain, I chartered vessels for the conveyance of no less than 1,400,000 quarters,[34] or nearly 314,000 tons, of different kinds of grain. This was principally wheat and Indian corn which was sent to the various ports in England, Ireland, and the Continent.[35]

I had, during that time, extended my system of working with other contacts at the various ports throughout the United Kingdom, Antwerp, Le Havre, Amsterdam, Rotterdam, and Hamburg. As the ships arrived at their respective destinations, I required the agents to ensure safety of these vessels. My name was soon established among the shipping merchants not only in London but also abroad.

In Liverpool, I had opened out another connection for carrying on the American trade, and had established as my agents two young men, Samuel and William Pearce, sons of the Vice Consul to the United States at that port. My arrangement with them was that they were to confine themselves exclusively to the chartering of United States vessels. I saw that these were rapidly on the increase, and that it was of the utmost importance for me to work with them. To secure this, I got acquainted with the leading houses in London; Sir John Guest & Co[36] and Thompson, and Forman & Co who were the largest shippers of rails[37] to the United States. These were the bulk of the freights which suited the American ships. I soon got command of them. The two Pearces found me ships, and so large a business did I transact in that branch that I remember, between 1 January and 1 April of one year, I shipped as Broker no less than 105,000 tons of rails from the ports of the United Kingdom to the United States.

Thousands of miles of railroad track were built, and the stock market entered upon a period of relentless growth which mostly favoured railroad stock. Thus, began a speculative movement which lasted until 1846, when an economic crisis hit Great Britain. In the process, some merchants doubtless found new and profitable fields, but many must have been reduced to seeking a somewhat haphazard livelihood in speculative cargoes or in turning themselves into shipowners plying for charter. The competition of Continental countries, following our reciprocal trade treaties, resulted in several bankruptcies.

As a seafaring nation, Britain was the largest shipbuilding country in the world, and held supremacy at sea. Shipbuilding had gathered a pace to cater for goods transported to the major countries of the World, and especially Britain's colonies. 90% of Britain's trade in goods was transported by sea. Steam ships were beginning to make an impact. They started to replace wooden steam ships, and screw (propeller) steam ships began to replace paddle steamers.[38]

My Company had, by the end of three years from the time of commencing business, far outstripped all my competitors and had even at that time attained the position of one of the largest ship brokers in London.[39] In two years after that, I was again by far the first in that branch of business and chartered three times as many ships over the year, as did any broker in the city. But, at the end of my first three years, I had established a splendid and lucrative position, as my business yielded on average £10,000 per annum – all in commissions.

One event, among many during this time, stuck in my mind. On one fine spring morning I awoke about five o'clock fully refreshed with sleep but as it was Sunday, and too early to get up, I fell into a sort of dreamy slumber, and fancied I saw my uncle, Dr Schaw, come in the front garden gate. He had a stout staff in his hand and walked briskly towards the hall door. I dreamed that I ran downstairs to meet him and welcome him to my house.[40]

"No, no," he said, "Willie I can't come in, I've just come to say goodbye, for I'm off on a long journey and"– striking his staff upon the ground – "you see I am well prepared."

"Can I accompany you?" I asked.

"No, no," he replied, "the road is a narrow one, and your time is not come."

With that sentence he vanished from my eyes. The dream appeared as distinct as reality. When I woke, I related it to my wife. The Doctor had been ailing for some time previously, but I had not heard that anything serious was apprehended. The dream however struck me so forcibly that I wrote on the following day to enquire after the old man's health. But before I had received an answer, a letter reached me announcing his death at 6.30 on the Sunday morning at the identical minute, so far as I could judge, when I had dreamt that he had called to say goodbye![41] These dreams, or visions of second sight, have been curious subjects of speculation throughout all ages but this was one of only two times it happened to me.

23 Shipowner and Father

I had, prior to 1849, invested some of my profits by taking a share in one or two ships. I had, however, still a considerable sum of money in the bank and my business continued to increase. I therefore decided that as I made money as a shipbroker, the most legitimate investment for my savings was in ships. If anyone could make them pay it was me. It was a trade I knew best.[42]

I wrote to builders I knew at various shipbuilding ports, enquiring their prices, terms, etc. The letters were all dispatched in one post and within ten days I had contracted for two ships to be built at Sunderland, two in Cumberland, one in Dundee, and two in Jersey, although the second Jersey ship was never built due to the builder's fault. These ships were all to be vessels of about 800 tons register, each with poop decks, and top gallants of much greater length than we had been accustomed to build. They combined great storage with speed.

The building contracts were not long completed before every shipowner knew of them. Following the depression of 1847 there was a great deal of gloom, however my action prompted them to think *"things cannot be as bad as we thought, when Lindsay is investing so much in ships."*

Word spread quickly to every seaport in the country and was like sounding a bugle to rouse our shipowners from their lethargy and despondency. The price of ships rose by 20 to 30 per cent, so I would have made a considerable profit if I had decided to sell. I completed all the ships, and very fine vessels they were in their day. I named them *Alipore*, *Barrackpore*, *Cossipore*, *Dinapore*, *Mirzapore*, and *Serampore*. All of them saw long service, except the *Serampore*, which was lost in a typhoon in Madras.

That year, 1849, my business of shipbroker had increased to such an extent that my clerks increased to ten or eleven. It had in fact become much the largest of its kind in London, and perhaps in the world. I needed a larger office, and after much bargaining I obtained one at a very reasonable rate.

Mr. Alderman Musgrove,[43] who shortly afterwards became Lord Mayor of London, called one day to offer me No. 8 Austin Friars. It was a magnificent office, certainly the finest accommodation in the city employed as a private office. It was, however, evidently too large for the requirements of almost any business concern in the city, and certainly much too large for mine at that time. I treated his application as a matter of a joke.

"You are the only man I see," he said, "likely to fill that office. You are knocking down room after room, until you can knock down no farther. You have got all the space the house will allow you, and yet it is not enough".

At last, I said, "Well then, what are you asking for this magnificent office as you call it?"

"Why," he replied, "it is worth £1,000 a year rental. And then there are the fixtures, and I know they cost £2,300. Such fixtures and fittings are not to be seen anywhere else in London. Those clocks, barometers, and wind-gauges faced in silver, and enormous machinery about them, cost £700. Just £700, themselves alone! Then there is the lease. There are 20 years to run. It is well worth £2,000, but I tell you what I'll do. You can have the lease for £1,000 and the fixtures for £1,500, and the rent £500 a year, and I am sure that is a bargain."

I had no thought of taking the office so I said in a joke, "I'll tell you what I'll do Mr. Musgrove. I'll give you £200 a year for the office. I'll pay you £200 down for the fixtures and I'll take the lease off your hands for I am sure it must be a heavy handful for you, Sir, in these times."

Of course, he treated my offer as a joke, and left me laughing, as there were a good many people in the outer office where the conversation took place.

I thought no more about the matter, but Musgrove seemed to have kept it in mind, as, three months afterwards, he reduced the terms to £500 a year rental, £1,000 for the fixtures, and £500 down for the goodwill of the lease.

"You remember my offer, Mr. Musgrove," I said laughing, speaking to him over the counter in the clerks' office, "£200 and £200, and I bear the responsibility for the lease?"

Four months later I obtained the lease on my own conditions.

With the business expanding so rapidly I also decided to take on a partner, Mr Edgar Stringer,[44] a young, diligent, honest shipbroker. Honesty is a capital that wealth cannot buy and Edgar Stringer without a penny was worth more to me than a capitalist would have been without honesty but possessing a million. I quickly trained him in my way of business.

The business of shipbroker had increased to such an extent that my coal agency was completely cast into the background. As my business grew, the shipments of Castle Eden coals also increased. But, as the agency gave me no trouble, I felt that I could not conscientiously continue to receive the salary of £400 per annum from the Company. Though the owners had acted ungenerously with me, when in Hartlepool, I felt no desire to do the same to them. I therefore relinquished the salary, assuring them that I would embrace every opportunity to put orders the way of the colliery.

There was news in my home life too. In less than twelve months from the time we had taken possession of Mornington Lodge, my good wife Helen gave birth to a fine little boy,[45] William Stewart Lindsay was born on 12 January 1849. He was to be our only child.

Part Two: Journey to Success

I remember I was consummately happy when Willie came into the world. I had given up all hopes of my wife having any children and, on that day when he was born, I did not go into the city, which was a most unusual thing for me at that time. I was invited round to our neighbours where I indulged somewhat in alcohol. When I heard that I had a son, I gave all the servants a sovereign each. And to the Doctor, who proved a good for nothing fellow, I gave ten pounds in addition to his usual fee.

As I have already said, when I cleared money in my business as a shipbroker, I invested my gains in ships as my most legitimate investment, and that which I best understood. I was then the owner of about 15,000 tons of the finest description of British shipping.[46]

I also invested money in various emigration schemes including one to the colony in Natal,[47] South Africa. Joseph Byrne[48] introduced a scheme whereby emigrants were transported to the country and received a quarter of an acre of land and were lodged for a month after arrival. The scheme was supported by the Government. Of the 250,000 British who emigrated each year in the late 1840s, 5,000 headed for Natal. Hunger, driven by the unemployment which followed the over-expansion in railway building, forced many to seek a better life in the colonies. Those from Lancashire were determined to grow cotton there. One of my ships, the *Coromandel*, was utilised. The scheme was successful in parts, although some settlers were provided with poor land.

My ships, the '*Pores*,[49] were a great advance in design at the time. Nevertheless, the Repeal of the Navigation Laws had made such extraordinary changes in the way shipowners must conduct their business. I saw it was necessary to make another vessel, and a much greater stride to keep pace with the progress of the rapid advance which Free Trade was making in other branches of commerce.

I resolved therefore to build a ship not merely of iron, but of far greater length than others had been accustomed to build. A good many iron ships had, it is true, been built by that time, but still there existed an immense prejudice against them. This prompted me to look closely into their merits. When I did so, I found that, in almost every respect, iron was vastly superior to timber for the construction of vessels.[50]

In the proportions of a sailing ship, it had been the custom, from times immemorial, to build them of dimensions so that the keel plus fore rake[51] should be 3½ times that of the breadth of the beam. If the breadth of the ship was 30 feet, the length of the keel and fore rake should be about 105 feet.

It struck me that the length not merely tended to increase the stability, but it also increased the capacity and the speed. Accordingly, I resolved to build a ship of 28 feet beam and of 180 feet keel and fore rake. This was a huge stride for a sailing ship. Instead of 3½ times it was close to 6½ times her breadth in length.[52] She was the largest iron-built sailing ship at the time.

Of course, I was pronounced mad. To build a ship not only of iron, but also of such outrageous proportions, was an innovation which the sedate old

W. S. LINDSAY & CO.'S LINE of PACKETS to AUSTRALIA.

The undermentioned First-class SHIPS, British-built, and owned by W. S. Lindsay (with the exception of the Gibson-Craig), will sail from London for PORT PHILLIP on or about the dates specified. The number of passengers will be limited in each, and they are fitted up with every modern improvement, for the Australian trade, in which all (with the exception of the two steam-ships) are already engaged. To call at Dartmouth, or a port in the channel convenient for passengers:—

HELEN LINDSAY, 545 tons register, 900 tons burden, B. Stacey, Commander, to sail March 25.

GIBSON-CRAIG, 1002 tons register, 1400 tons burden, W. H. Ellis, Commander, to sail early in May.

SERAMPORE, 907 tons register, 1300 tons burden, Hope Smith, Commander, to sail early in June.

COSSIPORE, 870 tons register, 1250 tons burden, F. Steward, H.C.S., Commander, to sail in July.

MIRZAPORE, 860 tons register, 1250 tons burden, W. Parker, R.N., Commander, to sail in July.

DINAPORE, 850 tons register, 1200 tons burden, J. D. Wilson, Commander, to sail in August.

CAROLINE CHISHOLM, Auxiliary Screw Steam-Ship, 2200 tons register, 2500 tons burden, A. A. D. Dundas, R.N., Commander, to sail in September.

ROBERT LOWE, Auxiliary Screw Steam-Ship, 2200 tons register, 2500, ———, Commander, to sail in September.

ALIPORE, 850 tons register, 1200 tons burden, B. D. Freeman, Commander, to sail in October.

BARRACKPORE, 850 tons register, 1200 tons burden, E. Underwood, Commander, to sail in October.

The undersigned having taken a deep interest in the trade to Australia, and having directed their particular attention to it by establishing an agency at Melbourne, and by employing some of the finest ships in this rapidly-increasing passenger traffic to that port, offer to those who desire to proceed to that flourishing colony a most favourable opportunity. Every possible attention will be paid to the health, comfort, and convenience of the passengers. Libraries will be on board each ship, and rules established to maintain order and cleanliness.

For terms of freight and passage or other particulars apply to

W. S. LINDSAY & CO., 8 Austin Friars.

R. H. STEVENSON & CO., 10 North St Andrew Street, Edinburgh, or 3 West Campbell Street, Glasgow, Agents.

Advert for Lindsay's ships to Australia, 1853.

school of shipowners could not endure in silence. My madness was thereafter the talk of the shipping world.

The building of the ship nevertheless progressed; it was in due time completed and advertised to convey passengers from London to Australia. The public seemed to have some faith in me, as nearly every berth in her was engaged before she came to London, from the River Tyne, where she had been built. She had 280 cabins including 60 in first class.[53]

No sooner had she reached London, in the winter of 1852, than a whole host of the old school visited her and the hairs of many of their heads stood on end when they saw her. Whoever saw such a craft in the shape of a ship? It was, in their opinion, a perfect tempting of Providence. To send such a vessel to sea with three hundred human beings or more on board ought not to be allowed. The government, they exclaimed, ought to put a stop to my folly. However, the ship was filled with passengers, and at the highest rates. Those who desired to go to Australia flocked to her and, despite the rantings and ravings of the old school, with that abominable bugbear called prejudice they preferred my ship to any other.

At last, she sailed – a ship full of passengers. A finer vessel and a more beautiful model never left the Thames. I was proud of her, and she bore my name, the *W S Lindsay*. She reached the Downs. There she anchored as it was blowing a strong wind from the Westward. It appears that the compasses had not been properly adjusted, and the captain telegraphed for me to come

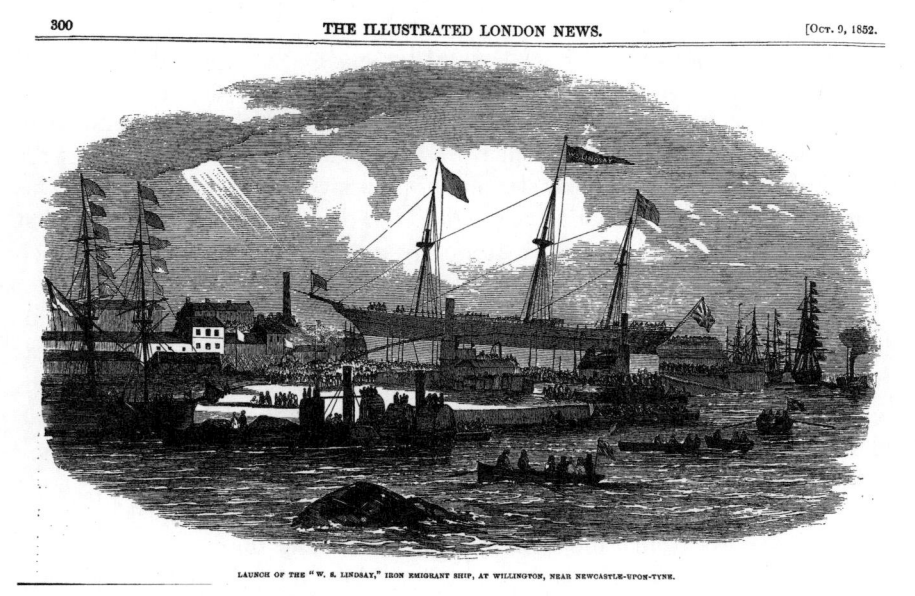

Launch of the *W S Lindsay* (Illustrated London News, October 9, 1852). © Illustrated London News Ltd/Mary Evans Picture Library. Picture number 12546776

down and examine them. The ship's compass varied on one side from 1½ to 2½ points, although it was perfectly correct on a level keel.[54]

The shipping folks in London heard that a telegraph had been sent to me and they at once arrived at the conclusion that, just as they had prophesied, the ship was proved to be unseaworthy. The telegraph had "announced that she was a total failure". Of course, this piece of gossip and scandal spread far and wide, and the clamour raised against me for sending such a ship to sea was almost intolerable.

The Captain and the Officers told me that they never had been in a finer sea-boat. They were willing to go round the world in her. The passengers also were quite contented. But to me the prejudice was a serious matter. I might easily have disregarded it. Indeed, I felt that the lives of those on board were not in any more jeopardy than those on any other ship. In fact, I felt the risk to be less. However, should any accident happen to her, should she encounter a hurricane and founder as other ships under similar circumstances might founder, it would be said that the crew and passengers were lost by my folly and that, in fact, I was their murderer. No language of condemnation would have been too strong for the bigots, if any accident had befallen the ship.

The responsibility was too serious to ignore therefore, and I recalled the ship. I never issued a more galling order. I was acting contrary to my own better judgement. I was surrendering my conviction, to the opinions – or rather prejudices – of others, when in reality I repudiated and despised them. I knew that they would have a fine laugh, and many a hearty sneer, at my expense. It was indeed a most galling order. I was acting diametrically opposed to my own impulses. My eyes were not closed in sleep the night I issued it.

The financial loss too, I knew would be considerable, as all the cost of the ship's outfit would be sacrificed, and I should be under the obligation to provide for all the passengers whilst they remained here and find them other vessels to convey them to their destination in Australia. The cost of the work,[55] in addition to their transfer and other unavoidable contingencies, was immense. However, I bore it all patiently. I felt that I was only suffering what most men are doomed to suffer who boldly step ahead and adopt that which is new, or in advance of the age.

To add to my labour and annoyance, I was summoned by two or three of the passengers before the Lord Mayor. What rendered this more irritating was that I discovered that these passengers were encouraged to adopt proceedings against me by some of my numerous enemies, and those of the worst kind, who were always professing friendship to my face.

The newspapers reported on the case:

Mr. Lindsay stated that the *W.S. Lindsay* cost him one third more than any other ship of the kind he had built; it was three times more efficient for immigration purposes than any ship hitherto used for the conveyance of passengers. Notice was given to all parties that the ship will sail on the 6th,

Part Two: Journey to Success

instead of the 1st of December, and she sailed on the following day, and as soon as he had heard of the variation in the working of the compass he started at midnight for the Downs and enquired of the Captain and mate if there was any danger in proceeding to sea. They expressed their readiness to do so, but as the pilot said there might be extra danger in a heavy sea, he (Mr. Lindsay) felt there was a heavy responsibility upon himself, and he would not risk the lives of the passengers, or the property of the underwriters, by allowing the *W.S. Lindsay* to proceed on her voyage. He, therefore, at great pecuniary loss to himself, ordered her into port again, so that he might feel at ease in his own conscience.[56]

In summing up, the Lord Mayor, Sir Chapman Marshall [57], said that my conduct had been highly honourable, and the case was dismissed.[58]

I may here put upon my opinions regarding pay of Masters of ships. Their charge is one of great responsibility and, as a rule the owners of British Shipping have paid little regard to their importance. When I first became a shipowner, I resolved to deal liberally with the commanders in my employ and remunerate them upon a higher scale than was customary. I have reaped the full reward of the liberal principle I adopted.

Several years ago, I purchased a vessel of 350 tons named the *Jenny Lind*. She had been owned previously by a narrow-minded person and the Master who commanded her appeared exceedingly anxious that I should employ him when I bought the ship. I declined. He was so anxious to enter my employ that he asked for £10 per month, then £8, then finally £6 per month. I made more enquiries in respect of him. He was not a man of much education, but

View of the Thames Estuary *c.*1865, attributed to William Adolphus Knell, with Lindsay's auxiliary steamship, the *W S Lindsay*, prominently anchored. © Philip Mould & Company.

View of the Thames at Greenwich also attributed to William Adolphus Knell. With the *W S Lindsay* anchored in the background. © Philip Mould & Company

I found him to be reputedly industrious and thoroughly honest. I then sent for him.

"Lloyd," I said, "you are very anxious, I see, to remain on the *Jenny Lind*. Now," I continued, "I will not give you £10 per month, nor £8, nor £6, as none of these sums can you keep you, your wife and family in a respectable manner. However, I will give you £14 per month and when you are away your wife can draw half of it monthly. You are to go away with the *Jenny Lind*, and just imagine her to be your own ship."

Lloyd sailed with the vessel. The shipping trade, for some years after I purchased her, was in a very depressed state. Nevertheless, the *Jenny Lind* made money at a time when similar vessels belonging to other buyers made a loss. In the course of four and a half years she had cleared much of her cost. The main, if not the only cause of profit, was the great economy, prudence, and industry which Lloyd had displayed. When I appointed him to the command of the *Jenny Lind* at the unexpected high rate, he was too overwhelmed to thank me. All he could utter was "I hope by my conduct to show you my gratitude." He did so. He stayed in my service for many years.

I may here mention a case of a different kind. Bailie Mitchell[59] of Glasgow was the owner of some eight or ten beautiful and valuable ships, all of them of the highest class and from 700 to 1,100 tons register. These vessels traded principally between London and Liverpool, and the bailie seemed to have so high an opinion of me that, when in London, they were solely under my charge, and I might employ them on any voyage I deemed fit. In fact, the vessels were left under my charge to do with them as if they were my own property. I was not, however, able to appoint the Commanders of his ships.

Part Two: Journey to Success

The bailie was an excellent man in many respects, but he was 'penny wise and pound foolish'. On one occasion, when his beautiful clipper ship, the *Hamilla Mitchell*[60] was on the point of sailing on a voyage to Bombay, his Master did not take up the post. The bailie came in great haste to London. I offered to supply him with a Captain as I had generally a few good men on my list, who were waiting for a vacancy I might be able to offer them.

"What pay?" asked the bailie.

"£15 per month" I replied.

"What! £15 per month!" he exclaimed in the greatest surprise at what he considered an exorbitant sum. "He'll not get £15 from me. I can get twenty good men in Scotland glad to go as Master o' the ship for £8 per month."

I said nothing further, and a couple of days afterwards he introduced me to a rough looking fellow who he got from Greenock. One single glance at the man satisfied me that he was expensive, even at £8. I, however, made no remarks and the ship sailed on her voyage with the bailie's cheap Master in charge.

Some five and a half months after that I received a letter from a correspondent in Bombay informing me of the arrival there of *Hamilla Mitchell*, after a passage of 130 days. They advised freights to England at £4 per ton, and to China at 20 Rupees per candy,[61] but at the same time urging me to send out another Master at once, to take charge of the ship as she was in a fearful state.

"The Master," they wrote, "had been in a state of 'delirium tremens' through drink for more than a month. He had been for days in his cabin drinking raw brandy, and the crew were in a mutinous state. Matters were so bad that not one of the mercantile houses would use her to ship cargo, as none of the insurance offices would take the risk at whatever excessive rate."

On receipt of this letter, I forwarded it to the bailie with the following laconic communication – "Enclosed find distressing and important communication from our friends in Bombay which requires your immediate attention." So much for cheap Captains!

In due course, I received a power of attorney, authorising our friends to dismiss the cheap Captain, and begging me to return the ship with another Captain, without delay. I was not to stipulate one word about the wages I was to give him. I acted upon these orders, and by first overland mail I despatched the letter, and sent the new Master by the same route. Before the ship sailed from Bombay, the freights had fallen to 30 shillings per ton, and to 6 rupees per candy. At these reduced rates the *Hamilla Mitchell* was engaged.

Labour, talent, and expertise are marketable commodities precisely like any other article. If we want good and trustworthy Masters, we must pay for them in the same way.

The loss to the bailie on that voyage exceeded £2,000! All of which would have been saved if he had expended some £50 or £60 extra and sent a competent, trustworthy, and sober commander in charge of his ship.[62]

24 Free Trade

It was at this time that, having trouble sleeping, I commenced the study of our maritime laws and of other countries. It was dry work. Nevertheless, I soon got a relish for these studies as I saw that our laws, spread over some 300 years and comprised in numerous Acts of Parliament, were in a very bad state. Soon I published a work entitled *Our Navigation and Mercantile Marine Laws Considered*.[63] I wished to point out inconsistencies and to suggest reforms. The book had a fair circulation and went through a second edition which I published in the early part of 1851.

The first point I touched on was the fallacy of keeping our local shipping trade[64] protected. In my letters to newspapers, in reference to the Repeal of the Navigation Laws, I urged the opening of local trade. The original draft of the bill intended to do this, but the Government had struck out the clauses. It was a glaring error. I remember the American Minister at the time in England, saying that "if England will give little, America will give little; if England will give much, America will give much; if England will give all, America will give all."

It had been asserted by many that, even if England had then thrown open her local trade, America would not have thrown open hers. But it appeared to me that, had we done so, America could hardly have refused to open her local trade to our ships. Our shipowners lost out considerably by that short-sighted policy on the part of the government. A short time afterwards the gold mines of California were discovered. An enormous trade was opened between New York and Boston with the Pacific coast. No other ships therefore but American-built vessels could participate in that voyage which, although longer than from England to India, was still in the strict sense of the term a coasting or local trade. From that trade, the American shipowners derived immense profits. It was that trade which created those magnificent merchant ships, known as American Clippers.

These vessels obtained enormous freights from New York to San Francisco and, having no return cargo of their own, proceeded across the Pacific to China, where they could afford to take much lower freights of tea than we could, since we were excluded in the voyage from New York to the West Coast.

The next point which I wanted to highlight was the consolidation and revision of our maritime law. They are indeed in a most confused and imperfect state. Acts passed so far back as 1650 continued to be in force. Indeed, in such a state were our laws, relating to maritime affairs, that the most able lawyers in the kingdom could not disentangle them.

Maritime Law reform had perplexed the Board of Trade in that time. Even though aided by a host of barristers, no progress had been made. I intended to embrace all the laws into one Act, framed in simple language.

1) Registry. Registration, launch, and reception of cargo.
2) Commerce. Responsibility of owner of duties to shippers, loading the ship ready for sea.

3) Marine. The ship when at sea, duties and responsibilities of owners, Masters, and crew, general rules to guide all.
4) Division. Admiralty, salvage, consuls, Courts of Law, etc.

Still, it was some years before the Government set about the work of revision and consolidation. When they did, I was consulted and spent a great deal of time and effort on the subject. But, although my views were adopted in many respects, the revisions and consolidation have not been made as simple and clear as I could have wished. It was, however, a great step in the right direction and was of immense advantage to shipping.

The repeal of the Navigation Laws in 1849, however, re-opened our trade with foreign nations, and thus brought hundreds of vessels to our ports, which had never entered them before. It ended centuries of legislative protection for British Shipping.[65] In this manner I gained considerably more by new connections than I lost when orders for grain ships ceased. The Laws opened free trade (or carrying trade) across the oceans, but it excluded freedom for coastal (or local) trading.

I argued for all sea trade to be free. I said in my letters to the newspapers, writing in a homely style: "I am a plain man of business, daily to be found at my office in one of the city lanes, in the midst of my clerks, in the centre of a large dingy room. Business is my politics, not politics my business. If I have a leaning it is towards Free-trade principles."

Latterly, I soon learned that my "principles" as I laid them down were, however plausible, fundamentally, and radically wrong. Sound enough they no doubt were, if all nations had been prepared to adopt them; and, if they could have been applied to the world at large, no system could have been more perfect.

Unfortunately, Foreign States were not prepared to adopt free trade; and if we adopted retaliation against those which did not, we reverted to Protection in its most damaging form. Consequently, we pursued the policy most likely to suit our own interests, and we very wisely did not attempt to enforce it on other nations. Therein, the Government was right, and I was wrong.[66]

By now, my name had spread to most of the American, Norwegian, and Swedish ports, and I had become so well known throughout all the parts of the country that my new office was an excellent investment and business from all quarters came steadily to my door.

Whilst living in Mornington Lodge in Fulham, my income had significantly increased. We were happy there. It was a beautiful spot. We had in all about three acres of land; two consisted of grass, and the remainder of garden-lawn and courtyard. My wife enjoyed it very much, and her health and strength increased day by day. Our little boy also grew strongly. It is true, I had but little time to enjoy the garden, as I left every morning at eight o'clock, and sometimes before then, and seldom got home from the city before eight or nine in the evening.

In the summer, I enjoyed the drive by the omnibus to and from the office, but during the long cold winter nights it was wearisome work. Twelve hours of close, incessant labour at business day after day was enough, without the additional toil of an hour and a half's ride in a confined damp omnibus every night. This exertion was beginning to tell upon me. On wet nights in particular, often with damp feet and damp clothes, sitting on the bus in this condition for more than an hour, I felt that however charming Mornington Lodge might be in summer, the labour of reaching it on a winter's night after the labours of the day was more than my constitution, however strong, could well bear.

I had enjoyed four summers, and endured three winters, but I felt I could not well bear another. Accordingly, in the autumn of 1852, I looked out for a house in town. There was one part of London I had long preferred to all others. I had little idea, however, that I would have the means to allow me to occupy a mansion in Portland Place.

The house No. 28 was To Let, furnished, so I engaged it to see if a residence there realised my expectations. It did so. It was true we missed the garden, but we had the benefit of Park Gardens at the north end of the Place, and the open area of Regent's Park. I could also reach home in twenty minutes or half an hour after leaving my office, and dismiss all its cares and labours, which was a great advantage. I accordingly engaged the house No.17, which was then unoccupied, and set about furnishing it.

25 The Gold Box

I met, and had transactions with, many of the leading shipbuilders during the course of my business. Amongst them was George Henderson.[67] His brother, Patrick[68] had started a shipping company (later to become the Albion Shipping Company) in Fife, Scotland in 1834 aged 26. Patrick died seven years later and left the business to his brothers, one of whom was Captain George Henderson. One of the Directors in the firm was James Galbraith,[69] who later was one of the partners who took over my shipping company.

James reminded me of an amazing incident which happened to me a long time ago when I accompanied his predecessor, Mr George Henderson, on a visit to his native town of Pittenweem, a small fishing town on the East coast of Scotland. It was back in 1849.[70]

George Henderson, who has now been dead a good many years, had in his younger days been a sailor like me and took a great deal of interest in all shipping questions. I had corresponded at that time with the Morning Herald newspaper, opposing the Repeal of our Navigation Laws. In the midst of my fleeting fame, when all the Tory papers were singing my praises, and when the Shipping Gazette had an article about me and my letters almost every day, I accompanied my old friend George Henderson on a visit to his friends on the East Coast.

Part Two: Journey to Success

Pittenweem in Fife is very ancient. It is also a Royal Borough. Tory to the backbone, it would not recognise any London paper as an authority except the Morning Herald and the Shipping Gazette. When therefore my friend made it known that I was to accompany him to his native town, a reception supper at the home of the provost was prepared for me.

The Provost of Pittenweem, at that time, was a retired West Indies planter. He had his plantation in the Island of Jamaica before Free Trade or slave occupation had commenced. He had retired to his birthplace in Scotland to enjoy the fruits of his labours. Here he had become a personage of very considerable importance and he and his native servant, who he had brought with him, were objects of no small attraction.

It was in the afternoon of a fine autumn day that Mr Henderson and I left Leith in a steamer for this ancient Borough. The advertised time of the steamer's arrival was 7.30 p.m., and the arrangements were that I should, on landing, proceed to the house of the provost where I was to be introduced to the leading members of the Corporation, and have supper with them at 8 o'clock at the expense of the retired planter. The steamer, however, did not keep her time, for steamers were not regular in those days, and it was 9.30 p.m. when we arrived.

Mr Henderson and I had consoled ourselves for the delay with a glass or two of whisky on board, and it afterwards appeared that the members of the Corporation had been doing the same before supper while waiting our arrival. Therefore when we met both sides were in a very happy mood, and I had a most welcome, indeed, I might almost say, an affectionate reception from the provost and his servant who received us at the door. Supper over, and the table cleared for wine and whisky toddy, the Town Clerk rose and in a solemn voice addressing the provost said that he had a most important duty to perform, "a delicate and delightful one", which in sum and substance was – to inform me that the Corporation or council assembled had unanimously resolved to present me with the Freedom of the Royal Borough of Pittenweem for the services I had rendered to the cause of British Shipping. This announcement, for which I was in no way prepared, was accompanied by many protestations of their "admiration of my patriotism and ability and sound judgement". Though the Town Clerk spoke like a man who was in earnest, and the members of the corporate body thumped the table as if he was giving utterance to their thoughts, I treated anything beyond the supper as a joke, though I afterwards learned that they had been really in earnest.

Rising to respond, although perhaps not much more clear-headed myself at the time than the Corporation, I thanked the whole body most warmly for the high honour they desired to pay me. I said I felt it to be indeed a great honour to receive the freedom of such an award of the renowned Borough – but I understood that the Freedom of a Borough was always given in a gold box!

This seemed to be rather a clincher, for I saw the provost looking at the corporate members, and the members looking at the Town Clerk who, after a pause, rose, and scratching his head as if searching it for a reply, said that the gold box had not been taken into consideration. I was informed it would be necessary to call another meeting to consider that subject, as the finances of the corporation of the Royal Borough were not in the most flourishing condition! Whether this matter was ever again considered or not, I cannot say but, if it was, the gold box must have been beyond the corporate powers, as I never heard anything more about the Freedom of Ancient Pittenween!

We had a merry night, however, and my recollections of the place are the substantial supper; the red-nosed provost and his servant; women gutting and salting herring during a clear moonlight night and somebody rattling up a wooden stair which stretched over my head in the house of Mr Henderson's sister where I slept. Needless to say, I left with a headache at six o'clock on the following morning by the steamer for Dundee.

26 Queen Victoria's Rebuke

In 1851 we were living in Fulham, not far from Hammersmith gate. On my way to the city, I used to walk, now and again, in the morning, through the Crystal Palace which had just been erected for the Great Exhibition in Hyde Park. At that time Lord Granville[71] was Vice President of the Board of Trade. He and I had then a good deal of communication about various changes in our Navigation and Maritime Laws.

During one of my morning walks through the Exhibition, Her Majesty was present with the two boys, the Prince of Wales and Prince Alfred, and was attended by Lord Granville and other persons. As we passed, Lord Granville nodded, and beckoned that he wished to speak a word to me. We were then in the West End Gallery, and it so happened that we went into a room where there were several of models of ships, amongst them a model of one of my eight Indiamen.[72] I had ordered these to be built to take advantage of increased opportunities in trade as a result of the Navigation Laws, and they were the object of a good deal of discussion at the time in the Newspapers.[73]

Lord Granville, wishing to be out of the way of her Majesty, had stepped aside into one of the recesses where the models stood, and he and I were standing there when the Queen suddenly turned into the narrow passage where we stood. We were so close that we could not very well get out the way without some excuse, so we took off our hats and Lord Granville remarked that he had stopped me to obtain some information about some shipping questions then under the consideration of the Board of Trade.

The Queen seemed to be familiar with my name. She remarked that I had a model in the exhibition of one of my ships which she would like to see. Of course, I readily acquiesced, and we soon reached the model which stood five or six feet above the floor on a pedestal made for the purpose.

As the model stood too high for the boys to see, Prince Alfred, then a child of about five or six, asked me if I would lift him in my arms so that

Part Two: Journey to Success

he might see the rigging and other things about the model which attracted his attention. Having received Her Majesty's permission, I lifted the child in my arms and was explaining to him the different points when, boyish-like, he whispered in my ear that he would be "so very much obliged to me" if I would give him a small brass anchor which hung over the bows and had evidently been the object of his desire.

I asked the Queen if I might do so, but she said that I must not do so for if I gave him the anchor, he would next want the spars and the ship himself. She then took him from my arms and gave him as good a scolding for his greed as any mother ever gave her son. No boys were ever better drilled, or less spoiled, than those two boys seemed to be while under the control and guardian care of their excellent mother. If I have always had a very strong feeling of regard, and a high sense of loyalty, for the Queen, it is because she is not merely the best of monarchs but also the wisest of parents.

27 Caroline Chisholm

Caroline Chisholm was a remarkable woman in a remarkable age and who, during the six or seven years she was in this country, was well known to the public. She was a humanitarian who had engaged in her work firstly in India, then in Australia. Her fanatical devotion to the cause of female emigration resulted in her being one of the greatest pioneer women in Australia's history.[74]

I first met her in 1851, on a fine summer's evening in Gravesend where I had gone to dispatch one of my ships, then on the point of sailing with passengers for Australia. I had just landed from the ship and was walking up

An Australian icon: Caroline Chisholm on the back of the Australian 5-dollar banknote, 1974 series.

and down the wooden platform in front of the river belonging to Waits Hotel where I had taken my lodging for the night.[75]

Amongst others residing in the hotel was a somewhat stout lady apparently of about 45 or 46 years of age. She was pacing up and down the platform and was in close conversation with a lady and gentleman who had taken their passage on my ship. The gentleman, without knowing who I was, asked me some questions about the tide. This led to a conversation between us and the stout lady whom I looked upon as the mother or relative of some of the passengers going on my ship. I however soon discovered that she was a very shrewd woman who knew quite as much about a ship as I did. She told me of India and Australia and of the fearful amount of wickedness she had encountered on her travels.

When I returned to the hotel, I enquired of the landlord of the Hotel who she was. He seemed surprised I did not know. He told me she was Mrs Chisholm, of whom I had heard so much, and whose name I so frequently saw mentioned in the Press.

Strangely enough she had been making similar enquiries about me and, when informed of my name, sent her card with compliments and a polite request that I would join her and her son, a youth of about eighteen years, for a while after tea. As I had nothing particular to do that evening, I had pleasure in accepting her invitation, and I must say I spent a very pleasant two hours with them.

There was nothing very striking about Mrs Chisholm herself for she wore an old black gown, very much faded, and a plain straw bonnet with a single ribbon tied under her chin. She was as good a listener as she was a talker. Her eyes were bright and clear; her thin compressed lips and small mouth denoted her to be a woman of great energy and determination. Her charity work and love on behalf of others were very great.

She was the daughter of a small farmer in Northamptonshire, in which county she was born in 1808.[76] Her father died whilst she was very young and left her with her mother, who was a knowledgeable woman and who had to bring up the family on her own. At the age of 21 she married Captain Archibald Chisholm whom she accompanied to Madras where his regiment was stationed. It was there she first commenced her philanthropy. She started schools there for the female children of the soldiers. She taught them how to sew, to read and write and to become good mothers and housewives. She laid down simple rules for their guidance and raised those who proved to be the most exemplary and industrious to be governesses and mistresses over the others.[77] Her husband's health failing, she accompanied him together with her young family in about 1838 or 1839 to South Australia where his medical advisers had recommended him to settle.

Morality in Sydney at that time seemed to have been at the lowest ebb. A trade was entrapping young women who arrived there from England on the so-called behest of their relatives in the colony. Other females, who had come out as servants, were allured in the same way by the temptation of high

Part Two: Journey to Success

wages and other inducements and, when once astray in a strange country, were lost for ever.

Mrs Chisholm directed her attention to snatch these classes from ruin. For a long time however, her appeals and exertions were disregarded. The Clergy and the Authorities thought she was interfering. She applied to the then Governor and he was also of little help.

At last, after many demands, he furnished her with an empty store which, as she described, "was then only inhabited by rats". This she was allowed to furnish and use as an Institute where young women, when they first landed in Sydney, might have bed and board until they found their relatives, or procured respectable situations. People soon saw the value of this Institution and, after a time, were ready enough to give it their support and patronage.

In 1847 she returned to Britain, accompanied by her husband and her family. Her objective was to improve the conditions on board emigrant ships, particularly for single women. There were hardly any partition screens for the unmarried females. The result was that many a young woman, who left her native country pure and virtuous, arrived at the colony lost to all sense of shame and some of them utterly ruined for life.

Happily, only minor pressure was necessary to demonstrate to our government that such a state of matters ought not to continue longer, so that all the ships which have sailed for Australia have separate and enclosed berths fitted up for each married couple. The unmarried females have their cabins also at one end of the ship, and the single men at the other. This separation of the sexes during the voyage is due entirely to the efforts of Mrs Chisholm.

She next established "the Family Loan & Colonization Society" in London. It met with great success and was supported by many of our leading bankers and merchants in the city. Its main objective was to assist poor families to emigrate, and join their relations and friends in Australia, by granting them a Loan which they were to repay by instalments once they gained employment.

It had also another objective: to assist respectable female emigration for the younger branches of families whose parents had previously emigrated and had not accumulated sufficient means to pay for the passage of their children. Indeed, the desire of many servant girls to emigrate became so great that many of them left their current employment and would not work. Some of them however discovered that emigration, with the Society's aid, was not quite as easy as they had hoped, and they resorted to an immoral and lazy way of life.

Those that emigrated with the society's help were of incalculable benefit in the improvement of the population of Australia. There, the male population far exceeded that of the females, mainly following the Gold Rush. Here in Britain, on the other hand, the female population far exceeded that of the men, jobs for women were therefore scarce, and our streets still thronged at night with girls who resorted to prostitution. Through Mrs Chisholm's efforts hundreds of poor girls were snatched from a life of misery to become valuable members of society in Australia.

I had many transactions with Mrs Chisholm which required me to see her often during the two or three years she remained in this country. I saw that her aims were good.[78] My ships which were headed for Australia were always at her disposal to send as many passengers by them as she pleased. Over eighteen months, I sent out between 500 and 600 young persons to Melbourne for her, consisting mainly of daughters of small farmers or servant girls of good character. As a man of business, I found her connection somewhat valuable at times and, as my ships carried the bulk of her passengers, it would appear that she was more satisfied with the arrangements and accommodation provided in them than in other ships.

She was an extraordinary woman. When I offered to give her son a free passage in one of my ships, as a small return for her services, she would not hear of it, but would insist upon paying the passage money even though, judging by the means in which she lived, she could ill afford it. She seemed to have no regard to her own personal comforts. She lived in a dilapidated little house at Islington, poorly furnished. She was always dressed in the plainest and sometimes in the meanest clothes. Her children were clean and neat, and seemingly well looked after, but their clothes were of the coarsest and commonest description, and often patched and mended.

I cannot however discuss the character of this remarkable woman without relating an anecdote or two which came to my knowledge, and which display her character in a very favourable light.

Thousands of all classes used to visit her in her little lodgings in Islington where she had two entrances. The front door was, she said, for the aristocrats who always wanted something that she did not want, and the other at the back for servant girls and others who were anxious to emigrate. The room which served as her office was divided by a curtain where her clerk, a female, sat on one side at the entrance and Mrs Chisholm at the other, close to a window looking into the back yard.

During one of the afternoons when I visited her, a young man somewhat stylish in his dress called upon her. The curtain was only partially drawn across the room when he entered. Seeing a lady, he addressed her somewhat abruptly and haughtily with the remark, "I presume you are Mrs Chisholm?" She nodded.

I stepped aside when he entered to a corner of the other part of the room where the clerk sat, but I could not help hearing all that was said and, in fact, saw what took place as the curtain remained partially open.

"You send female emigrants to Australia," remarked the stranger in the same abrupt manner but with rather a patronising tone, as he drew a blank cheque from his pocketbook.

Mrs Chisholm bowed as she rose from her seat but did not offer him a chair.

"How much do you charge?" he continued, stretching his hand towards the table for a pen to insert the required amount in the cheque he still held in his hand.

Part Two: Journey to Success

"I have not been favoured with the name of the gentleman who honours me with his presence," quietly remarked Mrs Chisholm, without noticing his question or assisting him to obtain the pen from her table.

"Oh! I suppose that don't matter so long as you have the money," replied the stranger.

"It may not," she dryly said "but who is this young person in whom you feel an interest. What is she?"

"Can't exactly say," replied the stranger. "Nothing very particular."

"Have you bought a certificate of her character from the clergyman of the Parish to which she belongs?" enquired Mrs Chisholm.

"No" said the young man somewhat haughtily, "never thought of such a thing. All you want I suppose is the money to send her to Australia and here it is." As he spoke, he tossed the signed blank cheque upon the table and requested that she herself would fill in the amount of passage money while he was there.

"I require something more," Mrs Chisholm mildly replied, "but as you have no certificate perhaps you will be so kind as to say what you know about the person whose passage you wish to pay to Australia in a ship under my charge."

As she spoke, and especially with the words "you know", her keen bright eyes were fixed steadily on the stranger who evidently keenly felt the penetrating glance, for he blushed and then blustered out with a guffaw laugh, "damned particular".

"I am obliged to be particular in some cases, very particular indeed, and I fear your case is one of these." Then, after a pause, she continued her eye still intently fixed upon him "You are about to be married," she said with a sneering smile. "Are you not Sir?"

The young man's face blushed to the forehead for he thought she knew all about him, "and before you are married" she added with bitter emphasis "you wish to have this young woman out of the way. Is that not so? Your wife would not like to see her coming to the house!"

"I call that impertinent," said the stranger in anger.

"Not so impertinent" quietly replied Mrs C, "as is your conduct in coming to me, a wife and a mother, to ask me to assist you to remove some poor girl whom you have ruined."

Then leaning to her table, she took up his cheque and handed it to him as she bade him good morning with a look of pity and scorn which I am sure he would never forget.

I may here add another incident which took place. It is one still more characteristic of Mrs Chisholm. One day a blazoned carriage with a ducal coronet upon it drove up to her front door, and from it descended a noble Lord, for whom his footman demanded an immediate audience. He was however coolly, though politely, told to wait his turn. When it arrived, his Lordship wanted to know what would be the cost of sending out some 200 girls to Australia, and in what ship Mrs Chisholm would send them?

"But what kind of girls are they?" enquired Mrs C.

"A fair lot," answered his Lordship, "some of them rather good looking, some decidedly so, and of course some decidedly plain also, that you must expect in so large a batch."

"But that is not the point," said Mrs Chisholm. "Of what character are they? Are they virtuous and industrious? For you know, my Lord, I never send out girls in any of my ships unless I get a written certificate of character from the clergyman of the parish to which they belonged. But I will dispense with that in the present case if your Lordship will simply give me your word that they are good girls."

His Lordship hummed and seemed considerably perplexed. At length he stammered out, "Well Mrs Chisholm I cannot do that exactly: but they are a fair lot. Some no doubt good: others no doubt very good, and some may have their failings Mrs Chisholm."

"That may be my lord, but as your Lordship cannot give me your word upon the point Sir, I cannot have anything to do with them."

"But that is very awkward Mrs Chisholm," said his Lordship, "for I have assured the Guardians that sent me that you were sure to take them out and, if you do not, I shall forfeit my word."

"I am sorry for it my lord. It is a pity you made so rash a promise for, if you do not give me your word that they are virtuous and industrious, I will not take them however high the price you may be willing to pay."

His Lordship looked exceedingly foolish, and after much stammering and humming and hawing, let out the whole truth. As Mrs C had guessed, he told her frankly that they were two hundred of the vilest strumpets who for years had boldly resisted parish Officers of a large metropolitan district with which he was connected. They had become so great a nuisance to the place that at a general meeting of the vestry the Guardians had unanimously resolved to pay the cost of the passage to Australia from the Parish rates, in order to get rid of them at any cost.

"And so, my Lord," said Mrs Chisholm, "the worthy Guardians of your Parish thought the best way of accomplishing their purpose was to send them to the infant colony of Australia, no doubt in the conviction that they would make excellent wives for those liberated convicts which the Government, of which your father was a member, sent to people that country in the prosperity of which they profess to have so deep an interest. I wish you Good Morning, my Lord." Mrs Chisholm added, "Pray do not forget to tell the excellent Guardians of your somewhat densely populated Parish that they have made a great mistake in commissioning you to honour me with a call upon their business."[79]

I entered Mrs Chisholm's office a few minutes after His Lordship had left and that was the only time I had seen the equanimity of her temper materially ruffled.

There must have been angry words between them, but she never told me what had taken place. I learned it afterwards, word for word, from another member of His Lordship's vestry who graphically described the scene and concluded, a little sadly, "Unfortunately, Mrs Chisholm was not the woman to relieve us of our strumpets."

It had been my intention to send the young women, and Mrs Chisholm and family, to Australia in the *Robert Lowe* but the ship's construction was delayed. I then wished to use another ship I was about to build to be named the *Caroline Chisholm*.[80] But the Crimean War intervened. Instead, she sailed to Melbourne in one of my chartered ships, the Aberdeen built clipper *Ballarat*,[81] with the last of the females.

Prior to sailing, she sent me this note:

Sunday 12 March 1854.

If you would meet me on board the 'Ballarat' on Monday at twelve Mr Young will be there and we could then make the arrangements necessary for the girls.

My pledge and desire is to protect the young women as a mother would wish to do.

On Saturday a poor woman whom the Doctors say can only live a few weeks, sent her husband with her daughter to me to assure me that on her deathbed her greatest comfort was to think her child would be under my care knowing I would take care of her. She was cheerful, happy, and resigned and sent her daughter to me knowing that she had promised to obey me as a mother – our contract was signed by our tears; could anything be more solemn and binding. This case is quite sufficient to show you how I stand.[82]

She duly sailed to Australia to continue her work.

28 Auxiliary Steamers

A year or so after the *W S Lindsay* had been built in 1852, I decided to build other ships with similar extreme dimensions, and in which I determined to introduce the auxiliary screw propeller.[83] During my time at sea, I had noticed that sailing ships had an insurmountable difficulty to contend with, namely calm. However fine a vessel was, or however swift she might be if she had a breeze, she was as helpless in still waters as the most bluff-bowed collier.[84]

I had a melancholy instance in the Bay of Bengal in 1840, when as Captain of the *Olive Branch* we lay becalmed for a long time. We were sailing from Mauritius to Calcutta. It was a very tedious passage, increased to a most unusual length by being becalmed during more than thirty days. I never had a more perplexing time.

For a month there was scarcely a breath of wind and I do not think that during the whole period the ship made fifty miles of progress. One man died of scurvy, four or five more ill with it as to be quite unfit for duty and we were all affected, entirely through the want of fresh provisions.

Desperate for healthy food we spied a shoal of turtles in the distance. No time was lost in lowering the boats, and every man on board who was able to pull an oar, myself amongst the number, was quickly away in pursuit of the shoal. We had the good fortune to catch fifteen or sixteen splendid large prizes. All was joy and feasting on board.

For six days we had nothing but turtle soup; or turtle boiled, or turtle fried, or turtle roasted. We had turtle chops and steaks for breakfast, dinner, and supper. Our sick men were soon convalescent, and all on board were happily restored to perfect health. Then the sailors began growling. Even though turtle soup was an expensive delicacy when served in London, the crew tired of it and demanded to return to their usual allowance of salted beef and pork.

I also observed that when vessels made a long passage, it was almost always due to the lack of winds, especially on the route to India. On the equator, and to some degrees both north and south, calms continually stopped the progress of ships. It was then that the idea first struck me of putting a small auxiliary steam engine into the full rigged sailing ship.

For many years therefore I had seen the need to introduce some sort of power which would propel the ship whenever the winds failed. Some such plan had been introduced into two Indiamen, the *Vernon* and *Seringapatam*, by Mr. Green[85] the owner, but it was a clumsy cumbrous affair, and it failed. It was many years before I could see how practically and efficiently, I could remedy the evil.

In 1850 or 1851 a company was started named the General Screw Steam Navigation Company. They built a fleet of screw steamers, to trade between Southampton and Calcutta, calling at the Cape Verde Islands, Cape of Good Hope, Mauritius, and Madras on their way. They were built, and fitted, with powerful engines and with a small spread of canvas in proportion to their size.

It was clear to me that they would prove a failure, not in an engineering point of view, nor mechanically, but commercially and that they would never return a profit in that distant trade. It proved so. The space the engines occupied in the ship was so great, and the space required for fuel was so large, that there was little or no room left for cargo or passengers.

Moreover, these vessels were compelled to stop to refuel for two or three days at each of the stipulated ports on their voyage, so that what they gained in speed under steam was lost in detention at these places. Their passages were consequently not made in any less time than those of some of our fastest sailing ships.[86] The enormous quantity of coals these vessels required, and their cost, far more than absorbed the freight carried in the small space they had allotted for goods.

After a few years' experience the vessels were withdrawn from the trade with a great loss of capital to the shareholders. Though I held no interest in the company, I had naturally watched its movements, and it was then the idea first struck me of combining the sailing ship – the fully rigged sailing ship – with the small screw engine. I therefore undertook to build two purpose-built auxiliary steamships,[87] the *Robert Lowe* and the *Tynemouth*[88] in 1852, both with small auxiliary engines.

The story behind my design of the *Robert Lowe*[89] was interesting. I vividly recall a visit that year from a Captain Laughlin McKay[90] in my office. It became apparent that he was the brother of the celebrated American builder, Donald McKay[91] who, in his Boston shipyard, had built some of the fastest American sailing clippers.

He described to me some of the wonderful performances of these clippers, and he 'calculated' that, as the China Trade was now open to American vessels, they would soon drive all the English out of it. "But, fast as those vessels are," he said, "we intend to build one which I guess will lick all creation." I remembered his words "lick all creation". He showed me the drawings, and the lines of this extraordinary ship, which they had just started to build, and which they afterwards named the *Great Republic*. I memorized the drawings and made a model of the ship.

When Captain McKay called again a month later, I showed him the model I had made and explained that I had contracted two ships to be built along similar lines. They were, however, going to have the added advantage of an auxiliary 80 horse-power engine, and whilst McKay's ship, when becalmed, would be like 'a log on the water', my ships would 'go ahead at least 7 knots an hour'. They would also be more manoeuvrable in rivers and harbours.

The same critics of my earlier ship, the *W S Lindsay*, again predicted that these two ships that I was building, would prove a total failure and that I, with my new-fangled notions, was sure to go to the dogs. What was the good, they argued, of engines of only 80 HP in ships of 1,400 or 1,500 tons. Whoever heard of such a thing before? And once more they expressed surprise that my friends did not encase me in a straitjacket. But in spite of all these warnings, prophecies and sneers, the ships were built, and I was bold enough to be the sole owner, though they cost me £60,000 to put to sea. They were however worth more like £80,000 as I had them built when the cost of labour and iron were very low, and these ships have proved by far the best investment I ever made.

The *Robert Lowe* was launched in August 1854 and described in the Greenock Advertiser as 'the first auxiliary screw ship of large size ever built'.[92] The vessel was also described as a 'screw assisted sailing ship' or a 'Steam Clipper'. The article stated:

> The chief peculiarity of this vessel is, that she will be fitted with a screw propeller and engine of 80 horse-power ... to act as an auxiliary during calms, and by which she will be driven at the rate of several knots per hour. The screw can easily be unfastened from its place and hoisted by means of guides and a winch on deck, to a trunk or square recess in the ship's counter,

The *Robert Lowe*, latterly the *Iron Cross*. Image Courtesy of Malcolm Brodie collection, the State Library, South Australia PRG 1373/6/19

where it will be completely out of the water and offer no resistance to the vessel's progress. When its assistance is required, it can be easily lowered into its proper position.[93]

The delivery of the *Robert Lowe* by Shipbuilders Scott & Co[94] was late. The company knew that it was a loss leader, and they took on a more lucrative contract to build other ships. I was obviously unhappy and demanded an apology at the very least; none was forthcoming.[95] I therefore took them to court and in the process, the following year, won £20,000 damages.

My opponents were compelled to admit that they had no case and made an appeal to my feelings. Their solicitor withdrew from their defence but said "if you claim as damages the amount of loss, which it is clear you have sustained by my clients failing to complete their contract with you in the time stipulated, it will ruin them."

I had known something of the family of Scott & Co. When I was a sailor boy in Greenock, they were the leading family in the place. Charles, the son of the original head of the firm had succeeded his father in the business and indeed, with a son, constituted the partnership of the firm. Charles had married a lady of considerable position in his day and by her had a large family, chiefly of daughters, who had been brought up in a certain degree of affluence, and who were accustomed to move in the best society at Greenock. If I had refused to listen to the appeal made to me, I would have brought ruin upon the family.

They had treated my just claims with contempt. Nevertheless, I could not inflict total ruin upon them as a family. I have never made money by injuring others and never will if I can avoid it. My heart revolted at it. I therefore decided not to charge them any damages. I did not accept one farthing from them. They had to pay 100 guineas to the Poor of Glasgow, and they had to cover all legal expenses. They also had to furnish me with a letter admitting that they had done wrong. Had I pressed the damages the firm no doubt would have collapsed.

Their solicitor looked struck dumb with amazement. He apologised for the harsh way he had questioned me. My own Solicitor opened his eyes in astonishment as I delivered my sentiments on the case and regarded me as a man who had gone "daft" in thus making a present, as he said, of £20,000 to persons who had so deeply wronged me. The arbitrator too was astonished.

My brother-in-law Robert Stewart, who had known all the particulars of the case, when he heard how it had terminated, could not refrain from hinting something about my being too soft-hearted, too easy, too weak, etc. I had, however, the satisfaction of knowing that I had made the right decision. I felt too that I had more money than I could ever want, and that the additional £20,000, though it would make me a richer, could not make me a happier man.

Of course, not everyone had good words to say about me. I was said to be 'a conceited active fellow, eaten by vanity'.[96] I was not afraid to speak my mind. I challenged people if I deemed them lazy, although I felt I was firm but fair.

At the same time as the *Robert Lowe* was being built on the Clyde, her sister ship the *Tynemouth* was being built in Newcastle upon Tyne. Originally called the *Caroline Chisholm*, she was destined for the emigration trade. It was my intention to assist the philanthropist Mrs Chisholm in sending out single women to the gold fields in Australia which had been discovered in 1853.

When the *Tynemouth* had been launched in March 1854 the local press said: "If beauty of mould and fineness of lines are to be depended on, there can be little doubt that under canvas alone she will be almost a match for the swiftest American clipper afloat."[97]

The captain of the ship expressed his satisfaction with the ship and extolled the virtues of its auxiliary engine. If ever I had doubts in my own mind as to the great value of the auxiliary principle, the short cruise from Greenhithe to the Downs completely removed them. Under steam alone, and with her 80 H.P. engine, her speed reached 8¼ miles per hour. Under sail and steam, we got 12 miles per hour. The *Fiery Cross*, a vessel of 1,000 tons, but with a 500 H.P. engine, sailed with us, and the pilot informed me that the two vessels only parted company off Plymouth. When the winds were light and adverse, the *Fiery Cross* naturally shot ahead of the *Tynemouth*, but when the winds were fair the latter, having all the advantages of a full rigged ship, outstripped her under sail.

Part Three
Politics and Shipping
(1852–1854)

29 Monmouth Contest: Buying Votes

My focus on Maritime Laws opened my eyes to seek a seat in Parliament. It appeared to me that few in that assembly really understood maritime matters.[1]

I resolved that I should get elected on my own merits. I felt that only the free voice of the people should place me in that position. I wanted to obtain the people's votes without the slightest undue influence on my part. I would not employ lawyers. I would not open public houses, nor take bribes of any kind. In the opinion of many this was absurd and would be doomed to failure. However, I stuck to my resolution and, though I fought three of the hardest contests that have been fought in this country for many years, I never gave an elector a sixpence to influence his vote.

So it was that, early in 1852, my first contest for a seat in Parliament was for the Monmouth Boroughs in Wales.[2] Even though I knew next to no one there, I was encouraged by the former Liberal MP[3] to represent the party against the Conservative who was running.[4] I was determined to make a contest of it. Even if I could not gain the seat, I might enlighten the people and I should have the satisfaction of making my opponent exert himself. Newport had great potential as a port, especially with the rise of Welsh coal being used for steamships. On my arrival there I had a hearty reception from the humbler classes, and it was evident that I was 'the man of the people'. A public meeting had been fixed for the evening of my arrival when I was to explain my political views. The hall where the meeting was held was packed. The mayor, who was a Conservative, took the chair, but he soon showed his true colours by making a speech strongly in favour of my opponent. This caused a commotion, and a more impartial chairman was voted in his place.

Part Three: Politics and Shipping

It was the first time I had spoken in public but, impressed with the belief that the art of Public Speaking was not as difficult as many made it, I imagined myself in private and commenced addressing the audience with plain speaking. I knew if the subject was an exciting one, I should soon warm to it. I felt it best to speak my mind on the subject as I saw it. Accordingly, I have never on any occasion written a paragraph of what I intended to say in public.

I learnt much from that meeting. Someone in the audience tried to unsettle me by asking me a question on religious affairs that I knew nothing about. I turned the question to him, and the audience told him to be quiet. Ever since that time, whenever I am asked a question in public to which I object to giving a reply, either because it is impossible to give an answer or it would trap me, I make it a rule to ask the person if he would be so kind as to explain himself or repeat the question in another form. Usually, the questioner either does not understand it himself, or he is unaccustomed to speak in public, and flounders. Otherwise, if he does understand, and can speak, ten chances to one the audience will not listen to him.

Somehow or other I won the affections of the people at this my first meeting. They looked upon me as one of themselves. They had heard of my career and instinctively claimed me as their own. Perhaps I had a frank, free and easy manner with them, which people always like, and they saw that I was the representative of the popular cause, civil liberty.

After the meeting I was followed to the hotel by large masses of the people cheering lustily. Their enthusiasm must have been honest and sincere, as I publicly announced the conditions on which I would contest the borough. I would not employ paid staff and, to their credit, those who had supported the Liberal cause previously, joined my committee and worked without fee or reward.

My opponent, Mr Crawshay Bailey, was a gentleman of immense influence in the district. He was the head of an ironworks that employed 4,000 to 5,000 pitmen, miners, and workmen of various kinds in the neighbourhood.[5] He was backed by the Duke of Beaufort[6] and the house of Tredegar, headed by Sir Charles Morgan.[7] He had also secured the support of one or two leading families who in previous elections had supported the liberal candidate. Against such an array of strength a stranger had little chance.

Following this first meeting, he and his party were aroused from complacency, and commenced an active canvass of the electors. In the meantime, I had been holding meetings and was every day becoming more and more popular with the people. I did not fail to tell them the time had come to throw off the yoke of the aristocracy. I explained to them, in clear and simple language, the benefits of free trade and I believe I opened their eyes to many truths previously not revealed to them. Every day I grew more and more popular.

The wives also took part in the contest. They did so, not merely for their husbands, but for themselves and their children. They pondered over my printed speeches, and they saw that under the policy which I had advocated there would be a wider field for employment, better chance of higher wages for their husbands, more prospects of certain employment for their children, cheaper and better bread, tea and sugar, and cheaper dresses and clothing.

So strong had popular opinion turned in my favour that, at the end of our canvassing, it was quite clear, and much to my surprise, that I should carry the election by a considerable majority unless great undue influence was brought to bear on the electors. My opponents saw this. Almost every public house was thrown open by the opposition to any elector to eat and drink as much as he pleased.

After a two week break in London, some five days before the day of nomination to stand as a candidate for the election, matters were in a high state of excitement. Pressure put by the duke, together with Mr. Bailey's intimidation and scenes of drunkenness (created by the open public houses), raised the feelings of the population. Matters reached such a pitch that two days before the election all the shops in Newport were closed, and all business suspended.

I shall never forget the scene at Monmouth on the day of nomination. Mr Bailey was no orator, and his supporters knew that I should come off much the better of the two at the meetings, if we were both allowed a fair hearing. Their aim therefore was to create confusion. The more noise there was the better for them. Accordingly, long before the meeting commenced, the old Town Hall was well-packed with a hired mob, consisting of pitmen, miners, and fellows whose business it was to yell and roar whenever I commenced to open my lips. The moment I attempted to utter a word, a great red-headed fellow who seemed to be the leader of the gang, and who sat at a table prepared for the press, commenced yelling, and thrashing the table with a huge stick, beating time with his heels. Of course, the hired gang imitated their leader so that it was quite impossible for even the person standing close to me to hear one word I said. After the first few words I was silent, quietly folded my arms and looked on, merely remarking that they might thump away, as I was quite certain that they would be tired of thumping and yelling before I got tired of standing.

In that position, I stood unmoved for three quarters of an hour. At last, the red-haired fellow, who was in an awful state of perspiration, bawled out, "It's no use master, we can't stop him. He won't lose his temper for us, and the more we bellow, the more he laughs and the cooler he stands, so we might as well give up!"

Accordingly, dead beat, he laid down his stick, and said "You may begin now – You're the coolest young lad I ever met!"

So, I began. I pitched into the Duke of Beaufort for his interference in the election of a representative to the House of Commons. I certainly had no mercy on that day for Dukes in general and their treatment of the people, and I was especially indignant with the Duke of Beaufort in particular. I learned afterwards that the Duke of Northumberland,[8] who was at that time on a visit to the Duke of Beaufort, had been so annoyed at what I said that he afterwards told my old personal friend, but political opponent, Alderman Thompson[9] that, although my abilities or talents were such that I ought to be in the House of Commons, I should never have a seat there if he could prevent it.

But the scene in the Town Hall at Monmouth was nothing compared with what went on when we returned to Newport that evening. My Committee Room windows were smashed. There was fighting, brawling, and debauchery difficult to describe. Shouts of "Lindsay forever", "Bailey forever" resounded – prelude to numerous fights between the contending parties. Nor were the male sex the sole actors in these disgraceful scenes, for women fought as sturdily as the men. They drank quite as much and some of them yelled and swore a great deal more outrageously.

The night before the election was bad enough, but it was worse on the day of the election. By six in the morning everybody seemed on the move. Thousands had not been in bed during the night. My popularity was evidently on the increase. Mr Bailey now resorted to strong measures. On a pretext of keeping the peace, he brought down some 2,000 or 3,000 of his miners from the works in the neighbourhood, armed with bludgeons and sticks. This group planted themselves in various public houses and were regularly marshalled by leaders. This provoked the Townspeople so that they formed themselves into several bodies and made an attack upon Bailey's men. Fights of the most desperate description ensued. Masses of miners were led towards the polling booths, evidently to intimidate peaceable electors from voting for me.

Before 9 a.m. various defections took place so that, between corruption and intimidation, backed by violence, it was evident that I should lose the day.

To incite his gangs further Mr. Bailey sent in large quantities of beer in barrels. These stood opposite every "blue" door. These were worth fighting for, so my supporters in red colours, fought deadly combats with the Blues for the beer. The Reds, more often than not, won the fight and rolled away the barrels to the middle of the street, whereupon they opened them and let anyone indulge, both friend and foe. The whole town was soon in a state of intoxication. Matters were getting serious. I sent for the mayor. He could not or perhaps would not, take any decisive steps towards quelling the disturbances. He said the policemen and their specials could do nothing.

Windows of almost every public house in the town were smashed to atoms, and three of the public houses, in which many miners had been lodged, were gutted. Chairs and tables were broken to bits and pitched out of the windows. Windowsills and frames were utterly smashed. The beds were torn to shreds, and the houses left a complete wreck, with nothing but the bare walls standing. I never saw such Demons fighting as these Welshmen. Many lives would unquestionably have been lost if the military had not been called out. This was at last resorted to, but not until the most urgent requests were made to the mayor. The Officer commanding the soldiers performed his duty well. He would not allow his men to interfere except when he saw scenes likely to end in loss of life, if not checked. Then, and then only, the soldiers dashed in separating the people and striking them on the back, with the flats of their swords.

There was one scene, amongst many, I shall not easily forget. I was standing at the window of the Inn, where I had taken up my quarters. It looked onto the main street, which was crowded with people, and was close to the main polling booth. A stagecoach drawn by two horses, drew up, laden inside and out with peaceful electors who had been brought from a distance. No sooner were they recognised, than the mob made an attack on the coach, opposite me. The assailants stopped the horses and about a dozen herculean fellows caught hold of the offside wheels, and with one fling capsized the coach, and all the contents, right across the pavement, through the shutters of a large window in a grocer's shop.

Amazed at this feat, I could not help crying out for I concluded that every man of them was killed. Not they! They soon emerged from their position, crawling out beneath the coach, and from the ruins of the shattered windows like rabbits from a warren. Two of them had fractured bones, but that was all.

The women too were quite as pugnacious as the men. Two women met right opposite to the window where I stood. One woman had blue ribbons in her cap, and the other wore red. The two were great Amazons and were evidently quite drunk. One made a grab at the ribbons of the other's cap. The other retaliated. A clutching, scratching fight ensued, until each had made clean work not only of the ribbons, and the caps, but of the combs and pins in their hair. They soon became dishevelled. Their gowns next became objects of spoil and destruction. They tore each other's clothes off, even to their undergarments, which were literally ripped to pieces. The mob was delighted with the sport and formed a ring around them. Their appearance became revolting even to the most depraved taste. Fortunately, some police arrived and supported by soldiers, they bundled the two combatants into two empty cabs and carried them off.

But however desperate were the fights, or however depraved the scenes, there was one incident which told me how the heart of the masses pulsated. Although those in blue were hired to support my opponent, it was clear that their sentiments lay with me.

My headquarters, and that of my committee, were in the main street, and at a wide part of it. The headquarters of my opponent were about 300 or 400 yards distant. Between the two houses there was a dense mass of furious people. The situation was such that the two sides should not approach each other or else an almighty battle would start. The Blues were by far the most numerous and powerful as they included the whole of Mr. Bailey's miners, a perfect army in themselves, strengthened by large masses of men from the Tredegar Works. Around two o'clock in the afternoon I needed to see a

Part Three: Politics and Shipping

person who was at the headquarters of my opponent, and there was no other way of reaching him, except through this vast crowd of drunken miners.

"For God's sake Mr. Lindsay," exclaimed all my friends "do not think of leaving the house, and going in the direction of Bailey's Committee Room. You will be murdered if you do."

"No fear of that," I replied. "I know the people better. Whatever they might do to you, depend on it, they will not harm me." So, I set out on my errand, leaving my friends in amazement, who thought me quite mad.

It was truly an awful scene. Both parties had gathered there for a fight. The noise, the yelling and the swearing were altogether dreadful. I must say that when I got out of doors, I began to think that my friends were right but as it was very important that I should see the person I sought, and as I had rather ridiculed their warnings, I did not like to go back.

Accordingly, buttoning up my coat, I elbowed my way right through the thickest of the crowd, the hired mob of my opponents. I did not expect that any one of them would recognise me, but I was mistaken. It was whispered about that I was in the crowd, and large masses of Reds followed me, to protect me, as they said, against the Blues. I knew that if I allowed them to follow me, it would only lead to a dreadful fight, so I waved them back and went on my own way.

The moment I got amongst the Blues they opened out a passage for me. As I passed amongst those workmen and hirelings of my opponent all fighting and yelling was suspended. I could hear one say to the other "God bless him don't touch a hair of his head." I dare say if anyone, even of their own party, had offered to insult me, either by word or look, he would have been knocked down. I was quite touched by their response.

No sooner than I arrived at my destination than the fighting recommenced with redoubled fury. The noise and tumult increased as the hour of four drew near and, when the poll closed, the yelling, screaming, and hooting were truly hideous and alarming.

Mr. Bailey won by a majority of 100 or so votes.[10] It was clear to the people that he carried his election by unfair means. More than 200 voters who had promised me their support would not leave their houses. They were in fear of their lives. Others, in one case, an entire street, had been corrupted by bribery or were frightened away. As I had no idea that I would gain the seat, I was in no way disappointed.

My opponent had secured one or two hundred voters at the moderate price of £5 each. I saw too that a select number had stood out for more than £5 each but were turned away. Some of these disappointed traffickers came to me, and offered their votes for a sovereign a head, then they reduced this to ten shillings, and finally this was reduced to a pint of beer!

The election gained a great deal of interest at the time. It was so obvious that Mr Bailey had obtained his seat by bribery, corruption, and intimidation that under the advice of many friends I petitioned Parliament against the result. Mr. Bailey would, without doubt, have been unseated but, as the

General Election followed shortly after, it was found impossible to bring the matter to an issue before the dissolution of Parliament.

It was afterwards reported that that election cost Mr. Bailey £10,000. However, Mr. Bailey was a wealthy man, and could well afford it. I accomplished all that I wished to do, to enlighten the people (some of whom were politically naive), and to advocate the Cause of Free Trade. All this was achieved at very little expense, as the entire cost of my contest was under £500. I never grudged the expenditure. I proceeded to the railway station for my return to London after breakfast and was followed by more than five thousand people consisting of men, women, and children. Many a blessing and "God be with you" were showered on me that morning.

This was the first election I had witnessed; and from my experience at the Monmouth Boroughs, I formed no high opinion of our parliamentary system. I was determined, however, not to give in until I was elected elsewhere.

William Schaw Lindsay around the time of his electioneering days.

Part Three: Politics and Shipping

30 Dartmouth contest: Up against the Admiral

Scarcely had a month elapsed before I was approached by a deputation from Dartmouth inviting me to stand for that borough at the 1852 General Election, which was close at hand.[11]

I told them my conditions. No lawyers, no paid agents, no beer, no flags, and of course no bribery either direct or indirect of any kind. I would pay all the accounts myself, and only at the regular trade prices. Upon hearing this, they left me, and I heard nothing more of them for a week. I then received another visit. They wanted a good active member of Liberal politics.

I promised to pay them a visit in Dartmouth and, after that, would form my own opinion. A few days later I went there. It is an old place, of little trade and the people poor. There are about 3,000 to 4,000 inhabitants and about 295 electors. As soon as it was known that I intended to go down, Admiral Sir Thomas Herbert[12] (a Lord of the Admiralty under the Duke of Northumberland in the Derby[13] Administration) came into the field. Large placards, announcing his name had, on the morning of my arrival, been placed upon every wall in the town together with the important addition in blazing red letters, that Sir Thomas was a Lord of the Admiralty. Two days later a man-of-war steamer entered the harbour to enlist seamen for the Navy. These two circumstances produced an astounding effect upon the inhabitants. My supporters were not slow in responding and proclaimed on posters, in equally large letters, that I was the great shipowner!

When I entered the old Town, there was a great deal of noise and cheering, firing of guns, and strewing of flowers. The open carriage in which I rode on entering the place was full of bouquets before I reached the Inn where quarters had been prepared for me.

I protested against entering the town in any such manner but following urgent requests I reluctantly agreed as the previous Liberal candidate[14] had never entered the town, even on private business, except in a carriage and four with outriders. I would have much preferred the shilling bus which ran between the railway station at Totnes and the town of Dartmouth.

That evening a meeting was held. I presume that I must have spoken well, as there was an immense amount of enthusiasm, with cheering, clapping of hands, stamping of feet and cries of "he's the man for us!" Learning from my experience in Monmouth, I wanted some assurance before I would agree to become a candidate, and I had a document ready drawn up which I took with me.

On my way down to Dartmouth I had met my friend Mr. James Wilson,[15] now Secretary of the Treasury, and read my document to him, telling him my intentions. He laughed, and said, "Lindsay, you are a man of business, and can carry everything before you in ships, but if you expect to get electors to sign that document, you are sadly mistaken."

"Well then," I replied, "if they don't sign, I shall not stand, that is all there is to it."

"In that case," said Wilson, "you'll never get into parliament!" and he went on his way.

When my speech was over, and the electors proclaimed loudly that I was the man for them, I quietly said, "Gentlemen, you seem to agree with my sentiments so, that being the case, you will have no objections to give me some proof that you really want me and, if so, be so good as to sign this paper," which I pulled out of the tail pocket of my coat. "If sufficiently signed, I will stand, if not I will go back to London."

The document said:

To W. S. Lindsay.

We the Electors of Dartmouth, having heard you explain your political views, and approving of the same, hereby pledge ourselves to record our votes on your behalf at the first general election and to use all our moral influence to secure your return as our representative in Parliament.

This was something entirely novel to them.

"Mr. Lindsay," said one knowing old fellow, "I hardly think that's fair."

I reiterated my demand. Great cheers followed my expressions, especially from the women who were present, and the non-electors; and after that great numbers of the electors came to the table before the platform and signed – I think between seventy and eighty.

"Now then," I said, "we will have another meeting tomorrow night, so that you may still further understand my views. I will spend three days amongst you, and call and see as many of you as I can at your own homes and, if by the end of that period, the document is signed by a majority of the electors, I will stand as a candidate."

On the following morning I commenced my canvassing. In a small place like Dartmouth, within hours everyone knew about me and everybody, particularly the Liberals, expected to see me. The first man I called upon was Mr. Woolridge, or rather Colonel Woolridge. He was quite an important person in the town and was reputed to be a Liberal and had been Chairman of the Liberal Committee at the previous election. I expected his warm support and so did all those who had accompanied me. We were however all mistaken. The Colonel had already pledged himself to the support of Sir Thomas Herbert and, as everyone in Dartmouth knew this, he asserted, "his word was his bond", etc., etc. There is something in the wind I thought. My party was thunder-struck and some of them firmly suspected that he had been bought.

The next great man of the town we visited was an old gentleman who was a great politician whom many looked up to, and he was quite an authority in the church. He was determined to keep me some time answering difficult questions. These I answered assuring him that I would consider what he said.

But when he brought out a whole host of subscription lists to charities, I positively declined to put my name to any of them, on the grounds that it was nothing more or less than bribery and corruption under the form of a charitable contribution. He was however a Liberal man, who clung to his political principles, and he signed the deed. His signature was the means of obtaining a great many more.

It would be almost endless work to go through the whole list of those we called upon. They consisted of all sorts. Many of them turned up their noses at me, because I had once been a sailor boy. They knew all about me. In fact, they seemed to know a great deal more about me than I knew myself. With some I passed for a most extraordinary man. With others I was deemed an equally extraordinary impostor.

On the following evening we had another great meeting, which was still more enthusiastic than the first. The Liberals were roused. Their blood was getting up. The excitement rose to an unusual height. The Tories saw that my speeches were making a greater impression than usual upon the Electors; and as they could not muster a sufficient mob to make a noise in the hall, and prevent me from speaking, they had hired a brass band with two drums. The band was stationed outside close by, just behind the window where the platform had been placed. The moment I commenced to speak the band began to play; the two drums thundered away at a most outrageous rate. Of course, the Liberal party were wild with rage. But when the band commenced, I stopped my speech. I knew that they would tire, so I let them play until they were exhausted.

At last, they relinquished the contest in despair. I then resumed speaking and said all I had to say in quietness. The most difficult part was keeping the people inside the building under control, as they were very angry. It was no easy matter to prevent them from sallying out in a body and smashing drums and bugles to pieces, which of course would have led to a terrible fight as the band was supported by a strong group of Tories. After the meeting I once more produced the document, and some 30 or 40 more electors signed.

The next day was employed in further canvassing, and part of the following day we continued to solicit votes. By that time, I had seen all the electors whom it was necessary to visit, the deed was signed by this time by a clear majority of 10 or 15 – I forget the exact number, but it was a clear majority.

I then took my document to the mayor, and requested him to sign it, certifying that all names on it were duly qualified to vote as electors of the Borough. This he did. Not content with this, I procured the attesting signatures of two Justices of the Peace. I then sent the Town Cryer through the town to announce to the electors that I desired to communicate with them at 3 o'clock, before my departure for London; and that if they wished to hear what I had to say they could come to the space in front of the hotel and I would address them from the windows. Three o'clock arrived, and a numerous body of people assembled.

"I would make no promise when I came here," I said, "but as you have given me proof that you want my services, I consent to stand as a candidate. The Tories may save themselves the trouble of a contest this time, for this paper" said I, producing the document, "is signed by a clear majority of the electors, all pledged of their own free will to support me. I will come back again in about a fortnight and repeat my visit for a couple of days and I will be here in good time when the General Election is announced to run against Sir Thomas."

The Tories were in a great rage and vented it by commencing to smash some windowpanes in the Inn. The Liberals by way of retaliation fought against those who broke the windows. A couple of policemen, aided by two specials, soon sent the mob away home, indeed a Dartmouth mob was at its worst a very harmless and good-natured body.

In about fourteen days, as I had promised, I paid the electors another visit, but on this occasion, I went into town by bus, carrying my carpet bag in my hand to the door of the Inn, very much to the horror and astonishment, no doubt, of many of the old aristocrats, most of whom were indeed my opponents.

Some of the voters began to doubt whether I was really W.S. Lindsay "the great Shipowner" and that I was the owner of 22 first-class ships, had signed insurance indentures to the amount of £2,800,000, and had chartered 700 ships in a single year to all parts of the world. They did not believe me.[16] Indeed, several days later, two electors called on me at my London Office to check that I was who I said I was.

At last, Parliament was dissolved, and the general election commenced. I was in no hurry to proceed to Dartmouth. I thought that if I was there four or five days before the day of nomination it would be soon enough. I counted upon the pledge which I held from a majority of the electors. I was however mistaken.

The Admiralty Lord was there, and in full regalia, on my arrival. An Admiralty steamer moreover lay in the harbour, and she was then engaging men for the Service! The Officers and men were walking about the town, and the ladies and gentlemen were visiting the steamer. The captain was all smiles and sometimes the visitors had luncheon on board. Dartmouth had never been so animated before: the great Lord of the Admiralty and his great war steamer in the harbour: the sailors kissing the girls on shore just to induce them to persuade their brothers to enter the service; and the Officers in their smart uniforms, with their swords dangling at their sides, promenading the streets.

It was inferred that the harbour would be always full of war steamers when the Admiralty Lord became MP. The effect produced was immense. The Liberal party shrugged their shoulders and wavered. Despite their written pledge, I began to entertain serious doubts of my return.

Then the owners of the public houses became overgenerous. They gave beer, sometimes wine and even suppers to the electors, for which they would make no charge. The great brass band too played such popular naval tunes about the town and carried such splendid flags with the name of "Admiral Sir Thomas Herbert, Lord of the Admiralty for ever" inscribed on them.

Again, somehow or other, persons who had always been poor before suddenly became richer. Rents they owed to their landlord, the Mayor, Sir Henry Seale,[17] were settled. I am sure Sir Henry would not have granted a settlement without the cash having been paid. For, though a Baronet, Sir Henry was not overburdened with riches.

Although they had most of the advantages, the opposition were driven to desperate measures. I was walking up the main street, when I heard a terrible hubbub: men and women roaring and screaming and rushing to the market in a crowd.

"What's all this noise about?" I enquired of a woman who was frantic with rage.

"The matter indeed, Sir, don't you know, why, they are stealing our men."

Stealing men, I thought, I have heard of many kinds of robbery, I have never heard of such a crime, unless on the coast of Africa. But it was nevertheless true! The Admiral's Committee were kidnapping my supporters as fast as they could, with the intention of getting them out of the town until the Election was over. I found out afterwards that they had really got a great many away that night, for on the day of the election some of those who had signed the pledge were not to be found.

Others of my supporters were threatened to be turned out of their rented homes. Some abstained from voting for fear of reprisals. Most of them, however, adhered to their pledges, and I dare say the poor men suffered for being faithful to their principles and their convictions. The evening before the Election, more people swung in my favour for they had had an opportunity of comparing what I had to say with Sir Thomas when he had to speak.

On the morning of the Election, voting commenced at 8 a.m. At 9 o'clock, I was ahead, and at noon I was leading by 20 votes. It was clear to almost everybody that I should gain the election. But in the afternoon the screw was tightened. Threats, bribes, and undue influence of every kind were employed. Every hour after noon I lost ground and when the poll closed at 4 p.m. I lost the election by seven votes![18] I would have beaten him, had he not at last bought five of my supporters, and he paid a pretty price for them, and that turned the election. I do not envy any man of such honours. I have the affection of the people, which is far better.[19]

It was about 7 or 8 o'clock on the evening, that a stout rough-faced man met me on the stairs. He introduced himself as Mr. Cooke. "Mr. Lindsay," he said, "I have had the pleasure of beating you again." I was somewhat taken aback as I had never seen this person before. I could not help exclaiming "Indeed! Not you, but your wallet has beaten me no doubt," and I walked on.

Afterwards I found out that this man was a London barrister, that he was a kind of agent for the Duke of Northumberland, that he had been employed at the Monmouth election, and had been sent down to oppose me also at Dartmouth. The duke, who had been hard at work, was determined to stop me from being a Member of Parliament. But even dukes may be beaten. I decided, if I ever had another chance, to give the duke another battle.

31 Tynemouth Contest: A Close-Run Victory

Nearly two years had passed since I had contested Dartmouth, during which time I devoted myself to my increasingly successful business. I shipped 100,000 tons of coal and 150,000 tons of iron; whilst as brokers, during that famine year, my operations had extended to 300,000 tons of grain.[20]

The opportunity arose to compete for a seat where I had almost certain victory, but I declined. I had another objective in view. I wished to contest a seat in the domain of my old opponent the Duke of Northumberland on my own conditions.

During the General Election in 1852 there had been a bitter contest in the Borough of Tynemouth which had resulted in Hugh Taylor[21] successfully defeating Ralph Grey[22] (the sitting Whig MP) by 12 votes. It, however, was found that Mr Taylor's supporters had been bribing the voters and he was duly unseated the following year. Hence a By Election was called.[23]

Hugh Taylor was the nephew of the duke's head manager. Ralph Grey had for some time been the private secretary to Lord Palmerston. Mr. Grey had petitioned against the return of Mr. Taylor. Though he was certain to unseat him for bribery, he could not himself contest the seat again, as his own conduct had been impeached.

The duke's agents had not been slow to find a candidate as, on the very day the news reached the north that Mr. Taylor was unseated the name of Mr. Peter Dickson was announced. He was a London merchant of considerable wealth. Although he showed little energy, he was ambitious and had, during several months, been courting the friendship and support of the electors of Tynemouth.

When I was invited to stand, by the Liberal party, I consented on my usual conditions. I adhered most rigidly to my resolution not to spend one penny on drink and much less on bribery and corruption. I still determined to have none of the paraphernalia of flags, music and ribbons considered so necessary at a contested election. This seemed to capture the mood of the public. No inducements were offered, I may say, on either side. As usual so much falls on the candidates themselves. If the Conservative resorts to bribery the Liberal might feel he must do the same. If one opens the public houses, the other does likewise.

Publicans themselves told me that though, at the previous election, £3,000 was spent at their public houses they were considerable losers by the transaction. The windows, glasses and various articles destroyed, and the interruption of the usual trade, far outweighed any profits they may have made. I resolved not to open any public houses and was heartily supported by the publicans themselves.

People only want a good example to be set to them. If they behave badly, they are often made so by those who ought to know better. If they are demoralised, it is often by those whose duty it is to introduce laws for their improvement.

Part Three: Politics and Shipping

I knew that my most vigorous opposition would be by all who were under the influence of the Duke of Northumberland, and by all professing Conservative principles. The Borough of Tynemouth, like most other Boroughs, was divided into two parties, Liberal and Conservative. The former consisted mostly of the shopkeepers and tradespeople; the latter of shipowners and those who consider themselves aristocrats.

My opponent avoided public meetings. He was a poor speaker. He canvassed heavily though. He visited each voter at their own home, and many far more than once. My party on the other hand, held meetings where I explained my views. I also visited as many of the electors as my limited time would allow.

On the day of the election every shop in the town was closed, all business was suspended, and everything was as tranquil and orderly as if it had been a Sunday. The duke's party were bent on returning Mr. Dickson, and on the other hand most people were equally determined that the duke should not have his own way. For the first few hours I took the lead on the poll; at 11 o'clock I was some 50 or 60 ahead. After that hour, however, the duke's tenants poured in to vote. They arrived in coach and cart loads and were bundled into the polling booths like so many sheep driven into a pen. It was clear to me however that many of them were voting against their wishes. Between the hours of 11 and 1 o'clock my opponent polled double the number I did, and at 1 o'clock I was only eight ahead. The Tories felt assured of success, but my party were making very strenuous efforts.

Many voters, who had been confined for weeks or even months to their houses through sickness, were, at their own request, carried upon couches to the poll to vote for me. One poor man I remember fainted away when he had given his vote. Another voter insisted on getting out of his bed, but never recovered from the effort.

At last, when the poll closed at 4 o'clock and it was announced that I was elected by a majority of 17, the crowd burst forth into tremendous cheering. The people had elected one of themselves against the influence of the duke. Much against my will they requisitioned a carriage and pulled it through the town with me on it. Hundreds dragged the vehicle and a full 5,000 people followed. Their enthusiasm knew no bounds.

I arrived at the Hotel where I stayed. The crowd of more than 5,000 demanded a speech which I gave from the window of my room. The multitude consisted in great part of miners, sailors, keelmen[24] and workers of all kinds.

They had heard that the mayor, who was a Conservative, had acted most prejudicially, and had treated me badly. A deputation, representing the crowd and consisting of three massive fellows, a blacksmith, a keelman and a sailor, approached me and asked me if I would allow them to pull down the Mayor's House. I saw that the men were serious and that they really intended to do what they proposed. By their looks it would not be safe to contradict them, so I said "Now lads, if you want to pull the mayor's house down, I'm sure you could do it in half an hour. I think you ought to. But" I continued, "I don't see the good of pulling it down to-night, all the bricks would likely be lost and that would be a waste."

This got them thinking and posed a problem for them.

"Now that I am your Member," I continued, "I am thinking of building a cottage down on the cliff by the mouth of the Tyne where I can go with my wife for a month or two in the summer. I shall need bricks to build it and, if you will only wait a bit, and not pull down the mayor's house until I am ready to build it, I shall then be able to make use of his bricks!"

This proposal produced its desired effect. They thought it a good idea, and within half an hour the vast crowd had dispersed, and no attempt was made to destroy the house.

The same agent, who had opposed me at Monmouth and at Dartmouth was actively employed at Tynemouth by the duke. On this occasion, however, I saw nothing of him. But I afterwards learned that the duke admitted that I had beaten him fairly and won my seat by honourable means. A more severe contest had never been fought in the borough, and an additional hundred voters polled than at any previous election.[25]

A few days afterwards I took my seat in the House of Commons. My first impressions of that assembly were curious enough. The reality fell far short of my expectations. Men of great names and of worldwide fame as statesmen had no halo around them. They were plain mortals like me. They did not at all strike me at first as men of a superior order.

Any man, when first entering the House finds himself very insignificant. If he attempts any airs and graces, he only makes himself ridiculous. The House of Commons is a great leveller. Members sat very informally in the seats, indeed some lay, many seemed asleep. As I sat on the cross benches below the gangway where I took my seat for the first time, it did not seem to me to be worth half the time and effort I had spent being elected.

Whilst in the House though, I determined that I should speak on matters I knew about – shipping.

32 The Marchioness and her Dog

Lady Londonderry[26] in her day was one of the great leaders of fashion. In her younger days she was considered one of the most handsome and most beautiful of women. I cannot however vouch for the fact, for when I knew her from 1854 to 1863, she certainly did not represent either the figure of Venus or the features of a handsome Angel.[27]

She had not however at that time abandoned the position she had long held in the West End world. The magnificent saloons of Holderness House, her town abode in Park Lane, were then, as they have long been, a place of attraction for the elite of the Tory aristocracy – the Richmonds, the Stanleys, the Cecils and the oldest and proudest of the Conservative families were her frequent guests. Her evening assemblies were amongst the grandest and gayest in that smart quarter of the great metropolis.

I first became acquainted with her Ladyship in the winter of 1854. Following a request of Mr George Marshall, the shipbuilder, I had provided her favourite son, Lord Adolphus Vane-Tempest,[28] an Officer of the Guards then with his Regiment in the Crimea, with a general letter of introduction to the captains of my ships which were then engaged as transports in the Black Sea. The letter it appeared proved of considerable value to his Lordship for, during the hurricane which swept over the camp, he had found excellent quarters on board my steamship the *Robert Lowe*, then lying in the harbour of Balaklava. The recommendation thus afforded had proved so acceptable to Lord Adolphus that he had written to his mother in warm and grateful terms of my kindness, and she had therefore thought it necessary to call at my office in Austin Friars, to make my acquaintance and thank me in person for what I had done.

Austin Friars was, and is, a very large office. In it there are shipowners and masters from all nations daily congregated; sailors getting payment for their advance notes, and sailors' and Captains' wives drawing their husband's monthly money. In fact, between the hours of 10 a.m. and noon there is generally a large gathering in the hall of No. 8 Austin Friars. But amongst that crowd a Peeress is seldom if ever found and, as the clerks at the counter had not caught her Ladyship's name, I presume they had taken her for a Captain's wife. They had not perhaps been so explicit in their answer to her enquiry if I was free, as they might otherwise have been. She wrote a somewhat curt note saying that she had called and missed me.

I could not think of allowing her to again call, and therefore, in reply to her note, I wrote to say that if she would allow me I would do myself the pleasure of paying my respects to her in Park Lane any morning she might name. After much consideration her Ladyship named a very early hour to suit me on my way to business, and when I called a little before 10 a.m. she was in her own little reception room ready to receive me.

This room was at the extreme end of a long and magnificent suite of drawing rooms, furnished in the most sumptuous and gorgeous style. The servants were unusually polite and obsequious, but such was not the case with all the four-legged animals under her Ladyship's order. No sooner had the two-legged animals bowed me into the drawing rooms than I saw in the distance one of those spoiled curs known as 'Lady's dogs'. This brute eyed me with considerable suspicion. It did not seem to think that a stranger had any right to be in its mistress's drawing room at so early an hour and, as I approached the sanctum of her Ladyship, it flew barking at me and then, without ceremony, seized hold of the leg of my trousers. I shook it from me, but it renewed the attack and, as I had no fancy to be worried by even the lap dog of a Marchioness, I gave it a lift with my foot which sent it sprawling and yelling amongst the sofas, ottomans, and other fancy articles with which these magnificent rooms were thoroughly furnished.

Just then, when the pet dog of her Ladyship lay howling and screaming the Marchioness herself – it was the first time I had seen her – sallied forth from her sanctum in full sail to meet me and bid me welcome. She was tall, very stout, and very dignified. The flounces of her rich and profuse dress almost reached her waist. One eye rested upon me, but the other upon her yowling pet. The warm welcome she had made up her mind to give me was evidently modified by the reception I had given her dog, and it was clear that her face was flushed more with anger than surprise at the manner in which I had treated "Beauty'; for such was the name of her favourite dog.

"You are Mr Lindsay I presume," she said tossing her head like a bull when a scarlet cloth is shaken before it.

This was not the kind of reception I had expected, so I replied as curtly. "I am, and I presume you are Lady Londonderry."

But without any notice of my enquiry, she turned to the immediate source of her anxiety remarking in a much more modified tone "Don't you see you have nearly killed my dog?" picking it up in her arms as she spoke and endeavouring to soothe the howlings of "poor Beauty".

'Beauty' however was not to be thus easily pacified for the insult and injury I had inflicted, for when he had got his mistress as a protector, he struggled fiercely to get away from her arms to repay the lift I had given him. In reply to her Ladyship's enquiry about nearly killing her dog, I coolly remarked that she should not allow such brutes to run loose and attack her visitors.

At this point we stood stock still looking at each other and then she held out her unoccupied hand, for the left still retained to her breast the enraged Beauty, and with a laugh bade me welcome, saying that I was just the kind of man she expected to find me. I laughed too, hinting, though not actually saying so, that she was not unlike the lady I had contemplated meeting.

This ludicrous mode of introduction had the effect of making her Ladyship and myself as close in five minutes as if we had known each other for five or fifteen years. We were both alike in our way I daresay for, from that day, I had invitations to all her 'at homes', evening gatherings and to many of her dinner parties. I only made an appearance at the former on rare occasions for, at such gay assemblies as these, I cannot say I was ever at ease.

Twice I had the honour of paying her a visit at Seaham Hall, one of her country seats in the county of Durham. On one occasion I was her guest for a couple of days, on another for somewhat longer. On both occasions Earl Vane[29] and his Lady and their children were there, but no other member of the family. The Earl however was not her favourite son. It was Lord Adolphus and Lord Ernest, two thorough scamps, who were the idols of her heart. They could do whatever they pleased when at home, but Earl Vane, when he wanted to smoke before bedtime, had to rest satisfied with the open air or one of the outbuildings. During my time there he and I enjoyed a good smoke together in the scullery, before going to bed, unknown to the Marchioness.

Like most clever persons, Lady Londonderry had strong likes and dislikes. Amongst the latter was the Parson on her property at Seaham. She said that

Part Three: Politics and Shipping

Lady Londonderry, Frances Anne Vane, Marchioness of Londonderry and her son George Henry Robert Charles William Vane-Tempest, Viscount Seaham, later 5th Marquess of Londonderry (1821–1884). Portrait by Sir Thomas Lawrence.

William Schaw Lindsay

Lady Londonderry in later life when Lindsay first met her. Great-grandmother of Sir Winston Churchill.

he was so lazy that he had worn a hole right through the cover of the pillow of the sofa which stood in his study. When I visited the manse with Lady Vane, which she herself would never enter, she asked me to report any of the Rector's lazy habits.

I, on the other hand, was one of her favourites at the time. She drove me about the country to inspect her collieries and villages and would insist upon having my opinion on matters about which I knew nothing, much to my own annoyance, and I daresay still more to the annoyance of her people. If I gave an opinion, and it was different to what they had been doing, she told them of it.

She was herself however a remarkably clever woman, though very speculative. Upon the whole however she was not a bad businesswoman, and she was an excellent public speaker. I have heard her address a large assembly. Her speeches to her work people were practical and good – so much so that the London *Times* on more than one occasion considered them worthy of a place in its columns.

When first I visited Seaham Hall I daresay Lady Londonderry's servants considered me quite as strange and eccentric as their Mistress. On the first morning I had just got out of bed and was sitting in my shirt tails on a luxurious sofa, rubbing my eyes, for I was not thoroughly awake, when two tall footmen entered my bedroom. I gave my eyes an extra rub to make certain I was not still in bed or dreaming, for I could not conceive it possible that I was to be placed under the charge of two such magnificent fellows. Such however proved to be the case, for after numerous bows they informed me that by her Ladyship's orders they were to attend on me while I remained a guest at the Hall. I said it was very kind and considerate of their mistress to think of such a thing. Then, giving my eyes another rub, to make certain of the reality of their presence, I asked one of them to hand me my trousers which lay on a chair by the window.

"Now," I continued, putting my hand in the pocket of my 'inexpressibles' and pulling out two half sovereigns, "here is something for each of you and, while I remain at the Hall, don't let me see either of you in this room again at this time in the morning, or at any time of the day when I am in it. I daresay some employment of some kind will be good for you, as you seem to require work very much, so one of you may bring me, at 7 in the morning, hot water to shave and another to place my boots outside the door – I daresay you get somebody else to clean them – but don't come in here again disturbing me like the ghosts in Macbeth."

The two 'magnificents' looked at me with their mouths open, but they took the half sovereigns and walked backwards out of the room, bowing, staring, scraping, and gaping, as if they had seen a more extraordinary thing than any of Shakespeare's visions! And I daresay they, to this day, tell the story of her Ladyship's guest who would not be waited upon.

Lady Londonderry took her departure for another world in the spring of 1865. Some years before her death she paid much attention to religion; to the last though, I believe she would not receive any consolation at the hands of the indolent Rector of Seaham.

33 The University of Life

My education was so limited, and so imperfect that I had great doubts that my writings and speeches would prove either clear or instructive. Although I benefited from my few years at Ayr Academy while I was relatively young, I lacked many skills that others acquired from their time at educational establishments.

The largest portion of my education was obtained reading on board ship during my sailing years and during an idle hour after work. I envied those with whom it has been my lot to mingle, who possessed the 'knowledge' of other languages, which I had never an opportunity of acquiring.

I remember at one of those fashionable college dinners, a discussion arose on the relative merits of Oxford and Cambridge as seats of learning, and of the special advantages of their respective colleges.[30] During the dinner, a noble Lord, near to whom I had the honour of sitting, very innocently asked me at which of the colleges I had been educated? I replied "Focsle (Forecastle) College" with still more apparent innocence. His Lordship did not catch the words as I had run the two into one in accordance with its nautical pronunciation. I therefore repeated them more distinctly.

"Fore-Castle" he repeated after me with great simplicity and gravity. "I thought I knew all the colleges" he continued "at both places, but I really cannot recollect one by that name, Fore-Castle."

Though everybody round the table saw what I meant, the noble Lord had trouble understanding what I had said, and I was consequently obliged to explain that I meant the forecastle of the ship in which I served my apprenticeship. An explanation always spoils and blunts a joke, but nevertheless in this case it created a hearty laugh at the expense of the good-natured Peer who, when he understood what everybody was laughing at, joined heartily in the joke. The fashionable assembly did not seem to think the less of me because I had been trained at sea instead of at either of the Universities.

34 An Overworked Mind

I took my seat in the House of Commons as Member for Tynemouth, in March 1854, and was present regularly during the remainder of the session.[31] In fact, there were one or two questions of importance before the House in which I had a deep interest. One was the Consolidation and Revision of our Maritime Laws, a measure which I had long advocated, so I made sure that I was there to follow the debates.

My constitution was naturally a strong one. It must have been so, or otherwise I never could have stood the labour I had gone through mentally and bodily for so long. But it gave way at last. I remained as close to business as ever. My day consisted of rising every morning not later than seven. I breakfasted at eight. I was in the city by nine and at constant work during the whole day. From the office I proceeded to the House where sometimes I was compelled to remain until two in the morning.

By the end of that session[32] in Parliament, I felt the effects of all this. I thought that a run up to Scotland amongst the Highlands would put it to rights. But I was mistaken. My digestive organs got out of order. My liver grew sluggish in its action. I lost my appetite; could not sleep; my nervous system got all out of kilter, my head grew giddy, and in a word, I became quite a different man mentally and bodily to what I used to be. For the first time in my life, I was fairly laid upon a bed of sickness and, for a short time, became seriously unwell. Through the blessing of God, I recovered. But during nearly three months, I was away from business, and not allowed to do anything requiring close study. As I grew stronger, I found that I was miserable doing nothing. I accordingly commenced writing my Journals.

I corresponded with a few political colleagues, amongst them was Richard Cobden,[33] who achieved fame for the repeal of the Corn Laws in 1846. At the end of September, he wrote to me[34] saying:

I knew by your eye – the open window of the brain – that you were mentally overworked and told you so as plainly as I had any right to speak. If I had been your family doctor, I should have insisted upon a change in your daily habits which would have prevented your recent break-down.

Now ask yourself, what are your objectives in the world? They are really all comprised in the old toast "health, long life and happiness", the first being essential to the other two.

Now in your case, you devoted yourself too exclusively to success in business. You succeeded beyond precedent, for I doubt whether anybody before achieved so much in private enterprise prior to thirty-five years of age as you have done. You must, from this moment, close your account with Fortune, and resolve to be henceforth quite indifferent about the annual balance sheets in Austin Friars in the name of "W S Lindsay & Co". If you can put your firm on such a footing as to insure prosperity through the labours of others, do so.

You may transfer your energies to some other pursuit with safety. Turn your mind to politics, or mechanics, or chemistry, or the arts, or anything you please. Work up the romance of your own life into novels or poems. Change your occupation, and hard work will do you no harm. Nay, it will be better than idleness. But if you attempt to super-add to your private business the labours of Parliament, or of literary pursuits, you will hasten the catastrophe which you seek to avert.

Writing to my wife two weeks later, Cobden said: "Whatever may be the symptoms, depend on it they all proceed from an overworked brain. The sword has been cutting the scabbard. The remedy is not to be sought in inactivity, but in a total change of occupation."

These letters from Mr Cobden were devoted almost exclusively to the state of my health at the time they were written, and the best means of restoring and preserving it. They contained much valuable advice to any person like me who gives the brain more work to do than it could well and honestly perform.[35]

Anyone however who reads these remarks will no doubt be disposed to smile and say of me "and why did he himself not take the advice, for these notes were written when he was paralysed from overwork, and at a time when he was obliged to be lifted out of, and into, his bed." All this is too true, but I may reply to it by saying that all men must die sometime, and though a good many men die of wear and tear, a still greater number, about whom we hear very little, die of rust. If I could have my choice, I would prefer to wear away instead of rusting away. I recovered and carried on with my business and my Parliamentary duties, but after many years and a second warning, I acted on Cobden's advice and retired from business.

Prior to my illness I had interacted with Cobden on many occasions. As well-known as he was, he was under the impression that when the House debated any Maritime Affairs, they would listen to me rather than him. Of course, I knew this was not the case. In his letters he often encouraged me to

Richard Cobden (1804–1865), a great friend of Lindsay's.

take the lead. On one occasion he had given notice that he would speak on a Shipping matter. The House was packed in expectation of him speaking. I usually sat next to him, not far from the Speaker. In the afternoon that day, just before he was to speak, he went across to have a word with the Speaker and informed him that he was not feeling well and that I would take his place opening the debate and submitting his motion.

I was about to request that someone else do this, when the Speaker called out my name, to the surprise of everybody in the House. Quite perplexed, I got up. I slowly read the motion and then, in as few words as possible, gave a few of the leading arguments in favour of the motion.

When, however, the audience realised that Cobden could not take part in it, the House began gradually to thin and after a while the chamber was almost empty. The subject was one of great importance yet when it was known that Cobden would not speak very few people seemed to take any interest in it.

So it was, on instructions from my medical advisors, my wife and I left London at the end of September to stay in the Isle of Wight. Though we were first out of the steamboat, we found only one sitting room and bedroom vacant at the Pier Hotel, which we secured for a few days.[36] I have a distinct recollection of this place. Some 21 or 22 years ago, as a sailor boy, having sailed from London for the West Indies, my ship encountered very stormy weather in the channel. She suffered severe damage and lost some of her spars. To replace them, and repair other damages, and to escape the heavy gales, we anchored at the Mother Bank off Ryde. I was one of the four boys whose duty it was to row the captain to the shore. We used to land him at the end of the pier. Of course, I never got any farther than that, as I had to wait for his return. Though it was late in the autumn, the Town appeared beautiful, and the rough life I led on the ocean, and on a merchant ship, considerably enhanced the natural loveliness of the place. I, at that time, sat on the end of the pier, wondering if it would ever be my happy lot to settle down in a cottage, close to some such spot. After a few days in the hotel, I sought a more suitable house for a longer stay in the vicinity of the seashore. I found one at 3 Pier Terrace, close to the Hotel.

The situation in Ryde was indeed interesting. There was a constant change of scene. From my windows close to the beach, I looked out upon the harbour of Portsmouth opposite, about five miles distant. A little to the right was Spithead with its magnificent fleet of men of war, which included the *Hannibal* (92 guns), the *Powerful* (84 guns), the *Colossus* (64 guns), the *Ajax* (60 guns) and various steam frigates, sloops[37] of war and steamers.

To the left was the Mother Bank, the anchorage for wind-bound merchantmen and for many ships laden with sugar from Brazil and West Indies which call there to await orders as to the disposal of their cargoes. Around the pier were moored innumerable boats, barges, and vessels of various kinds, including many most graceful yachts, colliers from Newcastle, trading smacks and small coasters of every rig. There were cutters[38] for hire, and a whole fleet of small rowing boats of colours more various than the rainbow. From the pier end a steamer was to be found, starting to and from Cowes, Portsmouth, or Southampton every hour. And on the pier itself, a constant succession of pleasure seekers could be seen all day long.

Although I had not long been in the Isle of Wight, we returned briefly to Portland Place in London. I wished to see my ship the *Alipore*, docked in Deptford and commissioned, with two of my other ships, as a Troop Ship for the Crimean War. On our way there I read in *The Times* the deeply interesting news of the great battle of the Alma.[39] I saw it reported also that Sebastopol had fallen. I could not however put faith in the latter report.[40]

We only stayed one night, and at 3 p.m. started from home and commenced our journey in the open carriage to Portsmouth. My young son Willie and my sister-in-law Mrs. Craig accompanied us. We proposed to make a two days and three nights' journey of it. The weather was beautiful and continued. We drove through Kingston-upon-Thames and Esher and arrived at Chobham, after a delightful drive, at 6.30 p.m. There we remained for the night at an Inn.[41]

Our journey continued the next morning with a drive through Guildford and Godalming to Midhurst. This was the birthplace and the home of Richard Cobden. I had previously mentioned that I would be overnighting in the town and would be pleased to meet up with him. When we arrived at the

Inn[42] there was a note from him inviting me over to his house which was in the process of being renovated.

After dinner, as the weather was fine, I strolled over to 'Dunford', his house, about a mile and a half away. My wife and Mrs. Craig were too tired after the day's journey to accompany me. When I arrived, we had a long chat and parted at 10 o'clock. We met up again the following day, and on a walk, I learnt about his politics.

"But is it not melancholy to think" said Cobden, as he gazed upon the very beautiful and very extensive scene at our feet, "that, except for my small spot, and one or two other bits of land much smaller, the whole land around us as far as we can see on either side is in the possession of three men, no more! Yes, as far as you can see, and much farther, the land belongs to the Duke of Richmond, Colonel Wyndham, and Lord Egmont."

"You were remarking" he continued, "that you considered our labouring population very ignorant. But how can they be otherwise when the soil on which they live is monopolised by three men, so far above their status that they dare not approach within a hundred yards of their own shadow? How can our population have any stimulant for hard work? Even if they save money there is no land here that they would be allowed to purchase. The owners of the soil are much too great to take the trouble of seeing to the education of the children on their estates."

We concluded our walk and I returned to the Inn for dinner. The following morning Mr Cobden joined us for breakfast and then my party and I continued to Portsmouth, and the Isle of Wight. On the boat crossing I read a copy of *The Times*, and learnt of the failure, among others, of the Liverpool Shipowner Edward Oliver[43] with liabilities amounting to one million pounds!

His failure did not surprise me. I had known him for years but invariably declined to have any dealings with him. His business was nominally that of a shipowner, but he was more properly a dealer, or speculator in ships. Originally from Quebec, he secured a large amount of sailing ships which he anticipated chartering as War Transports to the Crimean War. The Government turned to many steamships instead. As a result, he filed for bankruptcy.[44] He had 100 sailing ships in all, which far exceeded anything which was ever held in this, or any other country, by any one single individual. The sale of his ships resulted in a collapse in ship prices the following year.

Over the next few days my illness returned. My malady I could hardly describe. My digestion was bad. My liver did not seem to exert its proper action. There was a great tightness over my stomach; a constant belching of wind, a giddiness with some pains at times, and a great confusion in my head as if my brain was becoming soft or, in some matters, losing its faculty as I could not always command my thoughts.

Letters from my friends were sent to convince me that I was not made of impenetrable stuff. How true it is that "all men think all other men mortal except themselves." I had to follow the advice given me by them and my medical advisers. Over the following three weeks or so I took the medicine which the Doctors prescribed, though I did not have much faith in it. I believed my cure was pretty much in my own hands.

During our stay we toured the island. There was much to enjoy: the silvery sea, the chalky cliffs, the wild and secluded ravines contrasting with the ridged chines running into the sea, the beautiful country, studded with white villas, or princely domains and endless green lawns with magnificent clumps of trees making the whole entity exquisitely lovely. I was not anxious about Austin Friars and did not think about business for a fortnight.

Towards the end of our stay, Cobden visited us and joined my wife, my sister-in-law and me on a visit to the dockyard and arsenal in Portsmouth. We were accompanied through these great establishments by the Rev. Mr. Berthon[45] of Farnham, the ingenious inventor of an extraordinary lifeboat.

The Royal Dockyard of Portsmouth is well worthy of a visit. To me it was an object of particular interest. I had only visited it once before, and that merely for a few hours. As I had anticipated I found everything in order, and upon a most gigantic scale, but the expenditure appeared to be lavish in the extreme especially in ship building.

We found some six or seven very large vessels on the stocks from frigates to battleships. Some of them had been sixteen years in construction and would still require a few years to complete. All of them were undergoing great alterations at an enormous cost. Some were in process of lengthening in midships; others at the bow; and all were having their stern frames torn down and rebuilt to receive a screw propeller.[46]

The sums of money, expended annually on experimentation were truly enormous and, whilst our existing system continued, we could not hope for a change for the better. At every change in Administration, we had a new Secretary of the Admiralty and a new set of Lord Commissioners, differing of course politically from their predecessors. Naturally they were anxious to show to their partisans how much better they could manage the naval affairs of the country than the previous Lords whom they superseded. Each in turn discovered that the ships on the stocks were too shallow, too narrow, too short, or perhaps too long, and alterations were then undertaken and, everything previously ordered, countermanded.

The anchors in stock were all condemned because they were not patented according to the last appointed Lords Commissioners. The great guns were considered useless and were ordered to be melted and recast in some other form. The store houses or engine shops were torn down to be rebuilt because the new first Sea Lord preferred the Gothic to the Elizabethan style.

Such was the case long before my day, and so it will continue, unless we have a complete reform. The remedy is very simple. We must have one responsible head over the affairs of the Admiralty. This Officer must not be subject to change at every expulsion of the Ministry but must hold office for life, advising good and effective service. This important Officer should be responsible to the Crown, and to the country, for every item of expenditure in the Dockyards. He should be subject to the control of the Crown only and to the Ministers for the time being, who would however have power to remove him but only for neglect of duty or proof of incompetency.[47]

From the Dockyard we proceeded on a visit to examine Mr. Cunningham's patent[48] for the reefing of top sails. I had often heard of this very simple and ingenious invention and had in fact been long in correspondence with Mr. Cunningham about it but, until then, I never had an opportunity of inspecting it. The invention fully realised my expectations and it should soon be brought into general use.

The following day Reverend Berthon called upon me to explain the principle on which his lifeboat was constructed and brought with him a model. I am at a loss to describe this most perfect and compact craft. It must be seen and examined to be thoroughly understood. On the water, and at a very short distance, few could discover any difference between his invention and an ordinary boat. It was however constructed on entirely different principles and composed of totally different materials. The outside skin and sealing were made of a preparation of canvas and India rubber, about an eighth of an inch thick, light but very thick, tough, and strong and perfectly air- and water-tight.

The boat herself was divided into eight separate and distinct air-tight compartments. The beams were hinged, as were the sides, which allowed the boat to collapse in an instant and hence compressed into one sixth of her width. I was indeed very much pleased with the ingenious invention of the Farnham Clergyman and recommended its use in all sea-going passenger ships.

As the morning was inviting and there was a good stiff breeze on the water, I was induced to test the sailing qualities of his lifeboat, which lay at anchor off the pier. I found her all I had anticipated, very stiff and exceedingly buoyant, and fast under sail. I had a cruise in her for three or four miles. She was indeed an extraordinary boat.

Shortly after noon that day, after four week's stay, we left Ryde. My health had for the moment somewhat improved, but it was with regret that I left the beautiful Isle of Wight.

Part Four
The Crimean War
(1854–1856)

35 Transport Ships

On my return to London on 20 October 1854, I learned, greatly to my annoyance and regret, the Government, after engaging my new ship, the *Robert Lowe*, had ordered a portion of the upper deck to be removed, as they believed her to be too top heavy. This was my favourite ship. She had been more than two years under construction by Messrs Scott & Co at Greenock, and I had spent all my ingenuity and skill on her design. She combined great capacity and speed with small tonnage, with the accommodation of a three-decked ship, but with the tonnage of a two-decker.

To make matters worse, the Admiralty Board themselves, the week before, had discovered their mistake, and had sent orders not to touch the upper deck, but it was too late. The axe had totally destroyed it, and in so doing had destroyed accommodation for 100 more troops on route to the Crimean War, and demolished that which cost me £1,500 in its construction, besides £821 in its destruction. A more wanton waste of the public money, together with an equally wanton destruction of private property, can scarcely be imagined.

The *Robert Lowe* combined all the requisites of a powerful sailing vessel with those of a steam ship. My belief in my Auxiliary Steamers proved their worth and made the Government significant savings. When compared to 'fully-powered' steamships, those that had bigger engines and carried more coal as a result, the auxiliaries were more cost effective both in terms of reimbursement for the amount of fuel used, and the cost of hiring them. In addition, the same number of troops could be transported.[1]

The *Robert Lowe* could accommodate, if fully laden with cargo, besides her coals 1,200 tons of cargo and stores, with 1,000 troops. Her sister ship the *Tynemouth* had often done this. Whereas the steamer *Indiana* of 2,300 tons, and the *New York* of 2,400 tons would not take more troops and cargo, though double the register tonnage of the *Robert Lowe*. As payment was made based on tonnage, I pointed this out to the Admiralty to readjust the payments, but they were unmoved.

The Crimean War commenced to support the integrity of the Ottoman Empire and to prevent Russian expansion,[2] called for transport ships to carry troops and supplies to the seat of war as soon as possible. I had also negotiated with the French to contract my sailing ships the *Alipore* and *Dinapore* and my auxiliary steamers *Robert Lowe* and *Tynemouth*. The British Government, however, approached me and I assisted them instead. As an MP, I was barred from entering directly or indirectly into British Government contracts, but I circumvented the restrictions by having the ships transferred to my partners.[3]

During the War I was drawing £70,000 per annum from our government for the hire of my ships,[4] although I must say that I was glad to see its termination. Though it did not appear so, the war played sad havoc with our commerce.

I had no sympathy for the Turks. I could understand the policy of a war to check the further aggressions of Russia. I could also understand a war to curtail its power, which might become dangerous to us, and I could understand a war undertaken with a view to establish a Free Republic of energetic and independent people in Turkey. But I could not understand a war waged for the purpose of maintaining the idlest and most miserable people, whose government, if left to itself must crumble to pieces from its own innate weakness.

How many of our fine fellows have fallen! It was mournful to see the best and bravest of them cut off in their prime, fighting to maintain a miserable people who, when all was over, could not govern themselves and who morally, socially, and religiously, had no sympathy with us.

On 22 November the *Robert Lowe* set sail from London to the Crimea. She called in to Portsmouth Harbour and I travelled down to meet her. I slept on board. It quite put me in mind of old times. Captain Bingham, who was not feeling well and whom I replaced, left the ship early in the morning with his baggage in a cutter which I had provided. I soon had the ship in the order ready for the troops who commenced to embark at 11 a.m. and all were on board by 3 pm. They consisted of 15 Officers, 13 Sergeants, and 683 men of various regiments – the 4th, 28th Rifles, Scots Fusiliers, 38th, 44th, and staff. She also carried many medical Officers, a party of Royal Engineers and a diving corps in charge of their under-water explosives, intended for operation against the sunken men-of-war at the mouth of the harbour of Sebastopol.[5] The embarkation of the troops was indeed a fine sight. The Officers appeared to be in as good spirits as the men.

The following day I rose very early so that by daylight I was ready to despatch the ship as soon as the government despatches came on board. At 9.30 a.m, Captain Pentreath,[6] who had replaced Captain Bingham, mustered all hands to get under way, and at 9.45 a.m. the vessel sailed with a fair wind and clear weather, under steam, her three top sails, courses, and jib. I accompanied the ship in a large cutter for a few miles out to sea. At 11 a.m.

we parted with her and had three most deafening and enthusiastic cheers from all on board.

All sail was then set upon the ship, and the noble vessel bounded away directly on its course to the Crimea at the rate of not less than 14 or 15 miles an hour. It was indeed a magnificent spectacle. The pure white sails spread to the freshening breeze. A clear blue sky formed a canopy above the curling waters. We saw her long, bright, black sides, her gracefully bent yards and yielding masts, and the gleaming heads of the troops taking their last long look of the land as it rapidly receded from their view.

Something seemed to whisper to me, as I parted from those noble fellows, that perhaps few of their number would ever again see their native land. My heart was sad. My knees had subconsciously bent upon the deck, and my folded arms rested upon the low rail of the cutter as I watched, lost in thought, my noble ship gracefully skimming over the slightly rippled sea, and bearing within her the lives of hundreds dear to those left behind.

That week we had an account of a dreadful hurricane[7] in the Black Sea which occurred on 14 November, and which played sad havoc with our transports. We waited anxiously for details. Particulars reached us a few days later. The loss of life and property was very great. One vessel, the *Ganges*, under the management of my firm, was amongst the list of those totally destroyed. She was a very fine ship and was owned by my old friends, Messrs David Thom & Co. of Leith. Happily, she was insured.

Though it would appear that the hurricane was more than usually severe, there had been sufficient warning of its approach and I am sure that, if proper precautions had been taken, the loss of life and property would have been much less severe.

To moor ships in 40 fathoms during the winter season, and in open water, was most imprudent on the part of the Naval Officer in command who had ordered them there. But then it appears that he paid no attention to the warnings made against the orders he had issued, energetic warnings on the part of the Masters of the transports. His conduct was culpable and was open to the severest censure, if not deserving a dismissal from the Service.

The vessels lost were the HMS *Prince* (a steamer of 2,700 tons, which had recently cost £105,000), the *Resolute*, the *Kenilworth*, the *Wild Wave*, the *Progress*, *Wanderer* and the *Malta (El Malti)*. The following went ashore at Balaklava and became complete wrecks: the *Pyrenees*, the *Lord Raglan* and the *Ganges*. The *Rodsley* met with a similar fate near the Katcha River and the *Tyrone* was lost at the mouth of the river. The *Danube* was lost in Kamisch Bay. Besides the above, the ship *Her Majesty* (775 tons), the *Asia* (1,210 tons), the *Glendalough* (988 tons), the *Harbinger* and the *Georgiana* all went ashore off Eupatoria.

My ship the *Tynemouth* had just landed wounded of the battle of Inkerman at Scutari, and had afterwards gone across to Constantinople in order to have some slight alterations made to her engines. She was there, snugly moored, during the time of the hurricane.

Captain Dundas of the *Tynemouth* wrote to me to say that he had taken on board, during very stormy weather, the extraordinary number of 1,220 Turkish soldiers, and 8 horses from Stamboul to Balaklava; she towed a brig laden with Turkish stores and 29 men and 27 horses. Also on board was his Excellency Omer Pasha,[8] the Turkish Commander in Chief. That is an enormous freight for a ship of her tonnage to carry and proved the great value of such vessels compared to full-powered steamers.

The captain had visited, with his brother George, the entrenchments close to the walls of Sebastopol and very nearly lost his life by the explosion of one shell from the enemy close to his feet. He gave a very gloomy account of the condition of our troops at the Crimea, and was of opinion that Lord Raglan[9] the Commander in Chief was quite unfit for the position he occupied. Every Officer he met complained in bitter terms against him.[10]

After Christmas I received letters from the *Robert Lowe* from Malta. All was well. She had arrived there on 4 January, after a passage of seventeen days against strong adverse winds the whole way. She proved all I expected of her. She then sailed to Constantinople and Balaklava.

Much to my surprise I also had letters from the Admiralty, forwarding copies of letters from Admiral Stewart,[11] the Admiral in command at Malta, complaining of the conduct of Captain Pentreath of the *Robert Lowe*, also of another of the Officers of that ship, and alleging neglect of duty, and intemperance of the former. I cannot believe the truth of this report. The *Robert Lowe* was only twelve hours in Malta and if he was intoxicated there, his letter written to me whilst there, did not resemble the production of a "drunken" man. I feared this was only another example of the way the Admiralty conducts business. Pentreath and Officers had, no doubt, been so busy that they had not been able to pay that marked and fawning attention to the person in command, which our haughty Naval Officers expect on board of Merchant Ships. This likely enough had brought about some cross words between them which led to the report sent home. If Pentreath had treated them to a dinner and given them plenty of wine, the official report might have been very different. However, I had to look farther into it. If true, Pentreath was unfit to command any ship. If false, it was a most disgraceful proceeding on the part of Admiral Stewart.

The following month, I visited the Admiralty three times and had long interviews with Sir James Graham.[12] I spoke my mind very plainly. I received news from the *Robert Lowe* at Balaklava. The accounts from Captain Pentreath were not such as I could wish, and I resolved to dismiss him and send out Captain William Congalton,[13] late of the *Ganges*, to take his place. Drink is still the curse of our Merchant Service. I was resolved that whenever any Master or Officer gave way to habits of drinking, I would not only discharge him but as a Member of the Marine Board, I would have him tried and deprived of his certificate.

In my capacity as an MP, I offered a few remarks on the management of the War: especially the state of the Transport Service. At the time I spoke there were

Part Four: The Crimean War

full 400 members present, and the most marked silence was observed. It was well to have the ear of the House on subjects that I was knowledgeable in.[14]

My ships continued to operate as Transport ships during 1855. I received further letters in February from the ships at the seat of War. Captain Congalton reported that he had taken over in command of the *Robert Lowe*, and that all was in order. The *Dinapore* and *Alipore* had arrived at Constantinople.

I was also forwarded a letter from Captain Dundas of the *Tynemouth* that month to say that he had taken more than 1,100 men, 30 horses and 350 tons of provisions and stores from Baltzik in Turkey to Eupatoria. He is an amusing fellow. Writing to his brother, and relayed to me, he said they encountered a nasty gale, the ship rocked badly, and in the middle of the night he had nearly been smothered by an avalanche of books. "If anyone had come in, I am sure they would have taken me for a librarian."

He then said that "Yesterday we passed a sailing transport only halfway across [the Black Sea], laying to, under close reefed topsails, which left for Eupatoria to my certain knowledge nearly a fortnight ago; when she'll get there remains yet to be demonstrated." He sang the praises of our auxiliary steamers. The ship then sailed from Eupatoria to Balaklava with 1,200 men, 56 horses, and 150 tons of provisions and stores.

In April, by orders of the French Government, we chartered the American Ship the *Great Republic* for their transport service, and she proceeded to Marseilles to embark horses for the seat of war. At that time, she was the largest merchant ship in the world registering 3,375 tons. Employing her reminded me of when I met the brother of her owner, Donald McKay, years before. We also chartered the American clippers the *Ocean Herald*, and the *White Falcon*.

Then on 2 May 1855 the *Robert Lowe* again sailed to the Crimea. Aboard was Florence Nightingale.[15] Eager to get to the hospitals there, she referred to the ship as the *Robert Slow*. On arrival, much to her dismay, Dr Hall,[16] Inspector-General of Hospitals and Chief Medical Officer in the East, resisted her setting up her headquarters ashore. Captain Congalton, on *the Robert Lowe*, allowed her to set up her headquarters on board ship which she duly did. The ship then sailed to Balaklava from Scutari with Miss Nightingale and 500 convalescents on board. From Balaklava the vessel sailed to Gibraltar to convey a regiment to the Crimea.

My other ships were busy as usual. The *Mirzapore* took hay to Balaklava. The *W S Lindsay* was in dry dock fitting her engines. She was being converted to an auxiliary steamer. The Sardinian Government[17] commissioned the ship for £2,500 to carry a cargo of provisions from London to Balaklava.

In the meantime, the *Tynemouth* was also in dry dock having her hull cleaned and painted. The *Barrackpore* discharged her cargo of tea and silk and commenced her fitting out for the navvies for the Crimea.[18]

The following month I breakfasted with Sir Joseph Paxton at Devonshire house and afterwards we proceeded to Gravesend together to dispatch three ships[19] with 1,000 navvies for the Crimea. They had just finished completing work on the Crystal Palace for the Great Exhibition, in Hyde Park, London. They are strong fellows, each of whom could do as much work in the trenches as any half a dozen of the best soldiers. If they had been sent out first, the work of throwing up the fortifications and trenches would have been completed much sooner, and we should have saved the lives of hundreds of our troops.

My ships moved about without accident and did more than their share of the work in the conveyance of the troops and ammunition to the seat of war. The *Tynemouth* completed her reconditioning and left the Thames for Plymouth, where she embarked the Land Transport Corps, and 45 commissioned Officers for Balaklava. The *Mirzapore* sailed with 262 tons of hay also for Balaklava. My Company also assisted in chartering ships, amounting to 90,000 tons, for the French Government.[20]

Of my own ships, I engaged in the War the following as troopships: The *Tynemouth* steamship (1,450 tons), *Robert Lowe* steamship (1,400 tons), *Alipore* sailing ship (810 tons), *Dinapore* sailing ship (790 tons) for the British. The *W.S. Lindsay* steamship (780 tons) was engaged for the Sardinian Government, and the *Mirzapore* sailing ship (846 tons) and *Barrackpore* sailing ship (820 tons) for the French. There were also the steamers *Pactolus*, *Orontes* and others in which I only held a small interest as owner with the Liverpool agents Lamport and Holt, who were the managing owners. So that in one way or another I had no mean part to play in this great and terrible war.

In September the *Tynemouth* and the *Robert Lowe* each took on their last trip 1,000 French soldiers, besides large quantities of stores, from Marseilles to the Crimea. The *W.S. Lindsay* also arrived at Constantinople after a passage of 19½ days from London against headwinds the greater part of the voyage, thereby once again proving the great value of the small auxiliary principle. She was contracted by the British Government for four months at £1.17.6 per ton, per month.

The following month the *Robert Lowe* arrived in Portsmouth from Gibraltar. I went down by train from London to see her. On arrival at the station, I saw three or four of the wounded Officers from the ship conveyed to the train in their cots on their way home. Poor fellows! They were sadly cut up. One had lost his leg, and an arm. A shot had carried away part of the jaw of another, and a third who was suffering from various wounds, lay, the picture of death. When I reached the Dockyard, I found that the sick and the wounded were being carried to the hospitals. A hundred of these gallant fellows were wounded at the attack on the Redan Fortress,[21] Sebastopol. It was a sad spectacle. These mutilated men exhibited the reality, the havoc of War.

I found the *Robert Lowe* in splendid order, and just as good a ship as she was the day she was launched. She was paid off, whilst far more costly ships were kept on. I was made to suffer for having attacked the Government for their mismanagement.

Part Four: The Crimean War

Not content with discharging the *Robert Lowe*, the Government listened to trumped-up charges against the ship. It was said "that 30 wounded or invalided Officers and 224 men on board had been so neglected that they remained without a bed or blanket among them, and one wounded Officer had nothing to lie on but his own Buffalo skin." These falsehoods were, of course, utterly disproved, and the charges wholly refuted. I compelled the Admiralty and the War Department to make this acknowledgement and full admission.

At the commencement of the New Year (1856), I visited the *Robert Lowe* in the London Docks, loading a general cargo for Constantinople and the Crimea. She lay alongside the same quay wall and in the same berth where, some 23 years ago, I was stationed in the old ship *Isabella*. I was then on board as an apprentice – a homeless, friendless boy, dressed in my red flannel shirt and dirty canvas trousers.

In March 1856, another of my ships, the *Alipore*, arrived at Portsmouth. She was paid off, as the Government discharged all the sailing transports as they arrived, in consequence of peace.

At the end of May, the *W S Lindsay* arrived from the Crimea at Portsmouth, with troops and horses, after a most excellent passage of only 15 days from Malta. I also received orders for her to refit and return with all despatch to the Crimea, for more troops and stores.

That concluded my ships' involvement as transport ships to the Crimea. They served the country well. They were however involved in further wars. In 1857, my new ship the *England* transported troops from Mauritius and took on troops stationed in South Africa.

Later, in 1860, *the Robert Lowe*, on charter to Shaw Savill, was employed as a troop carrier to transport soldiers to fight in the Maori Wars in New Zealand. The ship carried 700 passengers including 500 soldiers. The passage out took 82 days (15 of which under steam); this was four days faster than the standing record of *Spray of the Ocean* in 1859.[22]

During the Crimean War the correspondent of *The Times* in the Crimea, Russell[23] made mention of a curious incident in a paragraph of one of his letters, respecting a Russian dog which was the only living creature found in the Redan Fortress, Sebastopol when a detachment of our soldiers crept into it, at the break of day, on 9 September 1855, the morning after the great assault. The dog was clinging to its dead master, faithful to the last and it was ages before the Officer-in-charge of our troops could prevail upon the fondly attached animal to quit his master's remains.

It happened that my ship the *Tynemouth* was at that time in Balaklava harbour and was one of the vessels employed to take down the wounded from Scutari Hospital after the dreadful affair. It also so happened that the Officer, to whom I have referred, was in charge of the wounded, and the dog he had captured in the Redan accompanied him. The Officer, poor fellow, fell victim to cholera soon after the *Tynemouth* arrived at Constantinople. The faithful Russian dog was again left without a master and became the property of the ship's sailors. Nine months afterwards, when the *Tynemouth* arrived in London, the Captain related to me the history of the dog.

I took on the poor old faithful creature at my home in Shepperton and, as long as he lived, I gave him a comfortable home. He was a brown bushy-haired animal, somewhat bigger than a sheepdog. He was very quiet and very faithful, and the only fault he had, as my wife reported, was, that he was completely ignorant of the English language, and that he was too old to learn!

36 Underwater Explosives

During the Crimean War, the threat of attack on Balaklava Harbour, and the strategic importance of its position, was so great that the Russians could not risk any chance of the allies breaking through. The answer lay in blocking the harbour mouth at their base in Sebastopol Harbour. So, they sank second and third lines of block-ships, including frigates and transports, in the outer harbour. Eventually they scuttled all the remaining ships in the harbour, seventy in all, including the *Twelve Apostles*, the pride of the Russian Black Sea fleet, bearing the flag of the Admiral Commanding-in-Chief. In response the British decided to engage the services of divers to try to remove the obstacles. Amongst those chosen was John Deane,[24] one of the most experienced divers in Britain.

Following a request from Lord Raglan in the Crimea, Admiral Sir James Dundas[25] at the Admiralty ordered thirteen large cylinders each with 1,000 lbs of powder, and twelve small ones, to be sent out in my auxiliary steamer the *Robert Lowe* to blow up Russian ships sunk in the outer harbour.

On board the *Robert Lowe*, on her first voyage, were Deane and three assistant divers, together with diving equipment, underwater explosive cylinders, and timers. The ship also carried troops, twelve Officers and 763 men. It was my ship's first commission. The vessel also took a large supply of munitions of war, including four million Minie rifle ball cartridges, hospital stores and bedding, to be landed at Balaklava. She was ordered to proceed in October (1854) to Constantinople, and thereafter to convey invalids, of which there was a vast number.[26]

Twenty-five tons of powder was to be used each time in these submarine explosions, which were to be triggered electrically. It was thought that, in addition to destroying the sunken wrecks, these explosions would seriously injure the foundations of Forts Constantine and Alexander, and probably render them untenable.

Prior to the *Robert Lowe*'s departure, which was delayed, an advance party on the SS *Prince* departed on 27 October together with the 46th Regiment and a large consignment of winter clothing, including 40,000 suits, undergarments, socks, and gloves (valued at £500,000), for the besieging troops who were already suffering badly from freezing winter conditions. The equipment and winter clothing duly arrived at Balaklava on 7 November,

Part Four: The Crimean War

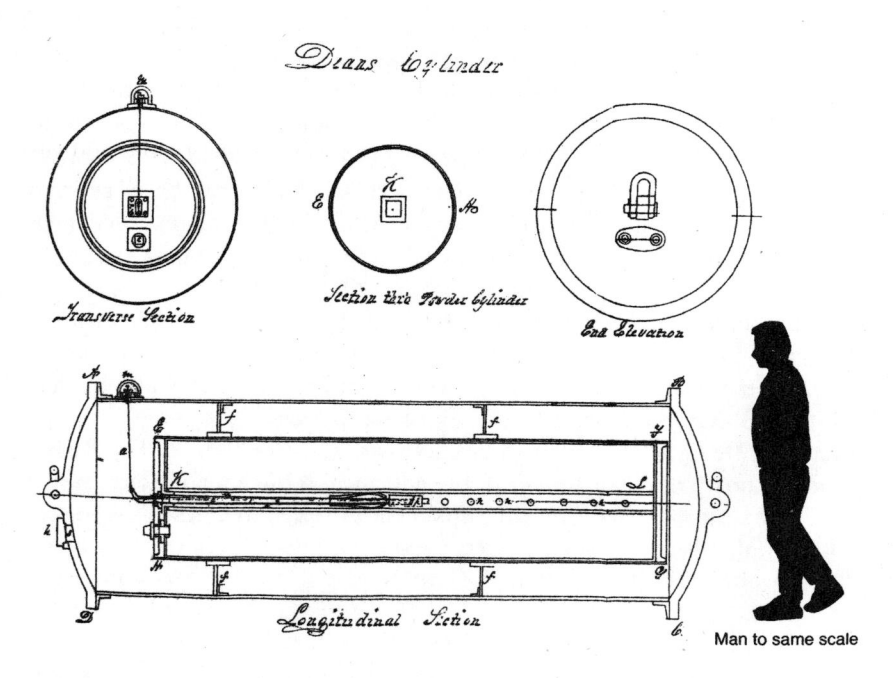

Drawing of one of the large galvanic cylinders. Bevan, J., *A Whitstable Diver's Crimean War.*

only to fall victim to the elements. The heavily laden steamship, together with most of its crew of 150, four sappers and diving equipment were all lost in the sudden horrific storm which descended mercilessly on 14 November 1854. Only one midshipman and seven men were saved.

Meanwhile the Admiralty was most anxious to have the *Robert Lowe* despatched, and I was equally so, but the contradictory orders which we received were most distressing. The cylinders had been made in Newcastle upon Tyne. The shipping of these cylinders had been a continued cause of perplexity. At the Admiralty there seemed no responsible head, but there were a hundred masters, all of whom we had to obey. These in turn were overruled by orders of a contrary nature from the Ordnance, and the Horse Guards then issued further orders still more contradictory and conflicting. Between them all, and for want of a clear system and responsible head, public money was wasted and the ships, with the regiments which they had to convey, were detained for weeks and even months.

From dock to dockyard and arsenal, the *Robert Lowe* had been knocked about for more than a month, and it was hard to say when she would get away. Though the ship was on full pay, I was annoyed by the situation, especially as the gallant fellows she had to convey to the seat of the action were so much wanted.

The ship eventually departed London on 22 November. When she arrived in Balaklava on 4 January 1855, having stopped off at Portsmouth, Malta and Constantinople on the way, the saga of the explosives rolled on relentlessly.

The cylinders should have begun to be unloaded at Balaklava on 30 January, but the plan was too optimistic. The bureaucratic process proved to be a lengthy and tedious one. They were still not clear by 5 February when Captain Peter Christie, Principal Agent at Balaklava, recorded in his "Return of Steamers for service of British Army" that the *Robert Lowe*, No. 134, screw vessel, with accommodation for 900 men and 12 horses, still had "powder cylinders on board, but will be available for troops when cleared".

The job was still not complete over a month later and it became such an embarrassment that it required a directive from Lord Raglan himself, dated 28 March 1855 to Sir Edmund Lyons,[27] to set matters right.

As it was, Deane was never allowed access to the block-ships. The Russian guns on the north and south sides of the entrance to the harbour were able to prevent any serious activity on the sunken ships. Even after the eventual fall of Sebastopol, when the Russians retreated to the north side of the harbour, the block-ships remained in range of their guns, and he was consistently denied access.[28]

There were, however, other valuable services that Deane rendered in the interim. In the Sea of Azov, and in the Straits nearby, were sunken ships that he and his team worked on. The Russians had also developed "infernal machines" which were underwater mines. They were secured to the sea floor and suspended to just below the surface. Deane and his team had to remove them.

Prior to leaving the Crimea, John Deane summed up his major exploits in a letter to Admiral Lord Lyons at the Admiralty on 27 June 1856. These consisted of his successful search for and recovery of twelve Russian Brass Field Guns and forty Carriages sunk by the Russians in the harbour in their retreat, and his blowing up of Sebastopol Docks and a Russian Warship.

He referred to his blowing up the hulls and machinery of the six sunken Russian steamers, and destroying the wrecks sunk to impede the passage of British ships through the Straits of Kerch. He surveyed and repaired ships' hulls which had been injured by the sunken objects and fitted new steam valves in them. He recovered a sixty-eight-pounder gun and 6½ tons of copper, together with lead and other materials, from the embarkation of the British Army. He also retrieved HMS *Royal Albert*'s moorings slipped by her on leaving Kertch Bay.

In his dives, Deane discovered at the bottom of the harbour a battery of field artillery, horses, men, and all, entangled in their harnesses and with their skeletons just hanging together in the network of leather. He fished up five guncarriages and two howitzers. They were filled with mud, but they were soon made functional. On the skeleton of one of the horses there were the bones of a driver, held together by the rags of his uniform, and with his foot still in the stirrup.

On his return to Britain, Deane arrived safely at Plymouth. He had travelled back from the Crimea on the *Robert Lowe*, the same ship that had taken him out there. On board the vessel, he was accompanied by thirty Officers, 838 men of the Land Transport Corps, six horses, 200 tons of shot and 160 tons of provisions. His contract with the Admiralty formally terminated on 18 August.

Also, on board the ship was 'iron ballast', apparently destined for London. This was a consignment of Russian scrap metal which was recovered during diving activities that Deane was disposing of. The exercise represented quite an entrepreneurial arrangement that included participation of the ship's Captain Congleton. The *Robert Lowe* duly arrived in London and the thirty tons of ballast was sold as scrap to Messrs Mitchesons of Limehouse at a handsome sum of £3 5 shillings per ton.

37 Tables without Legs

I remember when we drifted into that foolish War, and when orders followed each other in rapid succession from the War Office for the transport of troops, stores and munitions of every kind, Sir James Graham, first Lord of the Admiralty, was good enough to seek my advice on some technical matters connected with the large shipments which was then required to be made. In reviewing the situation with him I found that neither manifesto nor Bills of Lading were in use, so that there was no proper record of the contents of the cargo of each of the Transports dispatched to the seat of War.

I cited many examples of gross inefficiency by the Admiralty, all relating to the supply of ships for transporting horses, materials, and men to the Crimea.[29] When the soldiers were bootless in the Crimea, a ship loaded with boots and shoes was already out there, moored in the harbours of Balaklava and the commissariat there knew nothing about it. Consequently, the authorities at home were being urged to send out supplies.[30]

500 mess tables had been sent out for the use of the army in the Crimea. But when they arrived at their destination, they were found to be useless, as no legs had been sent out with them. There was no wood and no carpenters to make legs out there. After a search the legs were found in a store in Woolwich Dockyard.[31] Of concern, ammunition was shipped in the same compartment of a steamer with medical stores.

Worse still, a regiment stationed at the Cape of Good Hope was to be sent to Malta, to relieve one of the regiments on that island there under orders for the Crimea. The War Office, or the Admiralty, had transmitted orders to Calcutta to charter two large vessels at that port, to proceed to the Cape to embark the regiment required in Malta from the Cape. The troops were wanted urgently. The ships were chartered, at somewhere about £11,000 each, and proceeded in all haste to the Cape of Good Hope. But when they got there, it would appear that no orders had been sent to the regiment, and the ships could find no consignee who could tell them for what purpose they had gone there, or who had any orders for them. The consequence was that the ships, after remaining for a few days, and entering the usual protest against whomsoever it might concern, came home to England. They demanded to be paid, even though the troops were not on board, and received it. The regiment, so much wanted for the war, remained in the barracks in Cape Town!

On another occasion 3,000 horses, purchased in Britain for the use of the cavalry in the Crimea, had been kept waiting for ships, whilst a sufficient fleet for their conveyance was not only found, but had actually been offered on reasonable terms for their transport.

We had proved sadly deficient in the necessary arrangements for so gigantic an undertaking. We might have calculated on our army wintering outside the walls of that great Fortress in Sebastopol, nevertheless we made no provision for any covering for them, and no clothing to shelter them from the severity of a Russian winter. The *Robert Lowe,* when she arrived in Balaklava on 4 January 1855, was detained there for ten days with the troops on board, as there were no tents for them in the camp. The stores remained on board as there was nobody to receive them and no place to land them.

No one knew better than Sir James that the Executive departments of the Admiralty were greatly inefficient; and he even went so far as admit, when the Crimean War broke out, that unless there was a thorough change the departments would break down when severe pressure was brought to bear on it. Yet, he did not have the courage to make the requisite changes.

Any businessman could have foreseen what would happen unless a similar system was adopted to that of freight handlers. I therefore ventured to suggest that each ship should be furnished with a list of everything that was put on board of her, and a copy be sent to the War Office, together with a duplicate for the authorities on arrival. I recommended that Bills of Lading be available for any package put on board and I added that the Admiralty alone should be responsible for their safe delivery at the port of destination.

All these matters were so simple, that it was a surprise that they had not been adopted. But they were not. The heads of the departments at Somerset House had their own way of doing things and I daresay, when Sir James recommended changes to their 'established system', they rebelled for more than a year elapsed before any changes were made.

These were matters which some years afterwards came under my notice when I sat as Chairman of the Committee of the House of Commons on the Transport Service. From the enquiries that I then made I have no hesitation in stating that, had a proper system been adapted at the Admiralty and War Office when hostilities commenced, we could have saved at least three million pounds sterling in the cost of transport alone!

I wrote a pamphlet entitled "Confirmation of Admiralty Mismanagement"[32] highlighting many of these instances of inefficiency and referred to it at the meetings of the Administrative Reform Association that I attended. As might have been anticipated, I was violently attacked by Sir Charles Wood[33] and Sir James Graham who, during the course of the War, filled the office of First Lord of the Admiralty, but more especially by his senior Sea Lord, Admiral Berkeley.[34] They had no scruples as to the weapons they used. They attacked what I had said to explain away their faults and they raised counter charges against me to offset the faults of the Government.

I vented my dissatisfaction with the whole affair in a letter to Mr William Richmond, a colleague. I wrote to him saying that "Never did the House of Commons so well vindicate their rights, as the representative of the people, as they did last night, and though a staunch liberal in politics, I never had so much satisfaction as I had in speaking and voting against an administration who have left our noble soldiers to die uncovered, uncared for and unfed on the inhospitable shores of the Crimea."[35]

38 Transport Ships for the French

In February 1855 I travelled to Paris to discuss the chartering of ships to transport supplies and troops to the Crimea for the French. I met with Monsieur Pastré one of the leading merchants in France, and his son. The latter accompanied me to the Minister of Marine, Theodore Ducos,[36] as my interpreter. I found the Minister an exceedingly pleasant and unquestionably clever man. He was evidently one of those people elevated to his present high position by his abilities. He was not, I should think, more than 45 to 48 years of age.

Our conversation was confined exclusively to shipping, and he approved highly of my suggestions to establish a regular line of packets,[37] steam and clipper ships alternately, starting every week whilst the war lasted, from Marseilles to the Crimea. I further proposed that instead of continuing to have their hospitals at Constantinople and in the Archipelago, the vessels, rather than returning in great part empty, could convey back their sick to Marseilles. In the Crimea they would likely lose half of their invalids in the climate, and they would be subject to the malaria of the Crimea. In France they could receive superior medical attention. This point, he stated, would be submitted by him to the notice of the emperor.[38]

The Minister wanted my opinion on the French Transport Service in Marseilles and the state of their dockyards at Toulon. He provided me with letters of introduction to these places and requested that I visit him again on my return.

He was also eager that I should see the Minister of War[39] at once. Monsieur Pastré and I, on our arrival at the War Office, were invited into a great room, and in the utmost possible confusion stood a stout man of about 60 years of age without coat, waistcoat or cravat, his braces fastened round his waist. He had on an old fustian jacket, the cuffs of which were turned up. His hands were covered with chalk which he had been using to delineate some sketch on a large blackboard which lay on the floor. The room was hung with maps on which were marked in green, yellow and red patches the positions of the Allied Armies before Sebastopol. The patches were moveable, so it enabled him to indicate the relative changes of position taken by the Generals.

There were globes, charts, and maps in great profusion with the stations of the Russian army. The gentleman did not speak English, though he appeared to understand a few commonplace phrases. He at once entered into conversation with us which lasted half an hour, turning to his maps and pointing out the movements of the army, the store depots which had been established at Sinope and Constantinople, and the reserve division of the army of 20,000 men which had just been landed at the latter place.

He appeared, in fact, to know everything and when I remarked that every exertion must be made on the part of France and England, or otherwise the Emperor of Russia would prove too much for us, he replied with great composure, "Why we will put him in our waistcoat pocket"!

He seemed very interested and listened with great attention to the few remarks I made to him with regard to the conduct of the war, and the transport service, and upon taking my leave, he walked with us to the head of the outer staircase. After leaving I said to Monsieur Pastré "When can we see the Minister of War himself?"

"Why," he replied, "that was Marshal Vaillant himself, to whom you have been speaking this last half hour."

"That, Marshal Vaillant?" I replied in great astonishment, "What! That dirty looking man without the coat – he, the powerful War Minister of France, and one of her most distinguished Marshals?"

"Just so," said Pastré, "he is the man. He knows everything, and controls everything himself regarding the movements of our armies and, as you saw, he was tracing the dispositions of the troops from the dispatches when we entered."

"I am sorry" I said "that you did not give me the hint when we were with him, or I should have said more than I did. But mistaking him for some Master of the Navy who acted as a kind of practical adviser to the Minister, I fear I may not have displayed sufficient courtesy in my remarks."

Vaillant, however, was the sort of man with whom the management of the Army may be entrusted. He seemed to know thoroughly well what he was about and, in his vast operations was no doubt a very fit match for the autocrat of Russia.

In the evening I dined with Monsieur Pastré. He provided both the French and Egyptian Governments with all the stores required for their armies. I was surprised to learn that the entire standing army of France amounted to 750,000 effective soldiers. I urged upon the Minister of Foreign Affairs the necessity of despatching more French troops to the Crimea, and not to depend upon England, as our army was reduced to a mere brigade.

The following day, I was on the point of seeing the Minister of Foreign Affairs when Pastré called to say that Marshal Vaillant wanted to see me again. The Minister of War wished me to once again explain my views with regard to the management of the Transport Service and seemed so satisfied with them that he hoped I would place them on paper for the emperor. I of course most readily acceded to his request. On considering the subject, I set down a few important principles. In addition to recommending that the injured be treated in Marseilles Hospitals, I recommended that no more than one month's supply of stores be kept at depots close to hostilities in case of capture. Half the transport ships should be at sea while the other half should be loading goods in ports. Steamers should convey troops and clipper ships should transport stores and horses. Lastly an accurate log, on departure and arrival, should be kept of goods transported.

My recommendations were sent to Marshal Vaillant. My audience with him, and my recommendations, led to an audience with his Majesty Napoleon III.[40] It was the first time I met him. I daresay the emperor had sent for me to confirm, or otherwise, certain calculations of his own which he had been making as to the number of ships required to transport a given number of men, and so forth. After a long audience I remarked, at parting, "Sire, you had no need to send for me as you know more about ships and their capacity than I do."[41]

The fact is, he was thoroughly master of the subject and could tell me to a man the number of troops to be placed on a given ship and, to an animal the number of horses a ship of 1,000 tons could or should carry from Marseilles to Kamiesch;[42] the space required for each, and for their fodder and water, the height of deck requisite to allow for the toss of the horse's head, and the important, but not generally known fact that, though a horse must feel its own weight on its own legs at sea, it must also be slung, for if it lie down the chances are that it will not be able to get up again. At least, if the emperor did not know all about these things when I entered the Tuileries, he was the most apt scholar I ever met for he knew all about them before I left.

My firm engaged all, or nearly all, the ships required by the French Government for the Crimea, and we had about 90,000 tons of shipping under our sole management engaged as transports. They were some of the finest ships in the world. Out of the 90,000 tons, 75,000 tons were steam ships, many of them of 2,500 tons register. The bulk of the remaining 15,000 tons were the swiftest American Clippers afloat.

39 The Naval Scapegoat

Whilst much was transpiring in the Crimea, the Baltic Sea further north was a hotbed of activity too. The British Navy were engaged in holding the Russians at bay.[43]

Sir Charles Napier,[44] as long ago as 1840, had predicted that, owing to the aggressive foreign policy pursued by the Emperor Nicholas,[45] a war between Great Britain and Russia was sooner or later inevitable. He even wrote to Lord Palmerston, then Foreign Secretary, to say as much.[46]

In choosing the Commander-in-Chief for the Baltic Sea Sir James Graham, the First Lord of the Admiralty, recommended Sir Charles Napier. He was the most senior and experienced Officer available. His career at sea had been considerable and successful. His successful exploits, acting as Commander of the Portuguese Navy during the Civil War in Portugal in the 1830's, were notorious. His services for the British Navy in the Syrian campaign of 1840 were brilliant. He was also a pioneer of steam warships[47] which were to be advantageous in the Baltic.

In his letter to Queen Victoria, Sir James said that Napier

>...is an excellent seaman, and combines boldness with discretion. He has served in large squadrons, and he has commanded them. As a second, he may not have been submissive; as a chief he has been successful in command. This appointment will give confidence to both Officers and men, and his name is not unknown to both enemies and allies... Courage, genius, love of country, are not wanting and the weighty responsibility of a high command, without depressing him, would give steadiness to his demeanour.[48]

Sir Charles was unknown to me until I met him at a public meeting where I had to speak. After the meeting we were introduced to each other. He was just the kind of man I expected, a short thick-set man with a large round head – strongly marked features and a dogged resolute expression. He was perhaps the most slovenly dressed man, considering his position. White trousers and waistcoat which were always abominably dirty, and a very loose coat as shabby as his trousers, was his favourite attire.[49]

His abilities, his habits and his manners were a strange mixture. He was shrewd, keen and penetrating and very selfish, vain, but not without reason for he was a man of abilities much beyond ordinary men. In habits he was unsystematic and slovenly, though insisting on order and cleanliness in others under his command. In manners he was uncouth, and blunt often to rudeness. In some cases, his friendship was sincere and lasting, but he was not always to be depended on. He had a name, and in many respects deservedly so, which carried great weight with it, the name of Admiral Napier had great might both at home and abroad.

At first my opinion of him was that he was utterly incompetent for the high position in which he had been improperly placed. Sir Charles wanted discretion, judgment and perhaps courage. He seemed a great deal more a show-off than a real worker. His insubordinate conduct throughout his life towards those placed in authority over him did not endear him to others and he made many enemies.

The Baltic Campaign was, like the whole affair of the Crimean War, a gigantic bungle. We started our Fleet under the command of Sir Charles with the most useless and worthless crews that ever manned British Ships of War. We sent a class of ships totally unfit for the work we had undertaken.[50] They were undermanned too. The Admiralty even suggested that Sir Charles obtain crews from Scandinavian States. Ammunition was in short supply. Gunboats, required if an attack was made on fortifications due to shallow water, were not provided. No pilots were provided to guide the fleet through unknown waters. Finally, the weather, particularly fogs at that time of the year, was a hazard.

Nevertheless, there were high expectations, particularly from the Press, that the famous Admiral would deliver miracles. If, however, he took too many risks he could expose British ports to an attack from the Russian Navy.

Before the fleet sailed there was a great dinner at the Reform Club in honour of Sir Charles, with Sir James Graham in the Chair, at which a great deal of empty bluster and nonsense was talked.

During his campaign in the War Sir Charles successfully blockaded all the Russian ports, and sufficiently overawed the Russian Baltic Fleet so it never left the harbours. He also carried out several bombardment operations. His major success, in a joint operation with the French, was the capture and destruction of the Russian fortress of Bomarsund on the Åland Islands.[51]

The Government, however, raised a tremendous hue and cry against Sir Charles because he did not destroy Sveaborg,[52] or Cronstadt[53] as his ships could not reach it with their guns. There was much criticism by the press to which the Admiralty reacted by recalling him, even though he was faced with an impossible task. He had been in post for less than a year.

Nevertheless, Napier had achieved a great deal. The campaign "had successfully bottled up the Russian Navy for the entire first summer of the war. The Tsar had been denied an opportunity to reinforce his Black Sea fleet with additional ships. The 30,000 Russian troops posted in the Gulf had also been prevented from joining the army in the Crimea."[54]

In addition, Napier's constant training had welded the fleet personnel into a much more competent force for the next year's campaign; and not a single ship had been lost.

After the war he brought in his long-promised motion about the Baltic Fleet. This was in response to the harsh allegations of his ineptitude. As was anticipated by everybody in and out of the House of Commons, he had the worst of the encounter, when challenging such a practised speaker as Sir James Graham to single combat.

Sir Charles, with his usual imprudence, spun out his tiresome speech to three hours' duration, when he ought to have condensed it to half an hour or, at the utmost, an hour. The best way of judging the truth is by the written despatches of the parties. Sir Charles said that two Councils of War reported that Sveaborg was quite impregnable, and, upon these, he rested his defence. I concurred with him on this point and said so in the House. I, taking commiseration upon Sir Charles, and helping him all I could, advised him never to say one word about the Baltic campaign. He thanked me for my advice, adding "Nae doubt you are right, but that long-legged scoundrel of a hypocrite" – alluding to Sir James – "will be coming to shake hands with me some of these odd nichts after this, but if he does," (working himself into a fit of passion as he waddled through the Lobby to get his dinner with me, after the fight) "if he does," exclaimed Sir Charles, shoving with emphasis his not over-clean hands into the bottoms of his ample but dirty trousers, "if he does, I'll give him his answer."

Sure enough, about a month afterwards he had an opportunity of doing so. One night as we were walking together down the same Lobby, we met Sir James full in the face and, curiously enough and much to my surprise, Sir James put out his hand towards Sir Charley. Charley who has his own hands seldom out of his pockets, so far from withdrawing them, shoved them deeper and deeper still, and looked at his antagonist steadfastly in the face without uttering a word. I never saw a man receive such a snub and Sir James even, who has no feeling at all, seemed to writhe under it.

I cannot say that I had a very high opinion of Sir Charles Napier when he returned from the Baltic. There was much about his general conduct which I could not admire or defend but, having felt a certain amount of compassion for him when every member in the House turned against him, I could not help being somewhat of a friend in need to him.

During the War, Gunboats were built, albeit late in the day, to support the Baltic and Black Sea Fleets. In March 1855, I went down to Deptford to see the Gunboat to which Lieut. Pim has been appointed to the command. She was named the *Magpie*. I took her to be about 180 to 200 tons register, mounting one great 68 or 94 pounder gun upon a swivel in mid-ship, and 2 thirty-two pounders, having engines of 60 HP.[55]

I was however surprised to learn that the engines were high pressure. When will these Admiralty men learn common sense? Such boats were meant to slip in unperceived at night to attack forts or sink ships under fortifications, and with this object in view, to put into these boats high pressure engines which puff and roar when under steam like a locomotive so that they could be heard miles distant was indeed the height of folly.

There were thirty-three of them altogether, all upon the same construction, and all built within the last six months for the expedition to the Baltic. Perhaps our wise rulers anticipated that the very noise of these engines would so frighten the Russians that a single shot would not be necessary, but at the very sound our enemies would evacuate their forts![56]

The Baltic Fleet, and the debates about it, brought to my recollection our cruise to Cherbourg and the review of the English and French Fleets in that harbour after the Crimean War had ended. Old Sir Charles was there but merely in his capacity as a private member of the House of Commons, and as such he and I were shipmates on board of the P&O Company's steamship the *Pera*.

The French Admiral, out of courtesy to the House of Commons, was good enough to invite some of its members on board his ship. Amongst that number was Sir Charles Napier, Sir Fenwick Williams of Kars,[57] General Codrington,[58] and one or two others including myself.

Part Four: The Crimean War

I have said that Sir Charles was very slovenly in his manners, but in this instance, he carried his slovenly propensities to an extent for which I was not prepared. Williams and Codrington appeared in their full uniform, and we all expected that Sir Charles would for once change his usual attire. Not so. I had put on my best, and the other civilians had done the same but, when I made my appearance at the gangway of the *Pera*, Sir Charles did not at all seem satisfied, for he remarked that I was not altogether up to the mark, adding that it was through him I had received the invitation and that I might have put on a cleaner shirt and better clothes!!

I looked at him with amusement. He had on his usual so called "white" trousers which he had worn since he came on board, three days before. His hat was greasy and worn, and his old coat was minus a couple of buttons. But worse than all these, was a large hole in one of his stockings, which was conspicuous above the heels of his worn-out shoes.

I did not fail to remind him of his own attire, but in it he appeared before the French Admiral who, with his Officers, received us in full dress and with all that display and courtesy for which the French are so conspicuous. That however was not the worst part of the day's proceedings. Sir Charles was actually and, it would almost seem, willingly and perversely rude. He never even lifted his hat from his head to the Admiral and his Officers as they met him. Immediately after, as we were walking round the ship, he pulled from his pocket an inch rule and commenced to measure the sizes of various articles on board "taking a note of them", as he said, in an old pocketbook which he carried in his hand!

We were all thoroughly disgusted with his conduct and the French Officers were amazed and could not believe that he was really Sir Charles Napier, the Commander in Chief of the Baltic Fleet, of whom they had heard so much.

At that same Review I recall Sir Charles Napier had something else to say about First Lords of the Admiralty. Sir John Pakington[59] was an earnest and well-meaning statesman. On all occasions his aim was to perform his duty. Sometimes he had a mistaken notion of that duty. For instance, he would criticise the rig of the ships and the position of the masts, or the height of the gun ports, matters which a First Lord is not expected to know anything about, and which Sir John certainly did not understand, though he thought he did.

I remember at the Cherbourg Review[60] he considered it his duty as First Lord to see the ships of our Fleet properly arranged and anchored in line. With that object in view, he was being rowed about the harbour by a six-oared cutter, or rather gig,[61] which he himself steered amongst the vessels.

We were looking over the gang way of the *Pera* as Sir John passed in his gig. At every stroke of the oars Sir John bent forward under the popular impression that by so doing so he was assisting the rowers.

"Guid God" exclaimed old Charles as he passed – "look at him – just look at him – nae doubt he thinks himself a sailor!"[62]

About that time, I also remember when Sir Charles and Lord Clarence Paget[63] were staying with me at Shepperton Manor on the banks of the river

Thames, when Lord Clarence gave Sir Charles a row in the boat on the river. The boat was not one of a kind to which sailors are accustomed – it was shallow and flat and, though not easily upset, the slightest extra motion can lead to a sudden lurch on either side.

On the other side of the river a shoal sand bank projects on which many a pleasure boat has grounded and some of them at times capsized. Charles was seated in the stern with the rudder cords in his hands and, just as Paget was nearing the sand bank, he missed his stroke with one of his oars and the boat, which was being rowed against the stream, grounded on the sand bank, and lurched over. The lurch was so sudden that it threw Sir Charles right over

Sir Charles Napier (1786–1860). NPG 1460 National Portrait Gallery.

Part Four: The Crimean War

and, missing his grasp at the gunnel as the boat lurched, he fell right into the stream. The sand bank where he landed was not more than 6 or 9 inches of water. It was altogether a remarkable somersault, for the old Admiral fell onto his backside, and there he sat for a minute or two swearing at Paget.

"Can ye row a boat?" he roared in his anger "Pretty fellow to be Secretary o' the Admiralty," he exclaimed, boiling with rage, which the cold bath did not seem to have the slightest effect in cooling. He did not seem disposed to move from the position into which he had been unwittingly thrown by Paget until he had expended all his wroth upon him and every oath in the Devil's vocabulary.

Lord Clarence Paget (1811–1895). Mary Evans Picture Library.

Paget, who had an excellent temper, took the abuse with much good nature merely remarking that Charley's trousers, which had once been white, stood much in need of washing. That evening, after dinner the subject of conversation turned to the Crimean War when Sir Charles gave us his experience in the Baltic.

Amongst other incidents of the campaign he prided himself in the achievement that, though he did not capture nor destroy Cronstadt, he lost none of his ships as many people had said he would do: "*But*" he added addressing especially Mr Adams,[64] the American Minister, and looking hard at Lord Clarence Paget who sat opposite to him "that chief there" pointing to Paget, "got his ship on the shore – and did not ken how to get her off again for I had to gang and help him; and that was our 'only mishap'!"

Poor Paget did not know where to look or what to say but he prudently said nothing, and I saw Mr Adams felt for him as we all did, except Sir Charles who did not seem to feel that he had said anything that could injure anybody's feelings.

It was quite true that the battleship, which Lord Clarence had commanded in the Baltic, was the only vessel in the Fleet that ran ashore, and that Sir Charles had gone on board to give directions, but he had no need to relate the incident. Paget never forgave him for the insult and no wonder – they continued on speaking terms but nothing more.

Incidentally, I understood that Sir Charles Napier had declined the Grand Cross of the Bath. Our hero of the Baltic was once more in the dumps and scarcely knew how to vent his rage against Sir James Graham and the Admiralty Board. His refusal of his Sovereign's virtual pardon of all his misdeeds, his shortcomings, and egregious acts of vanity, was a perverse act and was indeed altogether something worse than bad taste; it was wilful ingratitude.[65]

40 Administrative Reform Association

On 26 January 1855 my parliamentary colleague, John Arthur Roebuck,[66] introduced a motion for the appointment of a select committee to enquire into the conduct of the Crimean War. Roebuck opened the debate falteringly and, after only ten minutes, he was answered from the government benches by Sidney Herbert.[67] Herbert's response was that of a Minister who felt he had neglected his duty, and yet it was a cowardly, unmanly speech.

Though I had only been six months in Parliament, hardly having uttered a word, I felt compelled to support my friend in a cause with which I strongly agreed. In a short speech I said that, as the government would not adopt the measures I thought necessary, I should give my support to the motion. I also felt that a large portion of our noble army in the Crimea had perished through neglect. In addition, the transport service was in an awful state. The ensuing debate resulted in Aberdeen's[68] resignation and his replacement by

Palmerston. Sir James Graham was replaced as First Lord of the Admiralty by Sir Charles Wood.

On 26 February 1855, I opened the debate on 'War and Admiralty Departments'. This was my first major Commons speech. During my speech, and another shortly afterwards, I condemned the transport service, whilst lauding its French equivalent.

In later debates I censured James Graham and Charles Wood. An acrimonious correspondence between Wood and me followed. We had many a contest in the House and during one of these, when Sir Charles was said to have demolished all my arguments, he made one of the most effective speeches he had ever delivered in Parliament. I must say at that moment I was completely lost for words. I had brought forward several cases of gross maladministration on the part of the Admiralty. Sir Charles replied saying "Those who live in glass houses should not throw stones." [69] He continued:

> I shall read to the House a letter from the Firm of which the Honourable Member is the head. In that letter we are told that the steamship *Tynemouth* shall be ready to sail on the 1 November. We made our arrangements accordingly.
>
> Now if any Honourable Member turns to the official list of sailings, he will find that the *Tynemouth* did not proceed to sea until the 25 November. How can the Admiralty be punctual in the transacting their business when the owner of the transports they engage deceive them in the manner of the Honourable Member's Firm had done?

I was of course silenced for the time and had to retire from the debate amidst the ironical cheers of the Whigs. But it was only for a time.

In searching amongst the letters of my firm, I found a copy of the letter that he quoted from. It was correct. He had however stopped short in his quotation and had omitted the following words which came after: "The ship *Tynemouth* will be ready to sail on 1 November, provided the Government send their stores on board."

Whether he intentionally left out these words or whether they had not been furnished to him by the clerk who made the extracts I cannot say. I should hope the latter was the case – but had they been quoted his argument would have been without force. Indeed it would have turned against himself for, as I afterwards showed to the House to the great discomfiture of Sir Charles, the *Tynemouth* was ready to sail on the 1st but did not sail until the 25th because, through some mismanagement on the part of the War Office and Admiralty combined, the Government stores were not sent alongside of the ship until the 24th and their shipment was only completed on the day she sailed.

Of course, my attacks on the Admiralty and Government made me very unpopular with the establishment. As once was said about me "Pure Scotch is very pleasant to read; but one soon tires of it in the House of Commons."[70]

This gross mismanagement of our Naval and Military Departments during the Crimean War induced many merchants in the City of London to form themselves into an association focussed on administrate reform. I was one of those actively involved in its conception. The speech, which I delivered on the Transport Service in April 1855, may have stimulated the association's formation. It was very extensively reported in the press throughout the Country and caused considerable talk at the time. At that meeting I had pointed out facts of mismanagement and inefficiencies. An army wasted away and destroyed by cold and starvation, at a time when prodigious supplies had been budgeted for, was a calamity which could have resulted only from flagrant incapacity or indeed from criminal neglect.[71]

Transport vessels of enormous tonnage, costing exorbitant sums monthly, were allowed to lie unemployed, rotting in port and harbour. Those in charge could not find the means of loading them. At the same time successive shipments were made from England to aid the army in the Crimea, but these were unavailable since no one seemed to be informed of the articles which had been sent.[72]

The first meeting of our Administrative Reform Association was held in the London Tavern on the 5 May 1855 and was very numerously and influentially attended. It far exceeded my expectations. Although the meeting was meant to start at one o'clock, the great room was filled by noon, and thousands left who could gain no admittance. The assembly consisted of substantial men, great numbers of them being our leading merchants. They were men from 35 to 60 years of age; men of position with a seriousness which showed they came to enter their protest against the present disgraceful state of matters.

The main objectives of the Association were highlighted. Inefficient, impracticable, and irresponsible management of State Departments should be addressed by a thorough change in the administration system. People of wide experience and practical ability should be recruited into these Departments. They should not consist of a monopoly of aristocratic classes.[73]

These objectives resonated well with the audience and at other meetings and support for the Association grew rapidly. Chaired by Samuel Morley MP, active Members included Charles Dickens[74] and Joseph Paxton. Some forty MPs were associated with the Association at one stage or another.[75]

A motion on the question of Administrative Reform was afterwards brought forward in the House of Commons by our Chairman, Mr Layard[76] but he did not handle it very well and no direct benefit was derived from it.

As might have been anticipated I was violently attacked in Parliament by the Lords of the Admiralty for my criticisms of their management. We had many a contest. In June, I published in length a rebuttal against the Admiralty's charges against me.[77] The publication asserted that:

> Government touts were going about the city for days after Mr. Lindsay's speech at Drury Lane was delivered, seeking, not for means of disproving

the charges which he had made against the Admiralty, but for any stories bearing on that gentleman's past career by which his character might be damaged!

I pointed out all that was wrong with the current administration and much more besides. I further illustrated the Admiralty's serious errors on their record keeping. The *Tynemouth* was returned as having made twelve voyages between the 10th of June 1853, and the 31st of December 1854. She made 20 voyages within those two dates. The return said that 713 tons of cargo had been sent; but I found that 1,063 tons were carried. Again, the Government said that six military Officers had been carried in that ship; she really carried 190 Officers. The return mentioned three horses as having been conveyed in the ship, she carried 124 horses, 270 sheep, and 15 bullocks. The return says she carried 324 soldiers; she carried no less than 4,306!

In my advocacy of Administrative Reform I endeavoured, as a plain man of business and with the earnestness of business, to speak the simple unexaggerated truth; and when statements, sufficient authority for which I produced, have been charged as 'virulent untruths not even founded on fact' and when unfair constructions have been elaborately put upon my motives and statements with the unmistakable intention of damaging my hard-earned position as a man of business, and which I value above all price, I have felt bound not to let those charges rest. I have no personal hostility to either the present or the late First Lord of the Admiralty, neither to anyone connected with the Government, but I owe a duty to my constituents and to the country to point out mismanagement and to carry through reforms.

The Government, however, had another card to play. The leaders of our movement were soon muzzled by accepting positions of office in the Government. Layard, Laing[78] and Lowe, all in time received appointments. Early on, I too was indirectly offered an office, that of the Vice President of the Board of Trade, by the Marquis of Lansdowne[79] and though there was the temptation of a 'Right Honourable' to my name[80] I ignored it. It was not good enough for me then nor did it suit me to give up the profits of my lucrative business. At least I, out of the four Ls[81] alone, retained my independence. I too might have been bought if they had offered me enough inducements at the time. It is true that position and title play sad havoc at times with frail human nature.

As it was, I felt obliged to protest that the Government's conduct during the War was an unnecessary waste of public money and that our Administration system stood greatly in need of reform and as a result the Marquis ceased to know me and even passed me by as a person he had never seen.[82]

As a result of the loss of important members of our leadership, our ranks were depleted, and our movement fell far short of our original hopes and expectations. It had been short-lived. In less than a year it became a spent force.

In time, various important reforms were however made. Our movement had made an impression upon the public which produced some good. Lord Palmerston in the Treaty of Peace[83] obtained all that we went to war for, and more, far more than I thought we should have secured, all the various circumstances considered. I felt it my duty, after the many attacks I had made on his Lordship's Government for their and their predecessor's mismanagement of the war, to state candidly what I thought of the conditions of Peace, and I gave Lord Palmerston credit for that which I conceived he merited. As a matter of course, I got abused, and broad hints were thrown out that I wanted office, or some personal advantage. Not so.

Part Five

Shipping Business Continues

(1856–1861)

41 Mail Service to Calcutta via the Cape

Towards the end of the Crimean War, I ordered three more purpose-built auxiliary steamships at an average cost of £24,500 each. The *Scotland* and the *England* were built on the Clyde and the *Ireland* was built in Hartlepool.[1] Although these vessels were smaller than my three other auxiliaries, the *Robert Lowe*, the *Tynemouth,* and the *W S Lindsay*, they were fitted with more powerful engines.

When the War ended in 1856, I foresaw that for a time there would be a great depression in shipping. It required serious and prompt consideration as to what was to be done with these six valuable vessels. There was a collective capital invested in them which amounted to nearly £180,000. I could not allow these ships to remain idle and unproductive; I had to decide which trade I could best employ them profitably.

Since the start of the War in 1853 there had been no steamers on the line between the Cape of Good Hope and India and the postal service on that route had been suspended for more than two years. I knew that once the steamers were released from the transport service, the public would call on the Government to re-establish postal arrangements to the South African Colony. Accordingly, I decided on advertising my six vessels as a line between London, the Cape of Good Hope, and Calcutta, calling at Dartmouth to embark passengers. I resolved to give the enterprise a fair trial for at least twelve months. I felt that once employed on that route my vessels would have the best chance of securing the Government contract to carry mail when they announced it.

The previous operation taking the monthly mail had been operated by the General Screw Company,[2] who had run the route, initially between Plymouth and Cape Town, and then latterly on to India, in 1850. The Company abandoned the line in 1854 as it was unprofitable. I thought that I could undertake the route myself.

There were several reasons why I felt that I would have more success than the General Screw Company. Their ships were over 2,000 tons, were fitted as fully powered steamers and were very lightly rigged as sailing vessels. Mine were half that size yet they held much more cargo and, as they were fully rigged sailing ships and only used steam as an auxiliary, I calculated that they would use one tenth fuel consumption in the journey to India. I also anticipated a higher average speed upon the whole voyage. Our ships would not need to stop for refuelling. Nor would we be required to keep coal depots along the route.

In addition, the General Screw Navigation Company reckoned on a capital of £590,000 to have undertaken the line. I found that the work could be done quite as well, if not better, with a capital of considerably less than a half of that sum.

My Company ran efficiently on a significantly smaller number of staff. The General Screw Company with a Chairman and Deputy, with 15 Directors, a secretary, an assistant secretary, and various managers, with an excessive staff of these and a numerous body of clerks, this was an expensive London Establishment. They also had another subordinate agency at Southampton where the ships loaded and discharged their cargoes and embarked and landed their passengers. This was a very expensive establishment consisting of highly paid superintendents and various other officials. My establishment was a very simple one. It consisted of two clerks and a boy, who together transacted all the business. Mr Bowman, the inspector, oversaw the construction of the ships, their outfit, and repairs, and I directed the whole operation. At Dartmouth Captain Bulley attended to the agency and he considered himself well paid at £150 per annum.[3]

The Screw Navigation Company was a Joint Stock Association[4] which could not successfully compete with an individual enterprise. Experience had taught me that twelve able men sitting as a Board of Directors were little better than a dozen blockheads and the more able the men, the more absurdly they acted in their collective capacity as a Board. Twelve men of equal standing and capacity are at so many cross purposes. Every man, or, at least, every other man, has a vision of his own which he pursues rigidly at times. Hours are occupied in discussions which often end in doing nothing or too often in inappropriate action.

The ships were not the property of the Directors. They held but a very small portion of the property and, although they did not intentionally squander away the capital confided to their management, it was somehow or other frittered away much faster than if it were their own. Then again, Directors and their friends had other business interests of their own apart from those of the Company.

On the other hand, one superior man and eleven lesser ones worked very well and the affairs of the corporate body under their management were better administered. I managed the ships myself. I had no cross purposes.

Part Five: Shipping Business Continues

No shipbuilder, nor engineer, nor provision Merchant could have any self-interested influence as I held more than three-quarters of the entire line of ships. My staff of Shipbrokers, who, as scouts, obtained cargo for the ships and acted on that sole purpose. I took great care that they worked hard for every commission they earned. It was for these reasons that I had faith in my Company's ships proving successful in this new route.

The announcement that I was to have Dartmouth as the port of departure came like a clap of thunder to the inhabitants. It was no more than I had promised four years earlier when I ran for election as MP. They thought that my expression to make the town a successful port was only a turn of phrase in a speech delivered for electioneering purposes.

I saw the opportunities that the harbour, which for some reason or other had been overlooked and neglected, was indeed one of the best as a port of call in the English Channel. In using the port, it would enrich the poor people as well as make it lucrative to myself.

The newspapers announced that the *England*, the first of the line, was to sail on 1 August 1856 calling at Dartmouth on the 5th.[5]

Fortuitously, within a week of its announcement the Government issued tenders for the conveyance of the mail from London to Table Bay, Cape of Good Hope, from thence to Mauritius, Point de Galle, Madras and Calcutta, with a return voyage vice versa – the packets to sail once a month. I of course tendered or rather I made Captain Dundas[6] of the *England* sign the tender as, under the existing law, my name could not appear as a government contractor whilst I held a seat in the House of Commons.

Royal Mail Ship *England*, The Lindsay Line; Dartmouth to Cape Town, Mauritius, and Calcutta.

About three weeks after lodging the tender, Captain Dundas was sent for to the Treasury. I accompanied him. My tender was the lowest. In fact, it was the only one the Treasury could entertain, for, though seven or eight others sent in their tenders, none but mine was prepared to carry out the conditions in its entirety. The contract was therefore assigned to me at the sum of £41,000 per annum.

The time allowed was 36 days from Dartmouth to the Cape, 14 days from the Cape to Mauritius, and 21 days from Mauritius to Calcutta, including stoppages at Ceylon and Madras. Similar periods were stipulated for the return passage and a penalty of £30 for the day over the time specified, £60 for the second, £90 for the third, and so on, increasing at the rate of £30 each day that the ships conveying the mail exceeded the period above stated.[7]

If the people of Dartmouth were delighted when the announcement appeared that my ships were to call at their port their joy knew no bounds when it was known that these ships were to convey the mails to the Cape and to various parts of India, thereby constituting it, not merely a packet, but a Royal Mail postal station in connection with our Indian dominions.

My visit to the port was the first that I had made since my defeat at the last General Election. They, who at that time called me an upstart and an impostor and all kinds of scurrilous names, were the foremost and the most eager to welcome me. I could not but feel compassion for Sir Henry Seale. He had four years ago treated me with the most supercilious contempt. I, who had been a common sea boy, sought to become the representative of the place of his birth, deserved, in his opinion, no better treatment.

The whole town turned out to receive me and the leader of the crowd was Sir Henry Seale himself. The Baronet was the first to greet me and the foremost to offer me his arm which, however, I respectfully declined. I preferred to accept the arm of Mr Hunt, one of the county magistrates, whose antecedents, morally, socially, and religiously were more in accordance with my own sympathies than those of the cringing baronet.

I issued a form of conditions of employing the sailors which differed from other shipowners' contracts. The chief feature was that the full wages was paid to each man on the day of signing articles[8] and at the end of the voyage five shillings extra per month was placed to the credit of each man who conducted himself well. This sum was paid into the Savings Bank which accumulated for his benefit and after three years' good service in my employ the profit was paid to him. This, with other inducements and rewards for good conduct, and the rigorous requirements of certificates of good character and ability, produced an excellent effect.

On the conditions laid down I manned the first three ships of the line and had more applicants than I could employ, indeed three times the number. Instead of the seamen, as previously, not being at their duty when the ship appointed was to sail, I found every man on board in a sober state at his post.

In the beginning the ships were more lucrative than I expected. The first, the *England*, earned, in outward freight and passage, including the mails,

Part Five: Shipping Business Continues

close to £9,000 but she was fortunate in getting her 'tween decks full of troops for the Cape. The *Tynemouth* earned gross £5,500 and the *Robert Lowe* £7,800. Each succeeding day the trade increased. The *Scotland* had all her cabins engaged and by the highest class of passengers.

The people of the Cape of Good Hope had been entirely without regular postal communication for more than two years. They complained loudly as their commerce must have suffered severely. They appealed to the Government, but the Executive were reluctant to assist them while they enriched themselves by local wars to which they did not contribute a farthing.

At last, however, the Colonial Legislative Council voted to finance the line, although the amount was too insignificant to induce any company to start a line of steamers. In this unsatisfactory position of affairs, to the surprise of everyone, and to the satisfaction of all who were interested in the Cape of Good Hope, I started my Line of auxiliary steamers. I sought no additional aid from them. I did not ask them to take shares in my ships or assist with their capital. In fact, I made no request whatsoever.

I expected, not unreasonably, that they would give me fair business support in return for the boon I was about to confer on them. I was mistaken. They shrugged their shoulders and told me that they could not afford to pay higher rates for freight carried by my steamers than they had paid for the sailing ships. In every way they endeavoured to grind me down, and when the *England* sailed at noon on 1 August at the appointed time, she did not have enough freight to pay her way if I had not by the merest chance procured troops and about 200 tons of government cargo which happily completely filled her.

In due course the second vessel the *Tynemouth* sailed on 1 September. I had a few more passengers in her but she went away with fully 600 to 700 tons empty space in her hold. These miserable Cape Merchants here in Britain – and I speak from experience, they are the most miserable and unscrupulous in the whole range of commerce which is saying a great deal – were under the impression that I would not sail with my ship more than half empty and that I would be compelled to yield and lower my rates to their asking price, which they knew perfectly well would not pay my ships. But they were wrong.

The *Tynemouth* sailed at her exact time to the minute all but empty. The *Robert Lowe* followed on 1 October. Passengers for her came forward much more freely and she was almost full. The general public also began to see their value and appreciated the regularity with which they were dispatched. I conveyed a large amount of bullion in her, upwards of £120,000 in gold. But though small packages and parcels were on the increase, I was still short of cargo and when the *Robert Lowe* sailed there was fully 400 tons of empty space in her hold.

The Cape Merchants were amazed when I preferred to leave empty rather than submit to their offers. I continued inflexible to all attempts to screw me down. It was a mere trial of strength and a question of time. I felt that they would have to give way before I did. The few merchants that conceded to my

Lloyds' survey report on the SS *England*. 1857.

moderate rates were likely to have a marked advantage over their rivals by getting their goods much sooner to market.

On 1 November, the *Scotland*[9] sailed and all her cabins had been engaged for a month before sailing. Her hold was as full of goods as could be, at my own rates, principally filled by the few enterprising men with the trade of the Cape. Merchants who had endeavoured to screw my rates down then came forward to accept my rates, but I declined them and demanded more.

When the *Ireland* sailed, she was not only full to overflowing with passengers[10] but she turned away nearly 200 tons of goods. Those merchants who had attempted to beat me down were most urgent that I should take their goods, at my own rates, urging that it would confer upon them a personal favour. What personal favour can those people expect from me?

Goods taken on the *W S Lindsay* (which I converted from a sailing ship to an auxiliary steamer) were charged at the same higher rate to these merchants, unless they were the few who frankly gave me their support from the beginning.

The Cape Merchants in South Africa seemed to be much the same as most of them here. No sooner did the *England*[11] make her appearance in Table Bay than they put their heads together to see what they could get out of her. They recognised that the line which, if carried out permanently, would prove of immense advantage to the Colony. But they put personal gain over benefits to the Colony. They at once advanced the price of coal by 60 cents and made the *England* pay 65/- per ton which had been selling the day before at 35/- per ton.

I have made it known to the people that I would not continue the line unless it paid me and that much depended on the support and fair dealing I received from them. My balance at the end of that year showed a realised capital of £200,000. But having realised this fortune by hard work and honourable dealing, I resolved not to lose what I have gained. I had, in this line of steamers, invested the largest portion of my capital. It was no ordinary undertaking for one man. If, after allowing for depreciation, I received a fair return for the capital employed, I would continue the line. If not, I would give it up, and send my ships into other and more profitable trades.

After twelve months, however, the ships could not maintain the regularity essential for the mail service, so I relinquished the undertaking. The ships had no mishaps or accidents and they had proved more efficient than sailing ships.

I began to realise however that the auxiliary steamships had certain drawbacks. In adverse winds they made little or no progress, a fact arising in great measure from their small steam-power and from the resistance their heavy spars presented to the winds. In addition, any advantage gained from having a greater space for cargo was counterbalanced by the maintenance of a staff of engineers and stokers who, during the greater proportion of the voyage, were unemployed.

42 Manor by the Thames

Shepperton Manor is everything a City Merchant could desire. I heard of it through a house agent at Isleworth. I had directed this agent to look out for me, with a view to purchase, some country property with a little land around it, situated on the banks of the Thames.[12]

I could afford to move to a larger house. The half-year accounts for W. S. Lindsay & Co. to 30 June 1855 show earnings of £80,724 after depreciation on ships of £10,272. The last six months of 1855 were the company's most profitable ever, with brokerage from the French reaching £20,000, of which my personal share was £8,000. Added to earnings of £30,000 as a shipowner, the profit for 1855, after depreciation, was £76,000.

Our public contracts for coal had amounted, during these last ten years, to 270,000 tons, and our private contracts, to about 300,000 tons, in all nearly 600,000 tons; shipped nearly all on long voyages. [13]

An often-overlooked fact was that the merchant ships of the British Empire, amounted at the close of 1855, to 7,744,237 tons, about as many as the sea-going merchant ships of all the rest of the world, and that the produce, manufactures, and goods they carried, exceeded in value those of all the nations combined.[14]

The Manor House, Shepperton, William Schaw Lindsay's home, which he purchased in 1856.

The more I saw of my purchase, the more I was satisfied. It was just such a place that I had been searching for over the previous two years. Together with the Estate I bought the Manor and 358 acres of superior arable land. I had little idea that I should ever possess such a mansion.[15]

It contained a dining room, drawing room, library, parlour and some seventeen or eighteen bedrooms, with offices and outhouses etc. The building was not more than thirty years old, so it will hold good for my life, and my boy's after me. The grounds are about the finest on the banks of the Thames.

I paid £26,000 for the entire Estate and I was told I had made an excellent investment. It was by the merest chance that I secured it as the property was not advertised for sale and very few persons, even in the immediate vicinity, appeared to have had an idea it was on the market. If it had been advertised, it is probable that I should not have secured it as I daresay the price would have been pushed up far above that I paid for it. I took possession of the Manor on 10 May 1856. The former proprietor was a Mr James Scott,[16] a gentleman of considerable property with a large family. He built the manor house in 1830. I had looked at other properties, but I realised that too large an estate would absorb too much capital from my business which is generally more profitable than an investment in land.

Shepperton estate embraces all the advantages of a place of "elegant retirement" from business. I could drive from the house in 15 minutes by way of Walton Bridge across the Thames to the Southwestern Railway station reaching the Waterloo terminus in 35 minutes.[17] From thence by cab to Austin Friars occupied another 15 minutes so that I was almost as conveniently situated in reaching the Office as from Portland Place and even more so than I had been at Mornington Lodge.

Part Five: *Shipping Business Continues*

I was able to quit the city and transport myself to a secluded country spot where the locals are as primitive in their habits as their forefathers were several ages ago. I am surrounded by pretty villages and the drives in the vicinity are charming.

Close to the yard gate of the Manor House is the village. It is much the same size and population as it was centuries ago. There are a few houses occupied by fishermen and labourers. It has a clean, neat, and well-frequented Inn, which the landlord tries to dignify with the name of hotel and in summer some of the best of families from London take up their quarters there.

The old Church in Shepperton bears every mark of antiquity and must have been built hundreds of years ago.[18] An old gallery in the church is the sole property of the "Lord of the Manor". My predecessors doubtless must have been exclusive aristocratic old fellows retaining all the rights handed down to them unimpaired from the days of feudalism. They could not sit on the same level with the people but must have built a gallery for themselves. They deemed not to enter God's house by the same gate as the parishioners but must have an entrance gate of their own together with a separate porch and a separate staircase all to themselves. I continued to use those specially appropriated conveniences and take my place in the "high seats of the synagogue" though I would have preferred to go in at the same gate and sit with them on the same level in church. If, however, the staircase and gallery should crumble away through decay in my time, which seems very likely, they will never be rebuilt by me. I made some improvements, and I did a little to improve the church with a stained-glass window.

Such then is the old village Church, raised high, as almost all old churchyards are, much above the level of the road, by the accumulated dust and ashes of successive generations. At this charming spot I found a resting-place, a haven of rest after my storms in early life. A vault beneath the old Church belongs to the Estate but I trust that when I am departed my bones may rest in the old Churchyard. I have no wish that they should occupy the so-called "family vault" but would rather that they should mingle with the bones of the villagers in the open air so that the green grass may grow on my grave.[19]

I should wish some simple words to mark the spot where my body is interred, inscribed on the headstone which covers all that may remain of my frail earthly form. A tomb of orphan's tears would be the greatest blessing I could hope for, and I might, thus wept over, sleep in eternal peace.

The neighbourhood of Shepperton is associated with many historic reminiscences. Some very celebrated men have lived and died near the spot. Some antiquarians assert that the Manor House stands on the spot where the Prætorium[20] of the camp of Julius Caesar stood. They make it out that his legions rested here after he had crossed the river nearby. I am afraid, however, that I do not rely upon such a 'visionary antiquarian' as Dr Stukeley[21] is called. Others, of far greater authority, regard the entire story as a fable and assert positively that Julius Caesar did not cross the river at this place at all.[22]

Very little is known of the life of the parish after the period covered by medieval manorial records. The village did not share in the 18th century fashion and prosperity of the river-side villages downstream, and in 1816 the houses were said to be 'chiefly of a mean and neglected character'. In the early 19th century, most of the inhabitants had lived in 'a state of great ignorance and depravity' with 'somewhat limited' means of employment.

The village was for some years the scene of riotous behaviour due to its popularity as a venue for illegal prize fighting, or bare-knuckle boxing.[23] The usual venue was the Range, a piece of common land between the Chertsey Road and the river. This site was picked because, being close to the river and hence the boundary between Middlesex and Surrey, those involved could make a quick exit to the next county if the local magistrates arrived to break up proceedings! In fact, so many of the gentry attended that a 'blind eye' was often turned by the authorities.

On the day of a big fight the local roads would be clogged with all manner of 'carriages, stagecoaches, carts, waggons and vehicles of every kind'.

A ring was marked out, and a yard square box marked out in the centre. Each fighter had to come 'up to the mark', or 'up to scratch' by the beginning of each round or lose the match. As each round continued until one man was on the ground, and the number of rounds was unlimited, these contests could continue for considerable amounts of time. Huge sums were wagered on these fights and afterwards local men came forward to fight for smaller purses, often in the Church Square.

Our village of Shepperton has for many years been much in want of a resident surgeon. The surgeon for the district parishes resided in Sunbury more than two miles distant from us and our poor people were not properly attended to.

To make matters worse our existing physician was seldom sober. When the 'Blue devils' at last carried him off to another world, I resolved to have a parish surgeon resident here and wrote to my fellow Magistrate[24] Mr Mitchison, in the hope of finding one. I explained that the population by the last census was somewhat over a thousand. From 1866 to 1874 or eight years, the deaths were 148 and, as proof of the remarkable healthiness of Shepperton, I may state that 33 of those consisted of persons who were upwards of 70 years of age, 20 of 75 and upwards, 14 of 80 upwards, 8 of 85 and upwards, and 3 who had reached the great age of more than four score years and ten. But while we have remarkable longevity, I ascertained that out of 148 deaths there were no less than 36 who died under 12 months and 49 children who died before they reached three years of age. I attributed a great number of the deaths of these children to have arisen from the want of medical attendance and I think it can be proved that the lives of many of them would have been saved had a doctor been within reach of their parents.

Mr Mitchison replied saying children less than 3 years of age would be less at risk with the proper medical attendance but also for the want of proper food and maternal attendance. What can we expect when we find large families, say 8 or 9, living in two or three small rooms?[25]

My appeal for a doctor however produced the desired effect and we soon had a parish doctor of our own, Mr Cattell-Jones, a young man of good promise, a grandson of the late Sir Benjamin Hawes.[26] He is getting on very well and I have made him my own family surgeon.

43 Brunel's Giant Ship

In the summer of 1857, the late Robert Stephenson[27] and I paid a visit to the SS *Great Eastern*. We were accompanied by Brunel.[28] The hull was then drawing towards completion and preparations for launching were about to be commenced. After thoroughly inspecting everything about the vessel Brunel asked me what I thought of her.

"Well," I replied, "she is the strongest and best built ship I ever saw, and she is really a marvellous feat of engineering."

"Oh," he said, rather testily and abruptly, "I did not want your opinion about her build. I should think I know rather more about how an iron ship should be put together than you do. How will she pay?"

"Ah." I replied, "That is quite a different matter;" and, seeing that I did not care to answer his question, he repeated it, adding, "If she belonged to you in what trade would you place her?"

"Turn her into a show," I said, with a laugh, "something attractive to the masses; for, if you insist on having my opinion about her commercial capabilities, it is only in that direction where you can look for profit. She will never pay as a ship. Send her to Brighton, dig out a hole in the beach and bed her stern in it, and if well set she would make a substantial pier and her deck a splendid promenade; her hold would make magnificent saltwater baths and her 'tween' decks a grand hotel, with restaurant, smoking and dancing saloons, and I know not what all. She would be a marvellous attraction for the cockneys who would flock to her in thousands."

And, as I saw he was far from pleased with my answer – no wonder – though given half in joke and half in earnest, I added, "As you would insist on having my opinion, I have given it to you candidly, for I really do not know any other trade, at present, in which she will be likely to pay so well." Stephenson laughed, but Brunel never forgave me.[29]

The giant ship was Isambard Kingdom Brunel's masterpiece, a ship able to sail to Australia without refuelling. Although christened *Leviathan* she was of course the SS *Great Eastern*.

As the largest and most advanced ship being built, five times the size any other vessel, she cost a fortune. The cost of building her, although estimated by Brunel to be £500,000, was budgeted at £377,000. The final cost was £1,000,000 and an additional £120,000 required to fit her out.[30] The launch itself cost £120,000 instead of the £14,000 budgeted.[31] In view of this Brunel and her backers were very keen to ensure she would prove profitable afloat and had asked my opinion.

Isambard Kingdom Brunel was one of the world's most famous engineers. His engineering feats changed the lives of thousands of people. With his father he built the first underground railway. He designed and built docks and suspension bridges. He built the Great Western Railway from London to Bristol incorporating tunnels and stations along its route.

Brunel built three great ships, 'firsts' in their day; the SS *Great Western*, a ship designed to extend the Great Western Railway to America by sea, and the first steamer to do so; the SS *Great Britain*, the first screw-driven and first iron-built, transatlantic steamer, and the SS *Great Eastern*, a giant steamship originally intended for the Far Eastern trade.

At the time I was advocating the use of power-assisted sailing ships (auxiliary steamships), others, including Brunel, were building fully powered steamships with a much smaller sail area.[32] In time, as more powerful engines were developed, sails on steamers would disappear altogether.

The SS *Great Eastern* story is well known to many. She was almost 700ft long, double hulled, a five-funnelled giant first proposed by Brunel in 1851. She could carry 4,000 passengers and her holds were to provide for 6,000 tons of cargo.

Whilst at Deptford I visited the yard of the builder Scott Russell[33] and had a peep for the first time at the Monster Ship which was being built.

My thoughts at the time were that no dock or port in the Kingdom would be able to receive her. When the owners wanted to repair her, or even to clean her hull, they would be required to build a dry dock for her and that might cost another million. Of course, she might find safe enough anchorage in Milford Haven and at other similar roadsteads,[34] but passengers and especially goods would not easily travel to such places.

Besides, if I were a shipper of goods I should much prefer sending them in a smaller vessel as I should be certain to have a speedier delivery of them and, if I were a passenger, I would never dream of taking a passage with 10,000, 5,000 or even 3,000 passengers on board, as in the event of a contagious disease breaking out, its ravages would be fearful.

I also question whether they would get anything like the speed out of her they anticipated. If ships have greater engines, and more of them, they will have a greater weight to propel through the water, and it is an error to suppose that the speed increases with the size beyond a certain limit, and that limit they far exceeded. I was sure she would be a monstrous failure. She would, however, be one of the wonders of the age.

From the start she was beset with financial problems. The original company and its backers went bankrupt, but the project survived. The huge vessel proved near impossible to launch. Built on the banks of the River Thames in Millwall she was a feature on the London skyline for 42 months. The sound of three million rivets being driven into her iron plating was constant and deafening.

Finally, after three months of trying, and on the third attempt in November 1857, the hulk made it to the water sideways. By September 1859

Part Five: Shipping Business Continues

the SS *Great Eastern* sailed on its maiden voyage. However, an explosion on-board caused eight deaths. Shortly thereafter Brunel had a stroke and on 15 September 1859 he died.

The SS *Great Eastern's* first transatlantic voyage from Southampton to New York eventually took place on 17 June 1860. This voyage and a few others returned profits; however, these were wiped out by accidents. On one transatlantic voyage she encountered a heavy gale which destroyed her two paddles and damaged her rudder. The giant vessel had to turn back home, and the passengers had to be reimbursed adding further to the loss. In 1862 she struck a rock while entering New York, which cost £70,000 to repair. She struggled to keep her losses to a minimum.

In 1864 the Director's report showed there was an outstanding debt amounting to £30,000, and an additional sum would be required for her maintenance. She was sold later that year for a meagre £25,000.

The Great Ship was then commissioned to lay transatlantic cables in 1865 but more than halfway across the Atlantic the cable broke. The following year she tried again. On this occasion the connection was completed between Ireland and Newfoundland. Subsequently she laid a couple more cables, including one from France to America, and in 1869-70 she laid one across the Indian Ocean. These were her only successful commercial ventures.

SS *Great Eastern* under construction. National Maritime Museum, Greenwich, London.

SS *Great Eastern* under full sail and steam, passing Dover.[35]

Significant opportunities were missed, however. Had she focused on emigration she would have been more financially viable; 800,000 emigrants came to the United States during 1861-65 alone. Equally, had she concentrated on transporting grain she would have been more profitable. She proved the point by importing five thousand tons of prairie grain in 1861 but did not follow this up. The vessel had more than her fair share of ill fortune. She was, however, a ship significantly in advance of others but too large to be a commercial success.[36]

My remarks, prior to the launch of SS *Great Eastern*, made regarding the commercial prospects for the ship, were a good deal ridiculed by the London press at the time. Public opinion was almost unanimous that this ship would be a great success. I remember the *Globe* newspaper expressing great surprise at a man of my "Common Sense" and nautical experience, talking such nonsense. My prediction however was correct. Years later, however, I wrote this:[37]

> It may be that a hundred or fifty years hence, the maritime commerce of the world may have grown to an extent sufficient to justify, with reasonable prospects of profit, another ship of the dimensions of the 'Great Eastern'.
>
> I can only write of the past and the present, leaving the future to be dealt with by those who may follow me, and, perhaps, all that posterity will be able to say against the enterprising promoters of the 'Great Eastern' may, hereafter, be condensed in the flattering eulogium, "Their ideas in regard to dimensions were in advance of their age – they were only before their time."

44 The Portuguese Loan

In the month of July 1857 I received, through a shipping company in London, an application to supply certain steamships for a Company about

Part Five: Shipping Business Continues

to be formed in Lisbon. I did not pay much attention. But the following month, when various merchants in Portugal contacted me directly and stated that the Company was to be formed under the auspices of the Government of Portugal, I replied asking for further information. The answer was favourable. I complied with their request and visited Lisbon for the first time a few weeks later.[38]

Immediately on my arrival I had an interview with Senor Carlos Bento da Silva, the then Minister of Public Works, in company with the gentleman who had invited me to Lisbon. During that, and other meetings, the prospects of the proposed undertaking were fully discussed. The Government of Portugal was evidently anxious that a line of steamships should be commenced with their settlements in Western Africa and with the Azores as soon as possible.[39]

The great stumbling block appeared to be the method of raising money to pay for the vessels that were required. At last, I agreed to supply the Portuguese with three vessels. I agreed to accept, in payment, certain credits[40] for one half of the purchase money and the other half in the shares of the Company about to be formed. When the Minister of Public Works had accepted my terms, I told him that I had no objection to sign the documentation once alterations had been made and then I would supply the steamships.[41]

Following delays, and seeking assurance that all would proceed, I again wrote to him in February (1858) stating that I would not dispatch the first ship, nor withdraw the other two from their current employments, until the Company is fully constituted, and the capital obtained.

At the end of that month his Excellency acknowledged reply of that letter stating that my wishes were being carried into effect; and on 28 March he addressed me as follows, not in reply to any further communication from me but of his own accord:

> Dear Sir, the contract and the Statutes of the Navigation Company are ready to be signed tomorrow or the day after tomorrow. We will let you know by Telegraph of the verification of this fact, and I rely on you to give your orders respecting the ship which ought to commence the voyage to the Azores and which ought not to be retarded. I am etc Carlos B da Silva.

He relied on me to deliver, and on receipt of that Telegraph, I dispatched, in good faith, the ship he so urgently required to start the service and in due course the other two steam ships followed.

Over the following months and years, I pressed for payment. None was forthcoming. The Portuguese Government changed regularly. The new regimes said that they were not party to arrangements made with former Governments. I asked our Foreign Office for assistance to obtain the money owed to me. But after initial approaches they said that it was not a government matter, it was a private contract. I considered raising it in Parliament and with the Prime Minister but decided to act cautiously.[42]

The shipping line failed, and the steamships were subsequently sold by Public Auction some years later. The sale of the ships more than covered the amount due to me but the amount £18,000 remained unpaid.[43] As for interest, I at last received £1,800 from the Portuguese Government.[44] The shares of the Company, of which I held 1,266, have been rendered worthless. They were originally valued at £25,320.[45] Hitherto every effort has failed to obtain settlement.[46]

To add insult to injury, in following years, the Portuguese raised loans in Britain for other projects, advertised through the press. I highlighted the fact, with letters to these newspapers, that previous loans were still outstanding, but my protestations were ignored.

In a letter to me, Lord Eslington[47] said:

> In my view of the case, the conduct of the Portuguese Government has been simply scandalous. It seems to me to be a monstrous proceeding on the part of the Portuguese Government, but how you wealthy and shrewd men of business can go and lend your money, or your ships, or your credit, to these damned Foreign Governments, I can't understand.[48]

45 Parliamentary Royal Commissions

Whilst in Parliament, I sat on several important Parliamentary Royal Commissions, including on Harbours of Refuge (1858-59), and on Manning the Navy (1858-59). I was also Chair of the Transport Service Commission (1859).

During my time at sea and in Hartlepool I had seen enough wrecks and saw the value of having sheltering harbours to avoid the worst of storms. There was a need for more of them. When the opportunity arose to partake in a Commission involving Harbours of Refuge I leapt at the chance. That Committee sat for two years. It was chaired by Rear Admiral James Hope.[49] I was one of the seven Commissioners.[50] Hope and I became acquainted during the Commission. For six months we were almost constantly together visiting the coasts of this country inspecting sites for Harbours of Refuge and taking evidence about them.[51]

Hope was an excellent companion and a clever man but on-board ship he carried his habits of discipline to an extent not at all appreciated by his naval colleagues. Though Washington[52] and Sulivan[53] were his equals on the Commission I was often amused to see the way he expected them to attend to his wishes because he was an Admiral, and they were only poor Captains. Sulivan used to laugh at it and always gave way, but Washington generally

Part Five: Shipping Business Continues

lost his temper and sometimes after one of these struggles, he would not open his lips to Hope for a week.

Admiral Hope was however an excellent sailor, and I should say first rate commander. Since we were together on the Commission, he has been Commander in Chief of our fleet in China and nearly lost his life to an engagement there.[54] After that he was Commander in Chief on the North American station.

Our Commission decided to arrange the harbours into two categories. Under the first we included harbours "which are required on parts of the coast which are often visited that are without any adequate place of safety into which vessels can run if overtaken by storms." Such harbours we termed, "Harbours of Refuge". Examples were Holyhead and Portland.

Under the second category we placed those harbours "rendered necessary for the purpose of saving life by the entire want of other than Tidal or Bar Harbours on an extensive line of coast, much exposed to heavy on-shore gales, and the most largely frequented by the class of shipping least capable, under such circumstances, of keeping off a lee-shore." These we termed "Life Harbours".

Between us we visited ports around the country to identify their needs. When assessing how they should be funded much depended on whether the harbours were utilised locally or not. The total estimated cost of the works recommended by the Commission, on the coasts of the United Kingdom, amounted to £3,990,000 of which sum £2,365,000 should be taken from public funds and the remaining £1,625,000 to be raised locally. We considered that it would take ten years to complete all of them and that Parliament should set aside not less than £250,000 per year for their construction. In the summer of 1858, we reported that we were unanimously in favour of the principle of grants of money for the improvement and extension of existing harbours and national grants for the construction of new harbours of refuge.

Although agreeing to the substance of the report Admiral Hope was unable to sign it as he had left England to assume the naval command on the East India and China stations.[55] Both Sir John Pakington, as First Lord of the Admiralty, in Lord Derby's Government and then Lord Palmerston in his own Government, admitted the need for harbours of refuge but they could not agree to such a large expenditure that was proposed.

Four times[56] I put forward a resolution in Parliament to carry into effect the Report of the Royal Commission, but each time it was defeated. Nowadays so large a portion of our maritime commerce is conducted in steam vessels; harbours of refuge are certainly of less value than they were. They are still required though.

Incidentally I had occasion to hear again from Admiral James Hope. He had been much criticized for his actions during the 2nd Opium War[57] when his assaults on the forts blocking the river to Peking ended in failure and he was forced to retreat. He wrote to me from Hong Kong explaining the course of events.

He said that he had taken the only course of action open to him, namely to silence and gain possession of the forts[58] and then to clear away the barriers. In the engagement he was severely wounded and three senior officers were disabled when gunboats were sent in to bombard the forts. Four gunboats were sunk and two other severely damaged.

Failure to take the Taku Forts was a blow to British prestige and the Admiral was called to account for it. Continuing in his letter to me the Admiral said:

> Where there is failure, blame must fairly attach, and you must not allow your regard for me to induce you to place yourself in a false position by an attempt to defend that which on calm consideration may appear to you indefensible.
>
> I was determined that if the thing was done at all, it should not be done by halves. Rely on it; it does not do to be deterred from the execution of a plan well considered beforehand, by slight difficulties.
>
> It is for the country to determine whether her Admirals are to confine themselves to operations which involve no risk. You know it was Nelson's dictum "When there is a doubt, fight". I followed and like him (at Tenerife[59] & Boulogne[60]), I failed, and perhaps with more excuses, as he possessed the advantages which I did not, of many years' experience of warfare previously.[61]

The second Parliamentary Commission I was asked to be a member of was the Royal Commission on Manning the Navy.[62] There was a need to have some representation from someone not in the Royal Navy but who had experience of seafaring matters and the merchant marine. I supposed that I fitted that role. The objective of the Royal Commission of 1859 was to inquire into the best means of manning the navy and especially as to the way in which seamen of the mercantile marine and the seafaring population of the United Kingdom might be made more readily and willingly available when required for Naval Service.

It was to include in what manner, and under what arrangements, seamen may be readily obtained for such purpose, either during peace, or in the case of sudden emergency of war.

The Commission was chaired by Lord Hardwicke.[63] Though I dissented from his report and that of my colleagues I never sat under a more agreeable and more impartial president. I was one of nine members.[64] I am sure that most on the Committee assumed that I would agree to their findings but on certain matters I disagreed and would not sign.

The Commissioners recommended that this country should have a Reserve of 60,000 men for an emergency, all of whom could be made available within a few months after the declaration of war. Included in the 60,000 men, they recommended the creation of a new Reserve Force to be drawn from the merchant service, which they styled Royal Naval Volunteers (since known as

Part Five: Shipping Business Continues

the Royal Naval Reserve) consisting of 20,000 men. The annual estimated cost of this would be £598,821.

While agreeing with my colleagues in many of their recommendations, I felt that their scheme was based upon precarious foundations.[65] I reluctantly declined to sign the report for these reasons:

1) I thought that my colleagues did not sufficiently realise the fact that steam had entirely changed the mode in which naval warfare would be conducted in future,
2) that as a maritime nation, a larger proportion of our military force should consist of men competent to serve either afloat or on shore, who should, in fact, be a sort of naval militia (Royal Marine Corps) trained in the management of guns,
3) that by garrisoning our seaports with men thus trained, we should have a very powerful and efficient reserve of gunners for our ships, whose places on shore could, on the emergency of war, be filled with either soldiers or militia and their places in turn, in the inland towns, filled by the Volunteers. In doing so we should not require to retain so many seamen in reserve,
4) that the reserve of seamen from the Merchant Service, which they proposed, would not be easily obtainable unless we invited their Officers to enrol in the Reserve and would be of little service unless we had enough competent men to command them.

My suggestions would significantly save on cost. However, the last was the only one of my suggestions which has been carried into effect. My letter of dissent was added to the official report.

Several years later there was another review into Manning the Navy. Having gone fully into the matter I prepared a paper to show that we had at present Officers and men afloat and in reserve sufficient to man double the number of effective ships at present in our Navy.[66] I pointed out how various large reductions could be made without in any way lessening the efficiency of the force. As expected, this was not popular with those in the Admiralty.

A rough draft of my scheme I have kept, but before sending a copy to the First Lord of the Admiralty, Mr Hugh Childers,[67] I also submitted to my neighbour Admiral Sir B J Sulivan [68] the whole of my plan. In almost every point he agreed with me.

I was also heavily involved with the Transport Service Commission in 1859, of which I was Chairman.[69] My experiences in the Crimean War in providing Transport ships for Britain and France, and in trying to improve the management of supplies, led to me being involved.

In Parliament I had moved for a Select Committee to inquire into the organization and management of those branches of the Admiralty, War Office, India Office, and Emigration Board, by which the business of transporting, by means of shipping, troops, convicts, emigrants, materials of war, stores, and any other similar services, was performed. I had in mind the adoption of a uniform system by which such services may be economically and efficiently conducted under the authority of one consolidated and responsible department.

Reviewing the system, we recommended certain reforms to the Transport Service. Principle amongst these was the separation of Transport from the Victualling (supply) department of the Admiralty, and the formation of "a distinct and separate Transport Office".

Our Commission showed that there was such inefficiency in the transport system during the Crimean War that the ships hired to transport troops (and supplies) was significantly underused. Instead of transporting 450,000 infantry, or 90,000 cavalry in a year, the ships transported 100,000 and 20,000 respectively. In addition, transports were kept utterly unemployed for weeks; large sums of money were thus wasted. The episode was just one example of the gross mismanagement of the war by the Admiralty and the Board of Ordnance during Aberdeen's precarious coalition administration.

I believed the great strength of the service lay in the mercantile marine. The maintenance of an efficient fleet of dedicated troopships would cost the nation far more than the employment of transport ships drawn from merchant vessels in times of War.[70]

46 Explorers and Republicans

Over the years I met several explorers and famous republicans. I refer to some of these now.

Commander Peter Belches[71] RN (1796–1890) Explorer in Australia 1827
I had met my cousin Peter Belches in Glasgow when I was a small boy. He was visiting my mother, his aunt. In his naval uniform he made a lasting impression on me. He easily lifted me on his shoulders. I received a letter[72] from him years later in August 1855 in reply to my communication stating whether he was my long long-lost cousin and the only surviving male cousin that I had. His letter was sent from King George's Sound in Australia.

He said that he had seen my name as a Director of a Bank[73] and as the name was given in full "William Schaw Lindsay" – Schaw being a very unusual way of spelling the name, the coincidence immediately struck him, and he became convinced of some connection. As a sheep farmer he wished to send some wool to England and my ships had been recommended to him. He said that he never dreamed that he was sending it to the little boy who had been on his knee when he was talking to his aunt the last time that he was in Glasgow. He continued, saying that my career savoured more of a romance than real life.

Part Five: Shipping Business Continues

He said that he had not been a fortunate settler, as his lot had been cast in a very barren nook in Australia. The discovery of gold nuggets had had a detrimental effect on his mortgage, and he had suffered as a result.

He continued: "My first trip to Australia was in the 'Volage' with Captain R.S. Dundas[74] who now commands the Baltic Fleet. I then joined the 'Success' with Sir James Stirling[75] who afterwards came here as Governor and I accompanied him, thinking to do great things" but instead he left as he found it, a poor prospect.

This was during the early days of exploration of Western Australia. In 1827 Point Belches was named after him. He also had the claim as the first to explore the Canning River. He got married, which kept him tied to the place. He had four children, two boys and two girls. He felt that there was no prospect for them there, which would compel him to lift his anchor soon.

He said that he often wished that he had never gone on half-pay and had remained in the Navy. The chances were that he would have got a command of one of the ships in the Baltic with his old skipper. He continued saying that he did not imagine that our Fleet would gain much there during the Crimean War. He said Admiral Dundas[76] was a first-class Officer, but what could he do against stone walls, particularly with ships that couldn't get alongside them? I replied advising him to go to Melbourne or Sydney instead of coming to Britain. I felt that prospects were better for him there.

Sir John Franklin (1786-1847) Arctic Explorer

In the search for the Northwest Passage to India and China two ships, the *Erebus,* and the *Terror,* disappeared in 1845 never to be seen again.[77] The Leader of that fateful voyage was Sir John Franklin,[78] the great Arctic explorer. His wife, Lady Jane, became increasingly concerned and she lobbied for a rescue party to search for the ships. Pressed by Lady Jane and others, the Admiralty launched a search for the missing expedition in 1848. I had met her half a dozen times at her lodgings in Pall Mall, and in 1860 during my visit to the USA, I spent an afternoon with her and her niece in Washington.[79] To the very last she was under the firm conviction that her husband was alive. Like most people though, I was of a very different opinion. I felt that the Government at least ought to grant her very moderate request for a ship which Admiral Napier had made on her behalf.

I could not have supported the fitting out of another expedition at the expense and on the responsibility of the Government, but when Lady Franklin and her friends resolved to have the responsibility and expense of another expedition themselves, I thought that Government could grant the use of a suitable ship for the purpose, more especially as that ship was not likely to be required for any other purpose. She contacted me in February 1857 to express her thanks for my support for Admiral Napier's motion to support her.

She said no amount of able speeches would have moved Sir Charles Wood from the decision he had come to not to support the motion. It was especially galling, she wrote, because a few days earlier the favourable views of Lord Palmerston and Lord Lansdowne prevailed. If Admiral Napier had been able to bring on his motion a week or 10 days earlier, she believed there should have been a quite different result.

When Lord Wrottesley[80] expressed his hope a year earlier to Lord Stanley[81] that she should be largely responsible for a private expedition (if the Government declined to undertake one itself), the answer was entirely favourable. She hoped for the loan of one of the Arctic ships, possibly the *Resolute*, which would be fitted with a screw propeller.

In her letter to me, she referred to her frustrations of the Admiralty keeping her in suspense a whole year and making her lose two, or she feared three, previous seasons for operations. She asked whether I would repeat my very effective speech in the House and trusted that it would put some pressure on the Government.[82]

Lady Franklin alluded to the fact that the £600,000 put down by the Government for Arctic expeditions could be reduced to a much smaller sum if all the facts were known but she indicated that she perhaps did not have the right to communicate the information that had been given to her. I never discovered to what she referred.

In a follow up letter in May[83] she said that she had been extremely vexed to learn that Lieutenant Pim[84] in his zeal for getting up another Arctic expedition, but without any previous communication with her, had been making use of her name in the City to form a committee for the purpose of raising a sum of £10,000 in aid of her funds.

In another letter to me in July she said that the Admiralty would refuse the remainder of the Arctic stores (from which Captain McClintock[85] had selected a considerable portion of the most useful) because hers was a private expedition. She said that she thought that this refusal had not yet been made public and she would be glad if it was aired in the House.

She continued saying that as long as the Admiralty thought they could prevent private expeditions by the refusal of everything, they did so, but when they found a vessel had been bought with private funds and that so distinguished an Officer as Captain McClintock had agreed to command the expedition, they relaxed their opposition and allowed some supplies.[86] I hoped that in some small way my support for her in the House of Commons had helped.

David Livingstone (1813-1873) African Explorer

David Livingstone[87] when he first started on his exploration into the interior of Africa did so as a missionary on behalf of the Dissenters of Scotland. When he returned to London, after his first and greatest expedition, I was introduced to him by Dr Archer of the United Presbyterian Church in Haymarket where I was a member. I afterwards met Livingstone on various occasions, and he once or twice dined with me at my residence in Portland Place.

Part Five: Shipping Business Continues

In 1857 he wrote to me concerning an appointment for his brother in Africa in the Union Mercantile Company of London. The Company had then just been formed to carry out the mail service between the Portuguese settlements in Africa and the Northern Country. Livingstone asked me to speak with his brother to suggest that his prospects would be better served accompanying him in his travels to the East Coast of Africa rather than work for a Portuguese Company in Western Africa. He hinted that he had little faith in the Manager of the Company. I duly met with Livingstone's brother and told him what Livingstone had said. His brother decided to accompany him to East Africa and Livingstone thanked me.

Years later there were conflicting reports of Livingstone's safety. There was little news of him from Africa. Other explorers however had disappeared only to reappear, so I was reassured that he was not lost. Du Chaillu,[88] for instance, on his first African expedition was not heard of for, I think, more than 2 years, and Livingstone himself was buried in the wilds for at least the same time, and during that time I believe he had no communication whatever with the civilised world.

In appearance, in manner, and in very many respects Livingstone was an entirely different man to my friend Du Chaillu.[89] Though hardy and resolute, he wanted the life, fun and energy of the latter, but his expression displayed the features of a determined man. In conversation he was slow and heavy but candid. He looked like a man who meant what he said and one who would not lightly break a promise once given.

His body was laid to rest in Westminster Abbey, and a pension of £200 per annum to his family was voted in by Parliament; an insignificant sum when we consider the great services he had rendered; but in such matters Parliament has never displayed a spirit of generosity.

Giuseppe Maria Garibaldi (1807–1882) Italian Republican and Shipmaster

The first time I met Garibaldi[90] was in my office. He was then the Master of an American merchant ship which was consigned to me for employment by his owners in the United States. I chartered the ship to proceed to Newcastle upon Tyne and there to load a cargo of coals for Aden. From there Garibaldi proceeded to Bombay where he took on board a cargo of cotton and seeds for Liverpool. He made an excellent and expeditious voyage and proved himself to be an able and economical shipmaster. The next time I met him was in 1863 when he was the guest of my friend Charles Seely MP[91] at his country house in the Isle of Wight. I spent a couple of days with him.

He was the same plain unassuming man; great success had not changed him, much less spoiled him. The man who had overthrown Monarchs, the idol of millions of men in many countries, who himself might have worn a crown, was still the shipmaster; with an ease and simplicity of manner which at once won the affection of any person who enjoyed the pleasure of his company. You could see immediately that he was a man of extraordinary energy and determination.

The mention of Austrian oppression and Russian despotism seemed to instantly arouse into action a spirit otherwise docile and in some respects childish and at the mention of the wrongs of Italy the most casual observer could not fail to see in Garibaldi a truly sincere and noble patriot.

He was a very early riser, and it was between the hours of 6 and 8 in the morning that I enjoyed his company most during my short sojourn in Mr. Seely's house. We had many things to talk about. Haug,[92] who had been his colleague in arms under Mazzini at Rome, had often been my guest while an exile here. Ernesto Haug had been one of Mazzini's Generals. I had a great deal of discussions when he was an exile in Britain and he used to speak in the highest terms of Mazzini.

I had also met Mazzini[93] on various occasions so Garibaldi and I had many odds and ends to talk over besides his voyage to Aden and Bombay. Garibaldi spoke of Mazzini in the highest and most affectionate terms – for which I was not prepared, for the two men, as men and as "patriots" are, in many respects, intensely different to each other. Each had in view the grand objective that Rome should be restored to Italy – Garibaldi seemed to live for that.

The worldly power of the Pope was then seemingly ending, but I questioned if Garibaldi would have been able to effect this great change without aid, in some way or other, from France or Italy. He however seemed resolved to restore Rome to the position she once held or perish in the attempt.[94]

Poor Mazzini – "King of Rome" – fit to be a King in many ways, and yet in some respects unfit to govern himself. It is true I did not know him intimately. We had met on perhaps eight or nine different occasions. Not more. Twice or thrice, he spent an evening with me at Portland Place. I had also met him at the houses of mutual friends, and I had seen him in his English home, poor – very poor – lodgings somewhere between Brompton and Chelsea.

There seemed to me to be always a mystery about him. In that respect he resembled one of his notes he wrote to me – no date, no name – no place and no very well-defined objective.[95] The note was altogether characteristic. It was written not long before Garibaldi made his great move for the Freedom of Italy, and I do not doubt that Mazzini played no mean part in that affair. Circumstances have since led me to think that Garibaldi received great assistance from him, and in a great measure acted upon his advice.

Mazzini was not the man whom I would have chosen as my leader. At times there was a wildness in his eye and an excitement in his manner which gave way to a wandering mind and incipient signs of derangement. But it was not so – at least his most intimate friends were not of that opinion - and though he was considered by them an enthusiast, they looked upon him as a man of great abilities and of the most honest intentions. Garibaldi told me that Italy had no more sincere or earnest patriot than Mazzini.[96]

So it was that I met and became friends with one of the greatest republicans of the day. In doing so I also had met others of his ilk.

Part Five: Shipping Business Continues

47 Bride Ships

Back in 1859 I approached the Colonial Office[97] to assist with transportation of emigrants to the new colony in British Columbia and to start a new mail service. A year earlier rumours of gold had prompted ten to twenty thousand men to move into the region from America and Britain. The Colonial Office's response was disappointing stating that it was too early to consider such an enterprise. In addition, they stated that the Colony, deriving revenues from the gold fields, should finance such a service themselves.

In 1862, however, two of my ships, the *Tynemouth,* and the *Robert Lowe,* were chartered by the Columbia Emigration Society in Canada who wished to convey prospective brides to Victoria, Vancouver Island, due to the shortage of females. In all the vessels transported about 80 brides, most of whom were successfully married.[98]

As well as providing future wives for the male overpopulated Canadian West, it lessened the numbers of women hit hard in the NW of England. Unemployment was rife due to a shortage of cotton for the mills. This was a result of the blockade of the South by the North in the American Civil War. In addition, the ratio of women to men was higher in England. The Columbia Emigration Society had been financially supported by Burdett Coutts, heiress to her grandfather's Coutts Bank. The idea of female emigration had first been suggested to her by Charles Dickens.

The first of two of my ships, the *Tynemouth,* set off from London Docks in June 1862. She collected additional passengers from Dartmouth. She had 292 passengers on board, 60 of them were sponsored single women. She was the first passenger steamer to travel from Britain to British Columbia. The *Robert Lowe* set off later in the year with 180 passengers, with 38 single females.

I was glad of the business. The American Civil War was on at the time, and I had decided not to conduct any trade to America whilst the War raged. Earlier, in 1855, these ships had been commissioned during the Crimean War to conduct supplies and troops to the Crimean War. Both ships had been built at the same time of a similar design.

The *Tynemouth* had been refitted in 1860. She was an iron screw steam ship and boasted three decks. Essentially, she was a clipper sailing vessel with an auxiliary motor. The first-class fare cost from 80 guineas, second class 40 guineas, and third class 30 guineas.

It was Captain Arthur Hellyer's first merchant ship command. Aged 46, he had been trained in the Royal Navy and had been recruited to undertake the voyage shortly before departure.

The single ladies had a Matron and a Reverend as chaperones. They were cordoned off and separated from the rest of the passengers.

Lasting 99 days, I was to learn that the voyage in the *Tynemouth* had been quite eventful. No sooner had she departed from Dartmouth than the vessel hit by a gale. The only cow was washed overboard hence denying milk for the children. Several pigs were hurt. Many of the passengers were seasick,

STEAM to the GOLD FIELDS of BRITISH COLUMBIA – For VICTORIA, Vancouver's Island (calling if required at San Francisco), the iron screw steamship TYNEMOUTH, A 1 9 years at Lloyd's 1,650 tons register, 600-horse power indicated ALFRED HELLYER Commander: will load at the Jetty, London Docks, leaving punctually on the 24th of May, and embarking passengers at Dartmouth on the 28th of May. This steamship having just been fitted with new engines and boilers, as well as all the most recent appliances for rendering her one of the finest passenger steamers afloat, offers a mode of transit to the above colony unequalled in speed and comfort as well as in economy. In order to ensure a rapid passage she will take only a very limited cargo, touching at the Falkland Islands for coals, fresh provisions, and water. The accommodation for the several classes is of a superior description, the dietary scale liberal, and every means will be adapted to promote the comforts of passengers. For freight or passage apply to W.S. Lindsay and Co., 8, Austinfriars, or 54 Old Broad-street, E.O.

Advert for the *Tynemouth's* voyage to British Columbia. *The Times* London, 9 May 1862.

one seriously and the captain was afraid she would die. The storm proved no threat to the ship, however.

During the voyage, in the middle of the South Atlantic several stokers and coal haulers, complaining of overwork, left their stations and let the boiler fires die. The ship was in the middle of a mutiny. The captain rounded up the culprits and detained them. This posed a dilemma. The ship had set off short of trained seamen. She was now in the doldrums near the equator, with no wind. Captain Hellyer had no option but to ask for the passengers' assistance in manning the boilers. Many volunteered, happy to be occupied with work to offset the boredom.

The ship sailed towards the Falkland Islands. The captain's tough action against the offenders seemed vindicated. However, one morning, several angry crewmembers grabbed him and threatened to throw him over the stern. One of the mutineers struck him in the face. The commotion brought the ship's Officers to the scene, but they were too afraid to intervene. Passengers soon crowded round to see what was happening and plunged into the fight. It was then that the Officers armed themselves with belaying pins and put down the uprising.

This incident caused additional problems. It was one thing encouraging passengers to man the boilers but asking them to handle the sails aloft was another. The task of sailing the 1,500-ton fully rigged ship in rough winds, with sails that had to be furled and unfurled on spars on high, was no job for untrained passengers. The situation looked hopeless. Two things saved them. Firstly, some of the passengers had been to sea in the past. They came forward to assist. Secondly, the trade winds at that time were set fair.

When all seemed settled, the ship faced another hazard. Another gale approached and soon became a hurricane. In the rough seas the longboat

Part Five: Shipping Business Continues

or ship's lifeboat, was washed overboard. Iron tanks in the hold, being transported for the railroads being built across Canada, broke loose, and smashed from side to side against the ship's hull, sliding on iron rails. Fortunately, the rails did not break loose, and the ships' hull held fast. Finally, the winds eased. The ship had survived. During the storm the passengers had been terrified. Confined to their quarters, with port holes shut, they emerged on deck, pale and horrified. Slowly their spirits rose with better weather.

In the meantime, one of the female passengers began to get sick and after a short while she died two days before they arrived in the Falklands. Smallpox was never confirmed, and she did not develop the disfiguring blisters that were a sign of the disease. She was buried on the island. The other passengers feared that an epidemic would follow but fortunately this did not occur.

After six weeks at sea, whilst most passengers happily enjoyed their time for two weeks on land, the chaperones of the single ladies decided that they should not leave the ship. One can only imagine their frustration.

The 16 men who had mutinied were brought ashore for trial. Knowing that rounding Cape Horn was still to come, Captain Hellyer testified that the seamen's confinement had been punishment enough and said that if they promised to do their work for the remainder of the voyage that he would take them on board. Most of them did. The vessel loaded coals and set off again on its journey. Rounding the Horn proved unproblematic as the seas were calm. This meant however that the auxiliary engines had to be employed and, before arriving in San Francisco, fuel ran very low. The ship just managed to complete the leg but not before any loose wood (such as deckchairs and the like) was used as fuel.

Their stay in San Francisco only lasted two days; enough time for half of the *Tynemouth*'s remaining crew to desert, which caused much concern for the captain. The single women were, yet again, detained in the ship. They were left seething as other passengers went ashore to get hot baths in a hotel and enjoy a good meal.[99] Again, the ship reloaded with coals and set off for Canada. As it steamed out the harbour several passengers were left behind due to a disparity about departure times. This was later to result in a fine of £20 that the captain had to settle.

After 99 days at sea, on 17 September 1862 the *Tynemouth* arrived in Esquimalt, the port for Victoria, British Columbia, during which the ship had faced two severe gales, mutinies, one death, and women who had to endure three months confined on board. Remarkably she was one month early.

While the *Tynemouth* was arriving in Canada, the *Robert Lowe* departed England from Gravesend. She sailed non-stop to Canada in 114 days, arriving on 10 January 1863. Compared to her sister ship, her voyage had been uneventful. In charge of the ship was Captain Congalton, who had served me well for many years. The ship transported three dozen uneducated teenage working girls from Manchester who had been sponsored. I was later to learn that six crew deserted and that two girls subsequently died of tuberculosis soon after the vessel's arrival.

48 Paxton's Wallpaper

One of my Parliamentary colleagues was Sir Joseph Paxton.[100] He was no common man. Affable and easy in his manners, homely and simple in his habits, and thoroughly warm hearted and sincere, he won the affection of every person who had the pleasure of knowing him. Though a man whom the Queen might, and did delight to honour, he was also honoured, esteemed, and loved, by all his work people, by whom he was known as the "grand old gardener".

If he was vain, as I have heard some people say, I never saw him display any signs of it. Like other men he no doubt had his failings, but they leaned to the side of virtue. Taken as a whole he was a thoroughly agreeable companion, a most excellent man, and a man ever ready to lend a hand to the struggling poor.

Though respected and esteemed for many years in the neighbourhood of Chatsworth, he was unknown to fame until 1851. The Crystal Palace in Hyde Park, which he had designed for the Great Exhibition, astonished and delighted all who saw it. The name of the designer of that truly dazzling and splendid building was then on everybody's tongue. My own first impression of the Crystal Palace – a most appropriate name – was of wonder and delight.

However, though the Crystal Palace earned for Sir Joseph Paxton his name and his fame, and though he may not be known to posterity by any other very great work than it, he was a man whose name should go down in posterity as a great benefactor of the human race.

During one of those evenings when the House of Commons was occupied with long and weary debates, Paxton, and I, when I had become an MP, used often to have a stroll together by the river Terraces. We would also smoke our cigars in the room downstairs given to the consumption of coffee and tobacco, and a glass of grog to those who liked it. We would compare notes and relate incidents of our onward struggles. It was during one of these occasions that Sir Joseph related to me an incident in his life, which in my judgment makes him a greater man than the designer of the Crystal Palace.

As everybody knows Sir Joseph Paxton commenced life as a young gardener in the service of the Duke of Devonshire in his beautiful grounds at Chatsworth. When he entered the service of His Grace, one of the oldest portions of the mansion was being demolished and was to be replaced by a building more in keeping with the other portions of that magnificent structure. It was his duty to assist in removing the rubbish from that part of the garden where the old building had stood. While employed, his curiosity was excited by a drawing on a piece of paper which had hung on the old walls.

While cleaning the dust and dirt off the piece of wallpaper which contained the drawing, he noticed that the cluster of plantains (or bananas) was double the size and contained in each bunch twice the number of bananas than any bunch he had ever seen or read about. He was curious to know where the original could be found. Taking the piece of paper to some person conversant with such matters, he ascertained that it was of Chinese manufacture and very old. He therefore concluded that this description of the banana plant must have been very plentiful at one time in China.

Part Five: Shipping Business Continues

Sir Joseph Paxton (1803–1865). NMM: LND 4–1, 462

Paxton then tried to obtain one of these plants. This was no easy matter to a person in his position. However, he made up his mind to do what he could. China was very far away of course. He knew no person in that far away country, but he remembered that a school companion of his had recently gone to Mauritius as a clerk to a Mercantile House on the Island. Mauritius, too, was a long way from China. However, it was the nearest place to it, where he knew anyone who he could communicate with, so he found out the address of his school companion and sent him the piece of wallpaper.

Paxton explained to his young friend what he wished and asked if he could assist him to find out if any banana plant resembling the drawing was to be found in any part of the Chinese Empire, or anywhere else in the East. This youth shared young Paxton's letter and the wallpaper cutting to his employers, who were merchants in St. Louis, and they very kindly sent it to their correspondents in Hong Kong.

Years passed away. More than four had elapsed since Paxton had asked his old school companion to assist him in the search. He had all but forgotten about the plant and his request, when one evening, on his return to his lodgings, he found at the door a large box which had been sent to him from China, marked outside 'roots' and 'carriage paid'.

When he opened it, he saw to his delight that it contained a dozen roots of the very description of banana plant which he had so long wished to obtain, and on the top, in a large envelope, the wallpaper he had sent to his school companion.

It would appear that this particular plant, which two or three hundred years ago had been very common in China, had somehow or other nearly died out, and it was only discovered after considerable research in a remote district to the eastward of Shanghai.

In the meantime, young Paxton had risen rapidly in the service of the 6th Duke of Devonshire, who throughout his life was his great patron and friend as well as employer. In 1836, when the banana plants reached Chatsworth, Paxton had been promoted to Head Gardener.

The roots were planted and flourished, and in the course of time became even more luxuriant, rich, and abundant in their clusters of fruit[101] than he had anticipated.

Among the numerous visitors to Chatsworth, and its magnificent gardens was John Williams,[102] the once celebrated missionary. Mr. Williams had long resided in countries where the bananas were the staple food for the people, and the roots that Paxton had imported and reared attracted his attention. Happy to meet the wishes of the great and good missionary, Paxton had a few roots packed for him and sent to the ship which Williams was about to embark to undertake his missionary labours on the shores and amongst the Islands of the Pacific Ocean.

It will be remembered that soon after Williams arrived at his missionary station in the South Pacific in 1839, he was massacred. However, the plants were not neglected, for these same roots were planted in the neighbourhood of Valparaiso. From there, their offspring were transplanted to Callao and Coquimbo. Although Williams did not survive to see these plants spread rapidly over the whole coast, they now form the staple food for the people who inhabit the western shores of the vast Pacific, and the numerous islands within the tropics.

The genius of Paxton, had, provided around the globe, a fresh and abundant supply of food for myriads of people. It has been said that he who can make two blades of grass grow where there was one, deserves to be ranked amongst the greatest benefactors to humanity.

Like the dates of Persia, or rice of India, and wheat of Europe, the banana is the chief source of food amongst large masses of people in tropical countries. The man who restored the use of this plant should be gratefully remembered, and held in long and affectionate regard, long after memories of the first Crystal Palace passed away.

49 Soporific Parliamentarians

In a letter to me my Parliamentary colleague Richard Cobden complained of the ventilation of the House of Commons.[103]. I wasn't surprised for I often suffered in a similar manner and during the last 10 or 12 years of his life, he was very much subjected to a feeling of depression on the brain, and especially a tightness across the forehead if he remained for more than an hour or two at one time in the House.

I often heard other members make similar complaints and no doubt the atmosphere of the House was at times very oppressive – much more soon after it was installed than later on.

Of course, in the construction of such a building, no expense was spared to make the ventilation as perfect as possible, and numerous plans were proposed. The plan adopted was the invention of Dr Reid.[104] It consisted of some very complicated machinery, which pumped hot or cold air, as the case might be, through the floor of the chamber in which we sat. The floor consisted of ornamental iron grating which was covered with coir matting.

Thermometers were placed in various parts of the chamber, which were examined every hour when the House was sitting, and according to the temperature we had a supply pumped up of either hot or cold air. The air came up either very hot or very cold, consequently honourable members used to have their legs either scolded with the hot air or frozen with the cold. Those members who did not wear Wellington boots suffered more, but everyone suffered if they remained in their seats while the pumping operations were going on.

The House soon rebelled against the frying or freezing process and one MP rose and emphatically declared that he would not allow the calves of his legs to be either pot boiled, or frost bitten any longer, and promptly demanded the patent atmosphere ventilating process should be forthwith abolished.

One speaker, I recall, was not more than three minutes on his feet till his voice suddenly died away and, with a look as if his tongue would not work properly in his mouth, he sat down with a thump on the seat by my side.

"Hello Sir James," I exclaimed "I thought you were going to make a great speech tonight."

"So I was," he replied after recovering his breath, "but there is something in the atmosphere of the House which, when I got up to speak, makes me feel as if I was choking and then my eyes get quite misty. The atmosphere must be really very bad. I had that speech 'well- tuned' thoroughly ready and said it over to my wife just before I came down here. But as soon as I got up, I thought I saw smoke coming out of the speaker's wig which increased to a blaze, and then I could not carry on – all my points zoomed into each other!"[105]

50 Insights on Four Prime Ministers

Though a committed Liberal, I was highly critical of Liberal administrations. When I entered Parliament as an MP, I felt that the Aberdeen Ministry[106] which held office, fell short of what a ministry ought to be which professes Liberal principles.[107]

Russell

Palmerston

Disraeli

Gladstone

Part Five: Shipping Business Continues

When the Aberdeen Administration was hurled from Office by an indignant people, they were succeeded by a yet more inefficient ministry under Palmerston. Those in the newly elected office wasted month after month of precious time in party squabbles amongst themselves, each contending for place and power, and when at length, an administration was permanently formed, one perhaps even more exclusively aristocratic than any which had preceded it, the same inefficiencies and the same favouritism which had disgraced the course of their predecessors in office were just as conspicuous as they had ever been. The plea set up to correct these delinquencies was rebutted with "better men could not be found."

The Palmerston ministry lacked men with practical minds and was formed of the scrapings up of the old Whig party, such as never had brains or genius exceeding the most ordinary mediocrity.[108] Nevertheless, I did not wish to see Palmerston's ministry replaced with one held by Disraeli. All hopes of reform from him were as vain as to expect figs from thorns, or grapes from thistles.[109]

Russell (1792–1878) Liberal Prime Minister 1846-1852, 1865-1866

Lord John Russell[110] was unquestionably an able and a clever man but, from what I have seen of his Lordship, I think that circumstances, and high birth, have had much to do in making him "a very great man". Had he not been the son of the Duke of Bedford I cannot suppose from what I have seen of him that he would have been twice Prime Minister of England; nor can I think that he, would have passed the Reform Bill of 1832 had it not been for the greater abler men whom he was at that period associated.

It must, however, always be said of Lord John Russell that on all great questions of progress during the last half century he took a lead, if not in the first rank, at least so as to earn for him the name of being the greatest little statesmen in history who, during that long period, have made their appearance on our political stage. Though somewhat critical, self-willed, and overbearing, he always rendered very material aid to the great measures of which Cobden and Bright[111] were the authors, and Peel[112] and Gladstone the ready and able converts.

Although taking an active part, it cannot be said that any of the measures necessary to accomplish the changes which took place, originated with his Lordship. Though his advocacy of them enabled them to be accomplished earlier than they might otherwise have been, they would all have been passed even earlier had Lord John Russell never made his appearance on the political stage.

I offer these opinions in no hostile spirit to his Lordship, as Earl Russell has always received me with as much courtesy and kindness as his naturally haughty, and at times somewhat repulsive, spirit would admit. Indeed, I have often in his recognition been favoured with three of his fingers when other members of the House of Commons, quite as good as myself, had only two, or perhaps not more than one! These were the measures of his friendship and familiarity.

The presentation of the expanded hand was only offered to his equals. Those persons who ought thus to be honoured were in his Lordship's opinion very limited in number. He graded his responses; a full hand – four – three – two fingers – or one finger depending on what esteem he held you in.

One finger was the common offering to the Commons – three or four to the Peers, and very few persons without these favoured circles ever had a finger at all or even a nod unless at Election times when he sat for the City – on such occasions he was condescending and friendly enough, and on one of these actually published a letter he had received from me with the conviction, I daresay, that it would secure for him additional votes among the seafaring population.

On all other occasions when his Lordship presented, as the case might be, one, two or three of his fingers, he would look at the person to whom he offered them, with an expression that read "now consider yourself highly honoured!" His small and withered face always bore the warning not to be too familiar with its owner.

One day Lord John Russell received me in his library at Chesham Place, and that morning presented me with three of his fingers: an unusual commendation, to a person in my position. Seating himself upon the edge of his own chair he gave me to understand that I was to follow his example and not cover the whole of it, which would be a sign of too great familiarity with his Lordship and his house. Then he smirked – the smirk consisting of half a grin and half a smile - and having done so he expressed a wish to know what brought me to his library in Chesham Place. Having heard what I had to say, he rose from the edge of his chair, smirked again, promised to "consider the matter" in a careless tone, gave another grin and smile and wished me good morning, presenting me with only two of his fingers on parting, as a hint, no doubt, that he did not agree with me, or that he did not intend to trouble himself with the question I had brought to his attention.

Dry and cold to a degree, and aristocratic to a fault, he drove away many men who would otherwise have been his warm supporters.

Palmerston (1784–1865) Liberal Prime Minister 1859-1865

History will have a great deal more to say of Russell than of Palmerston, for the one will leave the historian something to write about, whilst the other has gone and has left very little to write about.[113] Palmerston was the Minister of expediency, not of progress. He originated no measures by which his name can be remembered, and he gave a very lukewarm support to all these questions by which the names of Russell, Peel, Cobden, and Gladstone will be long remembered.

All that can be said of him is that he as a fine specimen of an English gentleman, and as a Statesman, or rather as a leader of the House of Commons he had a happy, way of expressing his thoughts, both in writing

Part Five: Shipping Business Continues

and in speaking, and in debate was ready and easy. Seldom, if ever, he lost his temper. Everything he said always appeared to be quite natural and altogether unprepared.

Throughout the whole of the Parliamentary Session when in power he was always to be found in his place – at half past four o'clock to a minute he would take his seat and remain there until the House rose. Then he generally walked home, it did not matter how late it was, unless it rained very heavily. This he did in his 80th year.

During the debates his custom was to sit with his arms folded, his head crouched between his shoulders, and his hat over his eyes as if sound asleep; and no doubt during the latter portion of his life he often was asleep in his seat. But he must have heard everything that was said for whenever a debate was wearing out, he would stand up, shake himself like a Newfoundland dog which had just come out of the water, and reply with good effect to all the leading arguments which had been used by the members who had opposed the views of his Administration. In this respect he was unmatched in the House of Commons. On great occasions when the House became excited, and its members were inclined to get out of order, no man could pour oil on the troubled waters with more happy effect than Lord Palmerston.

In his habits he appeared to be most regular when Parliament was sitting. His only relaxation was when the Speaker left the Chair at 3 p.m. for a quarter of an hour; he went to get some refreshment. At that time Palmerston would be found in the Tea Room with a large cup of beverage before him, and a thick lump of bread and butter in his hand which he was devouring with all the relish of a hungry school-boy, laughing and chatting all the time with anyone who happened to be sitting at the same table with him. In a word he was the most affable and most agreeable of men, but alas! he has gone and left no great measure of his own by which his name will be remembered.

When he died, he was Prime Minister and in the height of his power; so great was that power that for a year or two before his death it used to be a common remark "What will the Whig Party do without Palmerston". The general impression was that they would break up into fragments, and very many people looked forward to his death with gloomy foreboding. He died – suddenly – and for a moment there was a great ripple on the sea of life, as if a large stone had been thrown into the smooth waters.

He was buried in great pomp within the precincts of Westminster Abbey. Royalty and Statesmen of every shade of politics were mourners over his grave: the grave closed and with it the name of Palmerston. In a very short time, the sea was as smooth and tranquil as it had been before the stone was thrown. Not more than a year and a half after he was buried, we never heard Lord Palmerston mentioned.

An attempt to get up a subscription to raise a statue for him in Palace Yard, or anywhere else, entirely failed. Soon after his death a guinea subscription paper was put up at the Reform Club for a marble bust to his memory. It hung there for twelve months, and I have been informed that there was not a single subscriber to it!

I had occasion to visit him. Palmerston received me as if he had been for years on the most intimate terms. "Ah," he exclaimed as I was ushered into that well known political lumber[114] room of his, on the left-hand side of the hall as you entered Cambridge House. "Ah, glad to see you, come along give us your chat," and with such expressions made me feel instantly at ease in his presence.

That morning, as was usually the case with him, between the hours of 10 a.m. and 2 p.m., Palmerston was in the midst of his work. Great piles of papers were stowed away in the corners of the room, or lay in heaps on the table, and by his feet around the tall writing desk at which he stood with the pen in his hand.

He was dressed or rather he wore nothing beyond his shirt and a very loose pair of trousers which were kept in place by his braces which he had twisted round his waist. His waistcoat hung on his shoulders unbuttoned; his feet were encased in carpet slippers of the most spacious kind. As the morning was close and very warm, he had dispensed with his necktie, and the collar of his shirt was open.

"Sit down on the sofa there," he continued, after he had welcomed me by a hearty shake of the hand. "What news in the city?" and in this style he went on, so that I was quite at home with him from the moment I entered the room.

Having stated the object of my call, to which he listened with marked attention (as he did in all cases when an interview was granted), he then entered freely into the merits and otherwise of my proposal and frankly gave his opinion as if it was not a matter that required him consulting his colleagues or making his views a secret.

Even when he differed with the opinion you had expressed, you could not help parting with him in the best of humour and being satisfied with the interview. It was thus that Palmerston won the respect and esteem of many more members of the House of Commons than ever Lord John Russell could command, and many more votes were often given more out of respect for the man than faith in his political principles.

Disraeli (1804–1881) Conservative Prime Minister 1868, 1874–1880

Disraeli[115] became by far the most prominent actor on the political stage. Perhaps no actor ever played the part of Harlequin to such perfection, or with so much success, as Mr. Disraeli. In appearance this great political juggler was in all respects very much like the portraits which "Punch" every now and then gave us of him. He was just the old Jew cloths man; and though there are strong marks of a hint of intellectual development, numerous men very like him were seen every day.

Part Five: Shipping Business Continues

But Mr. Disraeli – or "Dizzy" – the name by which he was known in the House of Commons – was an astonishing man – no man more so in that great Assembly. Of Jewish origin and possessing neither the influence of high birth or great wealth – for he was at one time a very poor man – he had nevertheless long been the acknowledged leader of our proudest and most ancient aristocracy. His influence over them was truly surprising, more especially when it was well known that by some of them, he was personally despised – I might almost say detested.

During the 19th century no great party had been kept as well together as that which Mr. Disraeli led and ruled. They followed him through the most extraordinary and surprising changes, voting with him in favour of motions which a few months before they would have denounced in no measured terms. His power over his party was truly marvellous and stamped him as a man far above the ordinary run of men – indeed, no one ever doubted his great talents and abilities.

But what will history say of him? Not much beyond a passing notice of the fact that he was a political juggler of the most surprising skill and genius, for history can only record what a man has done, not what he has said ought not to be done. For more than a quarter of century Mr Disraeli opposed every measure of progress. His performances were amongst the most remarkable episodes of the political changes of the age.

He successfully attacked any Reform Bill introduced by the Whig or Radical Party on the grounds that it was revolutionary and dangerous, and then he passed a Reform Bill which went much further in favour of the people than any measure contemplated by Russell or Gladstone.

Gladstone (1809–1898) Liberal Prime Minister 1868–1874, 1880–1885, 1886, 1892–1894

Gladstone[116] was so far above the son of ordinary men. He neither required the accident of birth, nor of influential connexions, to make him what he was. In the face of great opposition, and against much jealousy, his genius and commanding talents had sound leadership of the House of Commons.

He was, beyond all question the leading man of the Liberal Party in the House of Commons and with the middle and upper classes. He was worthy of that position: he reached it solely by his abilities and if he had a failing as a Statesman it consisted in being in some things too clever.

In manners he could hardly be called like Palmerston "a charming man", but though at times curt, he was overall agreeable and obliging whenever he could be. He never procrastinated or said what he did not mean. He generally refused when he intended to do so, and not with the usual diplomatic "I shall consider the matter."

There are very few subjects of any importance likely to come under his notice which he had not considered and with which he was not quite as familiar, much more so perhaps, than those persons who came to him. Ready to a degree he picked up any subject with a facility truly astonishing. He would not in any instance arrive at sound conclusions, but he formed them sooner than most other men and in nine cases out of ten they would prove correct.

In this respect he was a striking contrast to Sir George Cornewall Lewis,[117] his predecessor when he was Chancellor of the Exchequer. I remember accompanying the late Mr Brown (afterwards Sir William Brown)[118] as one of a deputation to Sir George when he filled that office.

The object of the meeting was to recommend the adoption of decimal coinage in which Mr Brown had long taken a deep interest. Sir George received us in his usually quiet and quaint manner, listened as he always did very attentively to all we had to say, and then in his stuttering drawling way, wished us good morning without saying what he thought or even that he would consider our proposal.

"Ah," said Mr Brown as we left, "the Chancellor does not understand the question or at least he does not yet understand the advantages of decimalisation. It will take him a year or two to do so before he does."

Had our interview been with Mr Gladstone, he would have seen the practicability or otherwise of our proposals in less than half an hour and likely enough he would have shown himself much more master of the subject than any member of the deputation, even to its most minute details. In fact, there were few subjects he had not studied with care and on maritime questions I often found he knew more about them, even on their practical details, than I did.

One instance related to the construction of further Harbours of Refuge on various parts of our coast. These harbours had been recommended by a Royal Commission of which I had been a member and my motion was framed to seek Parliament's opinion on the recommendations contained in our Report. By the rules of debate the member submitting a motion for the consideration of the House is always allowed to wind up the debate – that is to have the last words before the division is taken.

There had been considerable discussions on the motion, and Mr Gladstone had made a long speech in opposition to my opening statement. In closing the debate, I briefly called attention to what appeared to me to be the weak points in his speech, at which he rose, contrary to the rules of the House. Members complained. Mr Gladstone however persisted in again addressing the House by way of "explanation" but, in truth, to endeavour to refute certain arguments of mine which had evidently produced a positive effect in my favour in the minds of various members, who, contrary to his expectation, had resolved to support my motion.

But while his explanation did not convert any members to his view, it exasperated a good many of those who perhaps had not fully made up their minds how to vote and the result was that I only just carried my motion in a House of 300 members by a majority of 17 against the Government. As a leader of the House, however, he was far from successful, as he had a habit of going too much into detail.

51 No Confidence Vote

By sticking to my principles, I sometimes landed in hot water and was unpopular. When the Prime Minister Lord Derby met the new Parliament in 1859, which had been called after his acceptance of office, he and his Conservative party were pledged to a measure of Parliamentary Reform.

The opposition under Lord John Russell, the Liberal leader, however, ever eager for place and power, would not consent that the Conservative party should be allowed time to prepare the measures to which they were pledged, and, as I think, with indecent haste he called the Liberal party together to consider a resolution to overthrow of the Government.

I felt it was not just, nor, as circumstances proved, was it for the interests of the Country, for Lord John Russell to form a coalition with Palmerston at its head to overthrow the existing administration.[119] Close on 300 members of Parliament assembled at Willis' Rooms[120] on the invitation of Russell and Palmerston. The former had his resolution prepared, though he himself was not to move it. The meeting was unanimous. In fact, I was the only member present who spoke against what I considered to be very hasty and unseemly proceedings. I said that as Lord Derby was pledged to reform, we ought at least to wait and see what kind of measure he presented for our consideration and approval.

Lord Palmerston expressed surprise that I could for an instant suppose that Lord Derby had any such intention, or that if he did present a Bill, it could be one which the Liberals could entertain. I replied that if he did not honour his pledge, then that would then be the time for us to turn him out. If that was the case, we as a majority, could either mould the proposed Reform Bill as we pleased, or if necessary, throw it out, and with it, the Administration. But neither Lord Palmerston nor Russell would entertain my suggestion for delay.

The course I had taken at the meeting was very soon known to Mr. Disraeli and the Conservative party – in fact he knew everything that had taken place at the celebrated Willis' Rooms meeting of the 5 May 1859.

He knew that I was the only Liberal member present who spoke directly against the course which was to be adopted. Disraeli had also heard of the complacent way in which Lord John Russell told the meeting that if the Queen sent for him, Lord Palmerston had agreed to serve under him. If, on the other hand, old Pam was sent for, Russell would serve under him. All these things Dizzy knew within an hour of the close of the meeting and I daresay he felt that the fate of Lord Derby's Government was sealed unless he could secure the votes of about twenty Liberal members. These votes were not to be obtained unless he distinctly pledged his government to certain measures of progress and Reform. Disraeli was ever ready to do more than Lord Russell to get and maintain place and power, and his first aim was to secure the votes.

The day after the meeting, Ralph Earle,[121] Disraeli's private secretary, favoured me with a call at Austin Friars. He called, so he said, though I did not believe him, to have my opinion on certain maritime questions, and stated that Mr. Disraeli would very much like to see me on that subject.

Although my opinion had more than once been asked by the Government on intricate shipping questions, I told Mr. Earle to tell the Chancellor that, although I had reason to suppose he wanted to see me this time about something else, I would call upon him that afternoon as he wished.

As I suspected Mr. Disraeli, knowing the part I had played the previous day, had thought that I was the most likely Liberal to secure him the votes he was most anxious to have. I told him frankly that I thought Lord Derby's Government ought to have a fair trial – that if he would pledge himself to certain measures, I would do what I could to secure for him a majority from amongst the Independent Liberals.

These measures consisted of a reassurance that they would introduce a Reform Bill which would meet the wishes of the country as represented by the moderate Liberal party. In addition, in regard to our foreign policy, they should in all cases be consistent with national honour and endeavour to maintain a strict impartial neutrality, interfering as little as possible with either the quarrels or affairs of other nations.

These conditions were laid out in writing and when approved by Mr. Disraeli (after having them for ten days in his possession), I pledged myself to do what I could to aid him. This document was signed by me and those other Liberal members, who after a time agreed to co-operate with me, and it formed the basis of our resolutions to vote on that occasion to maintain the Government. The original document with the signatures I destroyed in accordance with a pledge given to do so when the vote had been taken, but I kept a note of the substance of it.

The course however which Disraeli had taken, gave offence to many of the old school of Tories of his own Party. One of those who signed referred to the documents in a speech to his constituents, and foolishly added that Prime Minister Lord Derby and Mr Disraeli had also signed it (or words to that effect). This statement was taken up by the Morning Herald, and other newspapers, and of course Lord Derby and Mr Disraeli were obliged to deny that they had signed any such document.[122]

Mr Disraeli however endeavoured to get out of the matter altogether. He went as far as to say that he had not seen the paper, forgetting that in a letter addressed to me dated 24 May 1859, he had said "I return the paper of which I generally approve"! But Dizzy had his failings in this way when it suited his purpose.

Part Five: Shipping Business Continues

In due time the debate arrived, and continued, I think, for three or four nights. It was a long and very animated, and a very close and severe struggle. Seventeen members signed the document I have named, and five other Liberals promised to support the Government, but only twelve held to their pledge. The screw had been put on at such a rate by their party, and by their constituents, that eight of "my party", if I may so term it, on that occasion either voted against the Government or did not vote at all. The Tories lost by thirteen.

Had the rebel Liberals kept their promises on that occasion the Tories would have kept in office and from what has since transpired would have introduced a satisfactory measure of reform.[123]

Part Six

American Civil War

(1861–1865)

52 Atlantic Crossing

On 8 September 1860 I sailed on the Cunard steamship *Europa* from Liverpool to Boston U.S.A. Although I had visited a few American ports when I was a sailor boy, this was the first time I had visited on business. I was forty-four years old.[1] My objectives in visiting the country were threefold.

Firstly, for quite a while I had needed a change from the arduous duties of both parliament and business combined, so the visit was for health and pleasure. Secondly, for many years I had had many visits from American shipowners when they came to England. I wanted to call in on them in their country. My business with the United States was quite extensive and I was well known to almost all of them. My third and last objective was political. Although the newspapers of Britain and the United States made it appear that my visit was not official, it was however at least semi-official. My sole object was to settle various maritime questions which I felt were outstanding.

When I got on board a couple of hours before the *Europa's* departure from Liverpool, I found her as clean as a whistle, even though on the previous day she had shipped more than 1,000 tons of coal. Everyone seemed in the most urgent haste to have his or her things put away in their cabins before those of anybody else. My own cabin was a large and airy one. It had been allotted entirely to me, but finding a friend, Robert Chalmers[2] of Edinburgh, and his wife on board, who had a much smaller cabin, I placed mine at their disposal.

All the first-class cabins had been taken and the *Europa* had her full complement of passengers. There was the usual mixture, but conspicuous amongst the throng was a man who looked like a sporting character, and who was in a violent rage because the purser of the ship had informed him that he could not take a couple of dogs with him.

He had charged up the gangway without permission from the Cunard Company office. After a great deal of noisy altercation, he was told that to

Part Six: American Civil War

take dogs was 'against regulations'. The sportsman wound up by threatening to write to *The Times*. His threat seemed to calm him down, and although he was at great pains concocting the letter, I learnt later he never sent it.

A life at sea with nothing to do is indeed a monotonous one. Every day is alike. To eat, drink and sleep would seem to be the sum and substance of a passenger's existence on a long sea voyage. During mealtimes you keep the same seat for the voyage. Breakfast every morning at 8.30 to the minute, lunch at noon, dine at 4, tea at 6 and supper at 9 p.m. I often wonder how it is possible to eat so often, but some persons on board ship eat because they have nothing else to do and always seem to be hungry. I met several interesting people on the voyage and the twelve days passed quickly and pleasantly away.

I know of no feeling more pleasant than reaching a snug harbour after a stormy passage, so our arrival in Boston Bay was most welcome. It was made more interesting, not only on account of its beautiful scenery but also for its historical association.

Vessels of every size and description filled the many anchorages in that notorious bay. The celebrated Baltimore Schooners, with their graceful forms and tall and tapering masts were moored. There were also numerous stout Indiamans which had just arrived laden with the produce of the East, produce which had been taxed so heavily that led to the revolution which separated the Colonies from the parent country. Steamers, with their lofty saloons, reminded me of floating palaces, added life and novelty to this truly interesting scene.

Everywhere there were signs of advanced knowledge, combined with unusual vigour and energy. I felt that I was about to enter a country and mingle with a people who were at least our equals, and in understanding and skill perhaps our superiors. That was my first impression of America and the Americans.

Soon after I arrived in Boston, I spoke at a special meeting at the Boston Board of Trade. Here I presented my views on shipping with the aim of obtaining more aligned maritime laws between Great Britain and the United States. I outlined the various issues that were non-aligned.

In my introductory remarks, I said that I did not visit the United States as a diplomat, much less as a special envoy, as had been reported in some quarters, but I came as a man of business to converse with men of business about commercial matters in which both countries were deeply interested. My government was aware of my visit and sanctioned it.

I addressed various issues where there was discord between the two countries ranging from collisions at sea to privateering. There was a host of other issues to be addressed: rules of the road at sea, navigation lights, on-board crime and desertion, altercations, signing on of sailors, navigation laws and registry of ships.

I discussed all these points at the meeting, and I beseeched them to lobby their government in the hope that changes were made to their shipping laws.

William Schaw Lindsay

From Boston I proceeded to more Northern states, visiting nearly every seaport of importance in Vermont and Maine, and holding meetings where necessary. I therefore visited Portsmouth, Portland, Bath and Newbury port, Brunswick, Bangor, and other places in the state of Maine where a large portion of the shipowners resided with whom I had done business. In these places I was quite struck that the habits and customs of the people of these Northern States in many respects resembled the Scots.

I left the fine old Town of Boston and its pleasant inhabitants and travelled to the great maritime and commercial city of New York. That city can be reached from Boston by more than one route – by rail or by steamer and rail. As time was short, I took the former route. It occupied eight hours.

During my stay in New York, the city was graced with a visit from the Prince of Wales. A Ball was held in his honour, and I was provided with an invitation. Three thousand or so of the elite of New York and the neighbourhood were present. It is said that the fabulous sum of 500 dollars was given for a ticket by some rich blockheads who, not ranking with the aristocracy, had not received invitations. It was a very beautiful scene. Everything went off very well, except for the collapse, for a time, of a part of the platform due to the poor workmanship of some corporation contractor.

The ladies, however, despite the amount spent on their apparel, were not to my fancy. They fell short of the grace and beauty seen in similar gatherings in our own country. They had too much of the hot house plant appearance about them and if they would only follow the example of an English girl and take more outdoor exercise, they would become more beautiful women, and also stronger and more healthy mothers. Going on a fox hunt, with a leap now and again over a five-barred gate, would improve both their health and their beauty.

I left the "gay and glittering scene" at 2 a.m. At six o'clock the same morning I departed for the far West via the River Hudson to Albany, the capital of the state of New York and from thence to the far-famed Niagara. After my stay in Niagara, I took a short sailing trip to Buffalo, where I only stayed a few hours. It is the first of the astonishing cities of the West. Situated on the shores of Lake Erie it carries on an extensive trade, especially in grain with New York and with Europe. At the beginning of the present century, Buffalo was altogether unknown and the site on which it stands was then a dense forest. Now it is a busy handsome city with a population of 80,000. From Buffalo the railway skirts Lake Erie to Cleveland which is more modern but now the Lake port of the State of Ohio and contains upwards of 60,000 inhabitants.

From Cleveland the course of the railway runs along the banks of the lake through many thriving farms until it reaches the city and port of Toledo of the Western extremity of this inland sea. Though only founded in 1836, 24 years ago, Toledo is already one of the chief commercial stations of the vast lake trade and is the terminus of the Wabash and Erie Canal, the largest and most important of all the canals in the United States.

Part Six: American Civil War

From Toledo I proceeded by rail to Chicago, perhaps the most surprising city of the West. I spent three days there. The city has seen an astonishingly rapid growth which is not surprising when you consider the vast natural resources of the rich agricultural country for which it is the chief outlet. Its position signifies it to be the Commercial Capital of the Northwestern States. It is a central hub for railways, and it is conveniently positioned on the Great Lakes. It has the rich valley of the Mississippi on the one hand and the vastness of prairie country on the other where many million quarters of grain are now produced, which always finds a ready market throughout the world.

It was in Chicago that I learnt of the death of Herbert Ingram MP the founder of the Illustrated London News.[3] He died tragically with his son in a shipping disaster in the Great Lakes. Of nearly 400 persons on board only 98 survived.[4] His son's body was never found.

I then proceeded from Chicago to St Louis on the Mississippi and back to the Great Lakes and from thence to Toronto, Montreal, and Quebec. After that I travelled to New York and on to Baltimore, Philadelphia, and Washington. I then returned to New York from whence I took my departure in the *Persia* for England after a very pleasant and interesting tour of between two and three months.

During my visit I had the pleasure of meeting and conversing with James Buchanan[5] for an evening. He had been President for four years and I had known him in England. I never saw such a change in any man as Mr Buchanan. He was no longer the hale rigorous man who was our guest when he last visited Glasgow only four or five years ago. He had become aged, careworn, and infirm. His hands looked as if he had been affected with palsy and his lips had dropped.

All his former nerve and vigour had gone. I was told that this threat of separation on the part of the South, which was becoming serious, had quite changed him and he struck me as being in the broken-down state of health unable to cope with the emergency.

I remained in Washington for eight days. I also met General Lewis Cass[6] (Secretary of State), William Trescot[7] (Under Secretary of State), Howell Cobb (Secretary to the Treasury) and with many members of both Houses of the Legislature. I met up with Captain Raphael Semmes,[8] who was then Secretary to the Navy Board, or rather, the Lighthouse Board as it is called.[9]

I was also introduced, and had long conversations with, Abraham Lincoln,[10] the President Elect in his home in Springfield and with the Vice President Hannibal Hamlin[11] with whom I spent an agreeable evening at his farmhouse near to Bangor in the State of Maine. I had the pleasure of spending a few very agreeable days with Lord Lyons,[12] then our Minister for Washington, from whom I received kindness, courtesy, and assistance.

On my way to Washington, I had held various meetings with the Members of the Chamber of Commerce of the City of New York to discuss Maritime relations with their country.

William Schaw Lindsay

Above left and above right: James Buchanan, 15th President of the United States. There was a visible decline in his health.

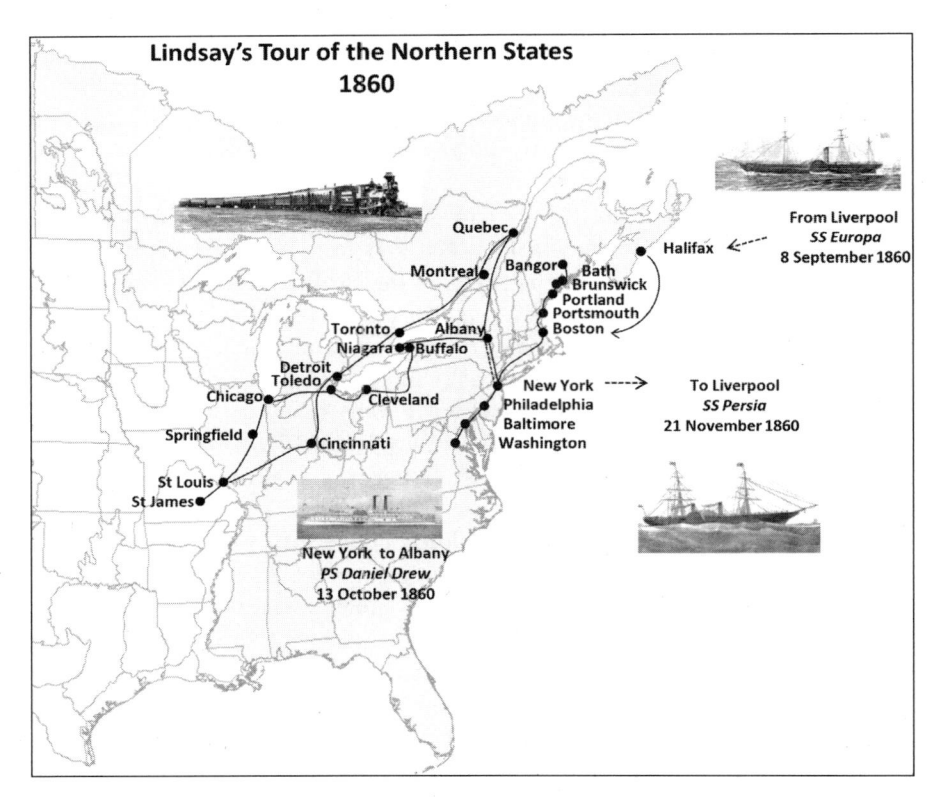

Lindsay's Tour of the Northern States, 1860.

53 Hudson River to Niagara Falls

New York is the commercial capital of the United States and must, I think, ever continue to be so. Its harbour is one of the finest in the world. At the time of my visit there were more seagoing vessels owned in New York than in London and Liverpool combined, excluding steamers. Indeed, the seagoing registered tonnage of the United States then exceeded that of Great Britain.[13] New York also carried on a direct trade with every port of importance in the world.

I do not know that I ever witnessed a finer sight than the view from the windows of Mr A. A. Low[14] in Brooklyn, with whom I dined and spent an evening. His home looked down on the East River and commanded a view of the whole bay, the entrance to the Hudson River, with the peninsula on which New York itself stood, and the rising city of Jersey in the distance.[15] As far as the eye could see there were forests of masts of vessels of every class, from the European liners and the handsome Indiamen to the fast and graceful Baltimore clippers and Cuban vessels.

Craft of every kind, with numerous steamers and ferry boats in which 300 people and a dozen carriages and other vehicles could be carried with ease, studded the Bay and views.

These Ferry Boats, plying between Brooklyn and the various other places, were most convenient and handsome affairs. On each side they were fitted with handsome saloons for the passengers, and in the centre, there was sufficient space for carts or carriages.

You may gain an idea of the City's trade from the following figures. The previous year the value of its imports exceeded two hundred million dollars and that year it expected upwards of one hundred million, while the receipt of gold from California was forty million dollars per annum.

I think that the sail from New York to Albany, up the Hudson River, is one of the finest of its kind in the world. It is greatly enhanced by the size and beauty of the boats on which you make the trip, and the conveniences, and luxury, of their cabins. The view of the great city, when we set off on a fine bright morning, is, with its domes and spires and busy hum of life, a sight of considerable interest.[16]

With Jersey City on the opposite shore and Staten Island in the distance, studded with beautiful villas, it forms altogether a most attractive scene. There lay moored fleets of great ships, towering steamers, and river craft of various kinds. We soon reached the "Palisades", precipices which rise in some places 500 feet above the river in an almost straight line from their base, richly wooded on their summits, and extending twenty miles along the Southern shore of the Hudson.

At the town of Sing Sing, which is thirty-three miles from New York, there is a succession of charming country residences. Here the river Croton joins the Hudson, and two miles further on the aqueduct which carries its clear water to the Metropole, commences. Perhaps no city in the world has a better or longer supply of water than New York.

This great work reminded me of one nearly as great which my brother-in-Law Robert Stewart[17] brought about when he was Lord Provost of Glasgow. He faced much opposition from Council Members but won through and enabled the city to be supplied with fresh water from Lake Katrine.[18]

Conspicuous from the river, and within a mile of Sing Sing, is the great prison of the State. I was told that the building for the male prisoners was about 500 feet in length with accommodation for 1,000 persons, and that for the females three-quarters as large. The whole site, with outbuildings and yards occupies about 130 acres.

Passing various pretty towns and villages we next reached Caldwell's landing at the foot of the Dunderberg Mountains, a very fine and extreme range, from which I was informed the view is truly grand and beautiful. The Hudson here in my opinion far exceeds in grandeur and in beauty any part of the Rhine. Though there are no views of feudal castles, there are the modern villas of the merchants of this great and free country.

Amid this mountain range stands West Point, the celebrated military school or college. Here the paddle steamer the *Daniel Drew* stopped to land and load passengers, the first berthing place since we started from New York fifty-four miles away.

We arrived there at 8.20am and had performed the journey in 2 hours and 12 minutes, for I timed it, or at the rate of 25 mph. I never was in a boat that steamed at anything like her speed, and I afterwards learned that the steamboat, American built and engines, was the fastest vessel in the world. I had no idea of her fame when I stepped on board and indeed, I had not previously heard of her. She was very much in appearance like the other ordinary passage boats on the Hudson.

Her saloon on deck was light, roomy, and elegant – and her form was graceful with a very fine wedge-like bow and remarkable clean stern. She moved through the water with great ease and hardly any motion, and her speed, as she passed the various points of land and vessels anchor, more resembled that of an express railway train than a steamer.

She was a paddle wheeled boat, however when she started the motion of the paddles was not felt and was barely heard by the passengers in the saloon. The very small wave rising from her bows was hardly disturbed as she cut through the water like a knife. I am forced to ask how it is that we have no similar boats in England. We have nothing on our rivers, or along our coasts, approaching the *Daniel Drew* in beauty, grace, elegance, comfort, and above all in speed.

But how is it that no country's vessel has reached a speed on the ocean much beyond the speed attained by the *Daniel Drew* on the river? The *Persia*, the vessel on which I returned to Britain is, I understand, the fastest ocean steamer in the world, and yet on the quickest run she could make across the Atlantic, she only managed 16 mph. Her great American competitor the *Vanderbilt*, on the same voyage, fell short of this speed as her average speed was just below 16 mph. The greatest average speed on the ocean then reached was only 16 mph, while on the river, 25 mph has been attained. The *Great Eastern* was an attempt at increasing ocean speed and her builders were certain that she would average at least 20 mph on a voyage to India. But her speed did not prove equal to that of the *Persia*.

We continued our journey to Albany, passing attractive townships, wonderful scenery, and magnificent mountain ranges. Albany is situated 145 miles from New York and the rapidity of the *Daniel Drew's* passage gave me five hours to spare before the train started for Niagara. I employed the spare time at my disposal in strolling through the Town or rather "City" as that is the name given to any place in America containing more than 10,000 inhabitants.

The much-overlooked pioneering work of Robert Fulton[19] whose early steamer, the *Clermont*, paved the way for passenger steamers, commenced in Albany on the Hudson River. I came across this amusing reference to him:

Fulton's first Steam Voyage, by R.W. Haskins.[20]

Some years since, I formed a travelling acquaintance, upon a steamboat on the Hudson River, with a gentleman, who, on that occasion, related to me some incidents of the first voyage of Fulton, to Albany, in his steamboat, the 'Clermont', which I never met with elsewhere. The gentleman's name I have now lost, but I urged him, at the time, to publish what he related, which, however, so far as I knew, he had never done.

I happened, said my narrator, to be at Albany on business, when Fulton arrived there in his unheard-of craft, which everybody felt so much interest in seeing. Being ready to leave, and hearing that this craft was to return to New York, I repaired on board and inquired for Mr. Fulton. I was referred to the cabin, and there found a plain, gentlemanly man, wholly alone, and engaged in writing.

"Mr. Fulton, I presume?"

"Yes, Sir."

"Do you return to New York with this boat?"

"We shall try to get back, Sir."

"Can I have a passage down?"

"You can take your chance with us, Sir."

I inquired the amount to be paid; and, after a moment's hesitation, a sum, I think six dollars, was named. The amount, in coin, I laid in his open hand; and, with an eye fixed upon it, he remained so long motionless that I supposed there might be a miscount, and said to him, "Is that right Sir?"

This roused him, as from a kind of reverie; and, as he looked up at me, a tear was trembling in his eye and his voice faltered, as he said, "Excuse me, Sir, but memory was busy, as I contemplated this, the first pecuniary reward I have ever received for all my exertions in adapting steam to navigation. I would gladly commemorate the occasion over a bottle of wine with you, but really I am too poor, even for that, just now; yet I trust we may meet again when this will not be so."

Some four years after this, when the 'Clermont' had been greatly improved, and two new boats made – making Fulton's fleet three boats regularly plying between New York and Albany – I took passage in one of these, for the latter city. The cabin on that day was below; and as I walked its length to and fro, I saw I was closely observed by one I supposed a stranger. Soon, however, I recalled the features of Mr Fulton; but without disclosing this, I continued my walk, and waited the result. At length, in passing his seat our eyes met, when he sprang to his feet, and eagerly seizing my hand, exclaimed, "I knew it must be you, for your features have never escaped me; and although I am still far from rich, yet I may venture that bottle now." – It was ordered; and during its discussion Mr Fulton ran rapidly but vividly over his experience of the world's coldness and sneers, and of the hopes, fears and appointments, and difficulties that were scattered through the whole career of discovery, up to that very point of his final, crowning triumph, at which he so fully felt he had at last arrived.

"And in reviewing these,"' said he, "I have again and again recalled the occasion and the incident of our first interview, at Albany; and never have I done so without its renewing in my mind the vivid emotion it originally caused. That seemed, and still does seem, to me, the turning point in my destiny – the dividing line between light and darkness, in my career upon earth; for it was the first actual recognition of my usefulness to my fellow men."

Such, then, were the events coupled with the very dawn of steam navigation – a dawn so recent as to be still recollected by many; and such as Fulton here related them, were causing a revolution in navigation, which has almost literally brought the ends of the earth into contact.

It was about six o'clock in the evening when I left Albany for Niagara by train in a 'sleeping car'. Our journey took thirteen hours and when I got up in the morning, we were drawing towards the railway suspension bridge which connects Canada with the United States and where the train stopped for one hour. The station is about two miles from the village and the falls. I took up my quarters in one of the large hotels on the American side which overlooked the mighty cascade. There are certain objects in nature which fill the mind with awe and make an impression upon it which never fades. Niagara Falls is one of them.

I have often heard it said that the bulk of the tourists are disappointed with the first sight of Niagara and that they have not been able to fully realise the extent and grandeur of the mighty cataract. Such however was not my experience. I was struck with surprise, and I may add wonder and awe. The moment my eye was able to embrace the falls they made an impression on my mind so instantaneous that I was for some time riveted to the spot where

I stood when first I saw them. There was a solemn and terrible majesty about them which instantly commanded my undivided attention.

It has been my lot to visit the four quarters of the globe and the two objects of nature, and the two of art, which have made the greatest impression on my mind are – Niagara Falls, Vesuvius, the unburied city of Pompeii, and Stephenson's vast railway bridge across the St Lawrence.

54 What the Dickens!

Beyond my business correspondence with American shipowners, and the ship masters who frequented my office in Austin Friars, London, my knowledge of the American people was both limited and superficial. Like too many of my countryman, I had attempted to study and appreciate their character through the writings such as the unjust and unwise production of Mrs Trollope[21] or Charles Dickens written many years ago. I did not know then, as I know now, that these works, though professing to give a true and faithful account of the manners and customs of the Americans, are little better than a caricature of a great and a remarkable people.

They however at the time had the effect of giving me an idea that the Americans were in many respects entirely different to the British, and that many of them were absurd and ridiculous in their manners and in their attire. I imagined their everyday wear was one of green coats with brass buttons, and cotton trousers, with wide-awake hats, with the addition of a red necktie and striped waistcoat on Sundays.

Such is the vague notion of what I expected to find in America, with the addition that every man I met chewed tobacco and squirted the juice from his mouth without much regard to his neighbour's comfort and none whatsoever to their carpets and the polished stones.

On my arrival in Boston these notions were however entirely dispelled. I found society there quite as good as some of our best society at home. They were better educated and, in some respects, class for class, more refined. The dress of the inhabitants resembled our own. They did not wear wide-awake hats and green coats with brass buttons, nor did they squirt tobacco juice from their mouths as Mrs Trollope or Charles Dickens had led me to believe. In New York and the other great cities, and especially in the former, I did see a few people that these writers had described, though only a very few, but not one in the extraordinary attire which was said to mark the true born Yankee.

Amongst the numerous letters which kind friends in Britain had supplied, there was one from Mr Cobden introducing me to Mr Banks,[22] then Vice-President of the Illinois Central Railway, in which Cobden and I were interested to invest in.

Mr Banks was anxious, as well as Cobden, that I should visit Chicago to inspect the railway and judge for myself of its capabilities and prospects. As it was my intention to visit the West anyway, I accepted letters of introduction from Mr Banks to the manager of the line at Chicago. When I reached Chicago, the manager wished that I should take a trip over the whole length of the line as far as St Louis on the Mississippi. He offered to send someone from his office to accompany me the whole distance and furnish me with any information I might require. I accepted his kind and courteous offer.

The train, which I had been recommended to take, left early in the morning. I was therefore up, not merely in good time, but I was at the station before any of the officials had made their appearance. As there was no person to take charge of my luggage, I placed my portmanteau on the platform and took my seat on it to wait the arrival of some of the porters. I had not to wait long before a porter made his appearance, carrying in his hand a kind of knapsack belonging to the person by his side. This knapsack attracted my attention. I turned to the owner who was dressed just as Mrs Trollope and Charles Dickens had so graphically described.

He was a middle-sized man, rather slightly built and he might be about 35 years of age. He had a free and easy way about him which was more conspicuous because he walked, or rather sauntered, along the platform. Both his hands were shoved right down to the very bottom of deep pockets in a very loose pair of yellow cotton trousers. He seemed to feel the chill of the morning, and no doubt kept his hands there for warmth. His dress was just what I had expected to see everybody wearing when I landed for the first time in the United States. His coat was of a pear green colour, and it had the brass buttons, with the addition of a bleach white collar, which I supposed to be his Sunday best. He had a waistcoat consisting of alternative red and yellow stripes. Around his neck was one of those fashionable ties. It was fastened close to the neck by means of a conspicuous ring and a large stone in it which looked like, though it was not, a monster ruby. His boots were laced in front and were very broad in the toes. On his head he had a wide-awake hat with a very tall crown. All in all, he was just the kind of Yankee which Charles Dickens had described and which I had hitherto looked for in vain.

Having thus quickly surveyed him, with much satisfaction, I was very surprised when he walked up to me and said, without any introductory remarks, "You're Mr Lindsay I guess," looking me hard in the face as if he had seen me many times before and twisting a piece of tobacco in his mouth as he spoke. I nodded my assent and asked him how he knew me.

"I just knewed you" he said "and, as you say you're Mr Lindsay, I may say that I am the guest that our Governor has sent to accompany you over the line. Come this way and have your traps booked."

In due course we had our luggage entered and took our seats on the train. I was delighted to have the company of so thorough a Yankee, for I thought that through him I would have an excellent opportunity of knowing more about his countrymen. He was indeed a fine specimen of the kind of man I had long expected to meet, for he cussed and squirted the tobacco juice from his mouth without much regard to either the dress or the feelings of his neighbours.

The train proceeded no more than a quarter of an hour on its journey when my companion commenced to inspect his knapsack from which he pulled out a large brandy flask, and at once unscrewing the cork and dusting the mouth of the flask with the cuff of his green coat, he begged me to have "a drink".

I however declined the invitation at so early an hour in the morning, at which he seemed surprised, remarking that it was the proper time to drink as it "removed the fog and the damp which collected in the stomach before breakfast". But as I did not see the advantages to be derived from an early drink in the light he did, he did not urge it upon me and putting his own advice into practice he took a long pull at the brandy, stroking his stomach with evident satisfaction as the liquor ran into it and drove the chill away which seemed to have been troubling his from the first.

"I guess" said he, after recovering his breath, "that if you were long in this country and obliged to turn out early in the morning, you would find a drink at this time do you a mighty deal of good"; and he confirmed this repetition of his advice with another drink and again rubbed his stomach, which after the second pull at the flask, seemed to glow with warmth.

From these remarks I do not wish it to be understood that my new-found friend was a drunkard – far from it, for during the whole of the journey that day the brandy flask was not again called into requisition. He evidently confined his drinks to the morning, but the chew and squirting was unceasing. Curious to know to what part of the United States my companion belonged, I made the usual enquiry in America as to the State he hailed from.

"State?" he said, "I guess I ain't from any State."

"Then where are you from?" I enquired, under the impression that as he did not hail from any State, he would be from one of the districts or territories in the far West not ripe for admission into the Union, and where the population was limited and somewhat rough and original like himself. But instead of informing me as I expected that he belonged to one of those districts from which the Red Indians had not been thoroughly rejected, he, to my surprise, informed me that he was from London.

"London?" I repeated after him, adding "I presume you mean London over the way" – pointing towards the North and referring to a town of that name in Upper Canada on the line of the Grand Trunk Railway.

"No, not that London," he said, "I mean London, your London. I knew you Mr Lindsay. I have often been in your office at Austin Friars – why, I was in the office" he continued to my amazement "of John Chapman and Co[23] the Shipbrokers of Leadenhall Street [24] – Don't you recollect me now?" But I did not then, though I recollected him afterwards.

"Well Mr Lindsay," he resumed, "I have now been here for seven years – your friend Mr Cobden got me the position in the Illinois Railway as John Chapman and Co, and I did not get on very well. I like my job so much that I guess I won't go back to the old country again. I have far more of my own way here than ever I had at home. This is the country for a man who likes independence as I do" and as he finished, he stuffed a fresh piece of tobacco into his mouth and looked at me as much as to say – "Don't you think I'm right?"

I did not presume to offer an opinion then but contented myself by looking at him and repeating the words "Leadenhall Street", "John Chapman and Co" and wondering who he could be. At last, he put my mind at rest by informing me that his name was Augustus Dickens[25] – brother to Charles Dickens! "Pickwick Dickens" he added by way of explanation as he saw that I was more than surprised by his statement.

For a time, I thought that the brandy had loosened his tongue and that he was joking, but the grave manner in which he conveyed the information, combined with the fact that Cobden had got him the situation he held, induced me to believe him. I could not however contain my surprise any longer and wound up our conversation by remarking that had he lived in Chicago twenty years before, when his brother visited the West, I could have sworn that he was the very man – the veritable Yankee – who Charles Dickens had in mind of Americans at home.[26]

On my return home, one night in the lobby of the House of Commons, I told the story to a fellow MP who, thinking that it was just banter, repeated it to Charles Dickens himself the first time they met. Dickens laughed heartily, remarking that he had a brother, a clerk in the Illinois Central in Chicago, and though he had not seen him since he left England, he thought it very likely that he had become quite the character which I had described. And as such often proves to be the case, for in my travels in America, I found many of my countrymen, who had had settled there for some years, have more of the so-called 'Yankees' in their dress and manners than the Americans themselves.

I recollect having many conversations with Cobden about investing in land along the railroad. I agreed with him entirely as to the prospects of the line, but we differed as to the time when the large prospective profits of the undertaking could be realized. He thought they were close at hand; I, on the contrary, held the opinion that, while all the land would in time find purchasers, they would rather belong to the next generation than to our own. In this instance my views came true.[27]

55 Lincoln's Ham

Mr Banks, who became General Banks, was a strong supporter of Mr Lincoln. During the civil war he was one of Lincoln's Generals, though not a very successful one. When returning from St Louis I spent a night in Springfield which was Lincoln's hometown.[28]

Mr Lincoln was at that time a lawyer in a good and respectable, but moderate, practice. His house was quite plain. The door was in the centre,

Abraham Lincoln. 16th President of the United States, photographed in February 1864 by Anthony Berger; the five-dollar portrait.

with a window above and a window on either side, above and below, with green venetian shutters. The green door had a brass plate on it, on which was printed in large letters "A. Lincoln".

Mr Lincoln had just then been elected President of the United States of America, and Mr Banks, who was on a visit to Springfield to see him, invited me to accompany him. I readily consented. The important meal with all Americans residing in country towns is tea at 6 p.m. As we called on Mr Lincoln between 5 and 6 o'clock, he invited us to remain with him to eat. I had travelled a long way that morning and had not had anything to eat since breakfast at 8 o'clock so I was very hungry. Nor had Mr Banks eaten. Mr Lincoln saw this and asked his wife, when we sat down, "to bring in the ham."

This request seemed to stagger Mrs Lincoln, who gave her husband a very significant look as much as to say that she would do nothing of the sort, and when he repeated his request, she exercised her household prerogative by remarking that "English gentlemen" – referring to myself – "were not accustomed to such solids at teatime."

Mr Lincoln however was resolved to satisfy our wants despite his wife's hints. In the room where we sat there were two doors and behind must have stood the kitchen and larder, for the President Elect stalked out of the one door and returned by the other bringing with him a large Virginia ham and laying it down on the table, to the horror of Mrs Lincoln but to the delight of Mr Banks and myself! We spent a very pleasant evening with Mr Lincoln despite his wife who seemed determined not to part with her ham.

When Abraham Lincoln was assassinated in April 1865, Andrew Johnson became the 17th President of the United States.[29] I heard it seriously whispered by men in high and responsible positions that Johnson had at one time some mysterious connection with the murderer or murderers of Mr Lincoln.

I have even heard it said by persons who ought to know that Johnson had been in personal communication with Booth a day or two before Mr Lincoln lost his life. But that the man, or men, who instigated or committed the murder, had any communication with any member of the Government of the South, or committed the terrible act in the interests of the Confederate cause is altogether unworthy of notice. They could have had no motive for such a dreadful act and the death of Mr Lincoln could in no way benefit any portion of the Southern people, or in any way tend to promote the Independence of the Southern States. That Johnson instigated the murder in the interests of the South is simply absurd and I know that the Southern leaders never held him in much esteem.

Lincoln's murder was no doubt committed by persons who had a personal hatred of Lincoln and Seward, or who, having suffered by the war, conceived the idea – the insane idea – that the murder of these two men would bring the war to a close and secure the independence of the South.[30]

56 French Naval Threat

Whilst the threat of Civil War simmered in the United States a very uneasy feeling prevailed in Britain regarding the French intention towards us.[31]

Many persons, who have however since that time changed their opinions, then had the greatest suspicion of the emperor and maintained that his professed desire to maintain peace with England was a mere cloak to cover his hostile designs against us. Indeed, so strong was this impression that if any member of the House of Commons, which I sometimes with others did, ventured to say that we thought the emperor was honest in his professed desire to maintain peace, and above all peace with England, we were often met with shouts of derisive laughter, especially by the old school Conservatives; but they were not alone. There were men high in office on the Liberal side of the House who had, or acted as if they had, quite strong suspicions of the emperor's honesty.

Mr Cobden referred to this subject, and to the increase of our naval expenditure, in many of his letters to me. I also received a good many letters from the French Senator Chevalier on the subject.[32]

The naval armaments of France were, at the time, the subject of much discussion in the House of Commons and elsewhere, and our own newspapers, which were supposed to represent the views of our government or rather Palmerston's views, never failed to magnify these assets, especially when our own naval estimates were published. The increase of French ships of war was the grand excuse for an increase of our naval expenditure. Many people in Britain concluded that Napoleon III was about to play the game which his uncle once contemplated, and to invade our shores.[33] Their suspicion was that he was arranging mighty armaments in the shape of Iron-clad ships, flotillas, and transports for no other purpose. Our own excessive expenditure tended in no small degree to confirm this absurd apprehension.

The Government therefore of Lord Palmerston, as well as the old school of Tories, had to a great degree encouraged the feeling of panic which prevailed in some quarters. Indeed, they were very much responsible for it, as Lord Clarence Paget with all his professions of peace was constantly insinuating that France must have hostile intentions against us or the emperor would not be increasing his navy at the rate which Lord Clarence Paget said he was doing. But it was to a purpose. Paget, as Secretary to the Admiralty, could not have carried his extravagant navy estimates through the House unless he had frightened members with some great bugbear of this view. In truth large sums of money were, one session especially, awarded solely on the grounds that we might maintain our maritime position with France – and that we should have a significantly higher naval supremacy.

Now no member of the House of Commons including Cobden himself would have offered the slightest objection to our naval expenditure had it been true as alleged by Palmerston and Paget that France was our equal in naval armaments – but it was not true – far from it and though the Government had the means of fully satisfying members of its truth or otherwise, they did not embrace the opportunity. Perhaps it was necessary however that Government had to maintain a certain amount of patronage without which it would be unable to exist, and therefore it asked for more money for our naval and military forces than the whole of our foreign relations required.

But whatever may have been the cause, our great naval expenditure at that time did a great deal of mischief beyond oppressing the people of both Great Britain and France with anger and unnecessary burdens in the shape of increased taxation. I say in France as well as with us because many persons in that country, seeing our great naval expenditure, thought that we intended to invade them! Monstrous as that idea might have appeared, it was even more logical than the report that the emperor had serious intentions of invading us.

Both countries were therefore at that time playing the game of "beggar your neighbour" on a larger and more dangerous scale than it had even been played before. The idea of France invading us drew extra sums of money from our pockets to be expended on Fortified Iron-clad ships and on our dockyards. On the other hand, that expenditure created alarm in the minds of many people in France and, to be protected from our imaginary invasion of their shores, the Government of France was obliged to make a greater show of expenditure on naval armaments that it would otherwise have done.

It was when this feeling was at its height that I had a remarkable and altogether unexpected conversation with the emperor in regard to the naval armaments of the two countries. I also had letters from Chevalier giving details of Naval Expenditure from 1852.[34]

He explained that in 1854, 1855, 1856 France spent large sums. The cause of it was very clear. During the Crimean War they had to spend a great deal because they had put all their ships to sea. They had to keep a fleet in the Baltic, and more importantly in the Black Sea. They had soldiers and ammunitions to transport to Sebastopol, as well as wounded to re-embark for France, and their army was more numerous than ours.

He also indicated that the analysis regarding naval ships in both countries was biased. It included French ships which were not fit for war and yet it discounted British ships which could be utilised. In addition, the number of French Iron-clads included those still in production or planned.

Chevalier wrote to me saying that the current naval expenditure, quoted by the British, was £12,000,000 for the French and £5,000,000 for the British. He said that this was completely incorrect.[35]

In the early part of January 1861, after I had seen the emperor regarding the Repeal of the Navigation Laws of France, I was required to visit Sicily on business of my own and was absent from Paris for 12 to 14 days. On my return Mr Chevalier told me that both the French Minister of Commerce[36] and the emperor wished to see me again on the question of these laws. On 31 January I therefore saw his Majesty at the Tuileries, but the information he required regarding the changes I had ventured did not occupy more than a quarter of an hour.[37]

When about to take my leave, the emperor said, in his usual quiet and apparently careless way of speaking when he wished to attain his object. "By the way Mr Lindsay you have been in Toulon since I saw you."

It so happened that when I reached Marseilles the steamboat for Palermo did not leave until the following day and having nothing to do in Marseilles, I took a return ticket to Toulon and spent a portion of the day in the arsenal and dockyards and sailed round the *La Gloire*, about which so much had

Part Six: American Civil War

been said and written, then at anchor in the Roadstead. I knew no person at Toulon and during the 5 to 6 hours I spent there I had no communication with anyone nor could I have supposed that any person there knew me. I was therefore very much surprised when the emperor remarked on my visit there. I hid my surprise and said that I had spent a few hours at the arsenal and dockyards on my way to Palermo. I added that as I had the opportunity I went to see if it was true that such a large sum of money had been spent on naval armaments as had been stated.

"Well, what did you see?" he laughingly asked though it was evident that he wished to obtain as much information regarding the state of the French and English naval forces.

I replied with the facts; that I saw nothing in the dockyard which in any way alarmed me as an Englishman, adding that I thought that John Bull would find our *Warrior* would be a match for two of his *La Glories*.[38]

He laughed and remarked that it was always the case with the English people, they never would admit that other people could produce ships superior to their own or allow any Nation to rival them at sea – or words to that effect. I said that that was one of our failings and that we were certainly very jealous of any rivalry in what we considered our Maritime supremacy.

"But" he said, "surely you do not think that I wish to rival the naval power of England?"

La Gloire: the world's first iron-clad warship, launched in 1859. Copyright: © National Maritime Museum, Greenwich, London, UK. PAH0973

HMS *Warrior:* Britain's answer to *La Gloire* Copyright: © National Maritime Museum, Greenwich, London, UK. PAH927[39]

This was bringing the question much nearer home than I could have wished or expected, but as it was put to me, I was obliged to answer it. I did so by saying that I certainly did not think so, but that there were a great many people in England who did. I then remarked that whatever I might say could be of little or no avail either one way or the other for such was the jealous spirit of our people in regard to any attempt on the part of the people of France to rival us that if he built one Iron-clad we would build two and if he built two we would build four and so forth; and that no amount of argument in the House of Commons or anywhere else could in that respect alter the fixed determination of the people of Great Britain to keep far ahead of France in Naval supremacy. I was thus candid with His Majesty and as my opinion was invited, felt it my duty to state candidly what I consented to be the true sentiments of the great majority of our people.

These remarks led to a lengthened conversation which the emperor concluded by the following remarkable confession:

> I desire peace – it is my intent and my most anxious wish to maintain it especially with England. I have seen enough of the glory, no, not the glory but the misery of war, and as the prosperity and happiness of my people depend upon peace why should I seek war? – but there are people in your country and a few here also who will persist in putting a wrong construction

upon my actions and remonstrance over disbelievers whatever I say in regard to my great anxiety to maintain peace.

I was much struck with the remarks and the way in which he made them. I saw that they were not mere words of fervour and that he was thoroughly in earnest in what he said. Indeed, he could not have had any object in deceiving a person in my unofficial and altogether uninfluential position; but I offered no remark beyond deploring the existence of this very unfortunate and pernicious misunderstanding and hinting that it might be well if something more was done beyond the expression of an anxious desire to maintain peace.

"What more can I do?" he said somewhat abruptly and then went on to remark that statements were made in England regarding his naval force which were very far from the truth – that many writers in the press and men of influence in Parliament greatly exaggerated his ships, not only their number but vessels merely ordered to be built of which the keels were not laid.

He then remarked that these were all published with a full description – and looking formidable on paper, the people of England got into a state of alarm and asked what he could do, and what his intentions were, with such a large fleet. Then making the matter more personal he said:

> You ought to know that when the Crimean war broke out, I had to depend on England for transports and that I had very few suitable vessels of war to send either to the Black Sea or the Baltic, and at this moment I wish to send a ship to China, but I find I have no vessel to spare for the purpose. If anything more can be done to satisfy the misunderstanding and put an end to any unnecessary apprehensive alarm, I shall be only too happy to consider any suggestion you may have to make.

When I had written to the Emperor's Private Secretary, Monsieur Morguard, to ask for an interview in regard to the contemplated change of the Navigation Laws, I had no idea that the interview would have led to a conversation of the character I have thus briefly and imperfectly described, consequently I merely remarked that I was not then prepared to offer any suggestion beyond the idea that if England on the one hand acknowledged France as her superior in Military affairs, France on the other might admit that England was superior to her as a Naval power and that some such understanding might form a basis to regulate in some degree the Naval armaments of the two countries.

The idea was somewhat crude but curiously enough when I mentioned it the same evening to Lord Cowley, he told me that the emperor himself had, during the Crimean War, made a somewhat similar suggestion to England but that it had gone no further. From what Lord Cowley stated I understood that the nature of the proposal was to the effect that if France had control of the combined military forces, England on the other hand should regulate to have entire command over the naval armaments.

As my own idea was somewhat similar, I was not surprised that the emperor appeared disposed to entertain it formally. I therefore, on my return to London, informed Lord Clarence Paget of the conversation and asked him to mention the matter to Lord Palmerston and Mr Gladstone. He did so; but many months afterwards I ascertained that Palmerston had thrown cold water upon it and had I believe told Paget that he would neither trust the emperor's word nor his bond. Mr Gladstone on the other hand had entertained the idea with much favour and had approved of a paper which Paget had sketched out embodying my ideas on the subject with suggestions of his own regarding this practical application. This paper he gave to me to take with me to Paris when I returned a week or ten days afterwards.

It would however appear that Paget afterwards became alarmed at his directives to me.[40] I presume he was afraid lest Lord Palmerston should find fault with him, though it is not easy to conceive why he would have done so. The agreement, secret or otherwise, if it would have been entered into, would at least have enabled the Governments of each country to have known the actual extent of each other's naval forces and if the relative and defined limits on each side were exceeded then they could have required an explanation and thus have put an end to a state of doubt and uncertainty. However, be it as it may, Paget would render no further assistance himself. He continued to encourage me personally to pursue this line, as merely his own private envoy, and he would "like very much if some such agreement could be carried into effect".

Though Lord Cowley had communicated to Lord Russell what had taken place and though his Lordship expressed to me his approval of some such understanding between France and England, when the Navy estimates were laid by Paget on the table of the House of Commons on the following July, they were as large as they had been the previous year and the excuse was still "the increasing Naval armaments of France"!

Upon this important point there was much controversy. Lord Palmerston and Paget with their followers repeatedly asserted that France was spending more money on her Navy than we were doing. And though it was repeatedly shown by me and other members of the House that the naval expenditure of France was barely one half of that of England, any statements that we made could not allay the alarm created by the authoritative statements of the Government – and did not do so.[41]

In his letter to me, Paget said that he read my letters with great interest. He could not rely on the statements put forth by the French authorities. He said that the year before he was in Toulouse and saw with his own eyes the French Iron-clad *Invincible* ready for launch, all but caulking which was being proceeded with by hundreds of hands. He said that she was just about to be launched so how could the French say she will not be ready for two years.[42]

My friend Cobden suggested that I visit the dockyards of France and "take stock". Even if I had accepted and acted upon his suggestion, I could not have expected the people of this country to have accepted my statements as facts in preference to the allegations of the Government.

I however conveyed to Lord Clarence Paget a special request from the Ministry of Marine of France that he would visit the French dockyards and judge for himself. He further added that every means would be placed at his Lordship's disposal for ascertaining the facts and that under the circumstances, the Government of France would feel much indebted to him if he would condescend to ascertain the truth instead of making statements based upon idle rumour.

Paget declined the invitation. The idea of the English Secretary to the Navy taking stock in a French dockyard was so novel and no doubt in his opinion absurd and preposterous that it could not for an instant be entertained. He even, indeed, became alarmed in case it could be known that such a thing had been proposed by the Minister of Marine of a foreign country and that I, an English Member of Parliament, should have been made the medium of conveying such an extraordinary proposal.

The consequence was that our naval expenditure continued, and the Government was enabled to retain their position by having the usual amount of patronage at their disposal. A matter, in their opinion, of mere consequence was the extra taxation and disruption of commerce which these false rumours created and encouraged.[43] But though Paget declined to visit the dockyards of France, other men of influence were ready to avail themselves of the offer which the French Minister had made.

At that time a Royal Commission was investigating our naval expenditure and two of its members, the late Lord Gifford[44] and Mr Dalglish[45] the member for Glasgow, accepted with pleasure letters of introduction from me to the Minister and visited all the dockyards of France. The two gentlemen went carefully and minutely into the whole question, and they returned to this country convinced that the cry of alarm raised by Palmerston and Paget had no foundation in truth. They learnt that the naval expansion of France in the dockyards was very far short of our expenditure. In addition, as far as that country was concerned, we were not justified in our vast outlay in ships and fortifications.

Such was also the testimony of other competent and important witnesses who visited the dockyards and arsenals of our great neighbour, but Palmerston turned a deaf ear to all such statements and under these circumstances I did not think it advisable to again name the subject of an agreement to the emperor. And thus, a matter which might have had happy results and led to a better understanding than that which existed between France and England, was stifled at the onset by the Prime Minister of England.

57 Onset of the American Civil War

During my tour through America, I did not visit the Southern States. I might have done so had time permitted, but I had little or no connection with any person in the South. I knew no one there except for three merchants[46] and they were all Englishmen by birth.[47]

Besides, although I had one or two urgent introductions to go south, when I reached Washington from the New York Chamber of Commerce, I felt that the maritime matters I had brought under the notice of the North were not concerns in which the Southern people had an interest. They had little or no connection with shipping.

But even if I had had the time at my disposal, I would not have visited the ports of the South then, as by that time there were rumours of the civil war (which soon after burst forth with such fearful fury). As the policy of the South was more in accord with my business sentiments than that of the North, I feared that my appearance might have caused confusion on both sides.

Though the differences between the two sections were often discussed in my presence, and I was often invited to offer an opinion, I declined to do so, especially in private company and while in America. I should never have thought of doing so in public. I could not however refrain from listening, so before I left the United States, I was somewhat familiar with the views on which the North and South differed.

Mr Cobb,[48] the secretary to the Treasury, but more especially Mr Trescot, were the only persons from whom I had heard the Southern view. On the other hand, the Northern view was continually poured into my ears. This constant denunciation of the conduct of the South, perhaps tended to enlist my sympathy in its favour, even though all my interests, and all my friends and business connections, were in the North.

A few months after my return from the United States, the Civil War was on the verge of breaking out. I received a letter from an esteemed shipping friend from the Northern States. He sought my views on the impending crisis. I replied as honestly as I could:

> The great problems to which you refer are now about to be solved – can the vast republic be held together without bloodshed? Events have already proved that it cannot.
>
> You are now about to enter upon the second and more terrible act of the rash drama, to see if the Union can be restored and held together by bloodshed and coercion. I daresay three-quarters of the people of the Northern States are of that opinion; and therefore, it may appear presumption on my part to offer any opinion; but you invite me to do so.
>
> Well then, when we look at history, when I consider the vast extent of your country, I find that the interests of the South are opposed to the policy of the North; when I see that the two sections of your people differ in feelings and associations, in fact differ in almost everything except language; and when I hear that they are resolved by the vote of their several State Legislatures, to arm themselves and raise a vast army, not

to coerce other States or attack the North, but to defend themselves, I cannot but feel that there must be a separation, and that no force which the North could bring to bear will ever re-unite the Southern with the Northern States. But even if re-united by force of arms, you cannot treat them as a conquered people. That would be contrary to the first principles of a republican form of Government. You cannot force them to be content and happy, and unless they are so, it is impossible for the Union to be held together.

My political feelings are all in favour of the people and that form of government which has been their form of government; but I cannot hide from myself the fact that thirty million people, spread over thousands of miles of territory, cannot be held together by a republican form of Government when a large portion of them are discontented and unhappy. Almost every friend I have resides in the North, and as the business of my firm comes from that quarter, I would, if I could, view the question as you do; but history, reason, and common sense appear to me, under the circumstances I have named, to be opposed to your views.

You will ask, what, then, is to be done? That question is not easily answered. But I will venture to say what I think you ought not to do, and that is, do not, I beseech you, march your armies into the South. If you do, there will be the most terrible bloodshed the world ever saw, and after all you will be farther from the object you have in view that you were when you commenced the carnage.

What then? The only answer I can give is to part, and part in peace; and I say so in the cause of humanity, and in your own interests, as well as in the interests of the world. Feeling, as I do, that the civil war can have but one termination; but separation will be easier now than it will be after you have roused every angry passion, sacrificed thousands of lives and millions of treasure,[49] and given a blow to your country and your commerce from which they will not recover in our generation.

I will not presume to offer an opinion in regard to the terms of separation, but the good sense of your people, and the spirit of justice which pervades their actions, will soon settle their contentions when the sword is laid aside! [50]

These were the words that I addressed to my friend, and which found their way into the public press in New York before the war began. My words were not heeded. On the contrary, I received many angry letters. I mention it with regret for I had many friends in the Northern States. I said these things in the cause of peace.

The movement for separation of the States was not the impulse of the moment. Those who suppose that this movement arose six or twelve months before the war were under a sad misapprehension.

Letter to the Dishonourable W S Lindsay MP from an angry Northerner in Boston, 12 June 1861. "Enclosed find sample of hemp used in America for hanging traitors." "Jeff's Knave-y: Seven wise men of Gotham went to sea in a bowl." NMM: LND 7.53[51]

    I conscientiously believed that the system of taxation, which the Northern States had carried out, had been a system of great injustice to the Southern States. As far back as 1828, they commenced a system of high tariffs. In 1833, the tariff was increased to such an extent that South Carolina entered her protest, and then threatened to do that which she has since done, to secede from the Union. She said, "We are ground down with taxes which the people cannot pay." Upon that, the Northern States entered into a 'compromise tariff'. That tariff subsisted for ten subsequent years, the taxation or high duties upon imports being gradually reduced, until, in 1843, protection ceased.[52]

But in 1846, Congress passed a higher tariff, passed too at a time when the Southern senators were not in the house. On many articles of that tariff, they imposed a duty of not less than 200 per cent. When the Southern States looked to the exports of America, and where these exports came from, they resisted what they considered to be oppression.

Exports amounted to 350 million dollars and if they analysed that account, they would find that, out of this 350 million, 250 million consisted of the produce of the Southern States, and upwards of 200 million consisted of cotton, while less than 100 million comprised the exports of the North.

In 1850, while the North and West had very materially increased the number of their representatives in Congress, the South had materially diminished. It then became a serious question with the people of the South, and they saw the effect of this in the rapid increase of taxation, or rather of protective duties; they felt that they were saddled with heavy taxes, while practically they had no voice in their imposition, because the majorities of the West and of the North swamped on almost every occasion the representatives of the South.

The South is a purely agricultural country, and its polity and interest is perfect free trade – to sell its cotton in the dearest market and buy the manufactures it required at the cheapest. But the interest, or the supposed interest, of the North was protection; and when the exports and imports of the United States are analysed, it is not very difficult to arrive at the main causes of the disruption. It was, in fact, taxation without representation.[53]

The consequence was that the Southern States, being in a minority in the Federal Legislature, had numerically no voice in the distribution of those taxes, though paying their proportion of those taxes as 2½ was to 1.

It was not surprising, then, that the South made a stand and said, "We will in future govern ourselves, as we have not the weight in the Federal Legislative, which we think we are entitled to have." They rebelled.[54]

Having some knowledge of that country, I saw from the first it was hopeless to attempt to subjugate ten million people resolved to govern themselves, and that force of arms would never re-unite the broken Union.

Consequently, when differences first arose between the Northern and Southern States, and long before I ever saw or heard of any person connected with the Confederate Government, I ventured to lift my voice in the presence of my constituents, at public meetings and in Parliament against a terrible war which I thought would be as in vain and futile as it was wicked; and by so doing my firm lost a great many more commissions from the North than they were ever likely to gain from the South.

During the War, which commenced in April 1861, I became friends with Mr James Mason, Emissary for the South. He always asserted that there had been deception, on behalf of the North in its handling of the South, at the start of the War. I asked him for proof.

In a letter to me, he explained that the State of South Carolina (Fort Sumter is in that State), sent three of her most distinguished Statesmen as emissaries to the Government in Washington in January 1861 on a mission of peace. Mr Buchanan refused to receive them in their official character and returned their communication they had addressed to him. Again, in February 1861, the same State, sent its Attorney General to Washington, as a commissioner with representative powers, and who in a like manner, was refused to be received by the Government.

The news spread rapidly throughout the Southern States. They, too, had been equally oppressed. The states of Mississippi, Georgia, Alabama, Florida, Louisiana, and Texas were forced by necessity to follow the example of South Carolina, and by the votes of the people, they declared themselves separate from the Union, from an oppressive compact which they could no longer endure.

It was towards the end of February 1861, that these seven states assembled in Congress in the city of Montgomery, in Alabama, and there formed the Provisional Government, of which Mr, Davis[55] of Mississippi, was elected the President.

The first act of this Government was to send commissioners to Washington, who, in the language of President Davis, had full power "to settle all

Jefferson Davis, President of the Confederate States.

questions of disagreement between the two Governments upon principles of right, justice, equity, and good faith".

The Commissioners arrived in Washington on 5 March 1861, immediately after President Lincoln had been inducted into office, and on the 12th of that month they officially communicated their mission to Mr Seward, Secretary of State. No reply was received until the 8th of the following month, and, when received, it was an abrupt refusal to treat with them. In fact, the Government of Washington would not even hear what they had to say.

At the earnest request of Mr Seward, "with a view to promote the peaceable settlement of all difficulties", the commissioners were persuaded, through the medium of Mr. Justice Campbell[56] of the Supreme Court of the United States, to refrain from pressing for an early answer to their communication. During the interval, the Commissioners were assured through the same source that Fort Sumter, which commanded the entrance to Charleston harbour and threatened that city, would be evacuated.

While assurances were given in the most solemn manner, the Government of the United States was secretly preparing a great naval and military expedition, its objective being the reinforcement of Fort Sumter,[57] and that this expedition had actually sailed for Charleston, while the commissioners were kept at Washington waiting for the "peaceable settlement of all difficulties" promised by Mr. Seward. The knowledge of this expedition reached the Confederate States only two days before its actual arrival off the port of Charleston. Fort Sumter was taken possession of by the people of Charleston in self-defence.

President Lincoln then issued his first proclamation, calling for a force of 75,000 men to "subdue the South". The men of the South flew to arms, not to make an aggressive war on the North, but to defend their homes and their hearths and the sovereignty of their states. Virginia, by the votes of her people, then joined the seven states which President Lincoln called for troops to subdue. North Carolina, Arkansas, Tennessee, Missouri, and Kentucky followed in rapid succession, and thus commenced the most terrible civil war recorded in history.[58]

Those in Britain most affected by the Civil War in the States were the cotton workers in the North of England. As the blockade tightened, so the supply of cotton dried up, and although a stockpile had built up, this rapidly diminished. The shortfall in supply resulted in unemployment and hardship for the workers. In Blackburn there were about 15,000 persons receiving relief, in Preston more than 12,000, and in Preston there were no fewer than 17,000 claimants upon the relief fund.[59]

The Confederate agents in Britain, notably William Yancey,[60] always thought that when the country became short of cotton, and when the people of the manufacturing districts were thereby thrown out of employment, Britain would be obliged either to force the blockade or make a move to end the war. However, he and many of his countrymen were wrong when they thought that cotton was King with us.[61]

Britain was not alone in the hardships caused by a shortfall in cotton. Emperor Napoleon III of France referred to the Blockade, saying that his people were suffering through the scarcity of cotton and were likely to suffer even more. He concluded by saying that if it met the views of the English Government, he would be prepared with England, to demand, and, if necessary, enforce, either the opening of the Southern ports or an efficient blockade.[62]

The emperor agreed with me that the blockade was ineffective. I had heard that more than 600 vessels had run the blockade from April until November 1861.[63] The inefficiency of the blockade would be justification for European interference. Napoleon told me that he would have the blockade lifted had England agreed. In the end the British did not want to risk lifting it for fear of provoking a war.

Mr Gladstone perhaps felt a greater interest in the American Civil War than any other member of Lord Palmerston's cabinet.

What his views were, I have no means of knowing beyond what he himself has said in public. He stated empathetically, within a year of the great struggle commencing, that had he alone had to decide the question, he would then have recognised the Confederate States.

I also think that Lord Palmerston was favourable disposed to do so and had the South at that point agreed to a plan where their slaves would then have been emancipated, even if it had been stipulated that the act was not to come into force for 20 years, I believe Lord Russell and the members of the cabinet would have changed their opinions in regard to the right of the Southern States to withdraw from the Union.

Mr Gladstone was always eager for information and at his request I wrote to him at great length regarding what appeared to me to be at that time the prospect of the War – I do not appear to have kept a copy of that letter, but I found a portion of the rough draft of it in which I state, writing on the 12 May 1861:

> Events have already proved that the Confederate States are a Nation – They have a legislature chosen by the people – a constitution, a government and an army – From all I can trace they are united to a man – resolved to govern themselves and to defend their States and their homes and maintain their constitution – They may be conquered or even annihilated but they can never be brought back to the Union so as to be of any practical service to it… They may by the point of the sword be freed back to the Union, but it will be but a nominal allegiance – They will ever be the Southern States – different in feelings – in association, and in everything to the people of the North.
>
> If the great powers of Europe make no move, this terrible War in America may continue for years – I do not think it possible now for the American people to settle it amongst themselves – the protest of Europe against its atrocities, by the acknowledgement of the South, or some such move, or

the sheer exhaustion of one or other of the contending parties, can alone bring it to it to a close.

In the latter case, from the determined spirit which is displayed, there must be an awful sacrifice of life, so awful that if the War continues for three years, which is much more likely than the "three months" which Mr Seward[64] predicts, there will be more lives sacrificed in the struggle than ever was sacrificed in any war ancient or modern – I think Europe ought not to witness without protest such a wanton desecration of human life.

I wound up my letter as follows:

From the numerous letters which reach me, I can speak of the depth & strength of the desertion of the people of the South to this cause. They are defending their states and their homes and will do so until all they have, even their lives, are sacrificed – we have done much to acknowledge them as belligerents, so let our Government with France now say they are a Nation. I am convinced that expression of opinion alone would at once stay the ravages of War with all its horrors and restore peace – peace in which we, not merely as a commercial, but as a Christian people, are deeply interested! I am [yours etc]

Mr Gladstone appears to have been struck with the letter for I found the following note from him in which he states that he will "at once" bring it to the members of the Cabinet.[65]

11 Downing Street, Whitehall
13 May 1861.

Dear Mr Lindsay
Many thanks for your letter. I have read it with great interest, and I shall at once bring it to the knowledge of my colleagues. Believe me
Very faithfully yours
W E Gladstone[66]

58 Threat of War with the United States

The Provisional Confederate Government sent Commissioners to Europe to convince them, particularly Britain and France, to recognise the Southern States as an independent Nation.

Mr William Yancey was appointed to the British post. I had not known Mr. Yancey personally. I had seen him and heard him speak when I was in Chicago during October 1860 but had not on that occasion been introduced to him. I was much struck with his power of speech and eloquent delivery. He had been for many years a member of the United States House of Representatives for his native State Alabama.

Yancey arrived in the summer of 1861, not long after the commencement of the War. As my Sunderland speech had been so liberally commented upon by the American press it was very natural that Mr. Yancey should be eager to meet me. I had a good deal of correspondence with him, met him several times, and he was often a guest in my home in Shepperton. Whatever he may have been in Congress, he displayed great judgment and prudence in the management of the difficult and delicate affairs he had to conduct in this country.[67]

I presume his appointment was *pro tem*, for not many months after his arrival, it was announced that Mr. James Mason and Mr. John Slidell had been nominated as the representatives of the South, the former to Great Britain and the latter to France.

When the news first reached this country that Messrs Slidell and Mason had been taken from under the protection of our flag on board the West Indian Mail packet the *Trent*, *The Times* published a strong article in favour of the course which the Government of the United States had adopted. The account of this illegal act caused a scene of the greatest excitement I ever witnessed in the City of London.

Commander Williams was the Officer in charge of the mails on board the *Trent* at the time. As the only representative of Her Majesty's on board it fell to him to protect the British flag and he did so in the true style of a British sailor. I met him shortly after the affair and although I forget his exact words they were in substance – "This ship is under the British flag and those who forcibly take it from any person under its protection, which Messrs Mason and Slidell now are, offers an insult to my Queen and Country which must and shall be resisted if they are not restored." What Williams said was the exact state of the law and was endorsed by the unanimous voice of Europe.[68]

Captain Wilkes,[69] who commanded the ship that captured the Commissioners and their Secretaries Messrs Macfarland[70] and Eustice,[71] returned them, without their families, to the Northern States to await their fate. This illegal act very nearly caused a war between Britain and the United States. The French promised their moral support.[72] After eight tense weeks the Commissioners were released and made their way to Britain.

On the morning the article in *The Times* appeared, I happened to call upon Mr. Yancey on my way to the City, and he was in a great rage, saying that John Bull had lost all his ancient pluck. He often referred to the incident, and did not hesitate to say, as Mr. Mason himself often said afterwards, that he was sorry they were set free. He knew if they had not been, we must have gone to war with America – and then the South would have unquestionably achieved its independence.

Part Six: American Civil War

"I am free," Mr. Mason used to say, "but what a pity, for had I not been, the South would have been free."

On the arrival of Mr. Mason in the spring of 1862, Yancey returned to the Southern States and had a narrow escape from capture on his way home. Within a year afterwards I heard of his death.

Mr. Slidell was the representative of the Confederate States in France. At the Court of the Tuileries, and though unacknowledged, he was received with much more courtesy and frankness by the emperor and his ministers than Mr. Mason experienced from Lord Russell.

The two Confederate Commissioners were men entirely different in their character. A Northerner by birth, Mr. Slidell had married a southern lady of fortune, and settled in the South. Warm and earnest in his attachments to the cause of independence, he lacked the shrewdness, perseverance, and placid endurance which Mr. Mason displayed in so remarkable a manner throughout the whole of that terrible struggle.

I frequently had the pleasure of spending a day with Mr. Slidell in Paris, but I always found him much more impatient and more desponding as to the results of the war than Mr. Mason, but he never complained, although his own financial losses must have been very great. The greater part of his wife's and his own property consisted of plantations, which the war rendered of little value. Property, savings, and investments in the South were rendered worthless by the war so that he and his wife must have suffered very severely in their fortunes.

When Mrs Slidell[73] and her young family – two daughters (young ladies about 17 & 19), with a son (a boy of 14) – reached London without her husband, I could not do otherwise than offer to tender her any assistance she might require. I did this considering her lonely position, and the interest I took in the cause in which her husband had embarked. They stayed a while with me in my Manor House. John Slidell wrote to thank me:

> I haven't words to express the sincere gratitude which I & my family entertain for your great kindness to them during their stay in London. Be assured, my dear Sir, that they will ever cherish the most vivid recollection of the very many friendly attentions of Mrs. Lindsay & yourself at a time when they stood so much in need of sympathy & encouragement.[74]

Mrs Slidell went to France to join her husband. Their oldest daughter married the son of Erlanger the well-known Banker of Frankfurt and Paris. He was a man of reputed great wealth and considerable commercial influence on the continent.

Except for the short time that Mr. Yancey was here, Mr. Mason represented the Confederate States in this Country throughout the war and remained here for about twelve months after its end. He then moved his family to Canada in exile. During the whole of his time in England I was on the friendliest terms with him. He was often my guest for weeks and sometimes for a

John Slidell, Commissioner to France, Confederate States of America. The Miriam and Ira D. Wallach Division of Art, Prints and Photographs: Photography Collection, The New York Public Library. (1860–1920).

Part Six: American Civil War

THE GREAT SURRENDER.

America surrenders the *great* Commissioners—England surrenders her great pretensions—Jeff. Davis surrenders his great expectations.

"The consideration is ample."—SUMNER.

THE PORTRAITS OF EARL RUSSELL, MASON, SLIDELL AND SEC'Y SEWARD, ARE PHOTOGRAPHY.

Published by E. Anthony, 501 Broadway, New-York.

The Trent Affair. Confederate diplomats James Murray Mason and John Slidell are shown aboard a vessel. On the left is England's Foreign Secretary Lord John Russell standing on land with one foot on the back of a lion and ripping up a piece of paper entitled 'Right of Search'. On the right stands President Lincoln's Secretary of State William S. Seward with Confederate President Jefferson Davis in the background.

month at a time at Shepperton. I have met few men whose companionship I have enjoyed more than that of Mr. Mason. Every person who really knew him could not fail to respect and admire him. Mr Mason during his stay in this country was very much respected. Even the most bitter opponents of the South had not a word to say against him. Cobden, though strongly against the South, always mentioned Mr Mason's name to me with the highest respect.[75]

In October 1863, the Confederates sent another Commissioner to represent them in Europe. Colonel Lamar[76] was a wealthy and very extensive planter in the State of Mississippi. He had been one of the members of the House of Representatives and when the Civil War broke out, he joined the Confederate Army and distinguished himself as a soldier. But his health gave way, and he was appointed Commissioner to Russia. He however never proceeded further than this country as he found on his arrival here that the Emperor of Russia had pronounced in favour of the North.

While in Britain, waiting for further orders from his government, he was often my guest at Shepperton and attended a meeting with me in the neighbourhood.[77] It was soon discovered who he was, and loud calls were made for him to make a speech. He did so and a report of the proceedings found their way to the London Journals. The fact that I had introduced Colonel Lamar to the meeting induced the "Morning Star" to make a virulent personal attack upon me, so personal that I was obliged to answer it.[78]

I may add that the "Star" was bitterly against the South from the first to last. It had also a grudge against me personally, for when John Bright and his brother-in-Law started the paper, they looked to me to assist them with the funds.[79] I declined to have any pecuniary interest in any newspaper upon principle and I think my stand was sound.

Soon after the commencement of the War, I received a letter from my old school friend, Mr Young, in Montreal, Canada.[80] In it he expressed his opinion about an invasion into Canada:

> The danger I see in the matter is that England may possibly interfere with their blockade or do something to recognise the Southern Confederacy. As soon as this is done, war will be declared by the N. States against England & the soldiers now being drilled in such large numbers for the South, may have their occupation in fighting England in Canada.
>
> I really cannot help thinking that if the Southern States go – the last thing that could happen to us here & in the other Provinces, would be to join the free States. This would be treason to say aloud, but I think it is true.

Even before the War started, the "New York Herald" had urged that the Southern States go their own way peacefully and it predicted an expansion of the South into Mexico. Therefore, it said, the North "should seek a counterpoise to these acquisitions of its powerful neighbour by absorbing Canada".[81]

During the *Trent* incident British troops were sent to the maritime provinces of Canada, and the British West Indian naval fleet was strengthened. Indeed, the lack of troops in Canada, even after they were strengthened, caused the

British Government to be continually cautious in their dealings with the Federal Government.

In June 1862, I wrote to Austin Layard, the Under-Secretary of Foreign Affairs stating that I would soon propose mediation in the Commons. I indicated that, having taken the opinion of both sides of the House, nine-tenths of the Members were strongly in favour of recognition.[82]

I added: "If the question is settled without our recognition of the South, you may rest certain that the Northern armies will be marched into Canada."[83]

As the War progressed my other friends voiced their opinions on it. Sir Fred Pollock[84] said: "The whole world was interested (this country especially) that all N. America should not be one great power – threatening all others."[85]

I echoed what Pollock said. In Parliament I said that I desired the disruption of the American Union, as every honest Englishman did, because it was too great a power and England should not let such a power exist on the American Continent.[86]

In fact, has it not been the boast of a large portion of the Americans that the day is not far distant when the stripes and stars of the Republic must float over every inch of territory now under a monarchy? These things must surely come to pass if the Union is thoroughly restored and maintained, and separation is the only thing which can prevent them.[87]

The threat of the Northern States marching into Canada was real. I still think that someday they will attempt it. When it arrives there may be too many people holding the opinion in Canada which Mr Young had expressed. The United States will yet be a source of far greater trouble to us than they could be if the South was free.[88]

59 Support for Confederate Independence

From the start of the War, I was determined to foster peace. As I mentioned I also felt that the South had a case for recognition. In Parliament I put forward a 'Notice of Motion for the Recognition of the South'. This notice stood for some time in my name on the orders of the day of the House of Commons. My Notice was effectively that an address should be

> ...presented to Her Majesty stating that the House of Commons viewed with regret the prolonged hostilities between the several States heretofore constituting the United States of America, with whom this country had long maintained friendly relations and that the House trusted Her Majesty would avail herself of the earliest opportunity for the recognition of the Independence of the seceding States – or for offering mediation so as to bring about an amicable adjustment of their differences on the basis of separation.

The motion was something to the above effect, though I do not have a copy of it before me and I do not recollect the exact words. I placed it upon the papers ready for immediate action should an opportunity arise through any decisive action in favour of the South, to recommend the House do something to attempt to halt the fearful havoc – but though every communication brought news of great actions and terrible carnage on both sides, it brought nothing decisive as I had hoped and anticipated.

The vast armies of the North were hurled back again and again, with fearful loss of life from their attempts to capture Richmond. Again, and again, their charge was renewed.

Under the circumstances it was vain to expect most in the House of Commons to go with me unless the leaders of the opposition were prepared, which they were not, to make it a party issue.

I had two meetings with Palmerston to gauge support for my motion. During the second, Palmerston explained that Russell "if not altogether against it, was not yet in favour of it."[89] To have brought forward the motion, and have it defeated, would have strengthened the hands of the North and injured the prospects of the South. To raise a discussion on so grave a question, mainly for the sake of discussion, could not have done any good. I had therefore no course left but to withdraw it. I did so with regret but with a feeling that under the circumstances I would best serve the interests of the South. Besides, the reason was ending. Many of the members who felt strongly on the matter were leaving for the season, and no news came from the South to lead me to hope for success.

The season ended and before Parliament again met, the armies of the South had been overwhelmed and their cause lost. By that time also I was laid up with my present affliction.[90]

During my conversations with Government Officials and interested parties during the War, I learnt there may have been a secret pact between the British Government and the Federal States of America.

Mr Disraeli told me that, from what he had heard, Lord Russell had given Mr Adams, the United States Minister to the United Kingdom, to understand that in no case would this country interfere. I had received somewhat similar information at the office of the Minister for Foreign Affairs in Paris, and through Chevalier, from whom I understood that a secret agreement had been agreed to.[91]

Mr Disraeli also went further and expressed regret "that steps had not been taken after 'Bull Run'[92] or about the time of the Trent Affair, either to recognise the South, or not to recognise the so-called blockade of the Southern ports". He added that the great majority of the Conservative Party was of this opinion; but he would take no steps to carry into effect the views he entertained. He stated that he had refrained from expressing them in public on the grounds that they had no desire at that time to distract Lord Palmerston's administration[93] and that questions of this character should be left entirely in the hands of the Government.

I believe that it was on the question of the emancipation of the slaves, that Mr Adams entirely won Lord Russell to his views and that he did, to some extent, pledge Lord Palmerston's Government at an early period of the war to the effect that the South would not be recognised if they remained in power.[94]

To harness support for the South, I was one of those Parliamentarians and Businessmen who formed the 'Southern Independence Association' in December 1863. Chaired by Alexander Beresford Hope, we wished to counter information that advocated the merits of the war in America, and to keep the British public aware of the policy and justice of recognizing, at the earliest possible moment, the independence of the Confederate States.[95]

In November 1863 I wrote to Mr Slidell explaining that Mr Mason, myself, and a few others had concluded our arrangements to launch the association to watch over the interests of the South in this Country. It was high time, for I thought our government grew colder and colder every day – I was quite at a loss to understand their policy. If they were not prepared to recognise independence, they ought at least to adhere to a strict and impartial neutrality.

The members of the Association were numerous and influential, consisting of many Members of Parliament and a few Peers who were on the Committee, but their efforts were of no avail. In fact, though anxious and earnest, they did not make the move in public I repeatedly recommended, and consequently their existence as an association was to a great extent a failure. Although I was vocal in encouraging separation, I felt that I did not have the time or gravitas to take leadership of the Association.

One area where we harnessed support for the South was via the press. Propaganda had a major role to play. The Confederate Commercial Agent, Henry Hotze,[96] founded a pro-South newspaper called the *Index*. Within two years of its inception, it served as the voice of British-based and the aristocrat-dominated Southern Independence Association. The two were interlinked.[97]

60 Blockade Running

I lost many friends in the Northern States whom I esteemed, and who were all very angry with me for supporting the South and advocating separation.

Soon after the commencement of the War, I wrote to a Northern sympathiser,[98] who was also a shipping associate in the United States, in response to a letter from him. I said that it was incorrect to say I ever supported the breaking of the blockade of the Southern ports; that would have been a declaration of war against his country, which I, in common with the vast majority of my countrymen, was most anxious to avoid. Our policy was non-intervention. We had too much of the "glory", or rather of the folly of war, to launch into it without some very strong cause for so doing; and we had too great a respect for them, to increase their troubles by a foreign invasion. I said that it was a great mistake to suppose that we rejoiced in their misfortunes.

I continued saying that he could rest assured England would take no steps, which would violate the law of nations, but she could not turn a deaf ear to the opinions and appeals of a community so numerous and so powerfully united as the Confederate States. I said that before long we must acknowledge them as an independent power. While I would not lift my humble voice against the breaking of the blockade, I did not hesitate to say I desired to see the Southern States acknowledged. The simple acknowledgement of the South by Great Britain and France would put an end to this terrible evil war and all its havoc.[99]

The blockade by the North was instigated to prevent goods, troops, and weapons from entering the Southern states.[100] It was proclaimed by President Abraham Lincoln in April 1861. It would also limit the export of goods, in particular cotton and tobacco. By doing this, the Union thought they could cause the economy of the Confederate States to collapse.

However, so convinced were the Confederate States that by starving Britain and France of cotton, they would enforce recognition of their status as a nation and thus achieve independence, that they embargoed the export of cotton.

This embargo drastically reduced the supply of cotton in 1861-62. The effect on restricting British and French clothing manufacture was slow to start as a stockpile had been built up prior to the War.[101] Ironically the effectiveness of the embargo only created the impression that the blockade was effective.[102] The embargo obviously severely reduced funds for the South. As a result, the embargo was soon abandoned. Mr Yancey wrote to me explaining the logistics of cotton supply and how the Confederates would manage the cotton situation.[103]

I know that it has been said that I was engaged heavily in the trade with the Southern ports. Mr Adams, the United States Minister to the United Kingdom, himself wrote a despatch to Lord Russell, in which he mentioned a list of twenty-four suspected blockade runners, and he actually put down twenty of them as belonging to me. I went to Lord Russell and said this was a most extraordinary statement, as I had never heard of one of those vessels. I declared that I had no interest, directly or indirectly, in anything connected with the Southern States.

It was perfectly true that I had been offered a very large amount of business with them, but considering my position as a Member of Parliament, and as a public man, I felt it would have been very wrong of me to take any steps contrary to the proclamation that had been issued by my Queen. That proclamation forbade me from rendering any material aid to any of the belligerents. Therefore, I felt it would be setting a bad example to the people if I had aided either the Northern or the Southern States. Consequently, I refrained from all transactions of a commercial or financial character with either of them.

Part Six: American Civil War

So much so, that during the War, when the firm of which I was the head engaged as brokers for one or two vessels, the object of which, I believe, was to run the blockade, I warned my partners and said that I could have nothing to do with it, and I retired from the head of that firm in 1863.[104]

Although I took no part in blockade running, my partners Edgar Stringer and Edward Pembroke, were heavily involved.[105] In November 1863, the *New York Times* carried an article on captured correspondence. The article published details of business transactions between the Confederates and interested parties in Britain. One of the documents showed an agreement between Colonel Gorgas,[106] Chief of Ordnance on behalf of the Confederate States, and Charles Reid & Co in London (and other parties) that five steamers would run from the port in Bermuda or Nassau to Charleston or Wilmington. The agreement was signed by Stringer.[107]

In a letter from the Confederate arms supply agent Caleb Huse[108] to Edgar Stringer he stated that the capital of Stringer's Company was £150,000 and he had already made use of the entire amount in the purchase of goods and steamers.

One incident of running the blockade springs to mind.

Mr A. D. Gifford was one of the very few men living in the Southern States who was known to me personally before the war. He was an Englishman by birth but had resided for more than 20 years in the neighbourhood of Richmond. He managed various coal mines in that district. Soon after settling in Richmond, he married Miss Jefferson, whose father was related to the celebrated Statesman[109] of that name.

I think it was in the year 1853 that I first became acquainted with Mr Gifford. He visited Britain to purchase iron rails for the Washington & Danville Railway, which was then being constructed, of which he was Vice President. He called on me to undertake the shipment of it. Five years after that he again visited England, and on that occasion he brought his wife with him, whom I introduced to Mrs Lindsay. During their stay we became good friends.

Strongly attached to the cause of the South, he came again to England, just as war was breaking out, to endeavour to interest his friends in this country in its cause. He succeeded to some extent and returned to Richmond with a shipload of stores of various kinds directed to the wants of the South. He returned to England again in November 1861. During that time, he wrote a note explaining how ineffective the blockade was. On his most recent journey he had sailed aboard the *Bermuda*,[110] a British Steamer, to Britain without incident. He said that if I should desire it, he would furnish me with a list of upwards of six hundred vessels which have passed out of the Confederate ports since the Blockade was established and he could give me the names of the vessels and that of their owners.[111]

Towards the close of December Gifford sailed for the South in a steamer he had chartered, laden with various descriptions of stores. That winter was a very stormy one and the ship must have foundered with all on board during one of the many violent gales which, in January 1862, swept across the Atlantic. Poor Gifford and the steamer in which he had sailed were never heard of again.

Mrs Gifford, knowing that her husband was to sail in December, anxiously looked for his arrival and, after the lapse of three months, wrote to me in considerable anxiety to know if I could give her any tidings of him. That letter never reached me. It was opened on its way through the Northern States – my name having attracted attention – and though it contained not one word beyond enquiring after her lost husband, it was, after a delay of nearly two months, returned to her. She wrote again, and again the letter was returned. She then called upon Mr Cridland,[112] who was at that time acting as the British Consul at Richmond. He heard what she had to say and knowing me by name, forwarded an enquiry from her to me through Lord Lyons, who at once despatched it to me in the Foreign Office bag. It was nearly 9 months from the time when poor Gifford had gone since his wife's anxious enquiry reached me in London.

Sometime afterwards I heard that Mr Gifford had lost his all and left his wife very poorly provided for. His support of the South had also significantly reduced his estate in value.

61 Building a Confederate Navy

The Confederate Government lacked a Navy. It was imperative therefore that naval ships were built or bought by the South.

To finance the building or purchase of ships, it was proposed that a loan be raised through the purchase of bonds. These bonds would be cashed in for cotton. The Confederate Government sent an agent[113] in July 1862 to Britain to negotiate the selling of the bonds. He contacted me and I then discussed the idea with James Mason the Confederate Commissioner. I suggested a fixed rate (of 4 pence or 8 cents) although cotton was selling for four times as much in Britain. Mr Mason informed the agent who returned to the Southern States to discuss this with the Government.

In the meantime, another Confederate agent, Commander Sinclair,[114] arrived in Britain to build a ship. He approached Mason who in turn suggested he see me. £60,000 in bonds was required and I was able through my contacts to raise this amount. These bonds were the first cotton bonds used by the Confederacy.[115]

This article was written in the "Raleigh Register" newspaper:[116]

Mr. Lindsay, MP and the Sanders Contract.

In reply to assertions recently made by an American correspondent of the Daily News, Mr W. S. Lindsay, M. P., states that neither he nor any member of his firm has entered into contracts with the Government of the Confederate States for the "construction of war steamers," or any other kind of ships. Mr. Lindsay says: "that in our shipping business, which extends over most parts of the world, my partners may as brokers have negotiated the sale of ships from English shipbuilders or shipowners to Mr Sanders (the Confederate agent), as we constantly do to many other persons, is very likely; but when any person invites us to negotiate for the purchase of a vessel, our sole duty is to find him, if possible, the description of the vessel he requires, and to see that he has the means to pay for her. For what purpose she is bought, or what became of her afterwards, are matters with which we have nothing whatever to do."

I suggested further ways of raising finance, through cotton bonds. Another proposal was put forward by a bank[117] in Paris; they had extensive branches throughout Europe, including London, and the Confederates decided to obtain funding through a loan organised through them.

The loan was an immediate success. During the first three days more than $16 million worth of bonds were raised, mainly in London,[118] The Bank derived considerable profit, estimated to be £1,500,000, from their sale.[119]

The bonds came at a considerable premium and shortly after rose to a premium of £10 per share so that those persons who had a portion of it allotted to them might have realised a considerable profit had they sold their shares. When the loan was introduced, I did not apply for any shares. No doubt had I done so a number would have been placed at my disposal. I however did not. I refused all business offered me by the Confederate Government as I did not wish it to be supposed that I supported the South for any financial or selfish motives. However, when the £100 stock fell to £40, I bought in the market about £2,000 as an investment. The newspapers made out that I lost £20,000 by the Confederate Loan![120]

After the War, I was sorry to see the failure of Fraser, Trenholm & Co who acted as bankers and commercial agents for the Confederate States. Though I never had any transactions with the house, and though I did not know personally any of the partners in the house, I frequently heard of them through Mr Mason and other gentlemen from the South.

For many years they had carried on a large and highly respectable business with the South. Their last duties were reported as amounting to one million pounds sterling. Their assets I presume could not be easily ascertained for very much depended upon the realisation of their vast investments in the Southern States. They were always considered to be a house of wealth and position. Their profits, if they had been able to realise them, must have been enormous during the great Civil War.[121]

Building the ships, iron-clad steamers, in Britain was fraught with difficulties.

The Northern States threatened war and there was always a threat of an invasion into Canada. It was said that ships would not be allowed to be built in this country for the Southern States; but should artillery and ammunition be refused to supply the Northern states from here? I could not see what could prevent the Southern people from being supplied with ships while the Federals continued to be supplied with arms.[122]

Legally, the building of the ships was permitted, as long as they were not fitted for war. If they were seen to be armed, then they could be in violation of the Foreign Enlistment Act. Politically, their building presented a great danger with our relations with the Northern States.

I received a letter from the Confederate Commissioner, James Mason, asking whether I would study some ship designs.

William S Lindsay Esq MP

Dear Sir

Mr John B Sandy, late a citizen, but not a native of the United States, has exhibited to me, and at my suggestion to Captain Semmes,[123] models, & drawings of inventions & improvements in steamers for action strictly intended for war purposes. I have not sufficient knowledge of the subject to form an opinion myself, but Captain Semmes I believe thought well of them – He has obtained patrons in the United States & will ask for the same in England.

Mr Sandy has made himself known to me, in a way that interests me to know whether his plans of construction, are really desiderata in naval architecture, & as I have thought the subject might interest you, have given him this letter – thinking if you could not look into the subject yourself, you might put Mr Sandy in communication with those competent to decide on the value of his plans.

Very respectfully & truly yours

J M Mason[124]

Six ships were to be built. Orders were placed with Lairds Shipbuilders in Liverpool. The CSS *Alabama*[125] was delivered but two other iron-clad steamers, or 'rams', were seized by the British Government. I wrote to the editor of The Times to the following effect:

The Stoppage of the Steam Rams
To the Editor of The Times

Sir, "Historicus"[126] has the pen of a ready writer. He has evidently the confidence of the Government and has become the medium of explaining to the public the reasons which induced Lord Russell to seize the Liverpool rams.

For these reasons I might not have ventured to question his conclusions if his facts could have been depended upon. But in this instance, he appears to have reared his superstructure upon a quicksand.

He says these vessels are without doubt for the Confederate Government and built to its orders, because certain "intercepted correspondence" makes it clear "that a special mission has been established and a special fund provided for the purpose of fitting out, equipping, and arming vessels in this country without Her Majesty's licence for warlike purposes against the dominions, ships, and goods of a foreign State."

"This is no matter of inference," he continues; "it is the express object for which the vote of the Confederate Congress was passed;" and therefore he arrives at the conclusion that Her Majesty's Government was perfectly justified in stopping certain vessels now in course of completion at Birkenhead, and thereby inflicting a heavy blow upon a very important branch of British Industry.

"Historicus" does not doubt the authenticity or accuracy of the "intercepted correspondence" sent by Mr. Adams to Lord Russell, and published in a blue-book by command of Her Majesty; and though I cannot enlighten him on this point I may state, for his information, that in the same blue-book there is another document sent by Mr. Adams to Lord Russell, in which a somewhat unwarrantable use is made of my name. The book is not at present before me, but I think this document professes to give a list of 22 vessels which were about to run the blockade, and my name, or that of my late firm, is given as the owners or agents of no less than 18 of these ships. Now, Sir, to the best of my recollection, I never heard of any of these vessels until I saw them published in the blue-book, and though I have had many inducements I never owned a ton of shipping or to the value of one sixpence in any vessel that ever ran or attempted to run the blockade.

So much for the value of the information and the accuracy of the documents furnished by the Federal Government, on the faith of which, I fear, Her Majesty's Government founds its American policy, maintains its "impartial neutrality", allows munitions of war to a fabulous extent to be shipped to the North, shuts the door against all communications, official or otherwise, from the South, and stamps the broad arrow upon every ship supposed to be for the service of a brave and an oppressed people, who have already given abundant proofs that they are a Nation. Is that neutrality? Is it justice, or is it English honour?

May not the "intercepted correspondence" be as inaccurate as the document to which I have just referred? I can at least assert in regard to that correspondence, in which my name is also introduced, that the "naval store bonds" referred to in it were not negotiated by me nor by my firm, and that not one of the "six vessels" was built or contracted for by me or by my late partners, or by any of our correspondents.[127]

If it was illegal to build and equip a vessel of war for the Southern Confederacy, it ought to be equally wrong to supply the Federal Government with "munitions of war". It will not be an easy matter to get an English jury to convict an English shipbuilder for constructing a ship of war for the Confederates, whom we have acknowledged as belligerents, whilst anyone may supply any number of ships of war to the Federals.[128]

To evade an unwelcome response from the Northern States, the British Government bought the two seized ships and employed them in the Royal Navy. The Confederates turned to France to build their ships, but that venture too ended in failure.

Captain Semmes, in the opinion of the Republicans of the Northern States, was a "Robber" and a "Pirate". If these men had extended their condemnation to any ship which captured or destroyed private property at sea, I would have been disposed to agree with them. But when the Confederate States were acknowledged as belligerents everything that Semmes did was perfectly lawful and no more than what the ships of the Northern States would have done had they had the opportunity. It will be sufficient for me to say that the feats of the Confederate ship the *Sumter*[129] surprised Europe, and with those of the *Alabama,* all but ruined the maritime commerce of the United States. Together with their high protective policy it has reduced their shipping from 5,000,000 tons in 1860 to less than half that amount. A statement made by the Secretary of France shows that at the close of 1866 there were very little more than 2,000,000 tons of shipping belonging to the whole of the American States. The name of Semmes will long be remembered by the maritime people of all countries and above all by Yankee shipowners.

It was early in 1862 when I first saw Semmes in England. Accompanied by Mr Mason, he walked one day into my office in Austin Friars and claimed me as a former acquaintance. His face was quite familiar to me, but I could not recollect his name. When he mentioned it I at once recollected him as Captain Semmes of the Navy Board whom I had, on various occasions, met when I was in Washington in 1860.

I had no idea that Semmes of the United States Board was the Semmes of the *Sumter* whose name, for some months, had been in everybody's mouth, so I joked with him for not being at his post when good men were in such great demand on the other side of the Atlantic. My astonishment may be imagined when I found out that my friend of the Navy Board had been very hard at work as Commander of the *Sumter*.

During his sojourn in London, he was often with me at Shepperton, and in fact passed a good deal of his spare time at the Manor House. But so thoroughly suited was he for the work he had in hand that all the time he was with me he never gave me the slightest clue as to his future movements, and when, within twelve days after we parted, I saw in the newspapers that the Ship Number 290[130] being built by Laird's in Liverpool had become the *Alabama*, and that Semmes was in command of her – the terror of the whole Northern States – I was even more surprised when he told me who he was at Austin Friars. The extraordinary exploits of that ship have been fully recorded, and I should say that the reported feats of Paul Jones[131] on the Ocean were even less surprising.

The fate of the *Alabama* is well known. In an engagement off the French coast, she was sunk by the USS *Kearsarge*.[132] Semmes spent six or seven months in England to recover his strength and have the benefit of good surgical advice. His hand had been shattered to some extent in the action with the *Kearsarge*. Some portion of that time he spent with me here at Shepperton, after that he returned home and took a conspicuous part in the masterly defence of Richmond.[133]

'Sinking of the CSS *Alabama*' by American marine artist Xanthus Smith, 1922.

It has been said by his enemies that Captain Semmes had realised a large fortune; but such was not the case. He might have done so but he did not, and he left the confederate service much poorer than he entered it.[134]

62 The Emperor's Messenger

In the course of 1861 and during the early part of 1862 I frequently visited the French Minister of Commerce,[135] the French economist Monsieur Chevalier, and His Majesty Napoleon III, regarding great changes then contemplated in the Navigation Laws of that country.[136] These changes, happily, have since been carried into effect.[137]

These visits were made, not only with the knowledge, but by the desire of my own Government.

The British Ambassador to France, Lord Cowley,[138] accompanied me during the first meeting, though on future occasions his Lordship's presence was not considered necessary, either by himself, or by the emperor, as the subject was one of a technical character with which he was not familiar, and consequently could not assist in its settlement.

On one of these occasions – 10 April 1862 – the Minister of Commerce mentioned, but not for the first time, the American War, and expressed his dissatisfaction with the so-called Blockade of the Southern Ports.[139] He then told me that the Blockade in his opinion was "not effective" and that consequently should not be respected. He remarked that the British did not seem to be affected by the blockade. I replied that I thought our people were likely to feel it much more than the French, as we were much more extensively engaged in the manufacture of Cotton which was being blockaded.

"If that was the case," he remarked with a half sneer and half smile, "then your government do not consider the matter of much importance by the way in which they have treated our communications to them on the subject."

He said that three or four months previously, he had written a summary of his views on it, which was submitted to the Emperor and his Minister of Foreign Affairs.[140] A despatch had been sent to the French Ambassador in London,[141] which he communicated to Lord Russell, but that nothing beyond an "evasive" reply had been received.

He further stated that in the early part of March, a month or so before I saw him, another despatch had been sent to England in which a very decided opinion was given regarding the Blockade. It recommended, as I understood him, that as it was not effective it would not be respected, but that no reply had been received beyond its simple acknowledgment.

On the following day – Friday 11 April 1862 – I had an appointment with the Emperor about the Navigation question but that did not occupy more than ten minutes.

When I was about to leave, His Majesty asked some questions about the American War, although themselves not of any importance, they led to a remarkable conversation and one, under the circumstances, I would rather not have heard. He told me that he and his Ministers for Commerce and Foreign Affairs had been speaking about the Blockade the previous evening. He said that England had not paid attention to his views.

He then mentioned that he could not understand why Lord John Russell had sent the substance of his despatches regarding the Blockade to the United States if he did not approve of them. He added that our Ambassador, Lord Cowley, always seemed to "throw cold water" on all his suggestions about the course which England and France ought to pursue. He was evidently very much displeased.

He intimated, as I understood him, that after the way in which he had been treated, he could not hold further discussions, or make any further suggestions, on American Affairs with our Government, unless he was satisfied that they were prepared to act with him.

The conversation lasted about half an hour. It ended with the statement that in his opinion the Blockade, not being effective, ought not to be respected and that he was prepared to join England in a remonstrance, and to enforce, if necessary, the opening of the Southern ports.

I need not say that I was very much surprised by what the emperor said, not at his views, but at his expressing them to me, especially in the manner he had done. I was however still more surprised when he requested that I could state to Lord Cowley what he had said and return to him any remarks which

Part Six: American Civil War

Lord Cowley might think proper to make in reply. [142] In effect I was to be a messenger, albeit a reluctant one.

That evening I dined with Lord Cowley at the Embassy, but as others were present, I had no opportunity of delivering the emperor's message, nor was I able to say anything beyond asking when he could spare half an hour to see him alone.

On the following morning I took breakfast with him and related all that had taken place, taking care to explain why I was the bearer of information which certainly should have gone directly to Lord Cowley from the Emperor or through his Foreign Minister. But Lord Cowley, though evidently much surprised at what he heard, did not seem to think it as strange as I had thought he would, that a private individual in my position should have been made the instrument of conveying the information to him. I understood that this was not the only instance in which the emperor had adopted a similar course. Remarking that his Majesty had curious ways of his own at times, his Lordship however said that he had never seen the despatches to which the emperor referred, and I think he went so far as to say that he had never even heard of them.

In other respects, Lord Cowley was much franker and more open than I expected him to be under the very peculiar circumstances of the case. It was very clear his views and that of the emperor were not in harmony. He thought the Blockade was not as effective as it was expected to be, but he was decidedly opposed to any more than a compulsory opening of it and opposed also to any joint official protest unless we were prepared to enforce our opinion. In a word, his policy was clearly against all interference of any sort on the grounds that it would involve us in a war. On the other hand, the emperor was evidently of the opinion that a joint interference or protest on the part of England and France would bring the war to an end and provide the South her independence, which he evidently wished, though he never said so to me.

In a letter to my brother-in-law in Scotland, I wrote describing the meeting with Napoleon. I told him that the mission was one of great confidence, so that I could not mention it even to him. The matter was one which Her Majesty would not confide to our ambassador, Lord Cowley. The 'Diplomatists' were privately very angry and very jealous of me. However, I continued saying that I appeared to have done the work so well, that the emperor, at parting with me, said "When you come to Paris always let me know. What can I do for you?"

"Nothing Sire," I replied. "The good of mankind and my country is the highest reward I can have."[143]

The emperor had arranged that I should see him again two days after my meeting with him. I was punctual for my appointment at 11am. The interview did not last more than a quarter of an hour that morning, as he was in full dress and his carriage was waiting for him. I told him, as I had full permission to do, in a very condensed form, what Lord Cowley had said, remarking that his Lordship had sent the conversation I had with him to Lord John Russell.

His Majesty seemed pleased with the way in which I had performed the very delicate duty he had imposed upon me but was evidently displeased with the views Lord Cowley entertained regarding the course which ought to be taken. To my astonishment he intimated that he would be glad if I would repeat to Lord John Russell and Lord Palmerston the conversation he had with me, in the same way as I had done to Lord Cowley and, if they had no objection, to convey back to him what they thought!

This was a duty which I certainly did not wish to perform. I endeavoured to evade it by remarking that it would not be necessary for me to do so as Lord Cowley had already relayed all that had taken place. The Emperor however thought otherwise – and though I told him, as plainly as a man in my position can tell a Monarch, that Lord John Russell was unlikely to see me on any such matter, he intimated that I should try – I then asked if I might convey his views to Lord Derby and Mr Disraeli as well, for on a question of so grave a character I thought they ought to know the nature of the conversation he had had with me. He approved of the suggestion, and we parted.

I felt that I was treading an unbidden path and on very delicate, if not dangerous, grounds and for that reason I went direct from the Emperor to Lord Cowley and told him all that had taken place as I had done on all previous occasions – adding that I would much rather be dispensed with the job.

I then saw Chevalier and the Minister of Commerce and, at their suggestion, saw the Minister for Foreign Affairs, whom I had met on one or two occasions before. I do not think that either of the French diplomats was very well pleased with the work I had in hand, though the Minister for Foreign Affairs was in no way surprised. But Lord John Russell had evidently got into a great state of anger and grandeur, for in reply to the note I sent to him when I arrived on Monday morning in London, I received the following grand and dignified reply by messenger.

Pembroke Lodge
Richmond Park
London SW

Dear Mr Lindsay

As the Queen has an Ambassador at Paris & the Emperor an Ambassador in London, I think the best way for the two Governments to communicate with each other is through the respective Embassies.

I am sorry you have had so much trouble – I shall always be ready to listen to any message the emperor will be pleased to send to the British Govt either thro' Lord Cowley or the Count de Flahaut & to give such answer as the Cabinet may advise & the Queen approve.

I remain, yours truly

Russell [144]
Secretary of State for Foreign Affairs

Part Six: American Civil War

Though it was clear by the foregoing note that Lord Russell had pulled up his shirt collar to the very fullest extent, and that he had resolved to see no one but Lord Cowley or the Count on the subject to which my note referred, I thought it advisable that I should again address him to explain why the Emperor had asked me to convey to his Lordship the substance of what he had said in regard to the Blockade. I therefore, on receipt of his dignified but not very politic communication, wrote to him explaining that if he agreed to see me I would be able to explain the reason why the Emperor had requested me to convey the discussions he had had with me on the proposition he would be prepared to make.[145]

This note however had no effect. Lord John Russell was resolved not to hear the reasons from anybody except through the usual channel, and the consequences might have been a serious rupture between France and England because his Lordship would not hear what the emperor had to say unless he strictly adhered to the usual etiquette of sending it through an acknowledged and full-fledged ambassador.

Mr Disraeli, Leader of the Opposition in the House of Commons, at once sent a reply to my note asking to see him. He arranged to see me.[146] I did not think it necessary to write to Lord Derby, the Leader of the Opposition in the House of Lords, and besides I knew he was very ill at the time.

I however mentioned in my note to Mr Disraeli that I was allowed by the emperor to make the communication to Lord Derby and himself. Mr Disraeli, when I saw him, made no hesitation about stating his own views in regard to the Blockade and the course which ought to be taken, and these views were in accordance with what the emperor had expressed, but he would not promise to support in Parliament a motion which embodied these views unless it was approved by the Government.

I left for Paris on the evening of 16 April, and on the following morning called upon the emperor's private secretary[147] so that he might inform the emperor that I was again in Paris. I also called at the Foreign Office. In the course of the afternoon, I had a message with a letter stating that the emperor wished to see me at 11 a.m. on the following morning – that is on Friday 18 April.

I arrived at the Tuileries a quarter of an hour before my time and sent in my name and was immediately received, although more than one deputation was apparently waiting for an audience.

I had so little to say that I hesitated to take a seat when he called me to do so, remarking that as I had seen neither Lord John Russell nor Lord Palmerston I had really nothing to communicate to his Majesty. He was evidently annoyed that Lord John Russell had refused to see me. He said that if I had written to Lord Palmerston the Prime Minister, the result, he thought, would have been different; however, he was disappointed that although the Government of Lord Palmerston, and especially his Lordship himself, had "professed great friendship" and an earnest desire to co-operate with France, they had not yet done so in various important matters.[148]

Though I had nothing new to communicate, the emperor had indirectly a good deal to say to me for he kept me nearly an hour, and his first bit of gossip – for Emperors, like other men, are at times fond of a little idle talk – was the state of perplexity with which our Foreign Office had been thrown by his conversation with me about America.

It would appear that when I left Paris on Sunday Lord Cowley had called upon the French Minister for Foreign Affairs to express his great surprise that the emperor should have sent "proposals" to England through me and not through the usual channel. This was a bit of wicked mischief on his part for he knew very well that I was merely requested to repeat the substance of a conversation to Lord John Russell.

But happily, I had explained to the French Minister that same evening before I left Paris, that if any such "proposals" were made to the English Government they would go through the usual official channel and that the emperor would not make these, or any other proposals, unless England was prepared to co-operate with him. The Minister then met with the emperor who confirmed what I had stated.

When I related to him what Mr Disraeli had said the emperor appeared to entirely agree with him and was evidently a good deal interested in the views entertained by the leader of the opposition. He did not see how Lord Derby or Mr Disraeli could act in this matter – but seemed very glad to possess the views of the latter on the American question, more especially as they agreed with his own.

Though the mission on which I had been sent was one of a character which I hope it may never be my lot again to undertake, and though it was not complete in its results and did not furnish the emperor with much information beyond that which he already had in his possession, it was gratifying to me to hear that he was satisfied with what I had done.

Though his Majesty did not ask me to do so, I wrote a letter[149] to Lord Palmerston on my return to London, explaining all that occurred. After what the emperor had said I thought it advisable to do so – besides, I felt that I ought to give his Lordship an opportunity of hearing what had taken place in regard to this extraordinary and delicate affair.

In his reply Palmerston reiterated that communications with the French Emperor should be made through the official channel.[150] I replied stating that I had endeavoured to carry out the emperor's wishes in as quiet a manner as possible, and now that my role, so far as I have been allowed to perform it, was at an end, it was neither my wish nor my intention to say anything more about it.[151] Copies of these letters I sent to my friend Chevalier to hand to the Minister for Commerce, for him to place before the emperor if he thought proper, and thus this matter ended.

The subject was never mentioned by me to anyone except to those persons I have named and to Chevalier, who knew all that had taken place from the Minister, and to Mr Mason, as the matter was one of considerable interest to the Confederate Government.

There the affair would have rested, and as far as I was concerned would never in my lifetime have become public or have known to other persons than those I have mentioned, except for a circumstance to which I must now refer.

Part Six: American Civil War

The affair was altogether of so delicate a nature that I never mentioned it even to my most intimate friends or relatives.

More than 12 months elapsed. The Civil War in America raged with greater fury than it had ever done, and the prospect of any hope of restoring the Union was much more remote than it had been the year before. In the early part of June 1863 Mr Roebuck (my colleague, Liberal MP for Sheffield), gave notice that on the thirtieth of that month he would submit for the consideration of the House of Commons the following motion:

> That a humble address be presented to Her Majesty praying that she will be graciously pleased to enter into negotiation with the Great Powers of Europe[152] for the purpose of obtaining their co-operation in the recognition of the Independence of the Confederate States of America.

Soon after this notice appeared a rumour arose – who circulated it I cannot tell[153] – that the Emperor of the French had changed his well-known views on American Affairs, and that he would not be prepared to join England in the recognition of the Southern States.

Had this rumour been true Mr Roebuck's motion would fail and under these circumstances it would not have been either prudent or politic to go ahead with it. Mr Roebuck, naturally anxious for the success of his motion, wrote to me to ask if I could ascertain if there was any foundation in the rumour. He said, "I wish I could see the emperor and ascertain from him if there was any truth in the report."

I handed Mr Roebuck's note to Mr Mason who sent it to his colleague Mr Slidell in Paris. The day that Mr Slidell received it, he happened to be favoured with an audience with his Majesty. He read Mr Roebuck's note to me to the emperor and sent Mr Mason the following reply to it:

> Paris 18 June 1863
>
> My dear Mason – I have just left the emperor. The interview was very cordial & satisfactory, & he authorises me to contradict, without qualification, the report that he is unwilling to recognise our government. I read him a portion of Mr Roebuck's note to Mr Lindsay & he said he would gladly receive those gentlemen if they came here, but after reflection he added he thought he could do something still more decided – viz make a formal proposal for joint recognition with England – that he would consult his Cabinet today – & that if it were decided now to make the proposal he would let me know in a day or two through M Mocquard[154] whether it would be desirable to see Messrs Roebuck & Lindsay. I shall prepare a note today of our conversation & send you copy of it tomorrow or next day – yours in haste signed John Slidell.[155]

I gave a copy of this note to Mr Roebuck, remarking to him "If any person during the course of the debate should say that France is not prepared to join England in the recognition of the South you may read this note to the House or a portion of it without giving the name of the Author."

But this did not satisfy Mr Roebuck. He expressed great anxiety to see the emperor himself and urged that I should accompany him. I called his attention to that part of Mr Slidell's note in which he remarked that the emperor would communicate with him should he think that an interview would be of any service. However, nothing short of seeing the emperor there and then, and having the contradiction from his own lips, would satisfy Mr Roebuck.

At very great inconvenience to myself, and with much reluctance, I accompanied Mr Roebuck to Paris. I was also induced to do so by the urgent request of Mr Mason who thought our interview would be of great service to the cause of the Confederacy. Mr Slidell was also of this opinion. On arrival in Paris, I discovered that the emperor had left for Fontainebleau. We reached that place on the evening of 21 June and on the following morning had a long interview with the emperor who at least expressed himself to be very glad to see us.

Roebuck had on many occasions, both in and out of the House of Commons, attacked the emperor's policy and himself personally and, from what I afterwards learned from Monsieur Chevalier, the Emperor felt much obliged to me for introducing him. I have no doubt he did so with a conviction that as Roebuck had sought the interview, and as he had him very graciously received, he could not with any decency again attack his Majesty in public, and such was found to be the case, for Roebuck's views entirely changed regarding the man whom he used to call "Napoleon the Little".

It was evident also that he wished to talk over the American question and that he was more convinced of the need to make some move jointly with England and show that these two Great Powers did not approve of the war. I gave him all the information I possessed on the subject and Roebuck stated his views at considerable length, for the emperor appeared to be much interested in them and remarked that he was more concerned than ever that the war, in which such vast sacrifices of life had been made, would not cause the restoration of the Union. In his judgement, to continue it would only lead to greater sacrifices and entail greater misery without producing the desired results. Such was the tenor of his remarks, which he concluded as follows:

> I believe the recognition of the South as an independent Nation would restore peace, & therefore I am most anxious in concert with England to adopt measures to recognise a people who have given such proofs of their abilities to maintain their independence & govern themselves.

Part Six: American Civil War

These remarkable words he addressed more especially to me, then turning to Mr Roebuck he said – "I fear I cannot make the formal application at present to England which you desire – I could have wished to have done so but in consideration I cannot now" – thus in a few words he refused to do what he had stated to me in April of the previous year.

The emperor spoke without hesitation and at a more considerable length than usual, as he is more in the habit of listening than speaking. When he had finished, he stated very dutifully that he had no objection to his views on this question being made known in any way we deemed best – adding "I wish them to be known."[156]

On 30 June, Roebuck brought forward his motion. He did this before a very full House, but in doing so he made a much more pointed allusion to our interview with the emperor than the occasion required. He not only repeated nearly everything he had said to the emperor, but he gave the House to understand that he had a message from his Majesty on the assumption that the House would listen to a message from a Foreign Monarch.

He also made some statements which startled the House and one in particular about which he himself was rather unclear as the emperor had only referred to it in passing. The statement to which I refer is the improper use made of the despatches which France had sent to England in the early part of 1862. On this point Roebuck was far from clear, especially as to dates and this consequently laid him open to a severe attack. The broad facts as he stated them were quite correct, in fact too true, but he was ignorant of the details for I had not mentioned them to him. But he had no reason to refer at all to that delicate affair. He only needed to say that if the House adopted his resolution, he knew that France would agree to act in unison.

He had no need even to state that he had seen the emperor for every newspaper in the Kingdom had some days beforehand announced the fact and therefore the members knew very well that what he stated in regard to the co-operation of France might be depended upon. But it was not so much what he stated but the way in which he gave the information which startled the House.[157]

Every newspaper in the Kingdom, and I might add, almost every newspaper in Europe and in America, had articles on this affair and on Roebuck's statements. I came in for a large share of the abuse though I had not opened my lips. There were loud calls for me during the debate, and I might add on every occasion for some days afterwards when the matter was noticed. It was not however until 10 July that I offered any remarks, and then only I said as little as possible.

Thus, the matter would have ended, Roebuck resolved to withdraw his motion following a long letter he received from Lord Palmerston expressing his earnest hope that the adjourned debate would not be proceeded with. We both saw Palmerston that day to close the affair.

It was necessary for me however to make a further statement, which I did on 13 July. I was cautious to say not one word more than was necessary to clear myself from the unfounded charges which had been made against me. I wrote to Lord Palmerston to explain my disapproval that the Under Secretary of Foreign Affairs, Mr Layard, raised personal matters about me and my actions in Paris.[158]

When I made my short statement on the 13th the House was very full, and the members anticipated that I would enter into a long explanation. I however contented myself in replying to points raised by Mr Layard by saying enough to clear myself. In my own justification I have been told that I might have said more: but I felt that it was far better that I should endure the reproach to which I was subjected, rather than reveal facts which must have produced very unpleasant, if not serious, consequences.

In fact, this matter had gone so far that if what Lord John Russell and Mr Layard had stated in their places in Parliament was true, then what the emperor and two of his ministers had told me must have been false; and for the reasons I have named I could not have misunderstood what they said for it was often repeated.

I was therefore placed in a very unpleasant, as well as in a very difficult and delicate position, and I therefore resolved to bear the condemnation rather than proceed with a statement to prove the false statements on the one hand and the veracity of the emperor and his ministers on the other.

It was far too dangerous and delicate a game to play considering the position of the respective parties and the risk of dishonouring friendly relations between two great nations on whose close alliance so much prosperity and happiness depends. I suffered, and I suffered in silence, and I never regret the cause I felt it to be my duty then to adopt.

So ended the chance for the Confederate States to gain recognition as a nation from Britain and France. In due course the tide of the war turned in favour of the Union.[159]

In later years Napoleon III was to declare war against Prussia.[160]

The engagements were of the most terrible description — in every one the armies of Prussia were victorious. The French army capitulated, and Napoleon became a prisoner in Germany! France then was in a state of revolution and was proclaimed a Republic.

What changes in a short month! But these are matters for the pen of the historian — six weeks before the war the emperor was by far the greatest man in Europe and had he then died history would have said of him that he was a far greater man than his uncle, for he had been the emperor of peace and progress and had done more to exalt and enrich France than any monarch that ever sat upon its throne. But what will history say should he die now?[161]

Whatever may have been the emperor's failings he had the interests of France at heart and the prosperity of the people of that country has been unquestionably far greater during the twenty-two years of his reign as President and Emperor that during any similar period of its history.

Nor should England say one word against him. Whatever may have been his motives he was one of the sincerest friends to England that ever occupied the throne of France. We have been large gainers by his commercial policy, and it was his letter which prevented war between this country and the United States of America over the Trent affair.

Part Six: American Civil War

Portrait of Emperor Napoleon III (1805–1873) in coronation robes, by Franz Xaver Winterhalter.

63 Suppliers' Greed

There were numerous Englishmen & Americans in this country who possessed great interest in the cause of the South, but who had no object in it beyond their own selfish interests. In a word, I had reason to fear that the South was plundered to as great an extent as the North, due to the greater risks they had to take. I have taken no part in supplying the North or South with materials because I would not have it said that I had any selfish or pecuniary interest in this great struggle.

In November 1863[162] however, I was urged to use my influence to have a contract carried into effect which the Confederate Government made with a Mr Chiles. He urged me to assist him. I considered the transaction carefully and assessed the facts. The contract was a large one. It was entirely for the clothing of the Confederate Army.

It consisted of the supply of 30,000 jackets, 30,000 trousers & 30,000 great coats – 60,000 flannel shirts, 60,000 pairs of drawers, 30,000 caps, 30,000 pairs of shoes, 30,000 heavy blankets & 60,000 socks & 10,000 yards of fine cloth. The person who had it in hand, a man from the South, had, in connection with one or two persons in this country, made up their minds to have an enormous profit for themselves whilst being relieved from all risk.[163]

I wrote to James Mason, the Confederate Commissioner, with the facts. The price his government agreed to pay for the clothing, to be delivered to Brownsville[164] was £410,000. I investigated and discovered that these goods could be purchased and delivered, including insurance with war risk & all charges, for £200,000 or say £210,000. The profit being £200,000!

But that was not all. His government agreed to pay on delivery of these goods, cotton at 18 cents per lb. Once in Britain the cotton would realise, after paying insurance & all charges, in round figures £1,000,000; so that the profit to the party with whom his government has made this contract is not merely £200,000 – it is £800,000!

I told him that somebody was using his government to an awful extent. Mr Mason said that I should also inform Mr Slidell, which I duly did.

64 Emancipation of Slaves

During my time at sea, I had of course come across slavery. Indeed, I had lived amongst them when I deserted my ship in Demerara in 1836 when I was twenty and they made me welcome. I found the act of owning of humans as slaves truly abhorrent. No one could abhor more than I do the system or custom or legislative enactment by which Man is empowered to sell his fellow Man.[165]

The slave trade had been banned in the United Kingdom and the British Empire in 1807. No more were British slave ships able to transport their human cargo from Africa to the West Indies and America. The act of

Part Six: American Civil War

Abolition followed in 1833.[166] It was a magnanimous measure I felt, and there is something truly exalted in the idea which, when as soon as a slave touched British territory, he became free. I felt, rightly or wrongly however, that the slaves in the West Indies should have been prepared for their freedom, as most of them had no idea of what freedom meant. They expected their masters to feed them and maintain them and assist them when sick.

A law should have been considered to free all the children of suspected slaves who were born after a fixed period. The twenty million pounds sterling which had been allocated to plantation owners should have been used to educate the children of slaves until they could work for their own living.

I had seen examples of slaves being set free by their master's, who respected them and supported their business. They became grateful free labourers and only a few quitted their master's service. Some slaves, however, expected their freedom as some recompense for previous wrongs, and as a result felt that they need not work.

I had frequently mingled with slaves. I had seen their conditions compared favourably with my own. In most cases they were more fortunate than when I was on board ship, under the control of a cruel mate, or when I had been destitute in Liverpool Docks. They had food and water, a roof over their heads; things I didn't have when living rough in the Docks. Rightly or wrongly, I felt the work they endured was less harsh than my treatment on board ship.

During the Civil War, politicians in the North made Slavery the constant theme of their speeches and insisted that the war must be continued until that institution was for ever swept away in the South. They alleged that the constant differences between the Northern and Southern members in Congress arose entirely on account of that question. The South they said desired independence solely to maintain Slavery and that the Union could not and would not be again restored unless the institution was entirely abolished. With these arguments they sought to incur the sympathy of Europe and especially Britain.[167]

But what are the facts? Mr Lincoln repeatedly stated on the part of the North that they had no intention of interfering with slavery as it existed in the South, much less abolishing it. The Government of the United States proclaimed freedom to the slaves in the hope that they would rise in rebellion against their master and thus assist in the subjugation of the South. It was for that purpose, and that purpose alone, that this famous proclamation was issued.

Nevertheless, the impression gained was that the main object of the war was the abolition of slavery. There could have been no greater fallacy.

The conduct of nine-tenths of the people of the Northern States towards slaves proved that they looked on them as a being of a lower race and unfit to associate with whites. Many instances that confirmed this came under my own notice while travelling through the Northern States in 1860.

One day while standing on the platform of the Railway station at Boston on my way to New York, a black man, dressed in the garb, and as circumstances proved, with the manners of a gentleman, approached to step into the same carriage where I had secured my seat.

"You are about to make a mistake I guess," said a white man – a Bostonian I presume who was seated close to the entrance to the cars – "the other car is the proper place for you," he continued pointing to the emigrant or luggage vans.

"I beg your pardon," said the black gentleman, for compared to the person by whom he had been so rudely accosted he was in tone and manners, indeed, a gentleman, "here is my ticket," producing a first-class ticket for examination.

"I don't care about your ticket" said the Yankee. "Just don't come in here – that's certain." And every white man in the car supported this person in his determination to exclude a man who was not of their colour. The black gentleman appealed to the conductor and this man conceded, to my disgust, with his white-faced brethren – so that the poor man was obliged to travel to New York with others of his colour in the emigrant van. Whether he had his first-class fare returned or not, I cannot say, but I am sure that any appeal from the conductor to the superintendent of the station, if there was one, would have been made in vain. I saw that every white man in that carriage would have left it if the black man had been permitted to enter and this was evidently well known to the conductor.[168]

I remember another case, but in this instance the person of colour did gain admission to the same carriage with her white "brothers", but in a manner I shall now explain.

I was on my way from New York to Albany, the capital of the state. All the carriages were very full, and the weather was warm and sultry. At one of the stations, when close to the end of our journey, a black woman entered the carriage in which I sat. All the others were full and as we had not many miles to go, I presume she was, for these reasons allowed to enter. I may explain that the American railway carriages are long, having a passage down the centre, with seats on each side and a door at each end.

The woman was very clean and respectfully dressed and she carried a fine little boy of her own colour in her arms. Her status seemed to be that of the wife of a superior mechanic. She was allowed to enter as I have stated, but that was all, for she was only allowed to stand, and no one offered her a seat.

The seat which I occupied was full but there was only one person on the seat opposite me, though the other seat was filled with a parcel and rug which evidently belonged to him. I turned to him and politely asked if he would allow me to put his parcel and rug aside so as to give a seat to the black woman who had evidently walked some considerable distance to the station and with the boy in her arms, who seemed much in want of a rest.

The passenger in the car looked at me with surprise as much as to say, how can one expect a white person to inconvenience himself for a black woman.

The man whom I had addressed merely remarked, "Wants a seat does she!" and concluded by attempting to joke about her excellent understanding – meaning that all black people had flat feet and were adapted to standing with ease even in railway carriages. I saw it was no use to have any conversation with him on the subject for he seemed in no way disposed to meet my request.

I consequently put his parcel and rug to one side, took the seat myself where they had been, and beckoned to the black woman to take my seat. She appeared to be very grateful. The whites around me seemed still more amazed at this further instance of a white man troubling himself about the comfort of a black and the man whom I had addressed looked at me very hard but offered no further remarks.

Their amazement however was greatly increased when I took the little black boy on my knee and dangled him in my arms. I did so for my own pleasure and to relieve the poor woman for a time of her burden. But when the little boy and I became friendly, which we soon did, and he began to put his little fingers through my long hair and his little black arms round my neck my fellow passengers looked aghast.

All this had happened in that particular section of America from whence arose the cry – "equal rights and freedom to the slave" – and when it reached me in England across the Atlantic, I thought of those things I have related and many others I could name. I said to myself, what a marvellous change has come over the people of the North in the short space of only three years! Can they really be in earnest to give in all respects equal rights to the blacks when they so very recently considered being altogether inferior to themselves?

The Northerners made the slave their instrument of restoring the South to the Union of the United States. As long as the Union could be restored, the state of the slave was not a matter of any consideration to most of the Northerners.

65 Overwork and stroke

In August 1864, I made my last speech in public as MP for Sunderland.[169] I wished to draw my constituents' attention to my views on the topics of the day. The two main topics were Free Trade and The American Civil War. The meeting was held at the Lyceum Theatre in Sunderland. It was very well attended.[170]

The Chairman introduced me and praised my efforts in improving the district, particularly the docks. He also credited me with inducing the Admiralty to include North Country coal in the list of their large requirements.

When I spoke, I firstly touched on free trade. Back in 1849, Britain had thrown open her ports to the ships of the world.[171] We had encouraged a large trade with all nations. I pointed out that ships were merely carriers of goods. The greater our increase in trading with other nations, the more goods we carry, the more employment there would be for our shipping business.[172]

Some other nations have not encouraged Free Trade. Portugal, Spain, France, and America did not reciprocate with us when we repealed the Navigation Laws. In resorting to protectionism, they have suffered.

I told the audience that it was likely that France would change and adopt Free Trade. To illustrate their dilemma, I said that that country seldom bought ships from other countries because the duty was so high that foreign builders were prevented from selling to the French. Our shipbuilders lost out, but so did the people of France. France required 80,000 tons of merchant shipping every year. In 1859 she only built 24,000 tons, in 1860 only 10,500 tons, and in 1861 only 4,800 tons.

My speech then continued turning to the American Civil War. I reiterated all the points that I had made in previous meetings. I pointed out that I had met several gentlemen who were now members of both the Confederate and Federal Governments and, as an onlooker, I arrived at certain conclusions. I referred to the fact that the South had complained about over-taxation and under-representation.

I added additional points. Workers in Britain had been seriously affected by the War. The price of cotton goods was twenty-five million before the war, it then became sixty million.

I said that France had long believed the friendly offices, not only of England and France, but of other European Powers, would be acceptable, and would aid the Government of America in solving the difficulty and in restoring peace.

Mr Adams, the Federal Government representative, had written to Lord John Russell to say that of 24 suspected blockade runners, he had put down twenty of them as belonging to me. I went to Lord John Russell and said that this was an extraordinary statement, as I had never heard of any of the vessels. I referred to other matters but ended the speech thanking the audience for their attention.

As I predicted, France reappraised her stance on Free Trade. Duties were to be abolished, and all the materials required in the construction and equipment of ships were to be admitted free of duty. Ships built, and fitted, in this and all other countries, were to be admitted, also free of duty.

Before the end of the year however, I fell ill. The pressures of the American Civil War, together with internal politics, and business affairs, weighed heavily on me, and in the end, it was too much. I had suffered a stroke. The newspapers referred to my sudden illness:

Alarming illness of Mr W.S. Lindsay MP

We regret to announce that Mr. Lindsay was seized yesterday with sudden and alarming illness, and up to the present time there has been no reported improvement in the condition of the hon. Gentleman. (*London Evening Standard*, 10/12/1864)

Part Six: American Civil War

Mr. Lindsay, MP

> Within the last few days reports which have been received with great and general regret have been in circulation relative to the serious illness of our able representative. We have made inquiries into the facts, and are sorry to state that the honourable gentleman, who has been staying for some time at Brighton for the improvement of his health, has had an attack of paralysis of the lower extremities. – *Sunderland Times*. (*The Globe*, 10/12/1864, *The Times*, 13/12/1864)

In January of 1865, I wrote to one of my Sunderland constituents to say that for the last month I had been under medical control. I had not been allowed to see my letters, but though still confined to bed, I had happily recovered as to be allowed again to take an interest in public affairs. The following week I wrote to another of my constituents to say that my doctors gave me every reason to hope that I would in time recover the complete use of my limbs and enjoy better health than I had done for many years past.[173] At the end of January I continued to improve and was recovered so that I could to leave my bed and to be up a few hours every day.

The *Newcastle Daily Chronicle* reported that there was very little doubt that I would be able to contest the Borough of Sunderland for my position as MP in the forthcoming election. But by mid-March I was exceedingly ill again. This time I would be confined to a wheelchair for the next 12 years. I was 49 years old.

My days in Parliament as an MP were over.

Part Seven

Maritime Historian and Author

(1865–1877)

66 Recovery

After my stroke I was very ill for a year, and it took me a long time to recover. On 19 December 1865 I reached fifty. Even if I was able to walk about like other people, and in an ordinary state of health, I would still feel that I was becoming an old man. After 50 the hill becomes very steep, and men seem to stumble down it very fast. The race of life from 50 to 70 must seem much shorter than from 30 to 50 and not half the length as that from 10 to 30. The sore on my back confined me to bed for more than 18 months after my affliction.[1]

During the winter of 1866-67, I found ample work for my spare hours. My correspondence did not exceed on an average four to five letters every day and did not occupy more than an hour or two, but I created for myself an abundance of work. There were lots of old papers to destroy and to glance over, before I parted with them. Then there were many letters worth keeping. To classify these and add to them, with reminiscences of my own, and recollections of bygone times, enabled me to get over the winter without feeling the time hang heavy on me.

On the contrary, I was so fully employed that the winter passed away as swiftly as ever, and as much as when I was able to take part in active life. My work, though neither profitable, nor, I fear, useful, was very pleasant and answered the purpose for which it was undertaken.

I was however getting short of something to do and, as an active mind needed to be employed – be it for good or evil – like many other people I resolved to keep a journal.

I kept one for a good many years, but it was very irregularly kept, and months at a stretch often elapsed without a note of any kind. I hoped to keep

Part Seven: Maritime Historian and Author

my present one much more frequently – at least I ought to do so for I had more time at my disposal – much more than I ever had before.

My health on the whole settled down and became pretty good, though at times I suffered very much from pains and cramps in my loins and limbs. I could not walk and was obliged to be lifted. This work, my man Jones did with comparative ease. Repetitive practice helped. I once heard of a man who, when his cow presented him with a calf, lifted it in his arms, and did so every morning until the calf became a cow. It did not appear any heavier to him than it was when a calf. Jones had a similar experience with me. I got somewhat stouter and heavier than I was when lifted from my bed just 12 months earlier, but he lifted me with quite as much ease as he did then.[2]

I have slept on a waterbed since my affliction a long while ago. I enjoy it. My breakfast is delivered in bed at 9 and after that I read the newspapers until ¼ to 12 when I am lifted into my chair in which I can wheel myself about.

When the weather is good and warm, I take up my quarter under a tree in the garden or have a drive for a couple of hours in the carriage, or a cruise on the steamer depending on circumstances. If cold or wet, I keep to my library and employ myself writing when I have nothing else to do, and as I do not go to bed until 9 p.m. I have consequently a great deal of spare time.[3]

67 Changing Tack

We are creations of circumstances. I knew I should never be able again to take any part, either in the business of the City, or in the affairs of Parliament, and therefore I directed my attention to matters within my reach, and to the improvement of my property and the people in the surrounding district. I had no desire ever to leave Shepperton.

The shipping interest was in a state of great prosperity, but whilst prices were high, I built no ships. On the contrary, I decided to dispose of the *Austin Friars, Shepperton, Woodham,* and *Medusa*. These ships had been managed by Mr Young[4] who recently died. Whilst they had done exceedingly well since they were built, on examining the accounts I found that a very large amount of return commissions had yet to be placed to the credit of their accounts. I had directed the special attention of the Executors to it. For instance, the commission on the last voyage of the *Austin Friars* from the North of England to Jeddah in the Red Sea, hence to Bombay and London, occupying 4 months, amounted to no less than £800. This included the £250 charged by Mr Young for management as agreed, but the remainder seemed to have been paid to brokers and agents.

The sale of the *Austin Friars* realised £17,400 and the *Woodham* £15,600. The *Shepperton* realised £13,400 and the *Medusa* £700. The four therefore fetched £47,100. The latter two were very fair prices, but not equal in proportion to what was obtained for the *Austin Friars* and *Woodham*. Prices have fallen since the vessels were sold. And I daresay, if these four ships had been sold later, the prices would have dropped by at least £800.

I foresaw a panic amongst the owners of steamships, or rather amongst the bankers who had advanced money upon them. Ten or twelve years ago the Bank of Scotland advanced £80,000 on the SS *Australasian* belonging to the European and Australasian Steam Navigation Co. That ship, I know, cost £140,000. The advance was not considered an imprudent one, but within two years of the time when it had been made, there came a slump which so terrified the Directors of the Bank that they foreclosed their mortgage, and in their terror sold her to Cunard & Co for £40,000. I can vouch for the fact as the transaction passed through my firm as brokers.[5]

At the same time as I was divesting of the interests in my ships, I realised that I could not continue with my Company. This realism had started in the American Civil War when I shunned any trade with the United States.

I negotiated with my partners, especially Edgar Stringer and Edward Pembroke, to sell my share.[6] The Company became Stringer, Pembroke & Co, although it was known still as Lindsay & Co. It soon became apparent that they needed another partner. I had known James Galbraith in his capacity as head of P. Henderson & Co. He then became senior Partner, and the Company became Galbraith, Pembroke & Co.[7]

In 1863, dispensing with the Company that I started in 1847 caused much friction between me and my partners.[8] I continued to get bills in my name rather than in the new partnership. When James Galbraith entered the arena, he was a calming influence.

The process of handing over the Company was painful and stressful. I needed to part with the Company that I had built from nothing. Money was due to me, and my partners resisted paying it. After a long-protracted negotiation, I wrote to Mr Galbraith in December 1869 to say: "Now to make a long story short, to end the vexatious matter I am ready without prejudice to accept £5,000."[9] The following month I wrote to Mr Galbraith again:

> To close, I hope for ever, a very unpleasant and very disastrous affair for me, I return herewith the counterpart of the agreement signed as you have drawn it up without any alterations and I may add that I do not think I should have agreed to these terms to any other man than yourself.[10]

It was hard to part with the Company with so little return.

The world of shipping was changing radically. The Suez Canal opened in 1869 and the route to the East significantly changed. No longer did ships have to travel via the Cape of Good Hope. Increased competition increased risks and reduced profits.

With the money from the sale of my ships and the money saved, I embarked on further house building, and farming. The advice offered by my good friend

Part Seven: Maritime Historian and Author

Richard Cobden all those years earlier to focus on a different business was finally coming to fruition.

When my shipping line commenced sailing from Dartmouth in 1856, I had bought seven houses and a Public House (the Lindsay Arms) there. As the line no longer ran, I sold these properties ten years later.[11] Following the Crimean War, I had purchased a property in Surrey consisting of Dorney House and the Lincoln Arms Hotel, with about 9 or 10 acres of land.

In the grounds of Dorney House I constructed 6 semi-detached villas and 6 semi-detached villa cottages. The situation was good with a fine view, and I let the former for £70 per annum and the latter for £35. They yielded a good return as my contract price for their completion, with garden walls and everything ready for occupation, was £4,500. The villas contained a drawing room, dining room and parlour, 4 bedrooms and dressing room with two superior attic bedrooms – kitchen scullery and all the usual conveniences. The builder was Mr Carter of Weybridge and Winchester, and as he had had great experience in his business, he finished the houses in good style.

Very many improvements have been made to the village during the last 10 or 11 years but we still had much to do in this neighbourhood. When I was in the process of identifying improvements to Shepperton, I asked Sir Joseph Paxton to design a "model" village for the settlement.[12] He duly did so. The large plans showed planned squares, gardens, and villas, and while the whole plan was not carried out, several of the houses were built, replacing the 'very wretched' one- and two-roomed cottages in the village.[13]

Latterly I invested in property where I had built three houses in 'Nanny Goat Lane' and built six more there. As a result, I had a good many houses built on my property, some of them on my own account and others by builders to whom I made an advance, holding the houses as security for the repayment.

To find out what a house cost I built one. I found all the materials myself, and contracted with the workmen of the village, who were out of employment. I paid them weekly three-quarters of the wages they would have received when on daily pay and the balance of the contract price when the work was completed.

I was surprised to find the low price at which timber deals, glass, paint, and especially all hardware materials could be obtained for cash, and I found that the house, which I have already let on lease, had cost me much less money than I would have paid for it to any builder.

Not only did I build houses, but I erected a cabinet maker's shop on which I made not merely the doors and other fittings for the houses, but a great deal of furniture as well. I quickly made 3 handsome wardrobes, and the cost was a great deal less than I could have purchased them for, while the materials and workmanship were much superior. I made all the furniture for the Bournemouth house, which was being built, as well as much that was required to furnish a house for my son Willie and his wife-to-be Annie.[14]

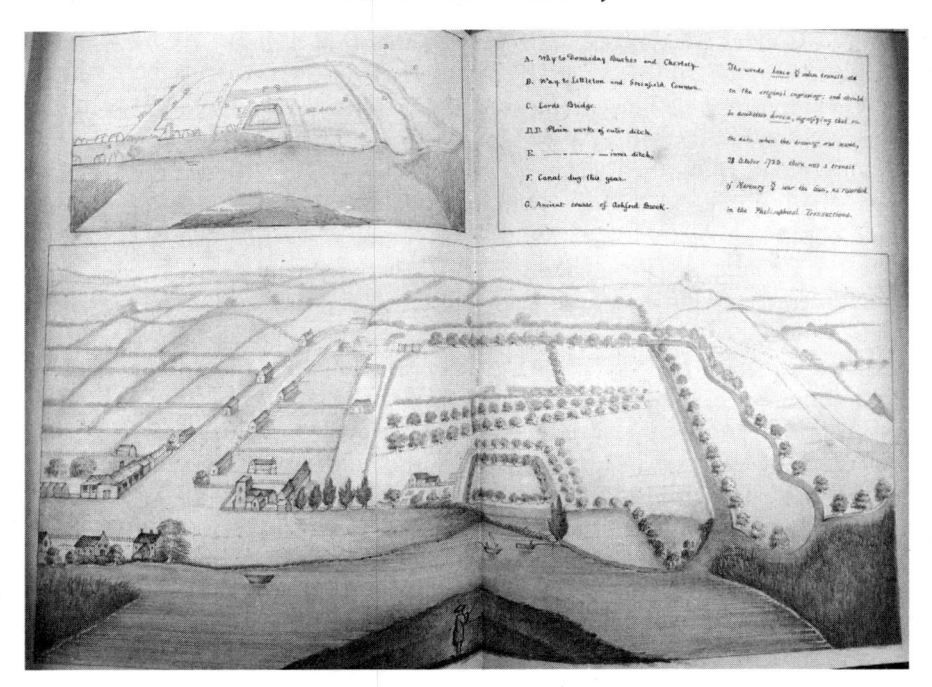

Map of Shepperton in Lindsay's journal. NMM: LND 5–4,559

I also had 440,000 bricks made out of a piece of land which people had said did not contain earth sufficient to make 300,000 and had still left earth enough on the same spot to make 3 million more.

I entered into arrangements with Mr Carter the builder to create a new home in Woodham of a superior kind; and also, four new model cottages. Those existing on the property were of the most wretched description built of mud and containing only two apartments not fit for human beings.

The old farmhouse was small and inconvenient and though not more than 70 or 80 years old was fast falling to decay. It was beyond repair. The bricks from it and from an old brick kiln on the property sufficed to build the houses I erected. I calculated on an outlay of £2,000 to make the property fit for a gentleman.

Mr Wheeler the builder roofed three of the houses he had contracted to build close to the Railway Station. At the beginning I could not say that I admired their appearance, but they looked better when finished. I contracted with Mr Easter to make additions to Halliford Manor House and the house and grounds were very materially improved.

I arranged plans for re-building and increasing the size of the girls' school at my own expense. The schools were finished, and I think the hitherto impossible feat of converting "a sow's lug into a silk purse" had been accomplished. While affording greatly increased accommodation to the children, they looked well and were a feature in our village instead as hereto a disfigurement. They proved valuable as a public hall and for 'penny readings'.

Part Seven: Maritime Historian and Author

In addition, I had a large hand in building the single-line Thames Valley Railway terminating at Shepperton station. It was opened in 1864, and at first eight trains ran each way daily.

When I bought the Manor House at Shepperton, the manor farm came with it. At first, I let the farm out[15] but I realised that I could not obtain the amount I wished when the lease needed to be renewed, I therefore took the farm into my own hands. I did so with considerable reluctance, as I was ignorant about anything connected with farming operations.

I appointed a bailiff, but I expected a loss, for though farming good land is a profitable business if commercially conducted, he had very extravagant notions and did not attend to his work as closely as I could have wished. However, whatever the result, I gained some insight into the business. The leading points I learnt needed attention were as follows:

1. Keep the land clean and free from weeds.
2. Put plenty of manure on it.
3. Keep as much improvable stock, sheep, and heifers, as the land will bear.
4. Adhere to the old mercantile maxim of buying when things are cheap and selling when high.
5. Use machinery instead of manual labour when it can be done without too great outlay for the work it has to do.
6. Sell your stock of sheep, cattle, pigs and poultry whenever they are fat enough for consumption and have reached their full size.[16]

And these six headings may be condensed into three – clean well, fertilize well, and buy well.

Such were the conclusions at which I arrived in my limited experience of farming; and one of them certainly was not attended to by my bailiff – he did not buy well. He bought sheep, in spite of my protest to the contrary, when they were double their present price; and I cannot anticipate any profitable results from farming under him.

In 1867, I bought a property in Surrey known as Woodham Farm. It consisted of about 144 acres. The land was good, but it was in a rough state. It was bordered on the one side by the Basingstoke Canal, and on the other, the main line of the London and Southwestern Railway. It was about two miles from Woking Station on the one side and two miles from Weybridge Station on the other. As the population of the district increases the Railway Co will be obliged to place another station between these two places[17] and if so, it will convert Woodham into building land and materially enhance the value of it. I had this in view when I bought it. The price I paid was £8,000, or about £55 10/- per acre, and as it was all freehold except for 3 acres, I think I made a very good investment. I daresay when my son is my age the land at Woodham may be worth £200 per acre if not more.[18]

The buildings on the farm are a disgrace. The five cottages are of mud – pure mud erection - and in these human beings reside within twenty miles, or half an hour by rail, of the great metropolis! I propose spending, one way and another, a good deal of money on the property and if I can induce the Southwestern Railway Co to erect a station on their main line at Byfleet corner, the investment cannot fail to prove an excellent one.

In 1872, I bought Pannels farm. I paid £10,300 for it. The farm consists of 137 acres, and I am disposed to think that my speculation, once again, will prove a very good one. It lies between Chertsey and Addlestone. The portion of it nearest Chertsey is not more than 200 yards from the Railway Station.

The farm is in a rough state though the land is very good, better than Woodham, but as people called it 'back land' I suppose that was the main reason why few persons thought of buying it. I saw however, that by cutting a road right through it from Chertsey Station to Addlestone, I should not merely render great service to the inhabitants of both localities by opening a way where one is very much required but should turn the whole into frontage on rising and undulating ground with a fine southern aspect commanding a beautiful view. I therefore had no hesitation in purchasing the farm.

I also bought another farm, lands of about 140 acres close to Chobham which I have been improving, by thinning the trees, grubbing the fences, cleaning the ditches, weeding, and draining.

The farms will prove a sound investment.

68 Tales by the Riverbank

My time sitting by the Thames riverbank at the end of my garden was frequently occupied talking with visitors. I invited politicians, friends, and relations to spend time with me to mull over news and events. During these visits I heard many amusing stories. Here are a few.

The Earl's Butler

Almost every man has a hobby, and the hobby of the Earl Kilmorey[19] during the last quarter of a century seems to have been to purchase honest estates on the banks on the Thames, improve them and then sell them.

All his improvements have been carried out in first-class style, and with the most exquisite taste. The Earl's pride was to work amongst his workmen, in a labourer's clothes and to be considered one of them.

One day a tramp, meeting the Earl in his workman's clothes in the avenue at Woburn, asked him if he knew if the Earl was at home.

"How so?" enquired his Lordship.

"Oh." said the tramp, "Now that I am through the gate, I can reach the house. I am sure to get half a crown from the old fellow if the servants in the hall only let him know that I'm badly off."

Part Seven: Maritime Historian and Author

"Good luck to you," said the Earl and they parted, the tramp continuing his way along the avenue, the Earl reaching the house by a short cut before him.

"Any luck?" said the Earl when they met again, about the same place half an hour later.

"Too right!" replied the tramp, producing half a crown and rejoicing over his good fortune.

"Was that all?" enquired the Earl, "Did you not get two of them?"

"Two! No." said the tramp, "Why did you ask?"

"Oh." replied the Earl, "The old fellow when he is in the right mood, and when needy chaps like you and I get to the house they often get five bob! You see I got a crown." continued his Lordship producing the coin from his pocket, "But he saw me and didn't see you, I suppose, and saw I was a hard-working man out of work, so he gave me more. The old Earl is a real good 'un to poor working folks when they are badly off." And with these explanatory remarks the Earl and the tramp again parted company.

On his Lordship's return to the house he called his butler who, after some cross questioning, confirmed that he had kept one of the half crowns to himself which the Earl had given to him to give to the tramp, and as he had reason to suspect that the Butler had for some time been helping himself in various ways, he had, on the spur of the moment, devised this plan to find him out. The butler and the Earl parted company that day.[20]

Thames Steamer's Smoke

My good friend Ayrton built a small steamer for me.[21] She was very complete and did him credit. Her cost altogether was about £250 including the various extras. Travelling with the stream she went 9 mph and against the stream 7½ mph.[22]

She could take twenty-one persons on board, although that was too many. She was fitted so that I could enter with my wheelchair. For that purpose, a portion of the side was made lower to the level of a platform. This platform was then lowered by a screw underneath to the level of the floor of the boat. By this means I was able to enjoy a sail with my friends on the river. It was certainly a great boon to me and added substantially to my enjoyment during the summers.

I had various cruises in the steamer. My usual trip was to leave the boathouse here at the Manor at 2 p.m. and go down as far as Kingston or Teddington, returning in time for dinner at 6 o'clock. At other times we left at noon, have our lunch at the 'The Bells of Ouzeley'[23] and generally go up as far as Windsor, returning here at 6 or 7 o'clock for a tea dinner. On all occasions I had friends, numbering from four to ten, who seemed to enjoy the trip. When the weather was unsettled, we still enjoyed the cruises as awnings were fitted to the boat to escape the heaviest rain.

I received a lecture from old Lord St Leonards,[24] whom I never saw to my knowledge, concerning my little steamer. It will be found in the following letter[25] from him which was worthy of preservation as the production of a remarkable man, now ninety years of age!

Boyle Farm
Friday [September 1871]

Sir,
When a steamer does not consume its own smoke and the wind brings its smoke into or across my grounds, unless my windows are all shut, which does not often happen, we should be forced to leave the house for a time and we should sustain much damage. I mention this in order to show to you why I am compelled to object to any steamer passing this house without consuming its own smoke.

Parliament has protected a house like this by forbidding steamers from passing without consuming its own smoke and making it liable to a fine of 5d.

Of course, I have no intention to take any legal steps but as your boat went up today without consuming its own smoke, I was compelled to send to the Bridge at the Palace to ascertain who it was that had passed this place and I find that you are the gentleman.

I request you to believe that nothing is further from my intention than to write a word which would give you pain; but I request you not to pass this place without consuming your own smoke.

Your faithful servant
[Lord] St Leonards [Sir Edward Sugden]

Of course, I sent him a polite note in reply saying that in future I should endeavour, in passing his lawn at Thames Ditton, not to allow any smoke to escape from the furnace that would be offensive to him, though I feared that a smoke consumer could not be fitted to the boiler of a vessel so small as mine.

My reply seemed to have satisfied the old man and my courtesy in sending him a copy of the essay on ancient galleys[26] appears to have gratified him still more, for in the three letters with which he honours me, he rises from "Sir" to "Dear Sir" and then "My Dear Sir".

A Royal Offering
Many years earlier, in 1858, before my stroke, Lord Clarence Paget and I were sitting on the round seat under the old elm tree which stands upon the banks of the Thames and close to my boat house. My little iron steam yacht *Neptune* lay moored in the river right opposite to where we sat.[27]

Our conversation in part referred to the Queen and her family and especially to the education of the Prince of Wales and Prince Alfred. Though the latter was then only a boy of 13 or 14 years of age it had been arranged for some while that he was to follow the sea as a profession. Some remarks which I had made regarding the education and training of youths in the position of the Prince of Wales and his brother struck Lord Clarence very much – so much so that he said he wished they could be brought under the notice of the Queen.

The little yacht *Neptune* could fulfil a role. I had no use for her.[28] She was a very pretty toy and would suit the two princes, either in the Isle of Wight, or on the river at Windsor. She was of little value to me as I had no spare time to have a cruise in her. The boat might be of some use to them in various ways.

Though both Paget and I know that presents were seldom or ever accepted, I proposed to offer her the boat. Paget forwarded my letter to him to Sir Charles Phipps[29] which led to the letters I have here inserted.

House of Commons
London
2 July 1858

My dear Lindsay

I enclose Phipp's answer – I confess I am not sorry for the result for I hope someday to have a cruise in the "Neptune" which I should probably never had, had she changed hands!

You have done a generous and loyal act and have given wholesome advice where few have opportunities or inclination to do so.

Very faithfully yours,
C Paget

Buckingham Palace
1 July.1858

My dear Lord Clarence

May I ask you to appraise Mr Lindsay that the Queen very highly appreciates the loyal and kind offer which you communicated to me from him, and that although the established rule precluded the acceptance of his yacht, the motives which dictated the will to present it to the Prince of Wales were very highly valued by Her Majesty. Indeed, I have seldom seen a better letter or one containing more sound sense and truth than that which you sent to me.

There is a fixed rule against the acceptance by the Queen or Royal Family of any presents, and any departure from this rule would be considered an invidious exception by those to whom it has been previously, or may be hereafter, noted.

The Queen feels she must therefore be obliged to decline Mr Lindsay's most kind and considerate offer.

Sincerely yours
C B Phipps.

A *Vicar Afloat*
On the subject of the Thames, in January 1877, we were experiencing floods in and around Shepperton. Water kept rising and was 6 inches deep at our

lodge gate and was close to the steps of the Hall door. We had to punt from the lodge to the railway station. At the Lords Bridge it was fully 7 feet above the crown of the road, and the water extended close up to the schoolhouse. The water was as high as it was in the floods of 1852.

Our Rector, Mr Martin[30] came to the Manor House to ask me if I would invite the Archdeacon and himself to dinner when he was to be inducted into his charge. I learnt he had bought the living for £9,000, a very high price, so, I suppose he could not very well afford to give the Archdeacon dinner. A week later I received a note from the Archdeacon[31] saying that he would be delighted to dine with me. I told the parson that if the floods did not go down, he must postpone the induction, as it would never do to fetch the Archdeacon in a punt.

A few days later, I received a note from the rector saying he wished to call and thank me in person but that he cannot reach the Manor House from the Rectory on account of the floods without climbing over the division wall between us, which would be quite as undignified as the Archdeacon going to his induction in a punt! Here is a newspaper cutting at the time that reflected on the floods.

Shepperton

The whole of the village of Shepperton is surrounded, and many of the inhabitants have been obliged to abandon their houses, while others are living in the upper floors and are in danger of being without even the common necessaries of life, as the tradesmen of the village are in the same predicament. On Sunday the curious spectacle was seen of inhabitants going to the parish church in boats, it being accessible by no other means. A congregation of about 70 assembled, many of them attracted by the novelty.[32]

69 Winter House by the Sea

In the winter of 1867, my wife Helen and her sister Christina decided to spend time on the South coast of England. They hoped that the sea air would improve my wife's ill health, which had plagued her most of her life. They chose Weymouth, but not finding suitable accommodation there, they moved on to Bournemouth.

So it was that, in joining them two or three months later, I moved from home for the first time since I was seized with my stroke three years earlier. Even in my invalid state the train journey was surprisingly easy.

Bournemouth, besides being a complete change from Shepperton, has many attractions. Its situation in the hollow of a chalk cliff, which faces the South, and with the sea for its Southern boundary, renders its temperatures warmer and equal than perhaps any other place in England, and its atmosphere less moist. It is surrounded with pine-clad hills in the midst of which are studded numerous detached villas which rival, in architectural beauty and comfort, any buildings of a similar kind I ever saw.

Part Seven: Maritime Historian and Author

The following year we again visited Bournemouth and thoroughly enjoyed it. It completely restored my wife's health. Altogether this place pleased us so much that I bought a house there. The climate is so excellent in the winter season. The house is situated on the East Cliff facing the sea and commands a beautiful view of the Isle of Wight and the Needles on the one hand, and St Albans Head and Poole Bay on the other. I paid £2,400 for it, complete with stalls etc, and I anticipate that the investment will prove a favourable one. If we had not been able to occupy it for a portion of the year, we would still have been able to let it at a profit.

As we did not intend to visit Bournemouth during the winter of 1871, I consequently let the house (Ravenscliff) for six months at 16 guineas per week. Indeed, I've always been able to find a tenant when it is not being used by us.[33]

I decided to build a new house nearby and sold Ravenscliff for £6,000. As it did not cost me more than £4,000, the sale yielded a considerable profit. It was difficult finding another site, and it took longer than I expected. I gave a young architect, Mr Ernest Porter, the task of drawing up the plans for the new house.

Meanwhile, my time at Shepperton Manor was spent in my established routine. I keep to my old habit of being called at 6.30 a.m. and reading books and newspapers until noon when I was hoisted out of bed by two men, for Jones my butler had an illness and was no longer able to lift me without assistance. I then had a long drive or a cruise on the steamer, depending on circumstances, and usually had an abundance of work of one sort or another. Nor did the work decrease.

At last, in November 1873, we inhabited our new house in Bournemouth. I called the new home "Ravensworth". The rooms we occupy have long since been put in order, and are very fine and very comfortable, although there are still a great many odds and ends to be completed about the house.

It contains 18 bedrooms, 6 sitting rooms, and no end of other rooms and other places. It is a very grand affair, the finest house in the place, and much too grand for us! It contains 43 apartments and, in the lodge, and over the stalls which are very large, there are another 7 or 8 rooms.[34] I have spent a very large sum on furniture. Bournemouth has doubled in size since we first came here 5 years ago. A great number of Scots people are buying or building houses in the town.

The builder, Mr Haggard of Bournemouth, has built many of the houses here, and has sold them all at a significant profit. Within the last three years, the increase in the value of house property has been very great. Although I made a fair profit on my former house Ravenscliff, I think if I had held on to it until now, I could have realised £8,000 instead of £6,000. The house which Admiral Sulivan built next to it, and sold only two years later for £3,500, has just been sold for £7,500. Hume Towers, which cost the late Sir Joshua Walmsley[35] about £10,000 in 1871, has since been disposed of by his executors for £20,000!

Now that I have almost switched away from Shipping, I have built the house as an investment. My present intention is to occupy it for 2 or

Cottonwood Hotel, Bournemouth, formerly *Ravensworth*, William Schaw Lindsay's house. Completed in 1873.

3 months each winter and let it for the remainder of the year, which I hope to do at a profit. I value the property as it stands, furnished, at £20,000, although I hardly expect to get anything like that sum. I intend to hold on to the house for some time, as property is rising in value here and nearly all the sites fronting the sea are now taken. But even if it does not yield a large interest on the capital invested, I see no reason why I should not enjoy myself in my old age, especially as others may benefit from my toil when I am gone, without displaying much wisdom or reflection.

We did not make use of the house every year. The sore on my back, which had developed when I had my stroke years earlier, flared up from time to time and prevented me from visiting.[36]

Housebuilding was an enjoyable amusement for me and kept me fully employed. I attended to everything myself, even buying and fitting curtains, and beds. If I did not, things would not make very rapid progress. My wife is not very fond of work, and our son takes very much after her in that respect.[37]

70 Admiralty Reform

During January 1868 the newspapers focused their attention once again on Admiralty mismanagement. This had been an interest of mine since the

Crimean War a decade earlier. The lack of accountability, and minimal control of expenses, troubled me.

I wrote to the Editor of the "Star" newspaper under a pseudonym,[38] saying that I hoped for success in the long-expected measures of Reform. The Government I understood may offset the Reform by offering an enquiry, which I said would only delay, or shelve, the question altogether.[39] The following changes I pointed out as imperatively necessary to combine efficiency with economy:

1. The abolition of the Admiralty Board.
2. The appointment of a Minister of Marine, or Secretary of State, who alone should be responsible to the country, and who, with the Under Secretary of State, should be the only two persons connected with the Admiralty who would be required to retire at each change of Government.
3. The division of the whole work into four great departments:
   first, to construct and repair our ships,
   second, to store and provision them,
   third, to equip and man them,
   fourth, to keep the accounts.
   Everything that the Admiralty was required to do could be embraced under these heads.
4. Should the Minister require the assistance of practical men, he should be empowered to summon, in the form of a council, the respective chiefs of these departments. These men, holding permanent appointments, and familiar with the details of their respective offices, would prove much more efficient and effective councillors than any Board of Admiralty, however able, presently constituted.
5. Place all our dockyards upon the competitive system and place a permanent superintendent at the head of each, vested with sufficient power to cause him to feel an interest and pride in the great and very important work under his charge, and in its efficiency and economy.

What I meant by the competitive system, as applied to our dockyards, was that, instead of lumping in our estimates for timber, or for iron, or for other articles required by the whole of the dockyards, there should be a separate and distinct account for each laid before Parliament, not in confused detail, as all the accounts were then, but in round figures.

For instance, the quantity of materials delivered to Portsmouth dockyard and the expenditure in wages for the year; these items would form one side of the account, and on the other should appear what the yard produced in new ships, and what, as far as practicable, it did in the way of repairs.

Similar accounts should be rendered by all yards; and thus, we would see what Portsmouth gave us for our money compared to Plymouth or any other yard; and thus, we should also afford the superintendents an opportunity of showing what each could do, and thus creating amongst them a system of laudable and wholesome rivalry.

In July I followed up with another letter to the same newspaper.[40] I wrote to say that although I was no longer a politician, and therefore I was no longer privy to private papers, I could grasp what was transpiring. I said that Parliament would soon be called upon to place at the disposal of the Admiralty Board, ten or eleven million pounds of public money, to be disposed of, I feared, as it had hitherto been, without accountability.

I said that whilst no nation at present intended to attack us, we were spending far more money on our navy than any other nation, and at the same time losing the supremacy we had always held in effective ships of war. Nor was that all. If these ships were required, the irresponsible and unreformed Board which professed to manage them would get us into the same chaos that it did in 1854 during the Crimean War.

I said Mr Seely MP made the grave charge against those who administered our naval affairs, that in four years – 1860 to 1864 – they received £1,870,000 for which they had not accounted in any shape or form. Nor did their lordships appear to have taken any steps to prevent the possibility of such a thing occurring again. Mr. Seely next charged the Admiralty with the most wanton extravagance in the constitution of our ships. In Parliament, he stated that the *Frederick William*[41] had cost the country £281,691 before she was ready for service. It appeared that the Board knew little about the cost of the *Frederick William*, or any other ship. Mr. Seely proved that the *Frederick William* cost somewhat more than the sum stated, and if they had charged depreciation on the machinery in their yards, and interest on the plant, she would be found to have cost the country £332,156. Had rent on the land, insurance, and other items also been included, the cost of the ship would have been at least £350,000 whereas Mr. Seely showed that such a ship ought to have been built for £134,450.

Admiral Robinson[42] for the Board said that the national dockyards were established on entirely different grounds to those private undertakings. Wherein, I asked, was the difference? Except that the private yards built and repaired ships for any person who employed them, whereas the national dockyards did the same work for the nation. They were established for that purpose, and for no other.

The Financial Controller submitted to the Board that "the commercial establishments existed to make as much profit as they could," and added with a wicked honesty which was amusing, that the Royal dockyards had no such object in view.

The Controller, however, did not deny that the *Frederick William* cost the country the sum Mr. Seely had named; but he said it arose from that gentleman's "theory of recording dockyard expenses differing from that adopted by the Admiralty", by which he implied that the Admiralty was not in the habit of recording what a thing cost.

The fact remained that before the *Frederick William* could be of any use, we had paid for her at least £281,691 when we might have had an equally good ship for less than half that money. Besides, any system which allowed a ship to remain twenty-four years on the stocks could not be a good one. The duty of the Admiralty, I conceived, should be to lay down such ships that would prove most serviceable to the nation, and finish them with all prudent and possible despatch ready for service. Our great aim should be to keep pace with the march of improvement with each successive ship, but it was impossible to do so if we kept our ships on the stocks until they became obsolete.

No amount of conversion can make such vessels equal to those of other nations which adopted the principles of being kept up to date. That our Admiralty Board had ever repudiated that common-sense principle is too apparent, for we were building sailing ships long after the screw was found to be essential for the purposes of war; and we were laying down wooden ships long after science and experience had clearly proved that they must give way to iron and armour plates. I ended my letter to the newspaper with: "Thus, it is that while we spend much more money than our neighbours, we do not keep pace with them."

Mr Seely soon discovered that I was the anonymous author of these letters. I had various letters from him – or rather from Mrs Seely, who on many things is the better man – highly approving of what I stated. The Tories however were still in power when he drew up his report and the result of course was that he was outvoted in all he proposed to do, and the situation was very much as he found it.

71 The Navy, Past and Present

I had always written letters on shipping matters to the newspapers and in 1870 at the request of the editor of the *Illustrated London News* I wrote an article for their Christmas number.[43] No fewer than forty tons of paper were consumed in that single issue, and it exceeded 200,000 copies. The article must therefore have come under the notice of a great many readers, but I fear it was too dry for many of them to have read it. This is what I wrote:

> Many of the ships of the past may still be seen at anchor in the vicinity of our Royal Dockyards. In their dismantled state they are clumsy-looking hulks; but they were noble craft when fully equipped and manned, and it was through their instrumentality, and their rough-and-ready crews, that England maintained her maritime superiority during the most critical period of her history. These were the bulldogs which, in days gone by, not merely protected our shores from any foreign aggressor, but swept the seas of the ships of any nation hostile to the British crown.

At the commencement of 1793, just before the French Republic bade defiance to Europe and involved the Continent and our own island in a terrible war, we had in commission 135 vessels of all sorts, of which 26 were ships of the line, measuring 44,000 tons. In 1800 they had increased to 468 in commission. In 1812, when at war with both France and the United States of America, our wooden walls had reached 621 in commission, of which 102 were vessels of the line, measuring 185,000 tons. Each of these three- and two-decked ships mounted from 60 to 120 guns and was manned by a crew varying from 500 to 600 of the most skilled, and perhaps the most daring seamen that the world in any age has ever produced. We then presented a front to all our enemies which they vainly attempted to destroy; but, though so powerful then, how insignificant was the force of that proud fleet when compared with the warships of today!

Not one of the three-deckers of our fleet of 1,793 mounted guns throwing shot of 24 lb. weight, except the 32-pounders on lower decks; and only five of the first-rates carried 18-pounders on the main deck, the great bulk of the guns then consisting of 6, 9, and 12 pounders. These guns were, however, superseded, soon after the declaration of war, by 24 lb. and 32 lb. carronades, which in their day proved most effective weapons. About the year 1838 the carronades gave place to guns of much heavier weight, and within a few years of that time the lower decks of our line-of-battle ships and the main decks of our frigates mounted 8-in guns. But simultaneously there was produced an instrument more terrible than the gun with its solid shot of 68 lb. weight. The shell, which in its progressive movements has entirely changed our war-vessels and, in a measure, altered the mode of maritime warfare, was then for the first time introduced into the Navy.

In the meantime, steam had become an important motive power. Paddle-wheel-steamers, which at first were limited to about 300 tons, were at last built of 1,500 to 1,800 tons register, mounting on their upper decks shell-guns of 10-in. bore. But these steamers, though valuable for skirmishing and for other purposes where sailing-vessels could not be employed, were otherwise found to be very inefficient in war, from the facility with which their paddles and machinery could be destroyed or disabled by the fire of the enemy; and consequently, they were superseded by the application of the screw. There then arose a vastly superior class of wooden line-of-battle ships, represented by the *Duke of Wellington*, of 700 hp, mounting 121 guns;[44] the *Jean D'Acre*, of 101 guns and 600 hp; and the *James Watt*, of the same engine-power, mounting 91 guns, the extra gun consisting of a heavy pivot on the upper deck. But, beyond these splendid ships of the line, we sent to sea a class of unrivalled frigates, of which the *Imperieuse*, of 500 hp and 50 guns, and the *Arrogant* and *Dauntless*, of 40 and 24 guns respectively, were excellent specimens. No country ever built nobler and at the time more powerful vessels than the frigates, of from

2,000 to 3,000 tons, which we launched from our dockyards, as it were, only the other day; and yet, within the last few years, these have been put aside by the iron-clad fleets of the present.

The *Warrior* was the first of this class. Though a magnificent ship, she is in many respects inferior to the *Sultan*. We have now – they seem the creation of yesterday—afloat and during construction, besides what have been ordered this year, no less than forty-seven of these gigantic armour-plated ships. Eleven of them have a uniform maximum speed of 14½ knots, or more than 16 miles an hour; eight have a speed of 13 knots; and thirteen will sail at the rate of 12½ knots, which far exceeds the average speed of the merchant vessels of our own or of any other country. Combined they measure 178,000 tons, propelled by 37,500 hp; and their 591 guns could throw a broadside of more than 62,000lb. of metal.

Nevertheless, in the face of this gigantic power, there are many persons who are constantly complaining that we are not sufficiently armed to maintain our maritime supremacy; others, again, tell us that, however powerful our armour-plated fleet, it would have been much more so had there been less variety among the ships and their armaments; but these critics forget that our fleet of the present is even now only an experimental one. War is still waged between the artillerist and shipbuilder. Messrs. Armstrong and Whitworth are still prepared to manufacture guns which will penetrate any armour-plate that the Admiralty can produce. The *Warrior* and *Achilles*-class were designed to carry 68 and 100 pounders, and were plated to resist guns of that size; but these vessels were hardly afloat before projectiles of 250 lb., 300 lb., and 400 lb. weight were created to destroy them; then we had to build ships of the *Bellerophon*, *Hercules*, and *Audacious*-class, to carry such great guns; and to plate them with armour sufficient to resist a shot or shell of the increased size. These, in turn, have already been found too weak to cope successfully with vessels which could throw a shot or shell of 600 lb. weight. Consequently, the *Monarch* and *Captain* were produced, with guns, fitted in a turret, capable of throwing in any direction, and for from five to six miles, projectiles of that enormous weight. Cased in iron armour, 7 in. and 8 in. thick, with a backing of 12 in. of East India teak, upon a skin of 1½ in. plate-iron, supported by a massive framework 10 in. deep and longitudinal girders of similar dimensions, one would suppose that a side was now presented which no shot could penetrate. But artillerists tell us they can destroy even ships thus built; and before Mr. Reed[45] left office, he submitted for the approval of the Admiralty, the plan of a ship with 18 in. of armour on the broadside and 20 in. upon her turrets. Indeed, we have seen it somewhere stated that the Russian Government already possesses a 20 in. gun, weighing 50 tons, and throwing projectiles of 1,120 lb. weight, with a charge of 130 lb. of powder. If any foreign nation can build ships to carry and effectively work such guns as these, our fleet may continue to be an experimental one for many years to come. And we may be required to build even larger ships than those submitted in the spring of the present year by Mr. Henwood[46] for the consideration of the members of the Royal United Service Institution, in which he proposes to place 1,000 pounders.

However, it is satisfactory to know that whatever the future may produce, we at present possess a maritime force which could bid defence on the ocean to any two other nations; and that if any three nations, backed by their fleets attempted to land their armies on our coasts, we possess a power which, we think, could successfully resist even so unlikely an invasion. But though we may deplore a vast annual expenditure on experiments – on ships to be built only to be surpassed as soon as they are launched – there is no help for it so long as other nations attempt to surpass us. We care not for the armies of Europe; but England, regardless of the cost, should have ever ready a fleet sufficient beyond all doubt to protect her shores and guard her now gigantic commerce. On these shores a foreign foe must never be permitted to land. For their protection a number of powerful floating batteries, which could be manned by our reverses and transported with ease to any given point, might answer our purpose better than seagoing ships of the *Captain*-class; and we can have no better police for the protection of our maritime commerce than the fleetest frigates the world can produce. We throw out these suggestions for consideration should the rivalry between the artillerists and shipbuilders continue to be waged.[47]

72 My Son, his University Life, and Marriage

Until his time at university my son's[48] life had been rather leisurely. His mother spoiled him and although I tried to encourage him to work hard at his education, he disappointed me.

He went to school aged six to a boarding school run by a lady[49] in St John's Wood. It was about two miles from our home in Portland Place and the number at the school was limited to twelve little boys. In 1861 aged twelve, he attended private schooling with a clergyman in Tooting to prepare him for Harrow, which he duly attended aged thirteen.

When he left Harrow aged eighteen, he went to a Military College but decided that a career in the Military was not for him so later that year (1867) he left to commence his studies at Magdalene College Cambridge. He promised faithfully to study hard for his degree. He had failings, however. I wished he could have considered things more and applied himself. I daresay if he had been left to depend for himself, he would have made more progress with his studies. In other respects, I had little reason to find fault with him for he had many good qualities.

I resolved however to withdraw him from Cambridge in the spring of 1868 as he appeared to drift away from studies. I wished to direct his attention either to farming or to business in the city.[50]

Though the University offered many, too many attractions, and he was anxious to remain, I found he was gaining no useful knowledge of any kind. On the contrary he was learning habits which might have proved the means of his ruin. I therefore adhered to my resolution to withdraw him, and I am truly glad I did so. In these University Towns every temptation is put in the way of young men who are supposed to have money to throw away. Tradesmen not merely grant almost unlimited credit to such youths but press their wares on them.

Wine merchants send a supply of wine, spirits, beer, and soda water, more than enough to satisfy the wants of twenty hard drunken men during term and charge the whole to the accounts of this one youth, expecting that his father will at once pay it, rather than have his son served with a summons.

But parents too often have themselves to blame by the large allowances they grant to their children. Frequently sent to the University not to obtain useful knowledge, but to get their sons into what is called "good society", the parents overstock their wine cellars, and supply anything which the young members of the "select class" guzzle and feast. I laugh at the plebeian donor and his son for their ambitious folly.

The masters of the Colleges are men with far too high a status to pay the slightest attention to what their pupils are doing. Some Tutors pay regard to their diligent students, and these in turn may benefit from this attention. However, students who are reluctant to learn may do exactly as they please. In my opinion, so long as they do not openly violate certain very mild or unimportant regulations, they are allowed to carry on in this manner.

Such is college life at Cambridge. When will the Reformers' broom be applied?

Opposite the river in front of the Manor House lies Walton-on-Thames in the far distance. It was on that side of the river in a large House that my son met his future wife Annie Ingram.[51] Annie was the second daughter and fourth child living of the late Herbert Ingram who was MP for Boston, who established the Illustrated London News, a paper which has proved a great success, and which became the sole property of his widow.[52]

Annie was just over eighteen years of age when they were engaged in 1869. She was not merely a very beautiful and accomplished girl, but she had evidently been exceedingly well brought up and was all one could desire in a daughter.

Mrs Ingram and her family resided at Mount Felix, a very fine house with about 20 acres of land close to Walton Bridge on the Surrey side which her husband purchased about 13 years ago.[53] In April 1872 the couple were married in Walton.

This event was just as important to me as to the young couple, for their future happiness depended on it. On the occasion there was a large gathering at Mount Felix – upwards of a hundred persons sat down to a sumptuous breakfast, and nearly double that number had a dance there in the evening.

I could not attend the wedding itself as my physical infirmities prevented me from getting into Walton Church where the marriage ceremony was performed. But I was at the breakfast, and that was the first time I had been into any other home than my own since I was seized with my affliction – more than 7½ years earlier. Everything went off very well.

Their honeymoon was spent touring the Continent. On their return I took on a furnished house for them for three months until they found a suitable house for themselves.[54]

As I hoped, William started as a clerk in the office of Messrs Aldridge and Co, an old East India firm, with the view of becoming a partner if everything went well. I was anxious that he should follow business pursuits as I was thoroughly convinced that there is no life as happy as the life of a man who is fully employed.[55]

At the time of his marriage, I conferred £10,000 for my son and his wife (and future children) on the understanding that Mrs Ingram would do the same. Unfortunately, she insisted that her £10,000 be for her daughter's use only. At the very least I wished that the interest on both sums be for their joint use, but this was not enacted either; as you may imagine this caused me much annoyance.[56] What can be worse than to start young people on the great voyage of married life with separate purses, which really means separate interests?

After the episode of the large sum I conferred on my son, without the same from Mrs Ingram, I warned them that unless this was rectified, they could not expect any further favours from me.

My relationship with Mrs Ingram however was soured further. I found myself having to protect against extravagant notions which she instilled in Annie without affording her the means of carrying them into effect. For instance, she made her the present of a Brougham carriage. Well, it was a mistaken kindness on her part to have done so, even if she had presented her also with the requisite means for maintaining the driver and horse etc. But as she did not do so, she did the young couple a positive injury, for on their income they had to get into debt. It would have been a much more sensible course if she had expended the money on furniture for a house, or towards a house itself, for at the time, they had neither home nor furniture, yet they had a Brougham!

Besides providing means to furnish their rented house as well as the rent itself for three months, I offered them Woodham House. Mrs Ingram made it clear that she wanted her daughter to have a house in London, which I was not prepared to agree to. My offer for a joint purchase of a house was refused too.

In February 1873 my grandson William Herbert Lindsay[57] was born. I wrote to my sister Helen in Scotland to say that of course my wife Helen and I were much pleased; and although I was not altogether pleased about some family matters of late, especially with the interference of Mrs Ingram, of whom I never had a very exalted opinion, I sent £100 to Annie as a small token of my love and regard for her, and so that she may buy a suit of clothes for the boy. How time whirls on! I was a grandfather at last![58] During that winter, William and his wife went "lionising" in Algiers, Northern Africa, where Mrs Ingram and her family took a house for the winter.[59]

The marriage was not to last though. In April 1875, three years after their wedding, Annie filed for divorce. William went to Germany. In a letter to me from there he said he shall have to go through the Bankruptcy Court for about £6000.[60] The following year he immigrated to New Zealand and in 1877 their marriage was annulled.

In a private letter to my sister in 1875, I wrote "The only hope of redemption for William is to send him to one of the large sheep estates in New Zealand and there let him find his own way in the world." I provided him with an allowance "with a credit of £10 per week, and whatever beyond that he can earn for himself".[61] I learnt, with some satisfaction, that when he arrived in New Zealand, he obtained a position as clerk in a solicitor's office.

73 Maritime 'Magnum Opus'

During my invalid years I catalogued my journals, which I had filled over the years, and wrote a novel based on them. It met with some success.[62]

Having had an interest in Shipping all my life and having time on my hands to be able to devote to researching Shipping through the ages, in 1867 I decided to write a book about Merchant Shipping.[63] The volumes contain every aspect of Maritime Shipping from ancient time to the present day. The larger portion of this work was devoted to the progress of Modern Shipping. Since the introduction of steam, the merchant navies of the world have increased to an enormous extent; and in comfort, beauty, and speed, the vessels of the present day immeasurably surpass those of any other period. Changes such as these were required to be fully described, and their results carefully recorded.[64]

With help from my contacts, and with Mr Birch[65] and Mr Newton[66] at the British Museum in London, I started work. During my research I had one notable success. There had always been a problem in solving how the ancient Roman galleys were configured. Through some close attention to drawings of pottery and tiles from ancient times, I solved the problem.[67]

I had considerable problems however trying to write about the history of the East India Company. This article in the Athenaeum goes some of the way to explaining why:

> The Worth of Historical Documents: It is well-known that when the business of the Honourable East India Company was transferred to the British Parliament, the first act of the new masters of the old house in Leadenhall Street was to make a clean sweep of the records of the company.
>
> They swept out 300 tons of these records to Messrs. Spicers, the paper makers, to be made into pulp. In this way, among other trifles, disappeared the whole history of the Indian Navy.[68]

After two painstaking but enjoyable years, I had completed two volumes. In 1872 the publishers and printers launched the books to the public. I was very sanguine of success. Who cares to read big books, especially about merchant ships in the age of steam and electricity? However, I did my best to make them instructive and readable books, and although they did not prove to be a financial gain, they filled up time which might otherwise have hung heavily on my hands. What a source of enjoyment that work offered me, who, because of my affliction, was obliged to float on a waterbed for sixteen hours out of the twenty-four!

Writing a "history" when the weather was wet, and improving a town with buildings when the weather was fine, showed that there was still life and vigour in the old wreck.[69]

The Big Book, which I called my Tombstone, or as learned men would call it my 'Magnum Opus', met with a reception from the public far beyond my expectations. It was favourably reviewed by the leading newspapers and letters from friends and readers.[70] As a result I devoted myself to the completion of the 3rd and 4th volumes. This was a typical review of my first two volumes:

> This work is to consist of four volumes, the first two of which are already published. Large and bulky volumes they are but we can promise our readers that there is nothing ponderous in them except the form... But the scope of these two volumes includes, as we have said, far more than the history of our own imperial and colonial navies, which we have hitherto been tempted to dwell upon... The labour of writing such a work must have been enormous... But it appears to have been a labour of love. There is, probably, no living Englishman, more qualified by study and experience to write a history of shipping than Mr. Lindsay... A book which can hardly fail to be the standard authority on the subject, if the concluding volumes are at all equal to those which it has been our pleasant task to notice.[71]

My remaining volumes were published in 1876. They became a source of reference for many years, and were housed in museums and libraries, here and abroad. The Royal Navy also ordered copies.

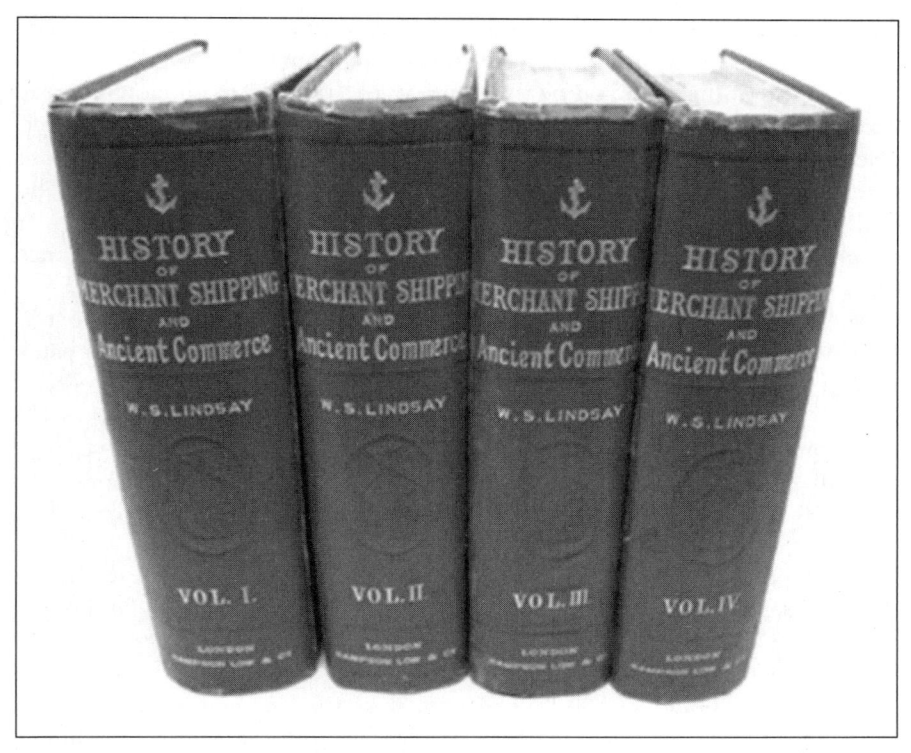

Lindsay's Four volume History of Merchant Shipping and Ancient Commerce, published by Sampson, Low, Marston, Low, and Searle in 1874 & 1876.

74 Coffin Ships

A subject that had always caught my attention was 'coffin ships'. I commenced gathering data at the beginning of 1877. I had in mind another book – 'The Annals of the Sea' – in which I wanted to present some facts about these vessels. By 'Coffin ships' I mean those that are so unseaworthy or overloaded that they are likely to flounder at sea and thus an insurance pay out could be claimed by the owner. The data was very hard to come by. Much of it had been hidden for obvious reasons.

I contacted my friends and acquaintances for any information that they may have. I received a letter from Mr Robert Bremner of the Glen in Bournemouth giving some instances that he knew of.

He said that alcohol was the cause of many problems. He explained that the "advance" system of paying sailors a month's wages, before they earn it is a downright curse and ought to be done away with.[72] Describing one journey he said that for the first week at sea after leaving Gravesend, half the men were not of any use, as they were suffering from the vile effects of drink and debauchery. One of them died from *Delirium Tremens*, the third week out. Three-quarters of them did not have sufficient clothing.

He said that they took on board either 50 or 100 tons of gunpowder near Gravesend. It was in small casks and stowed below and aft the main hatch below the cabin. There were about 100 jars of vitriol on deck over the fore hatch. They also had very many cases of brandy and whisky. In fact, he said, they were simply a floating engine of destruction. He added that he understood that Parliament was taking up the question of loading ships that carry emigrants with gunpowder.

Mr Bremner[73] collected several stories from a colleague Mr Webster. He said I was welcome to use them in my book if I saw fit. Mr Webster writes:

Let me tell you, Sir, that I have been knocking about at sea for 23 years in all kinds of ships from the collier brig, and the little opium schooner of 150 tons, to the mail steamer of 5000 tons, and have held all sorts of billets.

I will only mention such cases that come under my own experience. You, of course, know that a sound hull not over-laden will stand a good deal of knocking about before the ship will flounder.

Case 1: 'El Dorado', 1,800 tons register, ship, very old and well insured, arrived in Cork for orders. On the passage out to Galle with coals, ship overladen and straining herself to pieces running her Easting down, and making a great deal of water, a wind-mill pump and two hand pumps kept working all the rest of the passage. She was horribly provided with sails, ropes, and stores. Strict orders awaited the ship's arrival at Galle[74] that the captain was not to purchase any stores whatever. On the homeward passage, half allowance was served out as far as the Cape. From there to the channel only a ¼ allowance was given to us. The ship was constantly in the leakiest state. When within 500 miles of England, stores were all finished, and the crew pumping out water since they left Galle. At 12 o'clock one morning seeing a steamer's lights we insisted on the captain signalling for assistance. The steamer came to us, when instead of asking for canvas and stores, our own being spent and gone, the captain asked to be taken off the ship as he wished to leave her.

The crew of this heavy ship numbered only 23 souls all told, simply downright manslaughter. Three poor fellows died of sheer exhaustion on the homeward passage. The steamer sent a lifeboat to us, but before the boat came, the captain and the carpenter went below and drove out several treenails[75] under the water-line. The crew was not allowed to take any of their things with them, and some had kits worth a good deal of money which was very hard indeed. The crew were all landed in London where the captain was well received by the owners. This vessel was never intended to be saved but might have been if a few hundred pounds worth of canvas and

Part Seven: Maritime Historian and Author

stores had been laid out upon her. All the pump gear was thrown overboard before the men left.

Case 2: 'Flying Venus', 800 tons, an old tub that in six months would be out of class, with only part of one suit of sails on board. The boats were all rotten, but nicely painted, the rigging completely worn out, the masts rotten under the rigging, and the men employed to pump during the time she was wading in the East India docks, with a valuable cargo for Shanghai. She shipped her crew and was towed to Gravesend. Next day with the wind north-west, she sailed to the Downs.

In letting go the anchor the windlass and bitts[76] went to pieces, the chain ran out, and at 45 fathoms the end came up and slipped overboard. The sail was again set, and the course shaped to beat through Dover Straits, with the wind blowing fresh. When about two miles off the land, the fore topmast and lower mastheads went over the side damaging the hull a little in their fall. When a protest was entered at a notary's and afterwards extended, copying from the logbook the following entry: -

"While reaching down Channel, course -, wind -, and under three close reefed topsails, was struck by a heavy squall which threw the ship on her beam ends, wind and sea increasing. The topmast backstays were ordered to be cut away to save the ship, this was done, and the ship immediately righted herself when damage was found to be done to the hull, the port anchor knocked way by the fall of the wreck, carrying with it the windlass and 50 fathoms of chain cable."

Not one word of this being true. She was thoroughly refitted under the head of "General wearage".

She got an entire new set of anchors and chains and everything else of the very best. The whole affair was a complete swindle. This vessel is still running.

Case 3: 'Royal Oak' of Liverpool, 1,264 tons, journeying from Liverpool to Callao, she was laden with coal. She was an old American built ship in a most miserable condition. She left Wellington dock 4th March 1873, a heavy south-west gale blowing at the time. Frig's orders were to take the ship clear of the river and then leave her. 17 men in their bunks were drunk: mate ditto. The captain was in a chronic state of drunkenness bordering on the state of delirium tremens. Five boats were on board, with only three oars. The boats were not lashed, and ten casks of water were loose about the deck. Anchors on the forecastle head were not lashed either. The jibboom rigged in, and lower yards topped over. One of the crew deserted at the dock head.

The tug left her next morning off Point Lines in a strong south-west gale with heavy rain. The ship was never heard of afterwards. I may mention that it was one of the registered owners who was pushing this vessel to sea,

William Schaw Lindsay

in such bad weather, and in such a deplorable mess, and when told the bad state she was in, and that the captain and crew were drunk, said he did not "care a damn if all the crew were in the horrors of the sea; she must go, and be damned to her."

This man lives by buying up old traps with coals so that they may sink in a gale. This man has been well known to have had three of these sorts of vessels in port together.

When a survey is to be held on his ships, a few new sails, ropes oars etc are put on board. After the survey is over, these stores are taken away and immediately put on board the next ship to be surveyed, and then put in the store house, and so do duty in this manner, perhaps for years.

He is not the only shipowner in Liverpool who plays that game. It is the custom with them, when they call a survey, to enclose a 10- or 20-pound note to the surveyor so, of course, he goes through his work in a very blind-fold manner. Surveyors for Insurance Companies are bought over in the same manner.

Mr Bremner told me another tale:

Captain Clymn[77] told me of a friend of his who was loading jute in Bombay. As this article was very light, they were obliged to put some ballast in the bottom of the ship. The vessel could therefore be filled up to the deck with this light material.

In the course of loading the captain went down into the hold to see how they were getting on with the stowing of the cargo, when, while leaning against a tier of bales, he thought that one of them was damp. He ordered it to be pulled out at once and brought on deck, which, on being opened, was found to contain, in the very heart of the bale, a large quantity of the very finest jute thoroughly saturated with oil. In a few weeks this would ferment and heat, and so set on fire, consequently the cargo and ship would be burnt, and probably not a soul of the crew ever heard of, so the honest merchant who loaded the vessel would get his insurance money and continue his business as a respectable man.

Six or seven bales were found to be charged in this diabolical manner. The owner of the jute was immediately arrested, and who proved to be one of the leading Paris merchants in Bombay. He had hitherto been considered of the highest respectability and of course would have continued so but was stupidly found out. For his enterprising ingenuity he was sentenced to penal servitude, which was much too good for such a villain.

Of course, I had some experiences myself of these so called 'Coffin Ships'. When starting out as a ship's boy on the *Isabella*, I remember a carpenter saying, "This craft will be a coffin for some poor fellows."[78]

I also remember years ago a Shipowner of high reputation, on whose word I can implicitly rely, met another Shipowner, who, complaining of the bad times, during conversation said:

"And to make matters worse I have also had a bit of very bad luck."

"What was that?" enquired my friend.

"Oh!" said he, "a ship of mine I had just sold was lost the first voyage after I parted with her."

"Well," replied my friend, "and where was the bad luck there?"

"Where?" explained this "unfortunate" Shipowner, "why I bought her twenty years ago, and insured her at her full value, and had kept her so insured until I parted with her."

"And what made you do that?" enquired my friend.

"Oh!" replied he "she was an old ship, and an old-fashioned ship, and I thought that if she did happen to go to the bottom I might as well have a good and a new one in her place."[79]

One man campaigned against these overloaded and unseaworthy merchant vessels. Samuel Plimsoll[80] had the support of the public but he faced ridicule and obstruction from the government and from powerful ship owners of the time. He was determined to introduce legalisation to correct matters.

Little attention had been paid to loss of life and property at sea in British vessels until 1836 when a Committee of the House of Commons was appointed to inquire into shipwrecks. Their findings showed that losses were attributed in great measure to the imperfect classification of ships that had existed until 1834 (since when the Lloyd's Register was improved). Other reasons for shipwrecks were the incompetency of masters, officers and crews and their habits of intemperance; to the system of marine insurance; to the want of harbours of refuge; and to imperfection of charts (many of which were out of date). Since then, including in the Merchant Shipping Consolidated Act of 1854, a significant number of acts have been implemented to improve these and other reasons for losses.

As much as I could not but commend Plimsoll's laudable objectives, personally I felt that the Board of Trade need not interfere by passing laws that were not needed.[81] Indeed it is impossible to question the great value of service that the Lloyd's institution rendered. A few individuals for their own protection and for the protection of the public did more to save life and property at sea than all the laws which were passed.[82] If good-for-nothing shipowners despatched their ships to sea knowing them to be unseaworthy then they should be punished severely. It is the business of all insurance associations to see that the vessels they insure are seaworthy. Shipowners should not however be made to produce a government certificate which could then be used in their defence when a calamity occurred. There was already an official survey of emigrant and passenger ships; the Commissioners concluded that there was no need for a similar survey to be extended to all merchant ships.[83]

After years of campaigning, an Unseaworthy Bill[84] was introduced in 1875, giving strong powers of inspection to the Board of Trade and introducing a mark onto the hull of all ships to ensure they were not overloaded – the Plimsoll line.[85] This measure had to be entered in the ship's logbook and be left with the Custom's officer.[86]

By this Act, the Board of Trade were empowered, at their discretion, to detain any British vessel "which they have reason to believe is by the defective condition of her hull, equipment, or machinery, or by reason of overloading or improper loading, unfit to proceed to sea without serious danger to human life."

Epilogue

Sitting by the banks of the Thames the old man reflects on his life. The river's flow calms him. It is 1877. He is 61 and weary now.

As dangerous as his early days at sea were, it was then that he was most happy. The sense of adventure prevailed, and every day brought excitement and new risks.

Lindsay in later years.

His nine years at sea had been eventful. His employers had rewarded his hard work with a captaincy. He had avoided near-death events that had made him stronger. His retirement from the sea and his focus on ship-brokerage had resulted in him building a successful company. His knowledge of the sea aided him. Profits enabled him to own his own ships. Ships with a novel design; auxiliary steamships.

His interest in navigation laws and politics prompted him to run for parliament, and there he was able to focus on maritime matters. Wherever possible he sought to improve the merchant service and in some cases the Royal Navy. His involvement in the Crimean War and the American Civil War revolved around shipping, and drew criticism, although he felt his actions were in Britain's interest.

Although he has been very successful, during the latter part of his life his problems mounted up. Fate conspired against him. Too much work had exhausted him and led to an initial breakdown. He had been urged to turn away from running his shipping company and focus on something else. He had turned to politics but that wasn't without stress.

He couldn't give up his involvement with shipping, however. His involvement with projects such as his failed Shipping Line to South Africa, the fall in popularity of auxiliary steamers, the loss of his ships to the Portuguese Government, the loss of revenue of his shipping line by his refusal to conduct business in the United States during the Civil War, and his support for the Confederates, all of this must have resulted in his stroke.

He has refused to let his stroke get the better of him, however. Although he has been wheelchair-bound for twelve years, he sought different ways to fulfil his life. His improvements in the village had pleased him. He has built houses and turned to farming.

His diaries and journals are extensive; he has had time on his hands to focus on them. He has corresponded regularly with newspapers and with his parliamentary and shipping colleagues. His foray into writing novels has been successful and he is proud of his publication on the History of Merchant Shipping.

His marriage to Helen has been happy. In truth, though, it was her sister Christina who pulled his heart strings; he enjoyed her company and was delighted when she was around.

It is his son's impeding divorce that troubles him most. His son went through money like water. He frittered away money his father had given him. His career has been a failure. Work as a clerk, a farmer, and other professions had all failed. Now his marriage has failed too, and a costly divorce is taking place. In despair, his father has sent him to New Zealand, to become a remittance man, relying on a monthly subsistence cheque from his father. They will never meet again.

Happy that he has achieved much during his life, he is sad that he is not able to hand over his shipping business to a worthy son.

Epilogue

So, in conclusion, was Lindsay an entrepreneur? Yes. Was he well known in his day? Yes. Are his exploits worthy of remembering? Arguably so. Certainly, he ought to be better known in merchant shipping circles.

New historical data can be hard to find; but it is out there. We are fortunate that the unpublished journals of Lindsay's offer historical insights into the 19th century, notably first-hand descriptions of life at sea in a merchant vessel in the 1830s, the role of auxiliary steamers, political and maritime reform, and the Crimean and American Civil Wars.

I have just been reading a biography of Napoleon III.[1] There is little mention of the American Civil War, its blockade, recognition of the Confederate States, and Napoleon's involvement. Some may see this as an oversight, but how can one possibly capture all events in a person's life? The author must decide what to include and what to omit. In the case of Lindsay, his journals and documents contain so much information that I have had to focus on historical events pertinent to him, alongside some amusing anecdotes.

Adherence to strict Victorian values and rigid structures is apparent in the journals. This conflicted with a fast-changing world; one of inventions and expanding empires. Lindsay wished to improve out-of-date systems and structures, but this meant challenging established methods of running a business and ruling the country. His outspokenness made him many enemies but did not stop him doing what he felt was right. It cannot be denied that there is a degree of self-congratulation evident in the journals; Lindsay is more than happy to quote favourable reactions to his activities and his literary output. But it would be a harsh critic who would deny him the feeling of a life lived to the full.

Maritime history has tended to focus more on naval history rather than merchant shipping. There are several reasons for this but perhaps the main one is that naval records are much more prevalent. Naval records have guardians. Merchant records are much more easily lost as they tend to be held by owners, or defunct owners; they are more easily discarded. In addition, as the Royal Navy's role is the defence of the realm, it is seen as more important. Hopefully this book shows that there is an equally important function that merchant shipping fulfils. Today, ninety per cent (by volume) of goods travel by ship, as they did in Lindsay's time.

At Sea

Lindsay's journals confirm what we know of the harshness of a life at sea at sea during the 1830s. The risks involved were substantial. Life expectancy must have been significantly lower than many other occupations. Accidents such as falls from the rigging and drownings were common. Being washed overboard was a constant danger and many sailors could not swim. Diseases were prevalent. Much depended on the ship's destination. There was no cure for diseases such as yellow fever. Living conditions on board could cause ill health. Antibiotics had not been discovered so infections were the cause of many deaths. It was very unlikely that doctors were on board ship, especially on merchant ships, and the medical bags that captains carried were rudimentary. Pay was poor and much of it was wasted on drink. It was the influence of alcohol that led to many accidents.

There were dangers too that awaited the engineers and trimmers on steamships when dealing with boilers, faulty machinery, and high-pressure pipes. This was less of a case on auxiliary steamers such as Lindsay's, but the danger was higher on fully powered steamers that had larger boilers, and this could lead to fatalities.[2]

Further descriptions of sea life at that time can be found in Lindsay's novels.[3]

Business

Without doubt, Lindsay identified business opportunities and grasped them. To build up a shipping company from nothing, which in only a few years became one of the largest in the country, was an incredible feat. This was especially so for someone who had started life as an orphan with no money and no support. His decision to develop a business as a ship's broker paid dividends. As a man experienced in maritime matters, shipowners turned to him.

As the Industrial Revolution developed, so these opportunities grew. The transition from sail to steam meant that coal supply was of prime importance. Indeed, it was coal that in time turned the Royal Navy into the most formidable navy on earth.[4] Lindsay's connection with the Castle Eden Colliery and his breakthrough in identifying that P&O required coal at their coaling stations enabled his business to grow spectacularly.

Much of his business was based on ship-brokerage rather than profits from his own ships. Connections that he had built up enabled him to expand his brokerage business. In addition, opportunities arose that expanded his business: the Crimean War, the discovery of gold fields in America, Canada and Australia, as well as the general increase in emigration.

Although he was by no means the only shipowner building oceangoing ships utilising steam engines, he was a pioneer in the early phase of their development. He chose to use auxiliary steamers rather than fully powered steamers, but they quickly became obsolete. Other pioneers such as Arthur Anderson,[5] Isambard Kingdom Brunel, Samuel Cunard[6] and Alfred Holt built up businesses based on fully powered steamers. Advances, particularly the compound engine, which was much more efficient and used less coal than earlier engines, meant that the days of the auxiliary were numbered.

In the early phase, sailing ships used auxiliary engines, and then steam ships used auxiliary sails. Is it possible that today there could be a return to hybrid ships powered by small engines using no fossil fuels and mainly powered by sails?[7]

Lindsay was not a speculator and saw many of his competitors fall by the wayside because they invested in high-risk enterprises. He wasn't immune to financial mishaps himself though. His experience of handing

Epilogue

Bombardment of Kagoshima 1863 and the sinking of Lindsay's ship the SS *England* that he had sold to the Japanese. *Le Monde Illustré.*

over three of his ships to the Portuguese Government typifies the adage 'neither a borrower, nor a lender be.' As his friend commented, how could a shrewd businessman like Lindsay lend his money, ships, or credit to foreign governments? He certainly lost a fortune and spent nearly 20 years of his life trying to retrieve it, in vain. Other business ventures were unsuccessful. His line of steamers to South Africa failed after only a year and seemed to be the cause of much derision. In some eyes 'WSL' stood for Worst Shipping Line. On the other hand, his links to the Scottish Shipping powerbase assisted him in building his empire. Many of his contacts were Scots and he utilised these to his advantage.

No doubt he took a great deal of pride in his ships. He tried to incorporate the latest technology, such as their being iron-built and streamlined. In some respects, he was a man ahead of his time. He was an early adopter of a lengthier sailing ship. His ship the *W S Lindsay*, an ocean-going iron ship built in 1852, was six and a half times as long as its breadth and he was ridiculed by other shipbuilders for taking this approach. He faced considerable opposition to his design from the powers that be, the Admiralty surveyors, who insisted that modifications be carried out to minimise perceived risks. Other shipowners soon followed his example, however. Years later, HMS *Warrior*, the first iron-hulled ocean-going warship was based on the same dimensions.[8] But Lindsay was not the first to consider a longer ship design. I. K. Brunel's *Great*

Western, built in 1837, had a similar ratio, although she had side paddles that increased her breadth.[9]

At that time there was much competition in records for the fastest sailings. He would have been delighted when one of his ships, the *Robert Lowe*, set the fastest sailing record between New Zealand and London.

He sought to improve supply chain logistics in his business and recommended that the Admiralty adopt some of his methods in the Royal Navy. He wished to simplify systems, processes, and laws. This first started with his review of the complex Navigation Laws, but also applied to his participation in the Transport Service, Manning the Navy, and Harbours of Refuge commissions.

He was prepared to push his business boundaries. During the American Civil War in 1861 Lindsay decided not to trade with the United States. He therefore sold two of his ships, the SS *England* and the SS *Scotland*, to the Prince of Satsuma in Japan. The *England* was the first foreign private vessel sold to the Japanese.[10] The ship was seized and scuttled by the British fleet in August 1863, at the time of the bombardment of Kagoshima, and having been sunk in very deep water was never raised. The *Scotland* was still in Japanese service in 1870.[11]

Politics and Reform

For someone not born into aristocracy and who had made two failed efforts to be a Member of Parliament, his entry into politics was even more incredible than his business empire. Others would surely have given up.

Although a Radical Liberal, he always supported bills and motions that he felt were just. On occasions therefore he supported Tory initiatives. This made him very unpopular at times, notably during the No Confidence Vote in 1859. The Conservative government 1858-9 was led by Lord Derby in the House of Lords and Benjamin Disraeli in the House of Commons. Lindsay sided with the governing Tory Government, which was defeated by his party's (Liberal) votes.

His decision always to support Free Trade rather than protectionism was based on the assumption that all countries would support it. The United States preferred protectionism and the imposition of taxes. He admitted his mistake to Lord John Russell several years after he had challenged him on not supporting Free Trade with the US.

It is obvious that he moved in the right circles. His friendships particularly with Richard Cobden and the Marchioness of Londonderry enabled him to meet influential politicians and business people. No doubt he took great advantage of that. His diary notes on meeting the Marchioness (and his other friends) show that he was also a man with a sense of humour.

Lindsay stuck firmly to his principles and was not afraid to tackle difficult subjects. His criticism of the Admiralty during the Crimean War, the formation of the Administrative Reform Association, his backing of the Confederacy, his approach to the French Emperor during the American Civil

War, and his views on Manning the Navy, are just a few examples of when he landed in hot water.

Crimean War

His connections in shipping and in Parliament enabled Lindsay to supply transport ships to the Crimea. As an MP, he was barred from entering directly into British Government contracts. He circumvented this by disguising ownership of his vessels through a share system with his partners,[12] a practice that was often followed amongst MPs who were businessmen.

As proficient as he was in running his business, it is quite possible that he did not see the strategic significance of events and of Government policy. An example of this is his role in the Crimean War. Like others he may have seen that the main thrust of the War was to contain Russian aggression and its expansion into Turkish Territory. The War however was not only confined to the Black Sea.[13] It was a global conflict. Britain was determined to strangulate the Russian Navy so that it did not threaten British Naval dominance. It did this by decimating the Russian Navy, blockading Russian ports, and thus breaking the Russian economy.

His ships were utilised by the British and French during the Crimean War and as a shipbroker he secured contracts for many other ships for both countries. This led to his company achieving its highest year's financial revenue.

American Civil War

When it comes to publications on the American Civil War, some crucial political characters including Lindsay have not received much attention. Some articles, in particular by Michael Clark,[14] have referred to Lindsay's experience during the American Civil War, and Lindsay's journals throw a new light on reasons why the war commenced. His intentions were honourable. Whether his assumptions were correct, however, is another matter.

The causes of the war are complex. The obvious reason was slavery. However, in the early phase of the war, Lincoln did not proclaim emancipation; it came secondary to his objective of restoring the Union.[15] Lindsay thought there were other reasons for the war, notably increased taxation and political under-representation of the South. He believed in the right of the South to be independent and he did what he could politically to assist them.

Lindsay's views must have been influenced by James Mason and John Slidell, two of the Confederate envoys in Europe, as well as his own experiences in visiting North America. Although most of his contacts in North America prior to the War were with Northerners, his opinions must have been influenced to some extent by the Southerners. He wanted the war to be brought to a halt as soon as possible. He hated the waste in blood and treasure.

With his influence in shipping, he may have offered some advice regarding the design of Confederate ships. Instrumental figures from the South involved in building the navy and blockade running stayed in Lindsay's Manor House. These were Captain Ralph Semmes, James Mason, William Yancey, and Colonel Lucius Lamar. No doubt there were others that Lindsay met; possibly James Bulloch,[16] Commander George Sinclair, and George Sanders. Threatened by his position in Parliament, and the adverse reaction to his shipping business from the Northerners,[17] he handed over his company to his partners, and it was they who engaged in blockade running. Rather than become embroiled in building a navy or in blockade running, Lindsay chose to engage in a political strategy to obtain Southern independence.

Interestingly, the Confederate demand for naval ships in Britain and France was further complicated by an arms race of their own. Lindsay's discussions with Napoleon III convinced him that France was unlikely to go to war with Britain. Whether the country could rely on this is moot.

During the American Civil War, the North had a navy, the South did not. The North was able to blockade Southern ports to stop the export of cotton and the importation of goods and arms. Although the blockade was patchy, it did have a significant effect. Cotton was not getting through to clothes manufacturers in Britain and in France, resulting in unemployment and hardship for the cotton workers. This effect nearly led to both countries recognising the South as an independent state. Initially, the Confederates turned the blockade to their advantage. They restricted the export of cotton to make the British and French feel the effect on their industries and hence force them to recognise Southern independence. Unfortunately, as previously noted, both countries had stockpiled cotton supplies and did not feel the loss of imports for a year.

In blockading the Confederacy, the Union had unwittingly given them legitimacy as a *de facto* nation in the eyes of the French and British. As recognised belligerents, the Confederates believed they could purchase weapons of war from Europe.[18]

To counter the effect of the blockade, specialised ships were designed. These were fast steamers with a shallow draft and a low profile so that they were difficult to discern from a distance at sea. Secret agents from the South, notably James Bulloch, commissioned some of these ships to be built in Britain. They also commissioned advanced iron-clad ships. When these were discovered by the Government, their sale was blocked. These agents also bought existing British ships that could be adapted for naval warfare.

Britain was able to learn from the Confederate States some aspects of advanced ship designs. It became apparent that this advance rendered the British Fleet outdated and the British felt threatened.[19] But although American Naval design advanced, the American Civil War had a disastrous effect on the American Merchant Navy and British Merchant Naval power increased.[20]

Lindsay highlighted the suppliers' greed, but the blockade earned many blockade runners' fortunes.[21] $250,000 each way was a not uncommon return,[22] and a net profit of seldom less than 300 per cent could be the result. In the early years of the war the blockade was ineffective, so the risks of capture by the Federal Navy were minimal. The risks increased as the war persisted.

Epilogue

Lindsay also highlighted the problem of identifying whether ships being sold were bought by the South. In his communication to Milner Gibson[23] at the Board of Trade, who was fervently opposed to the supply of ships to the South, Lindsay wrote to say that it was difficult to keep track on the sale of ships to a third party which could then be sold on to the Confederates. How could shipowners know if their ships, sold in good faith, were then sold on? The answer lay with spies that the Union had engaged.

The British Government was reluctant to recognise the South as in doing so they could precipitate a war between Britain and the North. If that occurred Canada would be open to an invasion by the Union. Lindsay also pointed out that some of the Canadian politicians may be compliant in a merger with the Northern 'free' states.

The War was on a knife edge. As much as Britain was apprehensive about losing Canada in a war with the United States, the Union was just as apprehensive about fighting a war on three fronts, with the Confederates, the Canadians, and the British.

Lindsay also observed that the North was manufacturing-based and the South agriculturally-based. This prompted him to advocate and justify a separation. He hated the effects of a war, the damage in financial terms, and human terms, both in America and globally. But there could be another reason for him demanding a split, one that is more controversial. He saw the tremendous potential of a rapidly growing and prosperous Union, one that could pose a significant threat to Britain, Canada, and the rest of the British Empire.

How close was Lindsay to bringing about the recognition of the South as an independent nation? He was leading the cause in Parliament and therefore a substantial figure.

If his lobbying of the French Emperor had resulted in a close co-operation with the British Government, then both nations may have recognised the South. That was not to be. The British did not formally meet with the Emperor, presumably on the grounds that recognition of the South may have resulted in a war with the North, and that Britain would lose Canada to the United States. There was always a belief in some quarters that the South would win the war without outside help.[24] Nevertheless, Lindsay had at various stages nearly succeeded in forcing the issue. He had a vested interest in the South obtaining independence. He had bought the equivalent of six million pounds in Confederate bonds.

I have not included all Lindsay's notes on slavery. He abhorred it. Indeed, he was interested in helping the South achieve independence only on the understanding that slavery would eventually be abolished.[25] Emperor Napoleon III also found slavery repugnant.[26]

The historian Charles Hubbard summed up Lindsay's involvement in the American Civil War:

> Lindsay was a remarkable man. Unlike many Europeans who supported the Confederacy, Lindsay's sympathies came from the heart and were

not always based on financial self-interest. He believed that the Southern States were committed, as he was, to free trade. Even though his huge shipping interest would directly benefit from an independent South, his sympathies had already cost him dearly in his business dealings with the North. His contemporaries in Parliament and the British Press frequently accused him of "pecuniary or selfish motives." Lindsay was not born into the British aristocracy or the landed gentry but had conquered poverty by a combination of hard work, good fortune, and innate intelligence. He managed to purchase for himself a position of prestige and power and was willing to risk it all for the Confederacy.[27]

I have no doubt that the stress of handling his support for the Confederate South greatly contributed to his ill-health.

Lindsay retired from Parliament and sold his company to his partners Edgar Stringer and Edward Pembroke. They were joined by James Galbraith and the resulting firm still survives as one of the longest established shipbrokers in the world.[28]

Author
Of all his writings, I am sure that Lindsay was most proud of his four-volume *History of Merchant Shipping and Ancient Commerce*. He was fortunate to have connections, particularly in the British Museum, to help with this, but he singlehandedly drew together information that perhaps would otherwise have been lost.

His journals in the Caird Library at the National Maritime Museum number over 40 and some are 800 pages long. They contain an enormous amount of information on people and events. In this book I have only scratched the surface.

Appendices

Appendix I: Timeline

Date	Age	Event
19 Dec 1815		William Schaw Lindsay's Birth in Ayr
Apr 1816		Moves to Glasgow
22 Aug 1823	7	WSL's father Joseph dies
1825	9	WSL's mother Mary dies. Moves back to Ayr to live with his uncle
1831	15	Moves to Glasgow to live with brother Peter
1 Apr 1833	17	Departs Glasgow for Liverpool on steam packet *Glasgow*
7 Jun 1833	17	Joins *Isabella* as apprentice
1 Aug 1834	18	Slavery Abolition Act (1833) in British Empire, effective 1 August 1834
Nov 1836	20	WSL 2nd mate on board *Isabella*
20 Jun 1837	21	Coronation of Queen Victoria
20 Sep 1837	21	WSL 2nd Officer on the *Georgetown*
1 Jun 1838	22	WSL Chief Officer on the *Richard Bell*
Jul 1839	23	Meets future wife Helen Stewart at a schoolfriend's party
1 Aug 1839	23	WSL appointed Master of the *Olive Branch*
1 Sep 1841	25	WSL leaves *Olive Branch* & ends his life at sea
11 Oct 1841	25	Joins Castle Eden Colliery
1842	26	Lives in St Hilda Street, Hartlepool
Mar 1842	26	Working briefly in Limerick, Ireland

Date	Age	Event
14 Nov 1843	27	Marries Helen Stewart
Mar 1845	29	Moves to London. Office at 35 Abchurch Lane
1845	29	Founds W S Lindsay & Co
Apr 1845	29	Rents St Peter's Villa, Percy Cross, Fulham
19 Sep 1847	31	Uncle Reverend Dr William Schaw dies
Sep 1847	31	Moves to Mornington Lodge, North End Rd, Fulham
1847	31	Part owns first ship
1848	31	Californian Gold Rush
Oct 1848	32	Edgar Stringer joins W S Lindsay & Co
12 Nov 1849	33	Only child William Stewart Lindsay born
Sep 1850	34	Moves offices to 8 Austin Friars
1850-1	34	Six ships launched (the *'Pores'*)
1851	35	Meets Queen Victoria at the Great Exhibition
1851	35	Australian Gold Rush
1852	36	Moves office to 8 Austin Friars, London
Apr 1852	36	Unsuccessfully stands as MP for Monmouth
Jul 1852	36	Unsuccessfully stands as MP for Dartmouth
Sep 1852	36	Launches *W S Lindsay*
Oct 1852	36	Moves to 29 (then 17) Portland Place, London
5 Oct 1853	37	Crimean War commences.
30 Mar 1854	38	Elected MP for Tynemouth
15 Aug 1854	38	*Robert Lowe* launched
Oct 1854	38	Convalesce in Isle of Wight after illness
1854	38	WSLs ships used as transport ships for troops and supplies
2 May 1855	39	Florence Nightingale sails on *Robert Lowe* to Crimea
1855	39	Discusses troop transport logistics for the French with Napoleon III
1856	39	2nd Opium War commences; ends in 1860
30 Mar 1856	40	Crimean War ends

Appendices

Date	Age	Event
10 May 1856	40	Purchases Manor House Shepperton
1 Aug 1856	40	Commences his Shipping Line to South Africa
27 Mar 1857	41	Re-elected MP for Tynemouth
May 1857	41	Indian Mutiny commences; ends June 1858
1858	41	Canadian Gold Rush in British Columbia
Apr 1858	42	Sells three ships to Portuguese Government
31 May 1859	43	Became MP for Sunderland
8 Sep 1860	44	Leaves for Tour of USA
6 Nov 1860	44	Appointed Lieutenant, City of London
1860	44	Visits President Elect Abraham Lincoln
Jan 1861	45	Returns from USA
Jan 1861	45	Sells two of his auxiliary ships, the SS *England* and the SS *Scotland*, to the Prince of Satsuma, Japan.
31 Jan 1861	45	Discusses Navigation Laws & naval defence with Napoleon III
12 Apr 1861	45	American Civil War commences
14 Dec 1861	45	Prince Albert dies
1862	46	Retires from W S Lindsay & Co. Stringer takes over.
11 Apr 1862	46	First of four visits to Emperor Napoleon III to discuss American Civil War
Jun 1862	46	Two of his ships depart for Canada as 'Bride Ships': SS *Tynemouth* & SS *Robert Lowe*
9 Dec 1864	48	Has paralytic stroke
9 Apr 1865	49	American Civil War ends
15 Apr 1865	49	Abraham Lincoln assassinated
1867	51	Buys Ravenscliff, Bournemouth as holiday home
1872	56	Sells Ravenscliff
17 Apr 1872	56	Son William Stewart Lindsay marries Annie Jane Bescoby Ingram
9 Jan 1873	57	Emperor Napoleon dies in exile in England
17 Feb 1873	57	Grandson William Herbert Lindsay born

Date	Age	Event
11 Oct 1873	57	New house Ravensworth, Bournemouth built
1874	58	First two volumes of *History of Merchant Shipping* published
26 Apr 1875	59	Son William's wife Annie petitions for divorce
1875	59	Sends son to New Zealand as a remittance man
1876	60	Second two volumes of *History of Merchant Shipping* published
6 Jan 1877	61	Son William's divorce finalised
28 Aug 1877	61	William Schaw Lindsay dies at Shepperton Manor

Appendix II: List of ships owned, or part-owned, by Lindsay

Vessel	Built	Year	Tons	Classification	Share
Acacia	Hartlepool	1847	329	8A1	
Alipore	Sunderland	1850	811	?	64/64ths
Allandale	Sunderland	1847	300	9A1	
SS *Austin Friars*	Sunderland	1868	1,036	75A1	
Barrackpore	Sunderland	1850	816	?	64/64ths
Clarendon	Hebburn	1854	1,000	A1	40/64ths
Coromandel	Greenock	1843	660	12A1	
Cossipore	Dundee	1851	834	9A1	26/64ths
Dinapore	Workington	1851	1,200	?	30/64ths
SS *England**	Glasgow	1856	949	12A1	22/64ths
Ferozepore	Newcastle	1846	558	12A1	
Gibson-Craig	St.Johns	1851	980	6A1	
Gladiator	Sunderland	1851	435	10A1	
Harbinger#	London	1846	598	?	(£6000)
Helen Lindsay	Sunderland	1850	545	9A1	30/64ths
Helen Stewart	Sunderland	1848	400	10A1	£400
SS *Ireland**	Hartlepool	1856	807	?	64/64ths
SS *James Hartley*	Stockton	1856	705	12A1	

Appendices

Vessel	Built	Year	Tons	Classifi-cation	Share
Jenny Lind	Sunderland	1847	368	8A1	64/64ths
Maggie Leslie	Newcastle	1862	468	12A1	
Mary Stewart	Sunderland	1847	339	9A1	32/64ths
SS Medusa	Sunderland	1862	602	9A1	
Mirzapore	Birkenhead	1851	1,250	?	9/64ths
Moselle	?	?	650	?	
Moultan	Hartlepool	1849	429	9A1	
Nile ¥	London	1850	1,182	12A1	2/64ths
Orontes	Glasgow	1851	?	?	2/64ths
Pactolus	Sunderland	1852	317	8A1	
SS Robert Lowe*	Greenock	1854	2,250	?	64/64ths
Scamander	?	1854	753	?	4/64ths
SS Scotland*	Glasgow	1856	1,100	?	43/64ths
Serampore	?	?	1,300	?	
SS Shepperton	Sunderland	1868	1,033	A(B)1	
Shooting Star	Nova Scotia	1854	340	4A1	
Tally Ho	?	?	?	?	4/64ths
SS Tynemouth*φ	Newcastle	1854	2,250	?	52/64ths
Undine	Cartsdyke	1851	?	?	64/64ths
SS W S Lindsay*+	Northumberland	1852	1,280	?	64/64ths
SS Woodham	Hartlepool	1869	980	A(B)1	

Notes

* Formed the Lindsay RMS Line 1856: "I hold more than three fourths of the entire line of ships myself." NMM: LND 5-4, 815
# Built as a war steamship; purchased in 1857. 'The Index' 24 December 1863. Abandoned in 1860, Lindsay claimed on insurance but was only partially successful.
+ Converted to SS
¥ Lost with all hands 1854
φ Originally to be named the *Caroline Chisholm*

Lindsay states that he declined to classify any of his ships with Lloyd's although the classification had significantly improved since his day. Lindsay W S., *History of Merchant Shipping Vol III*, 631. Other shipowners were also critical of Lloyds.

295

Appendix III: Ships owned, or possibly owned, by Lindsay's partners

Vessel	Built	Year	Tons	Company
CSS *Atalanta**	London	1863	253	SPC - BR
CSS *Calypso*	Dumbarton	1855	535	SPC - BR
Canton/Pampero ≠	?	1863	?	?
SS *Charlotte* (CSS *Lamar*)*	Dumbarton	1864	632	SPC - BR.
Clara	?	?	?	SPC - BR
PS *Fergus* (CSS *Presto*)	Glasgow	1863	552	MTCL – BR.
Flora II *	Glasgow	1858	570	SPC – BR
Fire Cracker	?	?	?	?
Giraffe (CSS *Robert E Lee*)	Govan	1860	900	SPC – BR
Granite City	Dumbarton	1862	?	SPC - BR
Index *	Deptford	1863	363	?
Juno II *	Bristol	1853	298	?
Nutfield *	London	1863	531	?
Sir Colin Campbell	?	?	?	?

Notes
BR = Blockade Runner
CSS = Confederate Steamship
PS = Paddle Steamship
MTLC = The Mercantile Trading Company Limited
SPC = Stringer, Pembroke Company

* See also Wise S, *Lifeline of the Confederacy*
≠ See Long, *In the Shadow of the Alabama*, 125

Appendix IV: Voyages of the *Tynemouth* during the Crimean War with details of cargo and troops

CAPTAIN'S RETURN.

	DESCRIPTION OF VOYAGE OR SERVICE	OBJECT OF VOYAGE	Troops Officer	Troops Men	Tons of Stores	Cattle or Horses	From	To	Fuel Tons	Fuel Cwt.	REMARKS
1	England to the Bosphorus, Bosphorus to Varna	Ambulance Corps	5	314	713	3 Horses	18 June	18 July	202	10	Called at Gibraltar and Malta.
2	Varna to Constantinople	Invalids	10	158	—	1 Horse	4 Aug.	5 Aug.	10	—	Towed the Coal brig "Geneva."
3	To Sea of Marmora & back	To Tow	—	—	—	—	16 Aug.	16 Aug.	3	—	
4	Constantinople to Varna	To join Crimean expedition	—	—	5 Boats for Landing Troops.	—	20 Aug.	22 Aug.	28	10	Experienced adverse gales.
5	Varna to Baljick and back	Dispatches	—	—	—	—	24 Aug.	24 Aug.	6	—	
6	Varna to Baljick	To Water	—	—	—	—	25 Aug.	25 Aug.	3	10	
7	Baljick to Varna	Rendezvous	—	—	—	—	27 Aug.	27 Aug.	3	—	
8	Varna to Baljick	do. 44th Regiment	38	743	Camp Equipage and 126 gabions	13 Horses	4 Sept.	4 Sept.	5	—	Towed "Dunbar" Transport. Assisted H.M.S. "Cyclops" 24 horse, with 2 Transports in tow.
9	Baljick to Crimea	44th Regiment	do.	do.		do.	7 Sept.	14 Sept.	50	—	
10	Old Fort to Eupatoria	Rendezvous	—	—	—	—	19 Sept.	19 Sept.	2	10	Horse Boat in tow.
11	Eupatoria to Katcha		—	—	—	—	27 Sept.	28 Sept.	8	—	Towed "Palmerston" Transport. Bad weather, stood off all night.
12	Katcha to Eupatoria	For Cattle	—	—	—	—	13 Oct.	13 Oct.	6	—	
13	Eupatoria to Katcha and back	Important Dispatches	—	—	—	—	13 Oct.	14 Oct.	5	—	
14	Eupatoria to Balaclava	To deliver Shot	—	—	—	{15 Bullocks 270 Sheep}	18 Oct.	18 Oct.	5	—	
15	Balaclava to Scutari	Sick, Wounded, & Prisoners	18	309	—	8 Horses	31 Oct.	2 Nov.	8	10	Experienced very bad weather.
16	Bosphorus to Balaclava	Turkish Troops	62	1101	200	—	23 Nov.	26 Nov.	31	—	Brig in tow.
17	Balaclava to Varna	For Troops	—	—	—	—	5 Dec.	7 Dec.	20	—	
18	Varna to Eupatoria	Turkish Troops	53	1258	150	13 Horses	12 Dec.	15 Dec.	25	—	Experienced adverse gales.
19	Eupatoria to Balaclava	To Coal and with Horses	—	30	700 gabions	50 Horses	21 Dec.	21 Dec.	7	—	
20	Balaclava to Scutari	Sick	4	333	—	—	29 Dec.	31 Dec.	23	—	
	Total.....		100	4306	1063 tons, 826 Gabions.	124 Horses, 270 Sheep, 15 Bullocks.			461	10	

From Lindsay, *Confirmation of Admiralty Mismanagement*, London, 1855. This was an accurate account of the voyages that the *Tynemouth* made, with details of cargo and troops. These differed significantly from the Government return of services performed.

The Government, for instance, referred to a total of twelve voyages compared to twenty that were undertaken. They also stated the transportation of six officers rather than one hundred and ninety, and 324 troops rather than 4306!

Appendix V: Business affairs

Partners in W S Lindsay & Co
William Schaw Lindsay (1815-1877) Started Co 1845 withdrew 1862
John Gladstone (1799-1877) Joined 1845
George Gladstone (1828-?) Joined 1845 Aged 16 John's son
Edward Pembroke (1831-1911) Joined 1846
Edgar P Stringer (1822-1894) Joined 1848
Ole P Moller (1831-1888) Joined 1859 (?)
Chevalier L Serena (?-1885) Joined (?)
James Galbraith (1818-1885) Joined 1869

Lindsay's Directorships
W. S. Lindsay & Co 1845 NMM: LND 5-2, 15
South Sea Whaling Co 1850s NNM: LND 4-1, 665
Marine (Life and Casualty) 1850s
Chartered Bank of India, Australia, and China 1853 NMM: LND 5-3, 65
Safety Life Assurance Co 1854 NMM: LND 5-3, 17
St Katharine Docks, London 1850s NMM: LND 5-3, 416

Appendix VI: Estate of William Schaw Lindsay at his death in 1877[1]

Shepperton Manor

Manor Farm Shepperton

Watersplash Farm, Halliford

Halliford House, Lower Halliford

Laurel Villa, Halliford

Westfield House, Halliford (with coach house)

Ellesmere House, Halliford

Rose Cottage, Shepperton

Range House, Shepperton

The Limes, Shepperton (formally Manor Cottage)

Kilmiston Gardens, Halliford (Two cottages)

Kilmiston House, Halliford (formally 8 Highfield Villas, two cottages)

Highfield Villa, Halliford (delerict house, to be 9 Highfield Villas)

Dorney House, Weybridge (with coach houses)

1 Dorney Villas, Weybridge

6 Dorney Cottages, Weybridge

Rosedale, Weybridge (with coach house)

Lincoln Arms Hotel, Weybridge

Weybridge Lodge, Thames Street, Weybridge

Fairview, Thames Street, Weybridge

Holly Villa, Thames Street, Weybridge

Dolly's Farm, Chobham

Woodham Lodge, Addlestone

Pannells Farm, Chertsey

Ravensworth, Bournemouth (with coach house)

The Oxford Dictionary of National Biography states that Lindsay's wealth at death was under £45,000. His probate was published 29 September 1877

Appendix VII: William Schaw Lindsay's family tree

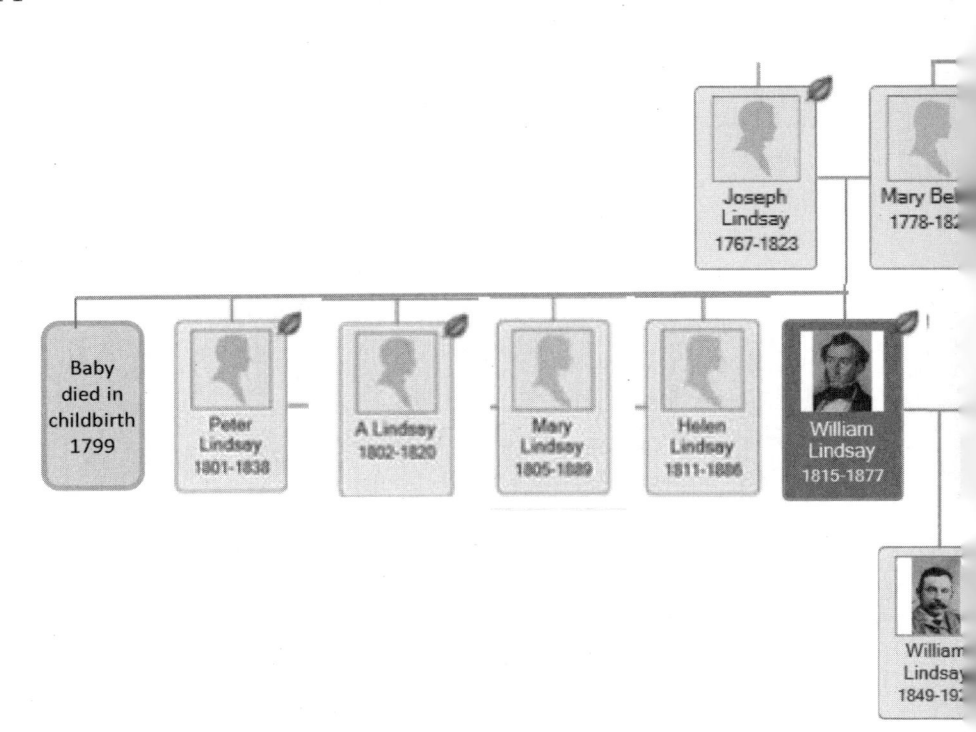

Appendices

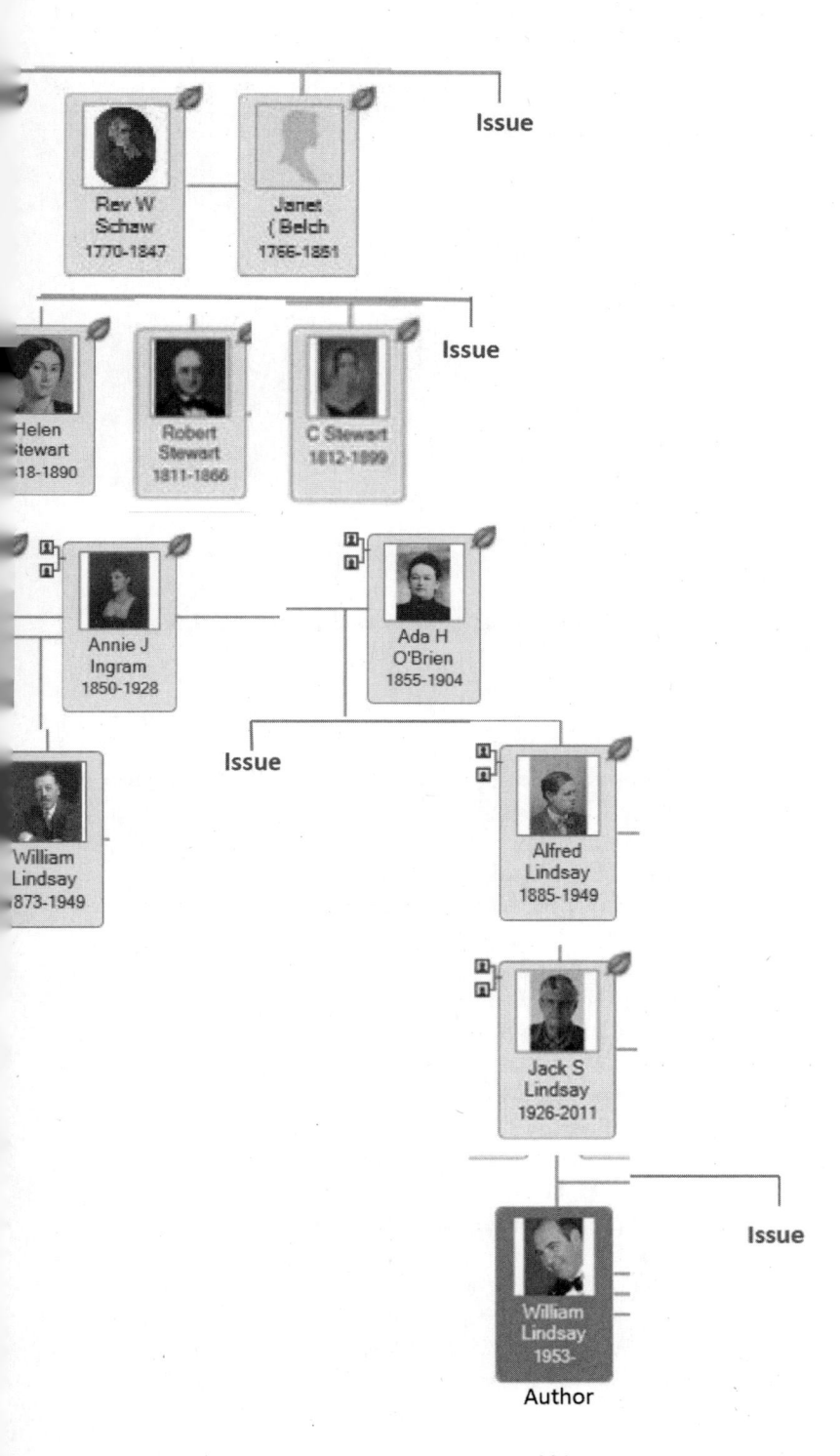

- Rev W Schaw 1770-1847
- Janet (Belch 1766-1851

Issue

- Helen Stewart 1818-1890
- Robert Stewart 1811-1866
- C Stewart 1812-1899

Issue

- Annie J Ingram 1850-1928
- Ada H O'Brien 1855-1904

Issue

- William Lindsay 1873-1949
- Alfred Lindsay 1885-1949

- Jack S Lindsay 1926-2011

- William Lindsay 1953-
Author

Issue

301

Notes

Foreword by J. D. Davies

1. https://jddavies.com/

Introduction: A True Story

1. Johnson, J., *Clever Boys of our Time who Became Famous Men*, 154. Published 1868.

Part One: At Sea

1. William Schaw Lindsay's unpublished Journal, Greenwich, UK. National Maritime Museum (NMM): LND 5-1, 7
2. Joseph Lindsay (1767-1823), Lindsay's father
3. Mary Lindsay née Belch (1778-1825), Lindsay's mother
4. The Napoleonic Wars: 18 May 1803-20 November 1815
5. Strawhorn, *750 years of a Scottish school, Ayr Academy 1233-1983*, Alloway Publishing Ltd, 1983, 43
6. NMM: LND/19, The Good Old Parson
7. Small, R, *History of the Congregations of the United Presbyterian Church, Edinburgh, 1904* p329, 538.
8. *The United Presbyterian Magazine*, 1851, 25
9. Lindsay's eldest sister Mary Lindsay (1805-1889), stayed with his aunt and uncle. She later married Reverend Dr John McKerrow.
10. Mary Lindsay née Barnet (1798-1837)
11. Helen Christie née Lindsay (1811-1886), Lindsay's sister
12. Thomas Christie (1787-1838)
13. Lieutenant Peter Belches (1796-1890) from Edinburgh. Later, in March 1827, Belches accompanied Admiral Sir James Stirling (1791-1865) on HMS *Success* exploring the Swan River, Western Australia. Point Belches is named after him. He left the Navy and settled in Albany, Western Australia.

Notes

14. Anchorage point at the mouth of the Clyde Estuary.
15. NMM: LND 3-7, 77
16. Johnson, *Clever Boys of our Time who Became Famous Men*, 147-55. See also NMM: LND 5-1,18
17. NMM: LND 5-1,19
18. The Mariners' Floating Church was an old frigate HMS *Tees*, a gift from the government to the Mariners Church Society, which had been towed to the Mersey from Plymouth, converted as a floating church, moored in George's Dock and opened for worship in May 1827. It remained there, maintained by the Church of England, until 1872 when weakened by extensive dry rot it sank at its moorings in 1872. See https://www.liverpoolpicturebook.com/2013/01/churches-and-religions-in-liverpool.html
19. Recently purchased by a Mr. George Anderson, a West India Merchant of the firm of George Anderson & Co of Demerara.
20. Thomas Tait (1800-1835), son of Thomas Tait and Margaret McIntosh in Glasgow.
21. Actually he was Malcolm McCaskill (1811-1840) Son of Kenneth McCaskell and Flora McIntosh in St Quivox near Ayr.
22. NMM: LND 5-1,30
23. *Report from the Select Committee Appointed to Inquire into the Causes of Shipwrecks: With the Minutes of Evidence,* Appendix and Index, ordered by the House of Commons 15 Aug 1836.
24. Gridiron: a frame of parallel bars or beams onto which a ship is hauled up.
25. NMM: LND 5-1,34
26. A boat hung on davits at a ship's quarter (ie located behind the beam and forward of the stern).
27. NMM: LND 5-1, 51
28. A two-masted ship, with a square-rigged sail to the fore.
29. See also Harris, *The Last Slave Ship*, Yale University Press, 2020.
30. WSL's journal says three weeks, but it must be three days.
31. The *Mountaineer* owned by George Anderson.
32. Actually, McCastle died some way along the Calcutta River.
33. John (or Jock) Dinning born 1803 was son of Neil Dinning and Elizabeth Kerr in Ayr. Jock's brother Alexander was the *Isabella*'s carpenter.
34. NMM: LND 5-1, 68
35. A barque is a type of sailing vessel with three or more masts having the fore- and mainmasts square rigged.
36. Sir Astley Paston Cooper (1768-1841). He was a British surgeon and anatomist, who made historical contributions to otology, vascular surgery, the anatomy and pathology of the mammary glands and testicles, and the pathology and surgery of hernia.
37. Michael McCarthy Keane (1800-1873)
38. NMM: LND 5-1, 78

39. NMM: LND 5-1, 92
40. NMM: LND 5-1, 203
41. NMM: LND 5-1, 94
42. *Newcastle Courant,* 23/08/1839.
43. Kharg Island
44. Lindsay's letter to his brother-in-law Rev Dr John McKerrow 25 December 1840
45. Mercury chloride mineral, a white powder formerly used as a purgative, used to empty and cleanse the bowels.
46. A tuberous vine also used as a purgative.
47. NMM: LND 5-1, 111
48. Indian soldiers employed by the East India Company or British Army.
49. Commodore George B Brucks, Acting Senior Naval Officer Persian Gulf 1835-?
50. 1st Anglo-Afghan War 1839-1842
51. NMM: LND 5-1, 159
52. NMM: LND 5-1, 174
53. Algoa Bay is near Port Elizabeth in the Eastern Cape.
54. Napoleon Bonaparte (1769-1821) Emperor of the French 1804-1814 & 1815
55. NMM: LND 5-1, 190

Part Two: Journey to Success

1. NMM: LND 5-1, 215
2. James and George Burns ordered their first steamer in 1825, quickly replacing all their sailing ships with steamers.
3. NMM: LND 5-1, 236
4. Margaret Reid née Stewart born 1820
5. Christina Craig née Stewart (1812-1899)
6. Helen told him that "one would require to have the patience of Job to wonder through his long-winded scrawls." He writes that "it cut my pride most sorely." Letter to his brother-in-law. 20 April 1842
7. Helen Lindsay née Stewart (1818-1890)
8. NMM: LND 3-2, 595
9. NMM: LND 5-1, 286
10. Cowan's Bank may have been Hunters & Co Bankers in Ayr where William Cowan was the managing partner. Description of Hunters and Co, Bankers, Ayr, Hunters and Company, Bankers, Ayr, 1657-1854. Lloyds Banking Group Archives (Edinburgh). GB 1830 HUN' on the Archives Hub website, [https://archiveshub.jisc.ac.uk/data/gb1830-hun], (date accessed: 21/07/2021)
11. Mageean, *Emigration from Irish Ports*, Journal of American Ethnic History Vol. 13, No. 1, European Ports of Emigration (Fall, 1993), pp. 6-30.
12. NMM: LND 5-1, 291

Notes

13. William John Vollum (1812-1849), Mayor of Hartlepool, and manager of Backhouse and Co Bank. *The Gentleman's Magazine*, 1849, Vol 185, 329.
14. Church rates were taxes formerly levied in each parish in England and Ireland for the benefit of the parish church. They were imposed by the occupier of the land.
15. Edward Turnbull (1821-1888), Solicitor, Mayor of Hartlepool 1849 & 1853
16. As a form of ballast
17. Lindsay called Helen 'Nell'. Letters to sister and brother-in-law. 22 May 1854
18. NMM: LND 5-1, 305. We can only take Lindsay's word for his success in achieving his first two aims. Documentation proving these is lost.
19. The Municipal Corporations Act 1835 was instigated to form councils in local government consisting of mayor, aldermen, and councillors elected by ratepayers. Hartlepool was not included in the 1835 Act but obtained the status in 1850.
20. *Sunderland and Durham County Herald,* 16 February 1844 refers to Hartlepool docks. See NMM: LND 1, 6
21. Life-saving apparatus in the form of a rocket. Invented by Henry Trengrouse (1772-1854). George Manby (1765-1854) also designed a similar apparatus using a mortar.
22. Note the similarities to the 'Great Gale' that hit the East Coast 24 years later. See Jones N, *The Plimsoll Sensation*, 70
23. NMM: LND 5-1, 312
24. Pig iron is obtained from iron ore by processing it with coke in a blast furnace, it is more easily transported.
25. 1844. See Fynes., *History of Durham and Northumberland Miners*
26. NMM: LND 5-2, 1
27. NMM: LND 5-3, 692. Letter to his cousin Lieutenant Peter Belch.
28. James Allan (c1811-1874). NMM: LND 5-2, 11. See also NMM: LND 3-1b,476. See also Smith., *Coal, Steam and Ships*, Cambridge University Press, 2018, 285.
29. NMM: LND 5-2, 23. Joseph Lumsden (1777-1865) and John Byers (1811-1866)
30. NMM: LND 5-2, 24 George Holt (1824-1896) and William Lamport (1815-1874) set up the firm. George's brother Alfred Holt (1829-1911) in Liverpool was Lindsay's consulting engineer *c.*1854. NMM: LND 5-3,104. Alfred and another of his brothers (Philip) founded the Blue Funnel Line. Alfred wrote of Lindsay as being "a strange mixture of energy, industry, self-reliance, egotism and pretence". Jones C W., *Pioneer shipowners II* (1938),132
31. NMM: LND 5-2, 17
32. The famine or Great Famine arose mainly in Ireland but in Scotland as well. A fungus caused the failure of the potato crop.

33. The Levant refers to a large area in the Eastern Mediterranean region of Western Asia.
34. A quarter of wheat would weigh about 494 lb.
35. NMM: LND 5-2,32
36. Sir Josiah John Guest MP, 1st Baronet, known as John Josiah Guest, (1785-1852) was a Welsh engineer and entrepreneur.
37. Railroad track
38. William Stewart Lindsay (2020) *William Schaw Lindsay and the Oceangoing Auxiliary Steamer*, The Mariner's Mirror, 106:1, 43-61, DOI: 10.1080/00253359.2020.1692577
39. Note that Lindsay was one of the largest ship brokers in London, not one of the largest shipowners. Duncan Dunbar (1803-1862) had 43 ships compared to Lindsay's 22. See Rhodes M, *Lion Rampant: Duncan Dunbar and the Age of Sail*.
40. NMM: LND 5-3,78
41. Reverend Dr William Schaw died 19 September 1847
42. NMM: LND 5-2, 111
43. Sir John Musgrove, 1st Baronet (1793-1881) was Lord Mayor of London 1850.
44. Lindsay ceded Edgar Pinchback Stringer (1820-1894), five years his junior, a third of his Company. NMM: LND 5-2,25.
45. William Stewart Lindsay (1849-1924). See also NMM: LND 6 (11)
46. NMM: LND 5-3,692
47. Hattersley., *The British Settlement of Natal – A Study in Imperial Migration*, Cambridge University Press, 1950
48. Joseph Byrne was born in Dublin in about 1800, the son of a small-time cattle-dealer, Joseph Byrne of Mount Argus House in that city. See https://shelaghspencer.com/josephbyrne/
49. The 'Pores were the six ships Lindsay named *Alipore, Barrackpore, Cossipore, Dinapore, Mirzapore, Serampore*
50. Many shipowners were fearful of iron. Some thought iron would sink. Lindsay, *History of Merchant Shipping* Vol 4, 91. Others felt that steamers would injure the flavour of fruit. Jones, *Pioneer Shipowners Vol 1*, 115.
51. Fore rake: That part of a ship's head which projects beyond or overhangs the forward end of the keel.
52. NMM: LND 5-3,182. Brunel's Iron ship the SS *Great Britain* launched in 1843 was also a proportionally long ship (and much longer than Lindsay's ship), so Lindsay was not alone in favouring a lengthy iron-built sailing ship. The SS *Great Britain* was a fully powered steamer (although she was adapted as an auxiliary steamer in later life); the *W S Lindsay* was firstly a sailing ship then an auxiliary steamer.
53. *The Newcastle Courant*, October 1, 1852. See also *The Newcastle Guardian*, October 2, 1852.

Notes

54. The iron in Iron ships was notorious for causing inaccurate compass readings. Lindsay, *History of Merchant Shipping* Vol 4,89
55. Said to be £3,000
56. *Lloyd's Weekly Newspaper*, 2 January 1853
57. Sir Chapman Marshall (1777-1862) was Lord Mayor of London 1839-40.
58. *The Economist* December 1852, NMM: LND-1, 94
59. A bailie is a civic officer in the local government of Scotland. They held a post similar to that of an alderman or magistrate.
60. There are two ships of that name; The *Hamilla Mitchell*, 540 tons, built in Peterhead 1850 and another of 958 tons built in Dumbarton 1864. I suspect that Lindsay was referring to the former.
61. One candy was 500 pounds weight
62. NMM: LND 5-1,98
63. For a list of Acts of Parliament between 1849-75 relating to Navigation Laws see Lindsay, *History of Merchant Shipping* Vol 3, 634.
64. Local shipping trade ie coastal trade. The movement of cargo and passengers, mainly by sea along a coast, without crossing an ocean.
65. Palmer., *Politics, Shipping and the Repeal of the Navigation Laws*, 1990
66. Lindsay., *History of Merchant Shipping*, Vol 3, 209.
67. George Henderson (1806-1852). Laird., *Paddy Henderson*, 25. See also King., *The Aberdeen Line*, 69
68. Patrick Henderson (1808-1841). Laird., *Paddy Henderson*, 29. See also Spong & Osbourne, *Shaw, Savill & Albion, A Fleet History*, 9.
69. James Galbraith (1818-1885), shipping agent and shipowner. See Laird., *Paddy Henderson*, 30. http://www.glasgowwestaddress.co.uk/100_Glasgow_Men/Galbraith_James.htm
70. NMM: LND 3-1b, 24
71. Granville George Leveson-Gower, 2nd Earl Granville, (1815-1891)
72. Indiamen: ships engaged in trade with India or the East or West Indies, especially an East Indiaman.
73. NMM: LND 3-1b (9)
74. See also https://www.rmg.co.uk/stories/blog five-women-who-made-it-letters-ws-lindsay-men-his-time
75. NMM: LND 5/3, 264
76. Caroline Chisholm (1808-1877) See also NMM: LND 4-1, 989
77. NMM: LND 5-3,272
78. See also McKie, 'How Caroline Chisholm worked to keep the strumpets at bay.' *The Age*, 2 April 1983.
79. NMM: LND 4-1, 989; NMM: LND 5-3,284
80. The *Caroline Chisholm* was renamed the *Tynemouth*.
81. *Ballaret* was one of Duncan Dunbar's ships. Rhodes, *Lion Rampant, Duncan Dunbar and the Age of Sail*, 276. The following year the ship recorded the fastest sailing times; 70 days to Sydney and return in 69 days.

82. NMM: LND 4-1, 1004
83. NMM: LND 5-2,191
84. Lindsay., *The Mariner's Mirror* 106:1 (February 2020), 43-6
85. Richard Green (1803-1863) was a wealthy philanthropist with a shipyard in Blackwall, London.
86. See also the *Nautical Magazine and Naval Chronicle*,1851, 211
87. NMM: LND 5-3,1
88. Originally named the *Caroline Chisholm*.
89. The *Robert Lowe* was named after the MP for London University, a former friend of Lindsay's. He became Viscount Sherbrooke (1811-1892), Chancellor of the Exchequer in Gladstone's government. See NMM: LND 4-1, 375
90. Captain Laughlin McKay (1811-1895) "was a quiet, mild-mannered, and even-tempered man with the innate qualities required to be a successful ship's captain." Nolan., *Clippers, the ships that shaped the World,* 75. See also https://archive.org/stream/nathanielmckay00mcka/nathanielmckay00mcka_djvu.txt ,27
91. Donald McKay (1810-1880), Canadian-born American designer and builder of famous clipper ships.
92. Unlike Brunel's SS *Great Britain* which was originally a fully powered steamship but converted to an auxiliary steamer in 1852, the *Robert Lowe* was designed and built as an auxiliary steamer.
93. *Greenock Advertiser*, 15/8/1854. See also *Greenock Advertiser,* 26/09/1854
94. Scott & Co traded until 1967 when it merged with Lithgows to form Scott Lithgow Ltd. Scott Lithgow Ltd was then absorbed into the nationalised British Shipbuilders in 1977.
95. NMM: LND 5-3,580 also NMM: LND 5-4,391
96. Layard to Lady Huntly, 7 May 1855, *Layard Papers*, B. M. Add. MS 38944/37
97. *Newcastle Journal*, 4 Mar. 1854; *London Evening Standard*, 15 Apr. 1854

Part Three: Politics and Shipping

1. The majority of MPs were landed gentlemen; the minority were businessmen. Even fewer knew about shipping.
2. NMM: LND 5-2, 130 See also NMM: LND 1, 31. The Monmouth Boroughs constituency included Newport.
3. Reginald James Blewitt (1799-1878)
4. Lord John Russell (1792-1878) was Prime Minister of the Whig Party (which soon merged into the Liberal Party) having been elected five years earlier.
5. Crawshay Bailey (1789-1872) was an English industrialist who became one of the great ironmasters of Wales.

Notes

6. Henry Charles FitzRoy Somerset, 8th Duke of Beaufort (1824-1899), styled Earl of Glamorgan until 1835 and Marquis of Worcester from 1835 to 1853, was a British peer, soldier, and Conservative Party politician.
7. Charles Morgan Robinson Morgan (1792-1875) was an English Whig peer. He was created 1st Baron Tredegar in 1859.
8. Algernon George Percy, 6th Duke of Northumberland, (1810-1899), MP (Conservative) for Bere Alston 1831-32 and for North Northumberland 1852-65; a Lord of the Admiralty 1858-59.
9. Alderman William Thompson MP (1793-1854), ironmaster and financier. MP for Callington 1820 and MP for London until 1832. Lord Mayor of London 1828–29. See also NMM: LND 4-1, 581.
10. The official returns showed that Lindsay lost by 235 votes.
11. NMM: LND 5-2, 156 See also NMM: LND 1, 113
12. Vice-Admiral Sir Thomas Herbert, (1793-1861)
13. Edward George Geoffrey Smith-Stanley, 14th Earl of Derby (1799-1869) was a British statesman, three-time Prime Minister 1852, 1858-59, 1866-68.
14. George Moffatt (1806-1878)
15. James Wilson (1805-1860) was a Scottish businessman, economist, and Liberal politician who founded *The Economist*. In 1853 he founded The Chartered Bank of India, Australia and China (of which Lindsay became a Director), which later merged with the Standard Bank to form Standard Chartered Bank in 1969. He became Liberal MP for Westbury, Wiltshire, in 1847. See NMM: LND 4-1, 385.
16. *Men of the Time: Biographical Sketches of Eminent Living Characters.* W. Kent & Co, London, 1859. See also *Sunderland Daily Echo*, 17 February 1877. See also Ronald McKie, *The Age*, 2 April 1983.
17. Sir Henry Paul Seale (1806-1897), Mayor of Dartmouth
18. The official return said Lindsay lost by 11 votes.
19. This General Election was a turning point in British politics. The Tory/Conservative Party became increasingly the party for rural aristocracy, while the Whig/Liberal party became the party for the increasing urban middle class. The result was extremely close; Lord John Russell's Whigs won the popular vote, but the Conservative Party won a very slight majority of the seats.
20. 1,200,000 quarters of grain. Johnson., *Clever Boys of our Time*, 153.
21. Hugh Taylor (1817–1900), colliery and shipowner, who was Conservative MP for Tynemouth & North Shields, 1852-3 & 1859-61. He resigned from Parliament to devote himself to his business interests and bought Chipchase Castle in 1862. See also NMM: LND 6 (38).
22. Ralph William Grey (1819-1869)
23. NMM: LND 5-2, 205

24. The Keelmen of Tyne and Wear were a group of men who worked on the keels, large boats that carried the coal from the banks of both rivers to the waiting collier ships.
25. Lindsay continued to represent Tynemouth until the April 1859 general election, when his advocacy for a repeal of the navigation laws compelled him to withdraw before the polling. "Because I would not say that I would do my best to secure what the shipowners wished they unanimously resolved to oppose my re-election." NMM: LND 1,156. He was returned, however, for Sunderland. NMM: LND 1,196.
26. Frances Anne Vane, Marchioness of Londonderry (1800-1865) was a wealthy English heiress and noblewoman. She was the second wife of Charles William Vane, 3rd Marquess of Londonderry (born Charles William Stewart); her great-grandson was Sir Winston Churchill. See also NMM: LND 4-1, 879.
27. NMM: LND 4-1, 879
28. Lord Adolphus Frederick Charles William Vane-Tempest (1825-1864), Conservative MP for Durham
29. Charles William Vane, 3rd Marquess of Londonderry (born Charles William Stewart; 1778-1854)
30. NMM: LND 4-1, 1
31. NMM: LND 5-2, 215
32. Most parliamentary sessions last for around 10 to 12 months, during which time each House sits for around 150 days.
33. Richard Cobden (1804-1865) was an English manufacturer, Radical and Liberal MP associated with two major free trade campaigns, the Anti-Corn Law League (repealing the Law that had raised food prices), and the Cobden-Chevalier Treaty (a Free Trade agreement between Britain and France). He was MP for West Riding of Yorkshire.
34. NMM: LND 4-2, 25
35. Within six months Cobden was to lose his only son. Lindsay helped him through difficult times that followed.
36. NMM: LND 5-2, 225
37. A sloop-of-war in the Royal Navy was a warship with a single gun deck that carried up to eighteen guns.
38. A cutter is a sailing vessel having more than one foresail or jib.
39. 20 September 1854
40. The siege lasted from 17 October 1854-11 September 1855 (349 days).
41. The Red Lion in Chobham
42. The Angel Inn in Midhurst
43. Edward Oliver was a ship-builder in Quebec who moved to Liverpool and became a major shipbroker.
44. Twenty-two of Oliver's ships were sold by auction in 1854, and fifty-two vessels were unsold in the auction.
45. Edward Lyon Berthon (1813-1899) was an English inventor and clergyman. See https://www.berthon.co.uk/berthon-blog/berthon/the-berthon-collapsible-lifeboat/. See also Hans Busk's Mars lifeboat NMM: LND 3-4, 8

Notes

46. In fact, changes to warships were driven by new technology, rather than incompetence. See Lambert, A.D., *Battleships in Transition*, Conway Maritime Press, London, 1984.
47. The call for a Naval Commander in Chief had been raised in an essay by Admiral Sir George Cockburn, posthumously published around 1852.
48. See also *The Capabilities and Advantages of Cunningham's Patent Mode of Reefing*, Woodward, Portsea, 1853. Henry D P Cunningham.

Part Four: The Crimean War (1854–1856)

1. NMM: LND, MLN/156/2-7
2. The Russians invaded Moldavia and Wallachia and refused to evacuate their troops.
3. John Gladstone, Lindsay's partner, received £4,260 per month gross as Lindsay's trustee.
4. Although significant, this contrasts with Duncan Dunbar's income for 1854 of £102,000; his ships were also chartered by the Government. Dunbar's assets however were massive; £605,000, which included his ships, warehouses and Wharf. Rhodes, *Lion Rampant: Duncan Dunbar and the Age of Sail*.
5. See below, 'Underwater Explosives'.
6. Likely to have been John Cundy Pentreath born 1819
7. Also known as the Great Storm.
8. 19 December 1854, *The Sun*. The article states it was Osman Pasha but it must have been Omer Pasha.
9. Field Marshal FitzRoy James Henry Somerset, 1st Baron Raglan (1788-1855)
10. In fact Lord Raglan was an effective commander, and a very capable manager of the Anglo-French alliance, but was only appreciated after his death in June.
11. Sir Houston Stewart, (1791-1875)
12. Sir James Robert George Graham, (1792-1861), Home Secretary 1841-1846, First Lord of the Admiralty 1830-1834 and 1852-1855. NMM: LND 4-1, 49
13. William Congalton (1827-1890) Son of John Congleton and his wife Diana of Aberlady, East Lothian.
14. https://api.parliament.uk/historic-hansard/commons/1855/mar/23/the-transport-service
15. Florence Nightingale (1820-1910)
16. Dr John Hall (1795-1866)
17. Sardinia joined France, Britain and Turkey in the Crimean War fighting against Russia.
18. Sir Joseph Paxton's Army Works Corps; men signed on for two or three years. They were mobilised into twenty-five-man gangs commanded by both gangers and uniformed Officers. The pay was thirty-five shillings a week for navvies, forty for gangers, and everybody was to get a twelve

pound bonus at the end. Dick Sullivan. *Navvyman*, Coracle Press,1983. See also Chadwick., *The Army Works Corps in the Crimea*, Journal of Transport History Vol VI, No 3, May 1964.
19. Including the *Barrackpore*
20. Howe, *Letters of Richard Cobden 1815-1847*, Volume 1. 2012, 54
21. A Redan is a type of fortification. It is V-shaped to obstruct an expected attack. The Redan or fortress (or bastion) at Sebastopol was attacked by British troops. They suffered nearly 1,500 casualties during the first attack and nearly 2,500 during the second.
22. Brett., *White Wings, Vol 2*,213; Waters, Shaw Saville Line.
23. Sir William Howard Russell, (1820-1907) was an Irish reporter with *The Times*. NMM: LND 4-1, 687
24. Bevan,*The Infernal Diver*, Submex, 1996. In 1836 John Deane discovered the shipwreck of the *Mary Rose* which sank on 19 July 1545.
25. Admiral Sir James Whitley Deans Dundas (1785-1862). See also NMM: LND 6 (27 & 28) and NMM: LND 4-1, 849.
26. NMM: LND 5-3, 50
27. Admiral Edmund Lyons, 1st Baron Lyons (1790-1858) Admiral Commander-in-Chief of the British Navy in the Crimea
28. The Commanding Engineer Lieut-Colonel E.T. Lloyd believed that the underwater explosives would not have been effective since the electrical charges were faulty. See *History of Royal Sappers and Miners*, Vol 2, 207.
29. Interestingly, Admiral Sir Charles Napier severely criticized the Admiralty in letters to the press a few years earlier for their mismanagement. Williams, *The Life and Letters of Admiral Sir Charles Napier, K.C.B.*, London 1917, 230.
30. A similar mishap occurred when shoes too small were sent to the Baltic Fleet.
31. NMM: LND 5-3,338
32. Lindsay., *Confirmation of Admiralty Mismanagement*, London, 1855
33. Charles Wood, 1st Viscount Halifax, (1800-1885), known as Sir Charles Wood, between 1846 and 1866. He served as Chancellor of the Exchequer from 1846 to 1852. See also NMM: LND 4-1,61
34. Admiral Sir Maurice Frederick FitzHardinge Berkeley, 1st Baron FitzHardinge, (1788-1867)
35. Letter Lindsay to Richmond 30 January 1855. See also https://api.parliament.uk/historic-hansard/commons/1855/jan/26/army-crimea
36. Jean-Étienne-Théodore Ducos (1801-1855) was a French politician and shipowner.
37. Packet ships were medium-sized boats designed for domestic mail, passenger, and freight transportation.
38. NMM: LND 5-3, 474
39. The Minister of War was Marshal Jean-Baptiste Philibert Vaillant (1790-1872) who held office from 1854-1859.

Notes

40. Napoleon III (Charles Louis Napoléon Bonaparte; 1808-1873) was the first President of France (as Louis-Napoléon Bonaparte) from 1848 to 1852 and Emperor of the French from 1852 to 1870.
41. Lindsay, *History of Merchant Shipping* Vol 3, 354
42. During the Crimean War, Kamiesch bay was used by the French as their main port of supply.
43. Lambert, *The Crimean War*, Manchester University Press, 1991, 166
44. Admiral Sir Charles John Napier (1786-1860). See also NMM: LND 4-1,287
45. Nicholas I (1796-1855) reigned as Emperor of Russia, King of Poland and Grand Duke of Finland from 1825 until 1855.
46. Williams, *The Life and Letters of Admiral Sir Charles Napier, K.C.B.* London 1917, 161. Napier was Captain, co-designer, and business partner of the world's first seagoing Iron ship, the *Aaron Manby* in 1822. Nancollas, *The Ship Asunder*, 198. See also Williams, 61.
47. Lambert, *The Crimean War*, Manchester University Press, 1991, 34
48. Williams, *The Life and Letters of Admiral Sir Charles Napier, K.C.B.* London 1917, 245
49. NMM: LND 4-1, 287
50. Lindsay contradicted himself; he is quoted as praising the Admiralty ships and Crews elsewhere. Nolan E.H., *The Illustrated History of the War against Russia*, Vol 1, 106, James Virtue, London 1857
51. After the Swedish Russian War of 1808-9, the Aland Islands and Finland were handed over to Russia. The Bomarsund fortress was built by Russia to resist any Swedish hostilities.
52. Sveaborg was the main port of Helsinki (or Helsingfors) in Finland.
53. Cronstadt was the port of Saint Petersburg (capital city of Russia at the time).
54. Troubetzkoy, *A Brief History of the Crimean War*, London, Robinson, 2006, 223.
55. Lindsay probably doesn't mean a 94 pounder, rather that the weight of a 68 pounder mounted was 95 hundredweight.
56. NMM: LND 5-3, 646
57. General Sir William Fenwick Williams of Kars (1800-1883). See NMM: LND 4-1, 453
58. General Sir William John Codrington MP (1804-1884)
59. John Somerset Pakington, 1st Baron Hampton, (1799-1880), known as Sir John Pakington, from 1846 to 1874. See also NMM: LND 4-1,179.
60. Cherbourg Naval Review, 6 March 1858
61. A gig is a light, fast, narrow boat for rowing or sailing.
62. NMM: LND 4-1, 178
63. Admiral Lord Clarence Edward Paget (1811-1895) was a British naval officer and politician. See NMM: LND 4-1, 409.
64. Adams, Charles Francis Sr (1807-1886) United States Minister to the United Kingdom. Son of John Quincy Adams (1767-1848) 6th President of the United States 1825-1829. Prominent during the American Civil War.

65. Although Lindsay says this, one can understand why Napier turned down the award. His treatment by the Admiralty, particularly by Sir James Graham, was appalling.
66. John Arthur Roebuck (1802-1879) MP for Bath then Sheffield. See NMM: LND 6 (16-17) also 4-1, 325
67. Sidney Herbert, 1st Baron Herbert of Lea (1810-1861) was a British statesman and a close ally and confidant of Florence Nightingale. See also NMM: LND 4-1, 967, Letter from Lady Herbert.
68. Lord Aberdeen, George Hamilton-Gordon, 4th Earl of Aberdeen (1784-1860)
69. NMM: LND 4-1, 60
70. Fletcher, *Parliamentary Portraits of the Present Period*, London 1862, pp 267-270.
71. Lindsay, *History of Merchant Shipping* Vol 4, 357. Lindsay states that the transport service for the War cost £15 million but with efficiencies that could have been reduced by a third.
72. NMM: LND 5-4, 205
73. NMM: LND 1, 286
74. Charles John Huffam Dickens (1812-1870).
75. Searle., *Entrepreneurial Politics on mid-Victorian Britain*. Clarendon Press, Oxford, 1993
76. Sir Austen Henry Layard (1817-1894) said "Lindsay was a conceited active fellow – eaten by vanity – with few of the tastes and feelings of a gentleman." Layard papers Add. MS 38,944. Layard became Under-Secretary at the Foreign Office. See also NMM: LND 4-1, 543
77. Lindsay, *Confirmation of Admiralty Mismanagement*, London, 1855.
78. Samuel Laing (1812-1897) was a British railway administrator, politician, and writer on science and religion. See also NMM: LND 6 (36)
79. Henry Petty-Fitzmaurice, 3rd Marquess of Lansdowne (1780-1863. He served as Home Secretary and Chancellor of the Exchequer and was three times Lord President of the Council.
80. Lindsay's letter to his brother-in-law 9 April 1855
81. Layard, Laing, Lowe, and Lindsay
82. NMM: LND 4-1, 4
83. Congress of Paris, 30 March 1856

Part Five: Shipping Business Continues

1. NMM: LND 5-4, 531
2. During the Crimean War their ships were employed as transport ships.
3. NMM: LND 5-4, 811
4. A joint stock company is financed with capital invested by the members or stockholders who receive transferable shares, or stock.
5. See also Mitchell, The *Cape Run* viii, Terence Dalton 1984

Notes

6. Adam Alexander Duncan Dundas (1822-1904). Son of James Dundas (1793-1881) and brother of George Dundas MP (1819-1880). http://www.dundasfamily.co.uk/dundas%20of%20dundas_2.html#adam_27th_of_dundas
7. Lindsay had suggested these penalties himself; Lindsay, *History of Merchant Shipping Vol 4*, 433
8. Contract of employment
9. Captained by Atkins. It was going to be Captain Wilson, then Captain Goodwin, but both were unavailable at the last minute.
10. In his book *Travels in Eastern Africa: With the Narrative of a Residence in Mozambique*, Lyons McLeod describes the voyage as appalling, and that WSL stood for Worst Steam Line.
11. Captained by Lieutenant Adam Dundas, second son of James Dundas, of Dundas Castle.
12. NMM: LND 5-4, 551
13. Lindsay, *Confirmation of Mismanagement*
14. Lindsay., *Manning the Royal Navy & Merchant Marine*, also *Belligerent and Neutral Rights in the event of War*, London, 1877, 107
15. See also Lindsay, *Shepperton*, edited by V. Brooking. 1994.
16. Eldest son of James Winter Scott, MP for Northern Division of Hampshire in 1832
17. In 1862, Lindsay was prominent in extending the railway line to Shepperton, thus further reducing the journey time.
18. A church has stood on this site since the 7th century.
19. The Old Churchyard was full before Lindsay died. He donated a portion of his land to form a new graveyard and it is here he is buried in a tomb. "At Shepperton I have presented to the Parish an addition to the cemetery, surrounding the whole with brick walls at my own expense. I have also laid it out as a garden and planted it with trees, and in it I have built a vault for my own use and my family, for that is a house we all require sooner or later."
20. An ancient Roman General's tent in a camp.
21. William Stukeley (1687-1765) was an English antiquarian, physician and Anglican clergyman. He had a significant influence on the later development of archaeology.
22. Although Lindsay didn't believe the story about Caesar's camp, he nevertheless turned his sitting room into a room modelled on a camp. He also used a motif based on a camp on his headed paper.
23. Allsopp, *Villagers lived a life of depravity*, Herald News, March 10, 1994. See also *Shepperton* by Lindsay, Lord of the Manor, The Sunbury and Shepperton Local Historical Society. March 1994.
24. As well as being a Local Magistrate, Lindsay was at one time a Deputy Lieutenant of London.
25. NMM: LND 3-4, 340

26. Sir Benjamin Hawes (1797-1862) was a British Whig politician. NMM: LND 3-4,166.
27. Robert Stephenson (1803-1859) was the only son of George Stephenson (1781-1848) who was acknowledged as the 'Father of Railways'. Robert built the *Rocket* in 1830, a locomotive that brought together many innovations.
28. Isambard Kingdom Brunel (1806-1859) the English civil engineer considered "one of the most ingenious and prolific figures in engineering history", Spratt, H.P., *Isambard Kingdom Brunel*. Nature 181, 1754-1755 (1958)
29. Lindsay, *History of Merchant Shipping*, Vol 4, 513
30. Dugan, *The Great Iron Ship*, 40 & 51. See also Lindsay WS, *History of Merchant Shipping* Vol 4, 540
31. Emmerson, *John Scott Russell*,128
32. Interestingly, the SS *Great Britain* was converted to an auxiliary steamer with success in her later days. Corlett, *The Iron Ship*, 121. See also Doe., SS *Great Britain*, 87 & 101.
33. John Scott Russell (1808-1882) was a Scottish civil engineer and naval architect.
34. A roadstead is a body of water sheltered from rip currents, spring tides, or ocean swell where ships can lie reasonably safely at anchor without dragging or snatching.
35. Lindsay, *History of Merchant Shipping*, Vol 4, 527
36. Lindsay's predictions were realised. The SS *Great Eastern* ended up a sorry sight in Liverpool docks as advertising hoarding for a department store in 1886. She was also turned into a show. Half a million visitors boarded the ship to see trapeze artists, a shooting gallery, restaurants and bars, and a music hall. She was finally sold for scrap in 1889-90. It took 18 months to dismantle her.
37. Lindsay, *History of Merchant Shipping*, Vol 4, 541
38. Lindsay was accompanied on the trip by a near neighbour of his, Judge Haliburton (Sam Slick) (1796-1865), and they met briefly with the King of Portugal Pedro V (1837-1861). NMM: LND 4-1, 491.
39. *The Times* 25 May 1858
40. Debentures
41. NMM: LND 3-1a, 46
42. In a letter to his brother-in-law Reverend John McKerrow in Scotland, Lindsay says "At Lisbon I was detained nearly two months on my own affairs. I have between £40,000 to £50,000 invested there." 3 March 1863.
43. NMM: LND 3-8,(1). See also Lindsay letter to George Villiers, 4th Earl of Clarendon, NMM : LND 3-4,46.
44. NMM: LND 3-4,45
45. The £18,000 plus the £25,320 equates to over £5 million today. Elsewhere Lindsay refers to £70,000 being owed to him. NMM: LND 3-7, 293.

Notes

46. After 19 years, from 1858 until his death in 1877, Lindsay received no payments, other than a small amount of interest.
47. Henry George Liddell MP (1821-1903) 2nd Earl of Ravensworth, Lord Eslington 1874-1878. Member for Northumberland South 1852-1878. See also NMM: LND 4-1, 565 also 3-4,70.
48. NMM: LND 3-5,139
49. Sir James Hope (1808-1881) was a Royal Navy Officer and Admiral of the Fleet. See also NMM: LND 4-1, 711 also 7, 587.
50. https://www.british-history.ac.uk/office-holders/vol9/pp41-62#h2-0031. See also https://lifeboatmagazinearchive.rnli.org/volume/04/37/report-of-the-royal-commission-on-harbours-of-refuge?searchterm=Yacht+Gan& page=1020 See also NMM: LND 4-1, 711
51. NMM: LND 4-1, 717
52. Later Admiral J Washington
53. Later Admiral Sir Bartholomew James Sulivan (1810-1890)
54. During the Second Opium War, 1859
55. Hope wrote to Lindsay from Hong Kong to say "I hope our labours in the Harbour Commission are not to be altogether useless – but fear that the large expenditure upon Naval and Military estimates will be much against the Harbours." NMM: LND 4-1,739
56. June 1860, May 1862, April 1863, and in 1864.
57. The Second Opium War was fought between Britain and France against China, 1856-1860. The war centred on issues relating to legalizing the opium trade, expanding general trade, and opening all of China to British merchants, After the War the Kowloon Peninsula became part of Hong Kong.
58. Taku Forts guarding the Hai River in China
59. The Battle of Santa Cruz de Tenerife in 1797 was a failed assault on the Spanish port city by Nelson.
60. The raid on Boulogne in 1801 was a failed attempt led by Nelson to destroy a flotilla of French vessels.
61. NMM: LND 7, 580
62. https://www.british-history.ac.uk/office-holders/vol9/pp41-62#h2-0031 See also Warner O et al, (1960) *Notes on Manning the Navy*, The Mariner's Mirror, 46:1, 63-72.
63. Admiral Charles Philip Yorke, 4th Earl of Hardwicke (1799-1873) was a British naval commander and Conservative politician. See also NMM: LND 6 (1).
64. See also Bolt, *The Sons of Neptune and of Mars: Organisational Identity and Mission in the Royal Marines, 1827-1927*. Thesis, September 2020. https://researchportal.port.ac.uk/portal/files/26919438/BOLT_UP753191_The_Sons_of_Neptune_and_of_Mars.pdf

65. Lindsay, *Manning the Royal Navy and Merchant Marine*, also *Belligerent Rights, in the Event of War*. Pewtress & Co, London, 1877. See also Calkins, *The Mariner's Mirror*, 46:1, 63-72, notes, 1960.
66. See *Illustrated London News* 6 August 1870; also *The Nautical Magazine* Vol XLV-No IX, 752-763.
67. Hugh Culling Eardley Childers (1827-1896) commissioned the unsuccessful warship HMS *Captain* in 1870; with his son on board, together with her designer Captain Cowper Coles it sank soon after its launch. He proceeded to various high offices including Chancellor of the Exchequer and Home Secretary. See NMM: LND 3-1a, 307.
68. One of Lindsay's friends, Admiral Sir Bartholomew James Sulivan (1810-1890) served with Sir Charles Napier in the Baltic during the Crimean War. See NMM: LND 3-7, 189. He made many invaluable surveys and charts of the shallow waters in which the fleet had to operate and led the bombardment ships into position during the capture of Bomarsund. In earlier years he served on the second voyage of HMS *Beagle*, from 1831-36, with Charles Darwin.
69. This was part of the Committee of Supply.
70. Lindsay sat on other committees, notably Mediterranean and Black Sea Freight (1863) NMM: LND 1, 372, Steam Coal Association Committee (1864) NMM: LND 1, 381. Anchor Committee (1859), Mechanics Magazine, 10 June 1859.
71. Belches also Belch, Belcher (1796-1890). Peter joined the Royal Navy on 2 February 1812. In 1814 he was severely wounded in a mistaken encounter with a British ship. He lived in Albany, Australia from 1827-1855. By 1861 he had returned to live in Cornwall, England and died in Plymouth, Devon, aged 94.
72. NMM: LND 5-4,403
73. Chartered Bank of India, Australia and China
74. Vice-Admiral Sir Richard Saunders Dundas (1802-1861)
75. Statham-Drew, *James Stirling: Admiral and Founding Governor of Western Australia*
76. Rear Admiral Sir Richard Saunders Dundas. James Belches' letter refers to the attack of the Russian fleet in Sveaborg Harbour during the Crimean War.
77. In 2014 and 2016, the wrecks of HMS *Erebus* and HMS *Terror* were finally discovered. Palin, *Erebus: The Story of the Ship*, Hutchinson, London, 2018. See also Coleman, E. C., *No Earthly Pole: The Search for the Truth about the Franklin Expedition 1845*, 2020.
78. Sir John Franklin (1786-1847) was a British Royal Navy Officer and Arctic explorer. Famously he lost his life seeking the North West Passage. See also NMM: LND 4-1, 909.
79. NMM: LND 4-1,909

80. Lord John Wrottesley (1798-1867), President of the Royal Society 1854-1858
81. Henry Edward John Stanley, 3rd Baron Stanley of Alderley and 2nd Baron Eddisbury, or Abdul Rahman Stanley (1827-1903), a historian.
82. Lady Franklin, failing to convince the government to fund another search, personally commissioned one more expedition herself under Captain McClintock. The expedition ship, the steam schooner *Fox*, bought via public subscription, sailed from Aberdeen on 2 July 1857. *The Aberdeen Journal* declared, "What the nation would not do, a woman did." McGoogan., *Lady Franklin's Revenge*, 362.
83. Lady Franklin to Lindsay 7 May 1857, NMM: LND 4-1,911
84. Bedford Clapperton Trevelyan Pim MP (1826-1886) was a Royal Navy Officer, Arctic explorer, barrister, and author. He became MP for Gravesend 1874-1880.
85. Sir Francis Leopold McClintock (1819-1907) was an Irish explorer in the Royal Navy, known for his discoveries in the Canadian Arctic Archipelago.
86. NMM: LND 4-1,909
87. David Livingstone (1813-1873) was a Scottish physician, Congregationalist, and pioneer Christian missionary, an explorer in Africa. His obsession was to find the source of the Nile River. See also NMM: LND 4-1,815 also 3-4,221.
88. Paul Belloni Du Chaillu (1831?-1903) was a French-American traveller, zoologist, and anthropologist. He became famous in the 1860s as the first modern European outsider to confirm the existence of gorillas, and later the Pygmy peoples of central Africa. See also NMM: LND 4-1, 805.
89. NMM: LND 4-1, 805. Du Chaillu was a good friend of Lindsay's, staying often at his Manor House in Shepperton.
90. Giuseppe Maria Garibaldi (1807-1882), Italian general, patriot and republican. He contributed to the Italian unification and the creation of the Kingdom of Italy. He is considered one of the greatest generals of Victorian times. See also NMM: LND 6 (43).
91. Charles Seely (1803-1887) was a 19th-century industrialist and British Liberal Party politician, who served as a MP for Lincoln from 1847 to 1848 and again from 1861 to 1885. He was one of the wealthiest industrialists of the Victorian era.
92. Ernesto Haug (1818-1888) was a naturalized Italian Prussian soldier, a fighter in the Italian Unification.
93. Giuseppe Mazzini (1807-1872), Italian politician, journalist, activist for the unification of Italy and spearhead of the Italian revolutionary movement. NMM: LND 4-1, 483
94. NMM: LND 4-1, End. Also NMM: LND 6, (43)

95. "As for Mazzini, he would continue to send out his assassins against Napoleon III until all foreigners, including the French troops occupying Rome and protecting the pope, were out of the country." Strauss-Schom, *The Shadow Emperor*, 281. No wonder he was incognito.
96. NMM: LND 4-1,483
97. Emigration correspondence: https://bcgenesis.uvic.ca/index.html.
98. Johnson, *Voyages of Hope, the Saga of the Bride Ships*, 2002. See also https://www.canadashistory.ca/explore/women/crinoline-cargo
99. The women's confinement on board ship may have been in part through fear of them staying in San Francisco rather than continuing to Vancouver.
100. Sir Joseph Paxton (1803-1865). A friend of Lindsay's who also knew him as a fellow member of the Administrative Reform Association. See also NMM: LND 4-1, 463.
101. These are known as Cavendish bananas.
102. John Williams (1796-1839) was an English missionary, active in the South Pacific.
103. Cobden to Lindsay 5 July 1857
104. Prof David Boswell Reid (1805-1863) was a British physician, chemist and inventor. He has been called the "grandfather of air-conditioning".
105. NMM: LND 4-2,165
106. George Hamilton-Gordon, 4th Earl of Aberdeen (1784-1860), Prime Minister 1852-1855
107. NMM: LND 5-3,156
108. NMM: LND 5-3, 554
109. NMM: LND 7, 133
110. John Russell, 1st Earl Russell (1792-1878), known as Lord John Russell before 1861, was a British Whig and Liberal statesman who served as Prime Minister from 1846 to 1852 and again from 1865 to 1866. See also NMM: LND 4-1,17.
111. John Bright MP (1811-1889) was a British Radical and Liberal statesman, one of the greatest orators of his generation and a promoter of free trade policies. He was one of Lindsay's friends as they agreed on free trade, but they opinions differed over the American Civil War. See also NMM: LND 4-1, 217
112. Sir Robert Peel MP (1788-1850) Conservative statesman who served twice as Prime Minister (1834-1835 and 1841-1846).
113. NMM: LND 4-1, 23
114. Lumber room: where furniture that was infrequently used was stored.
115. Benjamin Disraeli, 1st Earl of Beaconsfield (1804-1881), Conservative Prime Minister. See also NMM: LND 4-1,171.
116. William Ewart Gladstone (1809-1898), British statesman and Liberal politician. He was Prime Minister over four terms beginning in 1868

and ending in 1894. See also NMM: LND 6 (36) and NMM: LND 4-1, 31.
117. Sir George Cornewall Lewis (1806-1863) was Chancellor of the Exchequer 1855-1858.
118. Sir William Brown (1784-1864), British merchant and banker. A Liberal politician, he sat in the House of Commons from 1846 to 1859. See NMM: LND 6 (15).
119. Lord John Russell was Leader of the Liberals in the House of Commons and Lord Palmerston was Leader of the Liberals in the House of Lords.
120. Willis' Rooms, King Street, St James', were built in 1765, For a considerable time they were called 'Almack's. They were assembly rooms.
121. Ralph Anstruther Earle (1835 -1879) was a British Conservative Party politician. See also NMM: LND 6 (42).
122. Lindsay stated that it may be that Lord Derby never saw the document.
123. NMM: LND 4-1, 625

Part Six: American Civil War

1. NMM: LND 7, 10
2. Robert Chambers (1802-1871), Scottish editor, bookseller and scientist.
3. Herbert Ingram (1811-1860) MP for Boston Lincolnshire. See NMM: LND 6 (22). Ingram's daughter Annie married Lindsay's son William Stewart Lindsay in 1875 but divorced in 1877.
4. A full account of the tragedy is in Isobel Bailey's book on Herbert Ingram.
5. James Buchanan (1791-1868), America's 15th President, 1857-1861. See also NMM: LND 4-1,439.
6. Lewis Cass (1782-1866), Secretary of State, 1857-1860
7. William Henry Trescot (1822-1898), Assistant Secretary of State 1860. He joined the Confederates during the Civil War as a colonel.
8. Raphael Semmes (1809-1877) an officer in the Confederate Navy during the American Civil War. He was Captain of the CSS *Alabama*. Until then, he had been a serving officer in the US Navy from 1826 to 1860.
9. See also Hollett. *The Alabama Affair*, 6
10. Abraham Lincoln (1809-1865) 16th president of the United States, 1861 until his assassination in 1865.
11. Hannibal Hamlin (1809-1891), 15th vice president of the United States, 1861 to 1865.
12. Richard Bickerton Pemell Lyons, 1st Earl Lyons (1817-1887), British Minister to the United States 1858 to 1865.
13. Since Lindsay's visit in 1860, a decade later the tonnage of the United States had declined to little more than one half of what it was then.

14. A. A. Lowe and Brother were owners of the *Great Republic*, an extreme Clipper built by Donald MacKay in 1853. Abiel Abbot Low (1811-1893) was an American entrepreneur, businessman, trader and philanthropist who gained most of his fortune from the China trade, importing teas, porcelains, and silk, and building and operating a fleet of reputable clipper ships.
15. NMM: LND 7, 40
16. See https://www.hrmm.org/history-blog/a-scotsmans-journey-up-the-hudson-in-1860
17. Robert Stewart (1811-66), Lord Provost of the City of Glasgow 1851-1854
18. https://www.glasgow.gov.uk/CHttpHandler.ashx?id=32320&p=0
19. Robert Fulton (1876-1815) designed and operated the world's first commercially successful steamboat. Fulton's *Clermont* made its historic first run in August 1807 on the Hudson River. Lindsay sought to discover whether Fulton had Scottish heritage. Lindsay, *History of Merchant Shipping Vol 4*, Appendix 1.
20. Cutting from *Adventures, National Customs, and Curious Facts*. NNM: LND 2-12
21. Frances Milton Trollope (1779-1863), Author of *Domestic Manners of the Americans* (1832)
22. Nathaniel Prentice Banks (1816-1894)
23. John Chapman & Co, 110, Leadenhall Street, London, E.C., Ship and Insurance Agents. Established by Robert Chapman c.1809. In 1823 it became John Allan & Sons.
24. Well known as the location of shipping companies, notably the East India Company and P&O. Latterly it housed headquarters of Banks.
25. Augustus Newnham Dickens (1827-1866) was the youngest brother of Charles Dickens.
26. Augustus Dickens wrote a letter from the US on Lindsay's return to Britain. He refers to the possibility of Lindsay purchasing some farming land which Dickens offered to manage. It is stored in the University of St Andrews Libraries and Museums (ms38104).
27. Morley J., *The Life of Richard Cobden*, 685.
28. NMM: LND 3-1b 28
29. Andrew Johnson (1808-1875) was president from 1865 to 1869.
30. NMM: LND 7, 657
31. NMM: LND 4-2, 361
32. Cobden and Chevalier were instrumental in arranging a free trade agreement between Britain and France in January 1860. Michel Chevalier (1806-1879), was a distinguished Senator of France and its leading political economist.
33. Lambert, *HMS Warrior*, 12
34. NMM: LND 4-2, 395
35. Chevalier to Lindsay, 2 August 1861, NMM: LND 4-2, 427
36. Eugene Rouher (1814-1884)

Notes

37. NMM: LND 4-2,421
38. G. A. Osbon (1964), *The First of the Ironclads. The Armoured Batteries of the 1850s*, The Mariner's Mirror, 50:3, 189-198, DOI: 10.1080/00253359.1964.10657776
39. HMS *Warrior* was launched on 29 December 1860. An iron-clad, she was at that time the fastest, largest and most powerful warship in the world. Acting as a deterrent, she never fired a shot in anger. See Lambert A, *HMS* Warrior *1860, Victoria's Ironclad Deterrent*.
40. Paget to Lindsay, undated, NMM: LND 4-2, 383
41. Strauss-Schom contests this given the fact that 32 million Francs were set aside for the expansion and modernisation of the French Navy and building steam-powered iron-clad warships. He adds that the Emperor sought to match or to come close to matching the Royal Navy. Strauss-Schom, *The Shadow Emperor*, 168 & 279.
42. Paget to Lindsay, 19 February 1861. NMM: LND 4-2, 379
43. Gladstone to Lindsay, 25 May 1861, NMM: LND 4-2, 443. W.E. Gladstone, then Chancellor of the Exchequer, agreed with Lindsay that the British naval expenditure was a public danger. See also Gladstone to Lindsay, 26 November 1861, NMM: LND 4-2, 453 where he states, "I have always treated as idle the charge against the French Government of hostility to us."
44. George Hay, Earl of Gifford (1822-1862) was a British Liberal Party politician. MP for Totnes. He died whilst rescuing a workman about to be crushed by a tree.
45. Robert Dalglish (1808-1880) was a Scottish Radical politician. He was the MP for Glasgow 1857-1874. NMM: LND 3-4,26.
46. Mr A.D. Gifford of Richmond, Mr. Daniel Wheeler of Mobile (NMM: LND 7, 319), and Mr. George Arnold Holt of New Orleans.
47. NMM: LND 7, 13
48. Howell Cobb (1815-1868) United States Secretary of the Treasury 1857-1860. A southern Democrat, he became President of the Provisional Congress of the Confederate States 1861-1862. He was later a general in the Confederate army.
49. James Mason mentions in a letter to Lindsay that the debt of the Northern States on the Treasury books as of June 1864 was $1,740,034,639. NMM: LND 7, 389.
50. NMM: LND 1, 386
51. Jeff's Knave-y refers to Jefferson Davis the Confederate President's limited navy. Gotham refers to New York. It also appears to be an oblique reference to a cartoon entitled 'The wise men of Gotham and their goose' published in 1776 about British policies toward the American colonies during the American Revolution. cph 3a05308 //hdl.loc.gov/loc.pnp/cph.3a05308. The seven wise men may be an allusion to the seven original seceded states.

52. This is not quite correct. The Tariff of 1832 (not 1833) was in fact a slight modification of the "Tariff of Abominations" of 1828, but not sufficiently so to satisfy South Carolina. This turned into what was known as the Nullification Crisis.
53. Speech of W.S. Lindsay, Esq., in the House of Commons, on 18 July 1862 NMM: LND-7, 700, Appendix.
54. NMM: LND 7, 39
55. Jefferson Finis Davis (1808-1889) American politician who served as the president of the Confederate States from 1861 to 1865. He had been Secretary of War under President Franklin Pierce.
56. John Archibald Campbell (1811-1889). He had been nominated to the Supreme Court by President Franklin Pierce. He served as a mediator between three commissioners representing the Confederacy and the Lincoln administration.
57. Besides the *Powhattan*, 11 vessels, with 285 guns and 2,400 men, were ordered to be got ready, and by 11 April no fewer than 11,000 men had been sent from Fort Hamilton and Governor's Island in order to coerce South Carolina back into the Union. "A greater piece of duplicity and treachery was never perpetrated by any political minister." Manchester Southern Independence Association; NMM: LND 7, 780.
58. Neither Missouri nor Kentucky actually seceded, although there was support for secession in both states, both states had provisional secessionist governments in exile and representation in the Confederate Congress and both supplied troops to the Confederate Army.
59. Speech of W.S. Lindsay, Esq., in the House of Commons, on 18 July 1862.
60. William Lowndes Yancey (1814-1863) was a journalist, politician, orator, diplomat, and an American leader of the Southern secession movement. His time as Confederate Agent in Britain was mainly seen as a failure, but some felt he acted wisely. See Priestley, C., *The Civil War Abroad*, Chapter 4.
61. NMM: LND 7, 87
62. NMM: LND 7, 201
63. Jones, *Union in Peril*, 119. See also Hubbard C.M., *The Burden of Confederate Diplomacy*, 78
64. William Henry Seward (1801-1872), United States Secretary of State from 1861 to 1869
65. In a speech in Newcastle in October 1862, Gladstone said "Jefferson Davis and other leaders of the South have made an army, they are making, it appears, a navy; and they have made what is more than either, they have made a nation." He left an erroneous impression of being pro-Confederate. His speech provided a great boost to southern morale and hence infuriated the Union. Monaghan, *Abraham Lincoln deals with Foreign Affairs*, xii.

Notes

66. NMM: LND 7, 86
67. NMM: LND 7, 86
68. Commander Richard Williams, NMM: LND 7, 725
69. Captain Charles Wilkes (1798-1877) of the USS *San Jacinto*
70. Macfarland was then a man between 30 and 40 years of age, unmarried and had been a planter in Louisiana. The war had deprived him of all his possessions and when the struggle was over and his salary as Secretary ceased, he was without the means of living. In his distress he sought Lindsay's aid. Over time Lindsay gave him about £140. NMM: LND 3-1a, 172
71. George Eustis Jr. (1828-1872) was an American lawyer and politician.
72. Hubbard, *The Burden of Confederate Diplomacy*, 63. Napoleon III signified his support in a letter to the British Government.
73. Mathilde Deslonde Slidell (1815-1870) was born into a distinguished French family in New Orleans, Louisiana.
74. NMM: LND 7, 223
75. NMM: LND 7, 235
76. Lucius Quintus Cincinnatus Lamar II (1825-1893)
77. See also Monaghan, *Abraham Lincoln deals with Foreign Affairs*, 318.
78. NMM: LND 7, 691
79. Lindsay says of Bright "I have now known Mr Bright for 15 years, and though we have on various occasions differed in opinion ... I have never known him to be actuated by other than the purest and loftiest objects. The welfare of the people has ever been his aim. Through good and evil report, he has stood by them... But all these differences never altered my opinion of him. I still consider him as one of the ablest honest and most patriotic statesmen."
80. 17 May 1861, Mr John Young to Lindsay, NMM: LND 7, 80. John Young (1811-1878). Born in Ayr and schooled at Ayr Academy shortly before Lindsay, he emigrated to Canada. He was an MP of the House of Commons of Canada. See also NMM: LND 4-1, 456.
81. Jenkins, *Britain & The War for the Union Vol 2*, 26. *New York Herald* 24 January 1861 to 3 March 1861.
82. Sebrell II., *Persuading John Bull*, 81
83. Lindsay to Layard, Layard Papers, MS 38,988 (f.167), BL, 18 June 1862
84. Sir Jonathan Frederick Pollock, 1st Baronet, (1783-1870) Lord Chief Baron of the Exchequer 1844-1868. See also NMM: LND 4-1, 303. He ruled that the *Alexandra* was legally built, much to U.S. annoyance. Wilson W.E., *James D Bulloch*, 129
85. NMM: LND 7, 487. 11 October 1864
86. Jones., *Union in Peril*, 134. Mason, who was listening, was furious.
87. NMM: LND 7, 780
88. NMM: LND 7, 78
89. Jenkins., *Britain & the War for the Union, Vol 2*, 335. Lindsay was Vice President of the Association.
90. NMM: LND 7, 439. His stroke left him wheelchair-bound.

91. Howard Jones in his book *Union in Peril* states that Lincoln's administration warned England of war if it formally recognized Southern independence, 11.
92. The First Battle of Bull Run (the name used by Union forces), also known as the Battle of First Manassas (the name used by Confederate forces), was the first major battle of the American Civil War. The battle was fought on 21 July 1861 in Prince William County, Virginia. It was a Confederate victory, followed by a disorganized retreat of the Union forces.
93. After the battle of Bull Run, Prime Minister Palmerston wrote to his Foreign Secretary Lord John Russell suggesting that should further defeats for the Union Forces occur then the British together with the French should address the contending parties and recommend separation. Russell concurred. Hollett D., *The* Alabama *Affair*, 43
94. NMM: LND 7, 218
95. NMM: LND 7, 333
96. Henry Hotze (1833-1887) was a Swiss-American propagandist for the Confederate States.
97. Sebrell., *Persuading John Bull*, 2
98. Lindsay to C.M. Davis Esq, Portland, Maine, 1 September 1861, NMM: LND 7, 57
99. NMM: LND 7, 59
100. Lindsay described the blockade as "an infinitely stronger interference with private interests and private property than the right of capture at sea". *The Scotsman* (Edinburgh), 17 March 1862.
101. Jones, H., *Union in Peril*, 69.
102. Owsley, *King Cotton Diplomacy*, 235. See also Messner, *A Scottish Blockade Runner in the American Civil War*.
103. Yancey to Lindsay 25 August 1861, NMM: LND 7, 95. See also Bennett, *The London Confederates*, 28.
104. NMM: LND 1, 390
105. Edward Stringer had dealings with James Dunwoody Bulloch who was the agent tasked with building up the Confederate Navy. Bulloch distrusted him. Wilson, *James D Bulloch*, 110.
106. Josiah Gorgas (1818-1883) was one of the few Northern-born Confederate generals. He kept the Confederate armies well supplied with weapons and ammunition, despite the Union blockade. He worked closely with the Fraser, Trenholm shipping company that brought in shipments of ordnance by means of blockade runners. They acted as bankers for the Confederates; Wilson, *James D Bulloch*, 42.
107. *New York Times* 16 November 1863. Edward Pembroke, Stringer's partner was also involved. See Kent-Lemon D., *Blockade Runner*, 41.
108. Caleb Huse (1831-1905) was a major in the Confederate States Army, acting primarily as an arms procurement agent and purchasing specialist during the Civil War.

Notes

109. Thomas Jefferson (1743-1826) 3rd President of the United States 1801-1889
110. Built as the *Czar* in Stockton-on-Tees in 1861, the *Bermuda* was bought by Fraser, Trenholm and Company in Liverpool.
111. NMM: LND 7, 153 & 553. Gifford to Lindsay 28 November 1861 from the Burlington Hotel.
112. Frederick J. Cridland. NMM: LND 7,357
113. George Nicholas Sanders (1812-1873)
114. Commander George Terry Sinclair (1843-1930)
115. Owsley, *King Cotton Diplomacy*, 388.
116. 1 April 1863
117. Von Erlanger (1806-1878) was a Frankfurt politician and banker. In 1848 he founded the Erlanger & Söhne banking house, which later expanded to Vienna, Paris and London. His son, Baron Frédéric Émile d'Erlanger (1832-1911), founded the French branch of the Erlanger banking businesses, Emile Erlanger & Co. He married the Confederate Commissioner John Slidell's daughter, Marguerite Mathilde Slidell.
118. The bonds were launched 19 March 1863. Hubbard, *The Burden of Confederate Diplomacy*, 132.
119. Owsley, *King Cotton Diplomacy*, 403.
120. NMM: LND 7, 561. Reports showed Lindsay invested £20,000 in the Confederate Loan but he said he only invested £2,000. After the war he tried to recover this amount but to no avail. Lindsay's actual claim was for £4,000 and $65,000. St Andrew's University Library's special collection. ms38104_03-05. More than £6 million in today's money.
121. NMM: LND 3-1b, 12
122. NMM: LND 7, 709
123. This is the same Captain Semmes that Lindsay met in his tour of the United States in 1860.
124. NMM: LND 7, 265
125. During her two-year career as a commerce raider, CSS *Alabama* damaged Union merchant shipping around the world. The Confederate cruiser captured and burned 55 Union ships worth $4,500,000. (Some sources say 68 Union ships – See Hollett., *The Alabama Affair*, 93.) The U.S. government pursued the "*Alabama* Claims" against Great Britain for the losses caused by CSS *Alabama* and other raiders fitted out in Britain. A joint arbitration commission awarded the U.S. $15.5 million (approximately £3,000,000) in damages. See also https://sites.google.com/site/290foundation/css-alabama. Lindsay disagreed with this claim. NMM: LND 3-2,151.
126. Sir William George Granville Venables Vernon Harcourt (1827-1904), a pro-Union sympathiser who wrote several letters to *The Times*.
127. NMM: LND 7, 715, *The Times* 24 October & 28 October 1863

128. NMM: LND 7, 783 also 3-1b, 433
129. CSS *Sumter*, previously the *Habana*, was purchased by the Confederate Government in May 1861. Captain Semmes, her commander, seized 18 Union commerce ships. The *Sumter* was disarmed and sold at auction in December 1862 to the Liverpool office of Fraser, Trenholm and Company. *Sumter's* sail plan was changed to a ship rig and she continued her service to the Confederacy under British colours as the blockade runner *Gibraltar*. Captain Semmes then took charge of the CSS *Alabama*.
130. Ship number 0290 was a screw sloop-of-war built by Lairds in Liverpool for the Confederates
131. John Paul Jones (1747-1792) was a Scottish-American naval captain during the American Revolution who brought the fight into British waters. His marble and bronze sarcophagus at the United State Naval Academy has to be seen to be believed.
132. The battle between the *Kearsarge* and the *Alabama* was anticipated. The *Alabama* had sailed into Cherbourg for repairs, but the emperor had ordered the ship to leave harbour as he did not wish to antagonize the North. The *Kearsarge* was waiting for her. A Laird yacht, the *Deerhound*, waited nearby to take news of the expected *Alabama* victory (allegedly back to Lindsay, although this is debatable). She rescued Captain Semmes from the sinking ship. Monaghan., *Abraham Lincoln deals with Foreign Affairs*, 375. See also Priestley, *The Civil War Abroad*, Chapter 9.
133. NMM: LND 7, 469
134. Captain Semmes wrote to Lindsay after the War to identify future work prospects. See Semmes to Lindsay, 8 August 1865, NMM: LND 7, 477.
135. Eugène Rouher (1814-1884) Minister of Agriculture, Commerce & Public Works. See also NMM: LND 6 (37)
136. NMM: LND 7, 157. See also Lindsay, *History of Merchant Shipping* Vol III, 582, Appendix No 4.
137. For details see Lindsay, *History of Merchant Shipping*, Vol 3, 582. Also NMM: LND 11. The resulting treaty overturned "discriminating duties levied upon the vessels and their cargoes of either of the two nations in the ports of the other, and for procuring such alterations in the Navigation Laws of France as may tend to facilitate the commercial intercourse and strengthen the friendly relations between England and France."
138. Henry Richard Charles Wellesley, 1st Earl Cowley, (1804-1884), known as The Lord Cowley between 1847 and 1857, was a British diplomat. He served as British Ambassador to France between 1852 and 1867.

139. Lindsay suggested a scheme of establishing a line of steamers from Bordeaux to New Orleans. *Official Records of the Union and Confederate Navies*, Series II, Vol 3, 393.
140. Édouard Antoine de Thouvenel (1818-1866) was French Minister of Foreign Affairs from 1860 to 1862. He was pro-Union.
141. Auguste-Charles-Joseph de Flahaut de La Billarderie, comte de Flahaut (1785-1870) was the French ambassador to London.
142. NMM: LND 7, 157
143. Letters to Lindsay's sister and brother-in-law, 28 April 1862
144. NMM: LND 7, 165. Russell to Lindsay received 15 April & again on 24 April 1862, NMM: LND 7, 189
145. NMM: LND 7, 173. Lindsay to Russell, 15 April 1862
146. NMM: LND 7, 179. Disraeli to Lindsay 16 April & 21 April 1862
147. Monsieur Mocquard, Andre Adolphe-Eugene Disderi (1819-1889)
148. The Emperor had known Lord Palmerston since 1838. See Strauss-Schom, *The Shadow Emperor*, 2018, 57.
149. NMM: LND 7, 185. Lindsay to Palmerston, 21 April 1862
150. NMM: LND 7, 187. Palmerston to Lindsay 24 April 1862
151. NMM: LND 7, 189. Lindsay to Palmerston 25 April 1862
152. The Great Powers of Europe were Britain, France, Germany and Russia.
153. Possibly by Palmerston. See Owsley, *King Cotton Diplomacy*, 467.
154. Mocquard: the emperor's private secretary
155. NMM: LND 7, 193. Slidell to Mason, 18 June 1863
156. See also a report on this meeting in *The Public Life and Diplomatic Correspondence of James M Mason* by Virginia Mason, his daughter, 419.
157. See leading article in *The Times*. NMM: LND 7, 199.
158. NMM: LND 7, 201. Lindsay to Palmerston, 11 July 1863
159. Others tried to encourage the French to recognize the South, notably the former agent and representative of the Bank of England in the United States, John Cowell. He published a booklet in French giving reasons why they should do so. Amazingly, he also encouraged the French to strengthen their Navy. Priestley, C., *The Civil War Abroad*, Chapter 7.
160. Franco-Prussian War (1870-1871)
161. NMM: LND 3-1a, 276 & 296
162. Lindsay writes to say that he returned from Norway, but his notes are missing from his journals. Letter to his brother-in-law. 8 November 1863. Hilda Kirkwood said that they were being studied by a historian, but they are lost.
163. NMM: LND 7, 373 & 341
164. Brownsville, Texas
165. NMM: LND 5-1, 87

166. The Slavery Abolition Act 1833 abolished slavery in most parts of the British Empire. Excluded were the Territories in the possession of the East India Company.
167. NMM: LND 7, 483a
168. A similar case is recorded in Helen Doe's book *The First Atlantic Liner*, 82.
169. Lindsay switched Parliamentary seats from Hartlepool (1854, 1857) to Sunderland (1859).
170. NMM: LND 1, 384
171. With the repeal of the Navigation Laws in 1849.
172. Lindsay faced much opposition from many prominent shipowners, including William Imrie (1836-1906), Duncan Dunbar, George Marshall and George Frederick Young (1791-1870), for his support for Free Trade. Lindsay, *History of Merchant Shipping* Vol 3, 141. See also *The Times*, 30 November 1859. Meeting of parties having interests in British shipping.
173. *Newcastle Guardian and Tyne Mercury*, 7 January 1865

Part Seven: Maritime Historian and Author

1. NMM: LND 3-4, 282
2. A few years later, Jones, Lindsay's butler, had an illness and was no longer able to lift him without assistance.
3. NMM: LND 3-1b, 1
4. Alderman Richard Young of Wisbech MP (1809 -1871) was a British Liberal politician, merchant and shipowner. His son, John, acted for WSL for a while.
5. NMM: LND 3-3,111
6. W.S. Lindsay & Co was dissolved 30 June 1863. NMM: LND 2-11.
7. The Company still trades today in London as Galbraiths. https://www.galbraiths.co.uk/
8. NMM: LND 2-11-1, (19) & (37)
9. NMM: LND 2-11-1, (23)
10. NMM: LND 2-11-1, (33)
11. NMM: LND 24 & 26
12. Note from Hilda Kirkwood, archivist for the Lindsay family: "The large plans showing planned squares, gardens and villas were given to the Sunbury Council (Mr. John Brophy) *c.*1980. While the whole plan was not carried out, several of the houses were built in Laleham Road, Shepperton. Where the villas, built in the 1860s, stood (99-year ground leases) there are now blocks of modern buildings." The Lindsay Estate papers are lodged with the Archives of Greater London. See also a long obituary of Sir Joseph Paxton in the *Coventry Herald* of 30 June 1865. But all it says about Shepperton is: "A design bearing his name, the

Notes

laying out of Shepperton Park, near Hampton, in building-plots, is now to seen at the railway station."

13. Lindsay, *The History of our Village,* 1867
14. NMM: LND 3-3, 161 Annie Ingram
15. On a seven-year lease to Messrs Frances and William Merrick.
16. NMM: LND 3-1b, 16
17. Sure enough, a station was built in 1887 at West Byfleet, south of Woodham.
18. Writing in his diary of the acquisition, Lindsay said "Not in my time, nor in my son's, but in the next century, a great road will be driven west to link London through my lands at Shepperton and Woodham with the west." His prediction was realised in the M3 motorway.
19. Jack Needham, 2nd Earl of Kilmorey (1787-1880)
20. NMM: LND 3-1b, 209
21. Acton Smee Ayrton (1816-1886) was a British barrister and Liberal Party politician. He served as First Commissioner of Works under W.E. Gladstone between 1869 and 1873. He was a great friend to Lindsay and an executor in his will. See also NMM: LND 6 (18). This was probably the second of Lindsay's Thames Steamers that he had built.
22. NMM: LND 3-1a,258
23. The Bells of Ouseley, Old Windsor
24. Edward Burtenshaw Sugden, 1st Baron Saint Leonards (1781-1875), was a British lawyer, judge and Conservative politician. He became Lord High Chancellor of Great Britain in 1852.
25. NMM: LND 3-2,330
26. Lindsay, *On Ancient Galleys and Their Mode of Propulsion,* Taylor, London, 1871. See also Lindsay, *History of Merchant Shipping* Vol 1.
27. NMM: LND 6 (9) This was probably the first of Lindsay's Thames Steamers.
28. Lindsay was extremely busy with his company and his parliamentary business.
29. Colonel Sir Charles Beaumont Phipps (1801-1866) was a British soldier and courtier. He was appointed private secretary to Prince Albert on 1 January 1847. NMM: LND 6 (10)
30. The newly appointed Rector was Walter Martin, who stayed until 1890.
31. James Augustus Hessey (1814-1892) was a British cleric and Headmaster of Merchant Taylors' School, Northwood. He was appointed Archdeacon 1875-1892.
32. NMM: LND 3-7, 12
33. NMM: LND 3-2 595
34. Lindsay had a special lift built from the ground floor to his bedroom. He also had one fitted in Shepperton Manor.
35. Sir Joshua Walmsley (1794-1871) was an English businessman and Liberal Party politician.

36. NMM: LND 3-4, 282
37. Letter to Lindsay's sister Mary, November 1873
38. *Reform of the Admiralty,* to the editor of the *Star,* 27 Jan 1868, Nauticus (Lindsay).
39. NMM: LND 3-1b, 65
40. *The Board of the Admiralty*, to the editor of the *Star*, 8 July 1868, Nauticus (Lindsay).
41. HMS *Frederick William* was an 86-gun screw-propelled first-rate ship of the line of the Royal Navy. Ordered in 1833 as HMS *Royal Sovereign*, she wasn't launched until 1860.
42. Admiral Sir Robert Spencer Robinson (1809-1889) was a British Naval officer who served two five-year terms as Controller of the Navy from February 1861 to February 1871 and was therefore responsible for the procurement of warships at a time when the Royal Navy was changing from unarmoured wooden ships to iron-clads.
43. *Illustrated London News*, 24 December 1870
44. Flagship of Sir Charles Napier during the Crimean War (interestingly having a propellor lifting gear).
45. Sir Edward James Reed, KCB, FRS (1830-1906), British naval architect, author, politician, and railroad magnate. He was Director of Naval Construction for the Royal Navy from 1863 until 1870. He was a Liberal politician who sat in the House of Commons from 1874 to 1906.
46. Charles Frederic Henwood, was a naval architect and practical shipbuilder, and was trained under his father, an eminent naval architect and master shipbuilder in Her Majesty's Service.
47. NMM: LND 3-1a, 468
48. William Stewart Lindsay (1849-1924). Born in Brighton and died in Timaru, New Zealand.
49. Mrs Gardner's boarding school
50. NMM: LND 3-1a, 1
51. Annie Jane Bescoby Lindsay née Ingram (1850-1928). She later married Lieutenant-Colonel Augustus John English (1851-1909) in 1887.
52. Herbert Ingram died with his eldest son in the Great Lakes whilst on holiday, just before the American Civil War. Lindsay met him in America a fortnight before the accident. NMM: LND 7, Chapter 6. Ingram's daughter Annie later married Lindsay's son William in 1872.
53. NMM: LND 3-1b, 283
54. 19 Chester Square which they occupied was leased by Mrs Fenwick, the widow of Lindsay's respected colleague the late Henry Fenwick MP for Sunderland.
55. NMM: LND 3-3, 171
56. NMM: LND 3-3, 339
57. William Herbert Lindsay (1873-1949)
58. Lindsay's letter to his sister Helen Christie, 17 February 1873
59. Lindsay's letter to his brother-in-law John McKerrow, 10 January 1874

Notes

60. Lindsay's son's letter to him 5 April 1875. NMM: LND 3-5, 8.
61. Lindsay's letter to his sister Mary McKerrow, 7 June 1875. Lindsay's son had become a "remittance man".
62. Lindsay, *The Log of my leisure hours, by an old sailor*, Sampson, Low, Marston, Low and Searle, London, 1868
63. Lindsay's letter to his brother-in-law Reverend John McKerrow 19 March 1867
64. Lindsay, *History of Merchant Shipping* Vol 1, xviii. Also Marsden and Smith, *Engineering Empires – A Cultural History of Technology in Nineteenth-Century Britain*, Chapter 3, Palgrave Macmillan, New York, 2005.
65. Samuel Birch (1813-1885), Assistant in the British Museum 1836; Assistant Keeper of the Department of Antiquities 1844-1861; Keeper of the Oriental, British and Medieval Antiquities 1861-1866; Keeper of Oriental Antiquities 1866-1885. See also NMM: LND 3-1a, 247.
66. Sir Charles Thomas Newton (1816-1894), Keeper of Greek and Roman Antiquities, British Museum 1861-1885
67. Lindsay, *On Ancient Galleys and their Mode of Propulsion*, Taylor, London, 1871
68. NMM : LND 3-4, 19.
69. NMM: LND 3-4, 364
70. NMM: LND 3-4, 371
71. Pall Mall Gazette. NMM: LND 3-5, 6
72. NMM: LND 3-7, 297
73. Mr Bremner lists his port of calls on his journey around the world, as Gravesend, Melbourne, Java, Singapore, Hong, Canton, Shanghai, Japan, San Francisco, New York, Glasgow (via the Anchor Line, arriving October 1876).
74. Galle is in Sri Lanka.
75. A treenail, also trenail, trennel, or trunnel, is a wooden peg, pin, or dowel used to fasten pieces of wood together, especially in timber frames, covered bridges, wooden shipbuilding and boat building.
76. Bitts are paired vertical wooden or metal posts mounted either aboard a ship or on a wharf, pier or quay. The posts are used to secure mooring lines, ropes, hawsers, or cables.
77. According to Bremner, Captain Clymn was a rough, mean, and very much hen-hearted (cowardly) fellow.
78. NMM: LND 5-1,30
79. Lindsay, *History of Merchant Shipping* Vol 4, 249. Plimsoll in his book *Our Seamen. An Appeal* gives other examples of coffin ships.
80. In 1868 Samuel Plimsoll (1824-1898) was elected Liberal MP for Derby. Lindsay sent Plimsoll copies of his History of Merchant Shipping and received a letter thanking him. NMM: LND 3-7, 405.

81. NMM: LND 3-4, 269, letter 6 April 1874. Lindsay was not alone in thinking this. George Marshall agreed with him. See NMM: LND 3-5,472. Letter of 23 December 1875.
82. Lindsay, *History of Merchant Shipping Vol* III, 631. See also Lloyd's Register 250 years of service, 30. Lloyd's introduced their own guidelines for loading. Ibid,114.
83. Lindsay, *History of Merchant Shipping* Vol III, 488
84. This Bill became the Merchant Shipping Act of 1876. See also Lindsay, *History of Merchant Shipping* Vol IV, 246 and Vol III Chapter XVI, 463.
85. See Jones, *The Plimsoll Sensation.* "Apparently some 500 sailors were drowned unnecessarily every year, and in 1871 a Board of Trade report said that 856 ships went down within 10 miles of the British coast in conditions that were no worse than a strong breeze."
86. In December 1875 Lindsay gathered interested persons to a meeting in his house to discuss the Merchant Shipping Act; those invited included Lord Eslington, T.H. Farrer, James Laing, Charles Norwood, and George Marshall. Bernard Waymouth of Lloyds Register assisted with the invitations. NMM: LND 3-5,187,326, 418, 422, 472.

Epilogue

1. Strauss-Schom, *The Shadow Emperor*
2. See also Doe, *The First Atlantic Liner*, 89.
3. Lindsay, *Recollections of a Sailor.* Lindsay, *The Log of my leisure hours by an old sailor.*
4. Paxton J., *Black Gold*,114
5. Arthur Anderson (1792-1868) was a Scottish businessman and Liberal politician. He was co-founder of the Peninsular and Oriental Steam Navigation Company (P&O).
6. Sir Samuel Cunard (1787-1865) was a British-Canadian shipping magnate, born in Halifax, Nova Scotia, who founded the Cunard Line.
7. Indeed, the return of ocean-going auxiliary ships has already started. Groupe Renault has become a partner of Neoline, designer and operator of sailing cargo ships, to test a new maritime transport solution and reduce the carbon footprint of its supply chain. Press Release, November 27, 2018. See also construction contract signed for commercial sailing cargo ship, *The Maritime Executive*, 11 January 2022.
8. Lambert., HMS *Warrior*, 24
9. The *Great Western* was 212ft long (between perpendiculars) and 35ft 4in wide (without paddle wheels); Griffiths., *Brunel's Great Western*, 151.
10. Lindsay, *History of Merchant Shipping* Vol 4, 484
11. For details of the bombardment of Kagoshima, also known as the Anglo-Satsuma War, including the sinking of Lindsay's ship the SS *England* see https://en.wikipedia.org/wiki/Bombardment_of_Kagoshima

12. Clark, 'William Schaw Lindsay, The Largest Shipowner in the World?' Ships' shares (64ths) were divided between partners.
13. Lambert, *The Crimean War,* Manchester University Press, 1989. Also Duckers, *The Crimean War at Sea*, Barnsley 2011.
14. Clark, 'William Schaw Lindsay: Righting the Wrongs of a Radical Shipowner'; also Clark., 'William Schaw Lindsay, The Largest Shipowner in the World?'
15. Long, *In the shadow of the* Alabama, 27.
16. "In the autumn of 1862, Lindsay used his own money to advance Confederate captain James D. Bulloch, a naval agent, a sizeable loan to fund his effort to secure ships for the Confederate Navy in England." Pierpaoli P.G., *American Civil War: The Definitive Encyclopedia and Document Collection,* 1140. (I suspect this refers to W S Lindsay & Co rather than Lindsay himself.)
17. NMM: LND 7, 55
18. Wilson, *James D Bulloch*, 45
19. Wilson, *James D Bulloch*, 94
20. Owsley, *King Cotton Diplomacy*, 575.
21. Rhodes, *History of the United States from the Compromise,* Vol 4, 401. See also Lebergott, *Through the Blockade*, Journal of Economic History.
22. O'Flaherty, *The Blockade that failed*, 81
23. Thomas Milner Gibson (1806-1884) was President of the Board of Trade 1859-1866. See also NMM: LND 4-1,117.
24. Owsley., *King Cotton Diplomacy*, 578
25. Foreman., *A World on Fire*, 95
26. Strauss-Schom, *The Shadow Emperor*, 2018, 50.
27. Hubbard, The *Burden of Confederate Diplomacy*, 142
28. www.galbraiths.co.uk/heritage

Appendix VI

1. Middlesex Record Office. Acc 960. October 1978

Sources and Bibliography

Lindsay's Publications

Books
Lindsay, W.S., *Letters on the Navigation Laws* reprinted, Smith, Elder & Co, London,1849
Our Navigation and Mercantile Marine Laws Considered, Longman, Brown, Green, and Longmans, London, 1852
Lindsay, W.S. and Cobden R, *Remarks on the Law of Partnership and Limited Liability*. London, 1856.
Admiralty Administration, its faults and defaults, Longman, London, 1861
The Log of my leisure hours, by an old sailor, Sampson, Low, Marston, Low and Searle, London, 1868
On Ancient Galleys and their Mode of Propulsion, Taylor, London, 1871
History of Merchant Shipping and Ancient Commerce (4 Volumes), Sampson, Low, Marston, Low and Searle, London, 1874 and 1876
The History of Merchant Shipping: From American Independence to the Suez Canal (2 volumes), Bloomsbury, 2014
Recollections of a Sailor, Pewtress & Co, London, 1876
Manning the Royal Navy & Mercantile Marine; See also *Belligerent and Neutral rights in the event of War*, Pewtress & Co, London, 1877

Papers
Lindsay, W.S., *Confirmation of Admiralty Mismanagement*, London, 1855
Lindsay, W.S., and Cobden R., *Remarks on the law of partnership and limited liability*, London, 1856.
Our Merchant Shipping; its present state considered. Longman & Co, London, 1860
Practical letters on the navigation laws: addressed to the Right Hon. Lord John Russell, 1860
Nemo (Lindsay, W.S.), *Remarks on the Policy of recognising the Independence of the Southern States of North America and on the struggle in that*

continent, London, William Brown & Co, 40 & 41 Old Broad Street, 1863.

History of our Village or a few notes about Shepperton, Darling & Son, London, 1867

Shepperton, Brooking 1994.

Letters to his sister and brother-in-law. Unpublished. In the possession of the Lindsay family.

Further reading

Books

Adams, E.D., *Great Britain and the American Civil War*, 1924. https://www.gutenberg.org/files/13789/13789-h/13789-h.htm

Anderson, O.F., *The Administrative Reform Association, 1855-1857*, 1974.

Bailey, I., *Herbert Ingram Esq, MP*, Richard Kay Publications, Boston. 1996.

Blake, G., *The Ben Line*, Wm Thomson & Co, Edinburgh, 1956.

Bennett, J.D., *The London Confederates: The Officials, Clergy, Businessmen and Journalists who backed the American South during the Civil War*, McFarland and Co, Jefferson NC, 200.8

Bevan, J., *A Whitstable Diver's Crimean War*, John Bevan, Whitstable, 2020.

Bostridge, M., *Florence Nightingale*, The Woman behind the Legend, Penguin, London, 2008.

Burgess, Jr, D.R., *Engines of Empire, Steamships and the Victorian Imagination*, Stanford Univ Press, 2016.

Christie, Manson, and Woods., *Catalogue of Ancient and Modern Pictures, the property of W.S. Lindsay, Esq, deceased, late of Manor House, Shepperton*. Clowes and Sons, London, 1891.

Coleman, E.C., *No Earthly Pole: The Search for the Truth about the Franklin Expedition 1845*, Amberley, Stroud, 2020.

Connolly, T.W.J., *History of the Royal Sappers and Miners*, Vol. 2 (of 2), Longman, Brown, Green, Longman, and Roberts, London, 185.7

Corlett, E., *The Iron Ship*, Moonraker Press, Bradford-on-Avon, 1975.

Course, Captain A.G., *The Merchant Navy, a Social History*, Frederick Muller Ltd, London, 1963.

Cowell, J.W., *La France et les États Confédérés*, Hardwicke, London,1865.

Craig et al., *Chronometer Jack, The Autobiography of the Shipmaster John Miller of Edinburgh (1802-1883)*, Whittles Publishing, Dunbeath, 2008.

Denby, E., *Official Records of the Union and Confederate Navies in the War of the Rebellion*, Series II, Vol 3. Washington, 1922.

Doe, H., *The First Atlantic Liner*, Amberley Publishing, Stroud, 2017.

Doe, H., *SS Great Britain*, Amberley Publishing, Stroud, 2019.

Duckers, P., *The Crimean War at Sea*, Pen & Sword Maritime, Barnsley, 2011.

Dugan, J., *The Great Iron Ship*, Hamish Hamilton Ltd, 1953.

Emmerson, G.S., *John Scott Russell*, John Murray Publishers, London 1977.

Foreman, A., *A World on Fire*, Penguin, London, 2010.

Forster, E., *Churchill's Grandma*. The History Press, Cheltenham, 2010.
Fowler, Jr W.M., *Steam Titans*, Bloomsbury Publishing, New York, 2017.
Fynes, R., *The Miners of Northumberland and Durham*, J. Robinson, Blyth, 1873.
George, R., *Ninety Percent of Everything: Inside Shipping, the Invisible Industry That Puts Clothes on Your Back, Gas in Your Car, and Food on Your Plate*, Metropolitan Books, 2013.
Griffiths, G., *Brunel's Great Western*, Patrick Stephens Ltd, Wellingborough, 1985
Harris, J., *The Last Slave Ship*, Yale University Press, 2020.
Hoffs, G., *The Sinking of RMS* Tayleur, Pen & Sword, Barnsley, 2014.
Hoffs, G., *The Lost Story of the William & Mary*, Pen & Sword, Barnsley, 2016.
Hoffs, G., *The Lost Story of the Ocean Monarch*, Pen & Sword, Barnsley, 2018.
Hollett, D., *The Alabama Affair*, Sigma Leisure, Wilmslow, 1993.
Howe, A & Morgan, S., *Letters of Richard Cobden 1815-1847*, Volumes 1-3, 2012.
Hubbard, C.M., *The Burden of Confederate Diplomacy*, University of Tennessee Press, 1998.
Hurd, A., *The Merchant Navy*, Longmans Green & Co, New York, 1921.
Jeal, T., *Livingstone*, William Heinemann Ltd, London, 1973.
Jenkins, B., *Britain & the War for the Union*, 2 volumes, McGill-Queen's Univ Press, Montreal, 1974.
Johnson, J., *Clever Boys of our Time who Became Famous Men*, Gall and Inglis, London, *c*.1861.
Johnson, P., *Voyages of Hope, the Saga of the Bride-Ships*, Horsdal & Schubart Publishers Ltd, Victoria, 2002.
Jones, C. W., *Pioneer Shipowners* Vols 1&2, Charles Birchall & Sons, Liverpool, 1935 & 1938.
Jones, H., *Union in Peril*, University of Nebraska Press, 1992.
Jones, N., *The Plimsoll Sensation*, Abacus, 2007.
Kent-Lemon, D., *Blockade Runner*, Claymore Press, Barnsley, 2012.
King, P., *The Aberdeen Line*, The History Press, Stroud, 2017.
Kirkaldy, A.W., *British Shipping; Its History, Organisation, and Importance*, Kegan Paul Trench Trubner & Co Ltd, 1914.
Laird, D., *Paddy Henderson: the Story of P. Henderson & Company*, George Outram & Co Ltd, Glasgow, 1961.
Lambert, A.D., *Battleships in Transition*, Conway Maritime Press, London, 1984.
Lambert, A.D., HMS Warrior *1860, Victoria's Ironclad Deterrent*, Naval institute Press 1987, Revised 2011.
Lambert, A.D., *The Crimean War, British Grand Strategy against Russia 1853-56*, Manchester University Press, 1990.
Long, R.E., *In the shadow of the Alabama*, Naval Institute Press, Annapolis, 2015.
Lyons, McLeod., *Travels in Eastern Africa: With the Narrative of a Residence in Mozambique*, Hurst and Blackett, London, 1860.

MacGregor, D.R., *Fast Sailing Ships 1775-1875*, Nautical Publishing Co Ltd, Lymington, 1973.
MacGregor, D.R., *Merchant Sailing Ships 1815-1875*, Conway Maritime Press, 1984.
MacGregor, D.R., *The China Bird*, Conway Maritime Press, 2nd Edition, 1986.
Marsden, B., and Smith, C., *Engineering Empires – A Cultural History of Technology in Nineteenth-Century Britain*, Palgrave Macmillan, New York, 2005.
McGoogan, K., *Lady Franklin's Revenge*, Transworld, 2006.
Messner, J.F., *A Scottish Blockade Runner in the American Civil War – Joannes Wyllie of the Steamer Ad-Vance*, Whittles Publishing, Caithness, 2021.
Mitchell, W.H. and Sawyer L.A., *The Cape Run*, Lavenham Press Limited, 1984.
Monaghan, J., *Abraham Lincoln deals with Foreign Affairs*, Bobbs-Merrill Company, 1945.
Morley J., *The Life of Richard Cobden*, Chapman and Hall, London, 1881.
Nancollas, T., *The Ship Asunder*, Particular Books (Penguin), London, 2022.
Nolan, D.J., *Clippers, the Ships that Shaped the World*, Malbay Publishing, Bray, 2011.
Nolan E.H., *The Illustrated History of the War against Russia*, Vol. 1, 106, James Virtue, London 1857.
Owsley, F.L., *King Cotton Diplomacy*, University of Chicago Press, 1931.
Palin, M., *Erebus: The Story of the Ship*, Hutchinson, London, 2018.
Palmer, S., *Politics, Shipping and the Repeal of the Navigation Laws*, Manchester University Press, 1990.
Paxton, J., *Black Gold*, William Collins, London, 2021.
Plimsoll, S., *Our Seamen. An Appeal*, Virtue & Co, London, 1873.
Priestley, C., *The Civil War Abroad*, McFarland & Co Inc, Jefferson, NC, 2022.
Rhodes, J.F., *History of the United States from the Compromise*, Vol 4. New York, 1904.
Rhodes, M., *Lion Rampant: Duncan Dunbar and the Age of Sail*, Michael Rhodes, 2021.
Rogers, Colonel H.C.B., *Troopships and Their History*, Seeley Service & Co, Ltd, 1963.
Ruiz, M., *British Female Emigration Societies and the New World, 1860-1914*, Palgrave Macmillan, 2017.
Searle, G.R., *Entrepreneurial Politics in Mid-Victorian Britain*, Clarendon Press, Oxford, 1993.
Sebrell II, T.E., *Persuading John Bull*, Lexington Books, Lanham, 2014.
Spratt, H.P., *Outline History of Transatlantic Steam Navigation*, HMS Office, London, 1950.
Smith, C., *Coal, Steam and Ships*, Cambridge University Press, 2018.

Smith, E.C., *A Short History of Marine Engineering*, Cambridge University Press, 1937.

Spong, H.C & Osborne R.H., *Shaw, Savill & Albion, A Fleet History*, The World Ship Society Ltd, Windsor, 2011.

Starke, M., *Escape to the Sea: Tom Sullivan A.B*, Whittles Publishing, Dunbeath, 2008.

Statham-Drew P., *James Stirling: Admiral and Founding Governor of Western Australia*, University of Western Australia Press, 2003.

Strauss-Schom, A., *The Shadow Emperor*, Amberley Publishing, Stroud, 2018.

Strawhorn, J., *750 years of a Scottish School*, Ayr Academy 1233-1983, Ayr, 1983.

Sullivan, Dick., *Navvyman*, Coracle Press,1983.

Thornton, R.H., *British Shipping*, Cambridge University Press, 1945.

Troubetzkoy, A., *The Crimean War*, Robinson, London, 2006.

Tucker, S.C., (Ed)., *American Civil War*: The Definitive Encyclopedia and Document Collection, ABC-CLIO, 2013.

Watson, N., *Lloyd's Register, 250 years of Service*, Lloyd's Register, London, 2010.

Wilson, B., *Heyday, The 1850s and the Dawn of the Global Age*, Weidenfeld & Nicolson, London, 2016.

Wilson, E.W. and McKay, G.L., *James D Bulloch*, McFarland & Co, Jefferson, 2012.

Williams, H.N., *The Life & Letters of Admiral Sir Charles Napier*, Hutchinson & Co, London, 1917.

Wise, S.R., *Lifeline of the Confederacy*, University of South Carolina, 1988.

Zarach, S., *Galbraiths since 1845*, Galbraiths, London, 2020.

Journal articles

Aldis, O.F., *Louis Napoleon and the Southern Confederacy*, The North American Review, Vol. 129, No. 275 (Oct. 1879), pp. 342-360, University of Northern Iowa

Bolt, J.D., *"The Sons of Neptune and of Mars": Organisational Identity and Mission in the Royal Marines, 1827-1927*. Thesis. September 2020. https://researchportal.port.ac.uk/portal/files/26919438/BOLT_UP753191_The_Sons_of_Neptune_and_of_Mars.pdf

Braun, L.F., *The Roebuck Motion and the Issue of British Recognition of the Confederate States of America*, UCLA Historical Journal,17.1997

Calkins, W.N., *Notes on Manning the Royal Navy*, The Mariner's Mirror, 46:1, 63-72, Notes, 1960

Carter, T., *Mapping the knowledge base for maritime health: 3 – Illness and Injury in Seafarers*, Int Marit Health. 2011;62(4):224-40. PMID: 22544497.

Chadwick, *The Army Works Corps in the Crimea*, Journal of Transport History Vol VI, No 3, May 1964.

Sources and Bibliography

Clark, M., *William Schaw Lindsay: Righting the Wrongs of a Radical Shipowner*, The Northern Mariner/le marin du nord, XX, No. 3, (July 2010), 283-311.

Clark, M., William Schaw Lindsay, *The Largest Shipowner in the World?* History Scotland, Vol 12 No 2, 44-49 & Vol 12 No 3, 50-54

Clark, M., *Alexander Collie: The ups and downs of trading with the Confederacy*. The Northern Mariner XIX No 2 (April 2009), 125-148.

Cobden, R., *What Mr Cobden says about the invasion panic*, August 6th, 1859, Aberystwyth Observer

Fletcher, G., *Parliamentary Portraits of the Present Period*, London 1862

Lebergott S., *Through the Blockade: The Profitability and Extent of Cotton Smuggling 1861-1865*, Journal of Economic History. Vol XLI, No 4 (Dec 1981).

Lindsay, William Stewart, *William Schaw Lindsay and the Oceangoing Auxiliary Steamer*, The Mariner's Mirror, 106:1, 43-61. 2020. DOI: 10.1080/00253359.2020.1692577

Lindsay, William Stewart, https://www.rmg.co.uk/stories/blog/library-archive/lindsay-papers-caird-library 16 May 2018

McKie, R., *How Caroline Chisholm worked to keep the strumpets at bay*, The Age, Melbourne, 2 April 1983

O'Flaherty, D., *The Blockade that Failed*, American Heritage, 81, August 1955

Osbon, G.A., *The First of the Ironclads. The Armoured Batteries of the 1850s*, The Mariner's Mirror, 50:3, 189-198, DOI:10.1080/00253359.1964.10657776

Spratt, H.P., *Isambard Kingdom Brunel*, Nature 181, 1754–1755 (1958)

The Index, 1863

The Times, 1859-11-30. *Meeting of parties having interests in British shipping*.

Warner, O., et al., (1960) *Notes on Manning the Navy*, The Mariner's Mirror, 46:1, 63-72

List of Illustrations

1. Rev William Schaw *c*.1830: Lindsay's uncle. Portrait held by the Lindsay family.
2. Lindsay working his passage to Liverpool in the engine room of the steamer. Johnson, J., *Clever Boys of our Time who Became Famous Men*, London, 1868, 148.
3. Plan of the docks and basins in the port and town of Liverpool with the proposed alterations and additions. *The Penny Magazine* p.173, 1832.
4. Lindsay's Voyages. The Suez Canal had not been constructed in Lindsay's days at sea, so journeys to the Far East were via the Cape of Good Hope, South Africa. Author's illustration.
5. The *Olive Branch* on a stamp from Ciskei, South Africa, in a series on sail troopships. https://colnect.com/en/stamps/stamp/559093-Olive_Branch-Troop_Ships-Ciskei
6. *Olive Branch* Bill of Lading at Bushire 1841; The Lindsay family.
7. William Schaw Lindsay *c*.1850. Portrait held by the Lindsay family
8. Lindsay's wife, Helen Lindsay nee Stewart *c*.1850, shown with their son William Stewart Lindsay. Portrait held by the Lindsay family.
9. Lindsay's Sister-in-Law. Christina Craig née Stewart *c*.1850: Portrait held by the Lindsay family.
10. The Lighthouse at Hartlepool by J.S. Holmes. Hartlepool Museums and Heritage Service. Hartlepool Borough Council.
11. Robert Stewart, Lord Provost of Glasgow (1851-1854) after Daniel Macnee by David Gauld (1867-1936). Glasgow Museums Resource Centre (GMRC)
12. Advert for Lindsay's ships to Australia, 1853.
13. Launch of the *W S Lindsay* (*Illustrated London News*, October 9, 1852). © Illustrated London News Ltd/Mary Evans Picture Library.
14. View of the Thames Estuary *c*.1865, attributed to William Adolphus Knell, with Lindsay's auxiliary steamship, the *W S Lindsay*, prominently anchored. © Philip Mould & Company.

List of Illustrations

15. View of the Thames at Greenwich also attributed to William Adolphus Knell. With the *W S Lindsay* anchored in the background. © Philip Mould & Company
16. Caroline Chisholm on the back of the Australian 5-dollar banknote, 1974 series. https://banknotes.rba.gov.au/assets/images/australias-banknotes/other-banknotes/paper-5-both.jpg
17. The *Robert Lowe,* latterly the *Iron Cross*. Image courtesy of Malcolm Brodie collection, the State Library, South Australia PRG 1373/6/19.
18. William Schaw Lindsay around the time of his electioneering days. Photo held by the Lindsay family.
19. Lady Londonderry, Frances Anne Vane, Marchioness of Londonderry. Portrait by Sir Thomas Lawrence. Courtesy of National Trust.
20. Lady Londonderry in later life when Lindsay first met her. Great-grandmother of Sir Winston Churchill. NMM: LND 4-1, 879
21. Richard Cobden (1804-1865), a great friend of Lindsay's. U.S. National Archives and Records Administration 528678.
22. Drawing of one of the large galvanic cylinders. Bevan, J., *A Whitstable Diver's Crimean War*, Whitstable, 2020,19.
23. Sir Charles Napier (1786-1860). NPG 1460 National Portrait Gallery, London.
24. Lord Clarence Paget (1811-1895). Mary Evans Picture Library/ Illustrated London News.
25. Royal Mail Ship *England*. The Lindsay Line; Dartmouth to Cape Town, Mauritius, and Calcutta. www.southafricanphilatelyclub.com
26. Lloyds' survey report on the SS *England* 1857.
27. The Manor House, Shepperton, William Schaw Lindsay's home which he purchased in 1856.
28. SS *Great Eastern* under construction. National Maritime Museum, Greenwich, London.
29. SS *Great Eastern* under full sail and steam, passing Dover. Lindsay, *History of Merchant Shipping* Vol 4, 527
30. Advert for the *Tynemouth's* voyage to British Columbia. *The Times*, London 9 May 1862.
31. Sir Joseph Paxton (1803-1865). NMM: LND 4-1, 462
32. Four Prime Ministers: Russell, Palmerston, Disraeli, Gladstone. (Wikimedia Commons)
33. James Buchanan, 15th President of the United States. There was a visible decline in his health. Wikimedia Commons and Public Domain NARA 528318.
34. Lindsay's Tour of the Northern States, 1860. Author's illustration.
35. Abraham Lincoln, 16th President of the United States, photographed in February 1864 by Anthony Berger; the five-dollar portrait. Library of Congress.
36. *La Gloire*, the world's first Iron-clad Warship. Launched in 1859. Copyright: © National Maritime Museum, Greenwich, London, UK. PAH0973

37. HMS *Warrior*, Britain's answer to *La Gloire* Copyright: © National Maritime Museum, Greenwich, London, UK. PAH9277
38. Letter to the 'Dishonourable W S Lindsay MP' from an angry Northerner in Boston. 12 June 1861. "Enclosed find sample of hemp used in America for hanging traitors". "Jeff's Knave-y: Seven wise men of Gotham went to sea in a bowl." NMM: LND 7, 53
39. Jefferson Davis, President of the Confederate States. Brady-Handy photograph collection, Library of Congress, Prints and Photographs Division. LC-BH82- 2417
40. John Slidell, Commissioner to France, Confederate States of America. The Miriam and Ira D. Wallach Division of Art, Prints and Photographs: Photography Collection, The New York Public Library. (1860- 920).
41. The Trent Affair. Library of Congress.
42. 'Sinking of the CSS *Alabama*' by American marine artist Xanthus Smith, oil on canvas (1922). Courtesy: Franklin D. Roosevelt Presidential Library, Hyde Park, New York.
43. Portrait of Emperor Napoleon III (1805-1873) in Coronation Robes, Franz Xaver Winterhalter. Wikimedia Commons.
44. Map of Shepperton in Lindsay's journal. NMM: LND 5-4,559
45. Cottonwood Hotel, Bournemouth, formally Ravensworth, William Schaw Lindsay's house. Completed in 1873. Author.
46. Lindsay's Four volume *History of Merchant Shipping and Ancient Commerce*, published by Sampson, Low, Marston, Low, and Searle in 1874 & 1876.
47. Lindsay in later years. Etching photograph held by Lindsay Family.
48. Bombardment of Kagoshima 15 August 1863 and the sinking of Lindsay's ship the *SS England* that he had sold to the Japanese. *Le Monde Illustré*.
49 Appendix IV. Voyages of the *Tynemouth* during the Crimean War with details of cargo and troops. Lindsay, W.S., *Confirmation of Admiralty Mismanagement*, London, 1855.
50. Appendix VII. William Schaw Lindsay's abridged family tree. Author.

Index

1st Anglo-Afghan War 43
2nd Opium War 165
Abchurch Lane, London 66-8
Aberdeen, PM Lord George Hamilton-Gordon 144, 168, 180-181
Administrative Reform Association 134, 144, 146, 286
Addlestone, Surrey 258
Alabama 216, 220
Albany, New York State 192, 195, 197-8, 248
Albion Shipping Company 82
Alfred, HRH Prince 84, 260
Alipore ship 71, 119, 124, 127-9
Allan, James: Managing Director of P&O 67
American Civil War 173, 190-251 *passim*, 254, 282-83
Anderson, Arthur 284
Archer, Dr 170
Armstrong and Whitworth Company 269
Athenaeum, London 273
Austin Friars, London 71, 111, 117, 121, 156, 188, 199, 201, 234
Austin Friars ship 253
Australia 74-6, 85-95, 159, 168-9, 284
Australasian ship 254

Auxiliary Steamers 77, 91-5, 123-4, 127-8, 130, 149-55, 160, 173, 282-4
Ayr, Scotland 12-14, 22, 33, 52-4, 57-8, 115, 291
Ayrton, Acton Smee MP 259
Bailey, Crawshay MP 97, 98-9, 101-2
Balaklava 111, 125-30, 132-4
Ballarat ship 91
Baltic 137-41, 144, 169, 206, 209
Baltimore, Maryland 191, 193, 195
Bangor, Maine 192-3
Banks, General Nathaniel 199-200, 202-4
Barrackpore ship 71, 127-8
Bath, Maine 192
Beaumaris, Anglesea 32
Belches, Lieutenant Peter 168-9
Bells of Ouzeley Inn 259
Bento da Silva, Senor Carlos 163
Berbice 51
Beresford Hope, Alexander MP 227
Berkeley, Admiral Maurice Frederick FitzHardinge MP 135
Bermuda 229
Bermuda ship 229
Berthon, Reverend Edward 122
Bill of Lading 40, 44
Bingham, Captain 124
Blackburn, Lancashire 217
Black Sea 69, 111, 125, 127, 130, 139-40, 206, 209, 287

Blockade Runner 228, 250, 288
Bombay, India 38-9, 41, 43-5, 67, 79, 171-2, 253, 278
Boston, Massachusetts 80, 93, 190-192, 199, 214, 248
Boulogne 166
Bournemouth, Hampshire 255, 262-4, 275
Bowman, Mr 150
Bremner, Robert 275-6, 278
Bright, John MP 224
British Columbia 173-5
British Museum, London 273, 290
Brooklyn, New York 195
Brown, Sir William MP 186
Brucks, Commodore George Barnes 41, 43
Brunel, Isambard Kingdom 159-61, 284
Brunswick, Maine 192
Buchanan, James: President USA
Buffalo, New York 192
Bulley, Captain 150
Bulloch, Commander James Dunwoody 288
Bull Run Battle of 226
Burns, James and George 51
Bushire, Persian Gulf 40, 43-4
Byrne, Joseph 73
Caird Library, National Maritime Museum 290
Calcutta 36-7, 67.91-2, 133, 149, 151-2
Callao, Peru 178, 277
Cambridge, England 115, 270-71
Campbell, Justice John Archibald 217
Cape of Good Hope 32, 45, 48, 92, 133, 149, 151, 153, 254
Cape Town 38, 134, 151
Cass, General Lewis 193
Castle Eden Colliery/Company 59, 61, 63, 65-7, 72, 284
Cattell-Jones, Mr 159
Chalmers, Robert 190
Chapman, John Chapman & Company 201-2
Charleston, South Carolina 217, 229
Chatsworth House, Derbyshire 176, 178
Chertsey, Surrey 258, 299
Chevalier, Monsieur Michel 205-6, 226, 235, 238, 240, 242
Chicago, Illinois 193, 199-200, 202, 219
Childers, Hugh MP 167
Chiles, Mr 246
China 79-80, 91, 165, 169, 176-8, 209
Chisholm, Captain Archibald 86
Chisholm, Caroline 85-91, 95
Chobham, Surrey 119, 258
Christie, Helen née Lindsay 60
Christie, Thomas 15, 51
Christie, Captain Peter 132
Churchill, Sir Winston 114
Clermont riverboat 197-8
Cobb, Howell 193, 212
Cobden, Richard MP 116-121, 179, 181, 199, 201-2, 205, 210, 223, 255, 286
Codrington, General Sir William John 140-141
'Colehill', Jamie 22, 30
Columbia Emigration Society 173
Confederate States 211-249 and *passim*
Congalton, Captain William 126-7, 175
Constantinople 125-130, 132, 135-6
Cooper, Sir Astley 35
Coquimbo, Chile 178
Corn Laws 116
Coromandel ship 73
Cossipore ship 71
cotton 18, 45, 73, 171, 173, 215, 217-18, 228, 230-31, 236, 246, 250, 288
Coutts, Burdett 173
Cowan's Bank 57
Craig, Christina, née Stewart 56, 262

Index

Cridland, Frederick 230
Crimean War 91, 119-149 *passim*, 169, 173, 206, 209, 255, 265-6, 282-4, 286-7
Cronstadt, Russia 139, 144
Croton, River 195
Crystal Palace 84, 128, 176, 179
CSS *Alabama* 232, 234-5, 296
CSS *Sumter* 234
Cunard Shipping Line 190, 254, 284
Cunningham, Henry D.P. 122
Dalglish, Robert MP 211
Daniel Drew paddle steamer 196-7
Dartmouth, Devon 38, 103-110, 149-152, 173, 255
Davidson, Jamie 57
Davies, Colonel 41-3
Davis, Jefferson, President of the Confederate States 216, 223
Deane, John 130, 132-3
Demerara, British Guyana 22, 25, 29, 33, 356, 51, 246
Derby, Lord, Edward George Geoffrey Smith-Stanley, PM 103, 165, 187-8, 238-240, 286
Devonshire House 127
Dickens, Augustus 202
Dickens, Charles 146, 173, 199-200, 202
Dickson, Peter 108-9
Dinapore ship 71, 124, 127-8
Dinning, Captain Jock 33-4, 51
Disraeli, Benjamin, PM 180-181, 184-5, 187-8, 226, 238-240, 286
Dorney House 255
Du Chaillu, Paul 171
Ducos, Theodore 135
Duke of Beaufort 97-9
Duke of Bedford 181
Duke of Devonshire 176, 178
Duke of Northumberland 98, 103, 107-9
Dundas, Admiral Deans 130
Dundas, Admiral Air James 130
Dundas, Captain Adam 126-7, 151-2
Dundas, Vice-Admiral Sir R.S. 169
Earle, Ralph MP 188
East India Company 39, 41, 273-4
El Dorado ship 276
Emancipation of slaves 227, 246-8, 287
England ship 149, 151-5
Erebus ship 169
Erlanger, Baron Frederick 221
Eslington, Lord Henry George Liddell 164
Esquimalt, British Columbia 175
Eupatoria, Crimea 125, 127
Europa ship 190
European and Australasian Steam Navigation Company 254
Eustice, George 220
Falkland Islands 174
Fiery Cross ship 95
First Manassas, Battle of 226
Flahaut, Count Auguste 238
Flying Venus ship 277
Fort Sumter, Charleston 216-7
France 135-7, 161, 167, 172, 205-211, 218-222, 228, 233-9, 242-4, 250, 268, 288
Franklin, Lady Jane 170
Franklin, Sir John 169
Fraser Trenholm Company 231
Fulham, London 67-8, 81, 84
Fulton, Robert 197-8
Galbraith, James 82, 254, 290
Galbraith, Pembroke & Company 254
Galle, Ceylon/Sri Lanka 276
Ganges ship 125-6
Garibaldi, Giuseppe 171-2
General Screw Steam Navigation Company 92
Georgetown ship 35-6
Germany 244, 273
Gibraltar 67, 127-8
Gifford, Lord George Hay MP 211
Gifford, Mr A.D. 229-30
Gladstone, John 66

Gladstone, William Ewart PM 180-181, 185-6, 210, 218-9
Glasgow, Scotland 12-15, 18, 22, 51-4, 58, 60-61, 64, 67, 78, 95, 168, 193, 196, 211
Gorgas, Colonel Josiah 229
Graham, Sir James MP 126, 133, 135, 138-9, 144-5
Granville, Lord 84
Gravesend, Kent 85, 127, 175, 275-7
Great Britain ship 160
Great Eastern ship 159-162, 197
Great Exhibition, London 84, 128, 176
Great Lakes 193
Great Republic ship 93, 127
Great Western ship 160
Green, Richard 92
Greenwell & Sacker 48, 52, 54, 57
Greenwell, Richard 54, 58
Greenwich, London 78
Grey, Ralph William MP 108
Guest, Sir John 70
Hall, Dr John 127
Hall, Willie (Derby) 22, 26
Halliford, Surrey 256
Hamilla Mitchell ship 79
Hamlin, Hannibal 193
Harbours of Refuge 164-5, 186, 286
Hartlepool, County Durham 58-63, 72, 149, 164
Haug, Ernesto 172
Hawes, Sir Benjamin MP 159
Hellyer, Captain Arthur 174-5
Henderson, George 82
Henderson, Patrick 254
Henwood, Charles 270
Herbert, Admiral Sir Thomas MP 104, 105
Herbert, Sidney MP 144
'Historicus', (Sir William George Granville Venables Vernon Harcourt MP) 232-3
History of Merchant Shipping and Ancient Commerce 275, 290

HMS *Arrogant* 268
HMS *Captain* 269
HMS *Dauntless* 268
HMS *Erebus* 169
HMS *Frederick William* 266-7
HMS *Imperieuse* 268
HMS *James Watt* 268
HMS *Jean D'Acre* 268
HMS *Monarch* 269
HMS *Prince* 125
HMS *Royal Albert* 132
HMS *Success* 169
HMS *Sultan* 269
HMS *Terror* 169, 234
HMS *Volage* 169
HMS *Warrior* 207-8, 269, 285
Holt, Alfred 284
Hong Kong 67, 165, 178
Hope, Admiral James 164-5
Hotze, Henry 227
Hudson River 192, 195-7
Huse, Caleb 229
Illinois Railway 201
Illustrated London News 75, 193, 267, 271
Index newspaper 227
India 36, 38, 80, 85-6, 92, 122, 149-50, 152, 167, 169, 178, 197, 269 *and see* East India Company
Indiana ship 123
Ingram, Herbert MP 193, 271
Ingram, Annie 271-3
Invincible ship 210
Ireland 32-3, 57-8, 69, 161
Ireland ship 149, 154
Iron-clads 24, 205-210, 231-2, 269, 288
Isabella ship 21, 25, 30-33, 45, 50-51, 129, 278
Isle of Wight 39, 118-122, 171, 261, 263
Islington, London 88
Japan 286
Jefferson, Miss 229

Index

Jefferson, Thomas 229
Jenny Lind ship 77-8
Jersey, New Jersey 195
Johnson, Andrew: President 204
Kagoshima 285-6
Karrack, Persian Gulf 41
Keane, Captain Michael 36-7
Kearsarge ship 234
Kilmorey, Earl 258
Kirkwood, Hilda 329-330
La Gloire ship 206-8
Laing, Samuel 147
Lake Katrine 196
Lake Erie 192
Lamar, Colonel Lucius Quintus Cincinnatus 224, 288
Lamport & Holt Shipping Line 68, 128
Land Transport Corps 128, 133
Lansdowne, Marquis of 170
Layard, Sir Austin MP 225, 243-4
Leadenhall Street, London 201-2, 274
Lewis, Sir George Cornewall 186
Limerick, Ireland 54, 57-8
Lincoln, Abraham: President 193, 202-4, 217, 228, 247, 287
Lincoln Arms Hotel 255
Lindsay Arms 255
Lindsay, Annie née Ingram 255, 271-3
Lindsay, Alexander, brother of WSL 12
Lindsay, Helen, née Stewart, wife of WSL 52-60, 65, 72, 262, 272, 282
Lindsay, Helen, sister of WSL 15-16, 51, 272
Lindsay, Mary née Belch, mother of WSL 12, 16
Lindsay, Mary, sister of WSL 39, 51
Lindsay, Peter Belch 16
Lindsay, William Herbert, grandson of WSL 272
Lindsay, William Stewart, son of WSL 55, 72, 270-273

Lindsay's Light, The Heugh 62
Liverpool, England 16, 18-22, 25, 29-32, 45, 48, 50-51, 68-9, 78, 120, 128, 171, 190, 195, 232, 234, 247, 277-8
Livingstone, David 170-171
Lloyds 154
London Evening Standard newspaper 250
Lumsden & Byers 68
Lyons, Lord Richard 193, 230
Lyons, Sir Edmund 132
McCastle, Chief Mate 21, 26, 28-33, 51
McClintock, Captain 170
McDonald, Dugald 51
McKay, Captain Laughlin 93
McKay, Donald 93, 127
McKay, Willie 66
Madras 71, 86, 92, 151-2
Magpie gunboat 140
Maine, USA 192-3
Manning the Navy, Royal Commission 164, 166-7, 286-7
Maori Wars 129
Marseilles 68-9, 127-8, 135, 137, 206
Marshall, George 111
Marshall, Sir Chapman 77
Mason, James Murray 216, 220-221, 223, 227, 230-234, 240-242, 246, 287
Mauritius 38, 91-2, 129, 151-2, 177
Mazzini, Giuseppe 172
Medusa ship 253
Melbourne 88, 91, 169
Memes, Rev Dr John Smyth 13-14
Midhurst 119
Millman, Chief Mate Thomas 36
Milner Gibson, Thomas MP 289
Mississippi/Mississippi River 193, 200, 216, 224
Monmouth, Wales 96-110 *passim*
Montreal 19, 224
Morley, Samuel MP 146

349

Morgan, Sir Charles MP 97
Morning Star newspaper 224
Mornington Lodge, London 68, 72, 81-2, 156
Musgrove, Sir John 71-2
Napier, Admiral Sir Charles 137-144, 169-70
Napoleon Bonaparte 48
Napoleon III 137, 205, 218, 235, 237, 242, 244-5, 283, 288-9
Nassau 229
Navigation Laws 282, 286
Nelson, Lord Horatio 166
Neptune steam yacht 260-261
Newcastle 38, 58, 60, 64-6, 69, 95, 119, 131, 171
Newcastle Daily Chronicle newspaper 251
Newcastle Guardian and Tyne Mercury newspaper 62
Newbury Port, Maine 192
Newfoundland 161, 183
New York 80, 161, 192-199, 212-13, 222, 248
New York ship 123
New York Times newspaper 229
New Zealand 129, 273, 282, 286
Niagara Falls 192, 195, 197, 198-9
Nicholas I, Emperor of Russia 137
Nightingale, Florence 127
Ocean Herald ship 127
Ohio 192
Olive Branch ship 38-41, 43-9, 60, 91
Oliver, Edward 120
Palermo 206-7
Palisades, Hudson River 195
Palmerston, Lord, PM 108, 137, 145, 148, 165, 170, 180-187, 205, 210-211, 218, 226-7, 238-240, 243
Pakington, Sir John MP 141, 165
Paget, Admiral Lord Clarence MP 141-4, 205, 210-211, 260-261
Pannels Farm, Chertsey 258

Paris 135, 206, 210, 221, 226, 231, 237, 238-243, 278
Parson's Green, Glasgow 51
Pasha, Omer 126
Pastré, Monsieur 135-6
Paxton, Sir Joseph MP 127, 146, 176-8, 255
Pearce, Samuel & William 69-70
Pembroke, Edward 229, 254, 290
Peninsular & Oriental Steam Company 67
Pentreath, Captain H. 124, 126
Pera ship 140-141
Persia ship 193, 196-7
Philadelphia 193
Phipps, Colonel Charles 261
Pim, Lieutenant 140, 170
Pittenween, Scotland 84
Plimsoll line 280
Plimsoll, Samuel 279-280
Plymouth, Devon 95, 128, 133, 149, 265
Pollock, Sir Frederick MP 225
Pompeii 199
Porter, Ernest 263
Portland Place, London 82, 119, 156, 170, 172, 270
Portland Street, Glasgow 51
Portsmouth, Hampshire 59, 119-129, 132, 265
Portsmouth, New Hampshire 192
Portugal 138, 163, 250
Preston, Lancashire 217
Prince of Wales, HRH 84, 192, 260-261
Quebec 120, 193
Raglan, Lord, Field Marshal FitzRoy James Henry Somerset 126, 130, 132
Raleigh Register newspaper 230
Ravenscliff House 263
Ravensworth House 263-4
Redan Fortress, Sevastopol, Crimea 128-9
Reed, Sir Edward MP 269

Index

Reid, Charles Reid & Company 229
Reid, Professor David Boswell 179
Resolute ship 125, 170
Rouher, Monsieur Eugene 206n36
Ridley, James 13
Richard Bell ship 36-8
Richmond, Virginia 226, 229-230, 234
Richards, Thomas 22-4
Robert Lowe ship 91, 93-5, 111, 123-4, 126-134, 149, 153, 173, 175, 286
Robinson, Admiral Sir Robert Spencer 266
Roebuck, John Arthur MP 242-3
Rowell, George 59, 62
Royal Engineers 124
Royal Oak ship 277
Royal Scots Fusiliers 124
Royal United Service Institution 270
Russell, Lord John PM 180-185, 187-8, 210, 218, 221, 223, 226-8, 232-3, 236-240, 244, 250, 286
Russell, Sir William Howard 129
Russia 124, 129-130, 132-140, 172, 224, 269, 287
Sanders, George Nicholas 230-231, 288
Sandy, John B. 232
Satsuma, Prince 286
Schaw, Rev Dr William
Schaw, Janet, aunt of WSL 41
Scotland 12-13, 52, 79, 82-3, 116, 170, 237, 254, 272
Scotland ship 149, 153-4, 286
Scott, James Winter 156
Scott & Company 94, 123
Scott Russell, John 160
Scurvy 25, 92
Seaham Hall 112, 114
Seale, Sir Henry 107, 152
Seely, Charles MP 171-2, 266-7
Semmes, Captain Raphael 193, 232, 234-5, 287
Serampore ship 71

Seward, William 204, 217, 219, 223
Shanghai 178, 277
Shaw Savill Shipping Line 129
Shepperton, Middlesex 11, 130, 157-8, 220, 223-4, 234, 253, 255-7, 261-2
Shepperton Manor 141, 155-6, 263
Shepperton ship 253
Shipping Gazette 82-3
Sinclair, Commander George 230, 288
Sing Sing, Hudson River 195-6
Slidell, John 220-223, 227, 241-2, 246, 287
smallpox 175
South Carolina 214, 216
Southampton, Hampshire 67, 92, 119, 150, 161
Southern Independence Association 227
Spray of the Ocean ship 129
Springfield, Illinois 193, 202-3
St Andrews, Nova Scotia 25
St Lawrence River 49, 199
St Leonards, Lord Edward Burtenshaw 259-260
St Louis 178, 193, 200, 202
St Peter's Villa, Fulham, London 67-8
Stanley, Lord Henry 170
Staten Island 195
Stephenson, Robert 159, 199
Stewart, Admiral Houston MP 126
Stewart, Robert, brother-in-law of WSL 64, 95, 196
Stirling, Admiral Sir James 169
Stringer, Edgar 72, 229, 254, 290
Stringer, Pembroke and Company 254
Stukeley, Dr William 157
Suez Canal 32, 254
Sulivan, Admiral Sir Bartholomew 164, 167, 263
Sunderland 38, 58, 68-9, 71, 220, 249, ,251
Sveaborg 139
Sydney, Australia 86-7, 169

Taylor, Hugh MP 108
Taylor, Robert 'Ranting Rob' 13
Tait, Captain Thomas 21, 29
Tenerife 166
Terror ship 169, 234
Thames River 11, 37, 75, 78, 119, 128, 142, 155-6, 160, 258-261, 281
Thames Ditton, Surrey 260
The Times newspaper 119-120, 129, 174, 191, 220, 232, 251
Thistle ship 51
Thom, David Thom & Co 125
Thompson, Alderman William 99
Thouvenel, Monsieur Edouard 236 n140
Toronto 193
Toulon 135, 206-7
Toulouse 210
Transport Service 126, 134, 136-7, 144-7, 149, 164, 167-8, 286
Transport Ships 123-4, 127, 129, 135, 137, 167-8, 287
Trent ship 220, 223-4, 226, 244
Trescot, William 193, 212
Trollope, Frances 199-200
Tuileries, the 137, 206, 221, 239
Turks/Turkey 124, 126-7, 287
Turnbull, Edward 59, 61
Twelve Apostles ship 130
Tynemouth, Northumberland 108-110, 116
Tynemouth (Caroline Chisholm) ship 93, 95, 123-130, 145, 147, 149, 153, 173-5
United Presbyterian Church 170
USS *Kearsarge* 234
Vaillant, Marshal Jean Baptiste 136
Valparaiso, Chile 178
Vanderbilt ship 196
Vane, Charles William, 3rd Marquess of Londonderry 112
Vane, Frances Anne, Marchioness of Londonderry 113

Vane-Tempest, Adolphus Frederick Charles William 113
Vermont, New England 192
Victoria, HRH Queen 35, 84-5, 138, 176, 187, 238, 260-261
Victoria, Vancouver Island 173
Vollum, 'Old' William John 58-62
Vollum, Will 59
Waits Hotel, London 86
Walmsley, Sir Joshua MP 263
Washington, USA 169, 193, 212, 216-17, 229, 234
Webster, Mr 276
West Indies 22, 25, 29, 33, 35, 83, 118-119, 246-7
Westminster Abbey, London 171, 183
Weybridge, Surrey 255, 257
Weymouth, Dorset 262
White Falcon ship 127
Wilkes, Captain Charles 220
Williams, Commander 220
Williams, John 178
Williams, General Sir Fenwick 140-141
Wilmington, North Carolina 229
Windsor, Berkshire 259, 261
Wilson, James MP 103-4
Woburn, Bedfordshire 258
Woking, Surrey 257
Wood, Sir Charles MP 145, 169
Woodham Farm, Surrey 256-8, 272
Woodham ship 253
Woolridge, Colonel 104
Wrottesley, Lord John 170
W S Lindsay ship 75-8, 91, 93, 127-9, 149, 154, 285
Yancey, William 217, 219-221, 228, 287
yellow fever 25, 35, 283
Young, John 224
Young, Richard 253